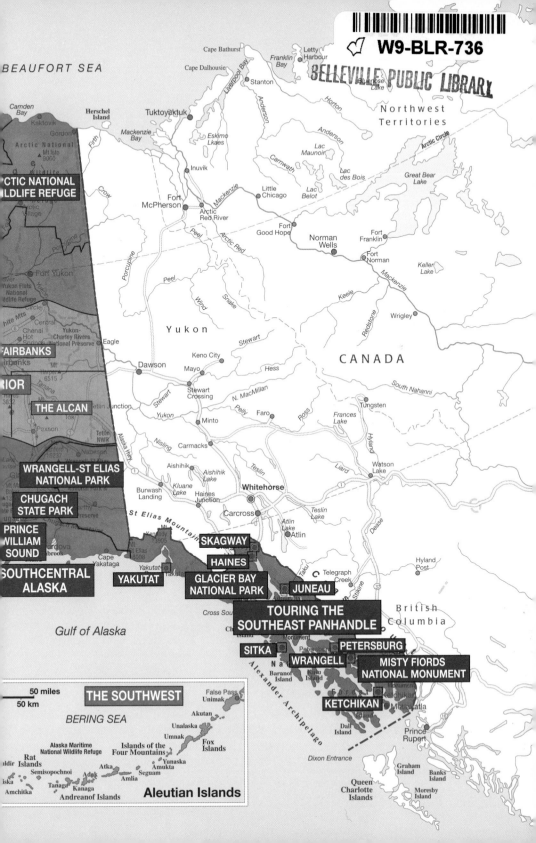

BEAUFORT SEA

Cape Bathurst
Cape Dalhousie
Franklin Bay
Letty Harbour
Liverpool Bay
Stanton

Northwest Territories

Camden Bay
Herschel Island
Tuktoyaktuk
Anderson
Bluenose Lake
Horton

Kaktovik
Gordon
Arctic National
Mt Isto 9060
Mackenzie Bay
Eskimo Lkaes
Inuvik
Anderson
Lac Maunoir
Arctic Circle

CTIC NATIONAL
WILDLIFE REFUGE

Firth
Crow
Fort McPherson
Mackenzie
Little Chicago
Lac Belot
Lac des Bois
Great Bear Lake

Arctic Village
Arctic Red River
Fort Good Hope
Fort Franklin

Fort Yukon
Peel
Porcupine
Mackenzie
Norman Wells
Fort Norman
Keller Lake

Yukon Flats National Wildlife Refuge
Peel
Wind
Snake
Keele
Redstone
Mackenzie
Wrigley

hite Mts
Central
Chenal Hot Springs
Yukon-Charley Rivers National Preserve
Eagle
Stewart

FAIRBANKS
rbanks
Mt 6515

Yukon

CANADA

Dawson
Keno City
Mayo
Hess
South Nahanni

RIOR

THE ALCAN
Stewart Crossing
N. MacMillan
Pelly
Ross
Frances Lake
Tungsten

Paxson
Tetlin Junction
Yukon
Minto
Faro
Nisling
Carmacks

WRANGELL-ST ELIAS
NATIONAL PARK

Aishihik
Aishihik Lake
Teslin
Liard
Watson Lake

Burwash Landing
Kluane Lake
Haines Junction
Whitehorse

CHUGACH
STATE PARK

St Elias Mountains
Carcross
Teslin Lake

PRINCE
WILLIAM
SOUND

Kennedy
Mt 13905
Atlin Lake
Atlin

Cape Yakataga
Mt Elias 18008
Yakutat

SKAGWAY

SOUTHCENTRAL
ALASKA

HAINES

Hyland Post

YAKUTAT
GLACIER BAY
NATIONAL PARK
JUNEAU

Telegraph Creek

Cross Sou
TOURING THE
SOUTHEAST PANHANDLE

British Columbia

Gulf of Alaska

Stikine

SITKA
Baranof Island
PETERSBURG
WRANGELL
MISTY FIORDS
NATIONAL MONUMENT

KETCHIKAN

Dall Island

Prince Rupert

False Pass
Unimak
Akutan
Unalaska
Umnak
Fox Islands

Alaska Maritime National Wildlife Refuge
Islands of the Four Mountains
Yunaska
Amukta
Seguam

Dixon Entrance

Graham Island
Banks Island

Rat Islands
Semisopochnoi
Adak
Atka
Amlia

Queen Charlotte Islands
Moresby Island

iska
Amchitka
Tanaga
Kanaga
Andreanof Islands

Aleutian Islands

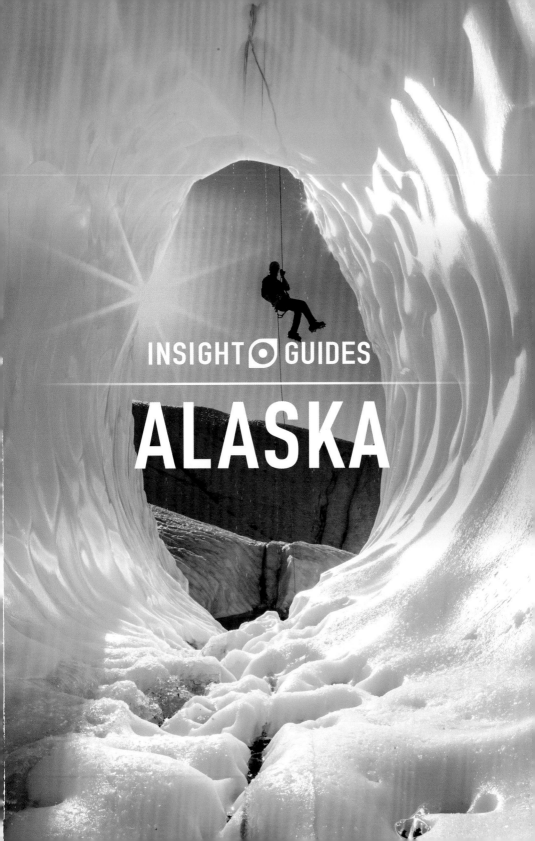

INSIGHT ⊙ GUIDES

ALASKA

PLAN & BOOK
YOUR TAILOR-MADE TRIP

BRAZIL

CHILE

ECUADOR

TAILOR-MADE TRIPS & UNIQUE EXPERIENCES CREATED BY LOCAL TRAVEL EXPERTS AT INSIGHTGUIDES.COM/HOLIDAYS

Insight Guides has been inspiring travellers with high-quality travel content for over 45 years. As well as our popular guidebooks, we now offer the opportunity to book tailor-made private trips completely personalised to your needs and interests. By connecting with one of our local experts, you will directly benefit from their expertise and local know-how, helping you create memories that will last a lifetime.

HOW INSIGHTGUIDES.COM/HOLIDAYS WORKS

STEP 1

Pick your dream destination and submit an enquiry, or modify an existing itinerary if you prefer.

STEP 2

Fill in a short form, sharing details of your travel plans and preferences with a local expert.

STEP 3

Your local expert will create your personalised itinerary, which you can amend until you are completely satisfied.

STEP 4

Book securely online. Pack your bags and enjoy your holiday! Your local expert will be available to answer questions during your trip.

BENEFITS OF PLANNING & BOOKING AT INSIGHTGUIDES.COM/HOLIDAYS

PLANNED BY LOCAL EXPERTS

The Insight Guides local experts are hand-picked, based on their experience in the travel industry and their impeccable standards of customer service.

SAVE TIME & MONEY

When a local expert plans your trip, you save time and money when you book, even during high season. You won't be charged for using a credit card either.

TAILOR-MADE TRIPS

Book with Insight Guides, and you will be in complete control of the planning process, from the initial selections to amending your final itinerary.

BOOK & TRAVEL STRESS-FREE

Enjoy stress-free travel when you use the Insight Guides secure online booking platform. All bookings come with a money-back guarantee.

WHAT OTHER TRAVELLERS THINK ABOUT TRIPS BOOKED AT INSIGHTGUIDES.COM/HOLIDAYS

Trip to Portugal

Every step of the planning process and the trip itself was effortless and exceptional. Our special interests, preferences and requests were accommodated resulting in a trip that exceeded our expectations.

Corinne, USA ★★★★★

Trip to Vietnam

The organization was superb, the drivers professional, and accommodation quite comfortable. I was well taken care of! My thanks to your colleagues who helped make my trip to Vietnam such a great experience. My only regret is that I couldn't spend more time in the country.

Heather ★★★★★

DON'T MISS OUT BOOK NOW AT
INSIGHTGUIDES.COM/HOLIDAYS

CONTENTS

Travel tips

TRANSPORTATION

A – Z

FURTHER READING

Maps

Inside front cover Alaska
Inside back cover Southcentral Alaska,
   Wrangell-St Elias National Park
   and Preserve and Katmai National Park
   and Preserve

LEGEND
◯ Insight on
◙ Photo story

THE BEST OF ALASKA: TOP ATTRACTIONS

▽ **Totem poles**. Tall and elaborately carved, totem poles are comparable to family crests and are used to tell a story or recall an event. The totemic symbols are often animals or birds – typically bears and eagles. See page 298.

△ **Denali.** North America's highest peak is surrounded by one of the world's greatest wildlife sanctuaries, Denali National Park and Preserve. See page 227.

▽ **Bald Eagles.** Alaska is the stronghold of bald eagles, which congregate in places where fish are plentiful. See page 76.

△ **Glacier Bay National Park and Preserve.** Sixteen tidewater glaciers flow down from mountain peaks and plunge into ice-choked fjords. The park is one of the best places to view bears, seals, humpback whales, and eagles. See page 144.

△ **Cruising.** Traveling along a stretch of Alaska's 33,900 miles (54,500km) of coastline by ship is a popular and often luxurious way to see wildlife. See page 91.

△ **National and State Parks.** With eight national parks and a state parks system of more than 3.2 million acres (1.3 million hectares), Alaska has tremendous appeal to outdoor enthusiasts. See page 185.

▽ **The Northern Lights.** These can be viewed most clearly in winter in the area around Fairbanks, which calls itself an 'auroral zone.' See page 263.

△ **Travel by rail.** Trains such as the McKinley Explorer, with glass domes or open-air viewing platforms, penetrate deep into Alaska. See page 92.

▽ **Fishing.** Prime fishing in pristine waters offers anglers a sporting chance of reeling in massive king salmon, leaping trout, halibut, and northern pike. See page 343.

▽ **Bears.** Getting close to brown bears allows you to recognize their individuality – some are aggressive by nature but others are mild-mannered. McNeil River State Game Sanctuary creates safe conditions for bear watching. See page 339.

THE BEST OF ALASKA: EDITOR'S CHOICE

Trans-Alaska oil pipeline is also known as the Alyeska Pipeline.

ONLY IN ALASKA

Arctic National Wildlife Refuge. Home to musk oxen, polar bears, and the Porcupine caribou herd, this refuge is the nation's largest and has the greatest biodiversity of any protected area in the Arctic. See page 284.

The Trans-Alaska Pipeline. Moving oil 800 miles (1,300km) from the North Slope to Valdez and across three mountain ranges, this feat of engineering is an important part of modern Alaska and can be seen from several state highways. See page 55.

Aurora Borealis Displays (Northern Lights). These heavenly light shows can be viewed only in the darkened autumn or winter skies that begin in late August. See page 263.

Alaska's Thermal Resort (Chena Hot Springs). Soak away your pre-conceived notions about a 'frozen wasteland' in outdoor and indoor steaming-hot thermal pools, in summer or winter. See page 263.

Land of the Midnight Sun. Communities throughout Alaska celebrate the summer solstice each year with parties and barbecues and, in Fairbanks, midnight tee time for golfers in natural light. See page 248.

BEST KEPT SECRETS

Lake Clark National Park and Preserve. A short flight from Anchorage or the Kenai Peninsula offers boundless recreational opportunities for wildlife viewing, river running, kayaking, hunting and angling, yet this national park is among Alaska's least known, and least visited. See page 324.

Richardson Highway. This scenic road from Fairbanks to Valdez provides spectacular views of Worthington Glacier, the many waterfalls of Keystone Canyon, and Thompson Pass. See page 257.

Ship Creek. This salmon-laden stream, within casting distance of downtown Anchorage hotels, is a favorite fishing spot for locals during lunch hour. See page 171.

Yakutat. Said by some to be one of the top, and certainly most unusual, surf beaches in the US, this is a great spot for serious surfing enthusiasts. See page 160.

A plane about to land on Lake Clark.

BEST SPOTS FOR BEAR-VIEWING

Brown bear.

Brooks River and Camp. Located in Katmai National Park and Preserve, the location is only accessible via plane or boat. Safe viewing platforms allow you to watch bears feed on spawning salmon near the Brooks Falls. Visitors may stay at Brooks

Lodge, or fly out on a day trip from Anchorage. See page 330.

Denali National Park and Preserve. Shuttle bus tours present visitors with excellent opportunities for bear-spotting. See page 227.

Kodiak Island. Famous for its healthy population of large brown bears. Bear-viewing tours will take you to see them in the Kodiak National Wildlife Refuge. See page 320.

McNeil River State Game Sanctuary. Created for the world's largest concentration of brown bears. Access is limited: visitors are selected by lottery. See page 335.

At Alaska Zoo.

BEST FOR FAMILIES

Alaska Zoo. A guaranteed safe, close-up look at Alaska wildlife. See page 175.

Crow Creek Mine. Try your hand at panning for gold at Southcentral Alaska's richest goldmine. See page 178.

Discovery Center. This award-winning hands-on science center within the Anchorage Museum features touch tanks, a planetarium, and reptiles.

. See page 172.

Alaska SeaLife Center. This is the place for people of all ages to get up close to puffins, sea lions, octopus, and more. See page 202.

Pioneer Park. This Alaska-centric theme park in the heart of Fairbanks includes a riverboat, historic gold rush-era structures, and carnival attractions. See page 247.

A pair of red-necked grebes near Anchorage.

FREE IN ANCHORAGE

Drive to Hatcher Pass. You can have a family picnic on the tundra, take a hike, or pick fresh berries on stunning alpine slopes. See page 217.

Navigate the Coastal Trail. Whether you travel by bike, in-line skates (or skis, in winter) or your own two feet, the 11 miles (18km) of the Tony Knowles Coastal Trail, from downtown Anchorage to Kincaid Park, makes for a delightful afternoon. See page 175.

Eagle River Nature Center. This center offers free nature programs, hiking trails, a viewing telescope, and natural history displays. See page 179.

Anchorage Coastal Wildlife Refuge. A broad, open expanse, just south of Anchorage, which provides an excellent wetland habitat for a variety of resident and migratory birds (and, sometimes, salmon spawning). See page 177.

Windy Corner and Beluga Point. At mileposts 107 and 110 on the Seward Highway, there are pull-outs that allow you to safely park and look for Dall sheep, which often perch on nearby craggy ledges, apparently watching the traffic go by. Telescopes help spot the inlet's beluga whales. See page 177.

Climb Flattop Mountain. Panoramic views of Anchorage, the Alaska Range, and the Cook Inlet reward the sweaty hiker. See page 183.

SPORTING EVENTS

Iditarod Trail Sled Dog Race. Known as 'The Last Great Race,' mushers and their dogs dash approximately 1,000 bone-jarring miles (1,609km) from Anchorage to Nome, crossing two mountain ranges, following the Yukon River for about 150 miles (240km), then traversing the pack ice of Norton Sound. See page 306.

World Eskimo-Indian Olympics. Hundreds of athletes from Alaska and the circumpolar nations gather each July in Fairbanks to compete in many exotic, and often painful, athletic events. These competitions are patterned after the traditional hunting, fishing and gathering culture. Endurance, observation, and a spirit of cooperation are all key ingredients in events like the ear pull, the knuckle hop, the Eskimo stick pull, and the blanket toss. See page 254.

Baseball under the Midnight Sun. During Fairbank's yearly summer solstice festivities, you can watch a baseball game (which has been played on June 21 for more than a century). It begins around 10.30pm and is played without any need for artificial light. See page 248.

Bald eagle near Homer.

Hiking towards Spencer Glacier.

BEST FOR BIRDWATCHING

Chilkat Bald Eagle Preserve (Haines). This preserve is home to the world's largest gathering of bald eagles, and hosts a festival each November. See page 151.

Kachemak Bay (Homer). Hundreds of thousands of shorebirds from as far away as Asia, Hawaii, and South America visit the picturesque hamlet of Homer during spring migration. The city hosts the Katchemak Bay Shorebird Festival each May. See page 207.

Pribilof Islands. These tiny islands about 200 miles (320km) north of Unalaska in the Aleutians are a nesting ground for nearly 200 species of seabirds, including feathered migrants from Asia. See page 343.

Creamers Field (Fairbanks). Originally a dairy farm, this official migratory waterfowl refuge now plays host to sandhill cranes, Canadian honkers, and ducks every spring and fall. See page 249.

Copper River Delta (Cordova). The delta is a birder's paradise, home to the entire population of dusky Canada geese, and the town of Cordova hosts a lively festival during May's migration. See page 191.

BEST RAIL TOURS

The Spencer Glacier and Grandview Tour. Traveling from Anchorage on the Alaska Railroad is a chance to see gorgeous landscapes, glaciers – even take a float trip – and be back in Anchorage in time for dinner. See page 203

The Hurricane Turn Train. Part of the Alaska Railroad, this track is used by locals to reach remote cabins. Passengers may get off the train at any point along the 55-mile (90km) trip to fish, hike, or enjoy a float trip, then flag it down on its return trip to Talkeetna. See page 216

Anchorage to Seward. This route also passes the Spencer Glacier and Grandview areas, but continues on to Seward, where you can take a day cruise into Kenai Fjords National Park. See page 203

Denali National Park and Preserve. Traveling to the park via train offers several good opportunities to view Denali, weather permitting. See page 231

Aboard the White Pass and Yukon Route Railroad. You can retrace the steps of the historic Klondike Trail of '98, from Skagway to the White Pass Summit (elevation nearly 3,000ft). See page 153

A child enjoying the exhibits at the Imaginarium.

MUST-SEE MUSEUMS

Alaska Native Heritage Center (Anchorage). This is the place to learn about Alaska's incredibly rich indigenous culture, art, and traditional customs. and see artists at work. See page 174.

UAF Museum of the North (Fairbanks). This museum at the University of Alaska has long been considered one of the top museums in the state. Exhibits include cultural artifacts, a huge mummified bison, a giant copper nugget, and more. See page 248.

Sitka National Historical Park. Wind your way through a beautiful, old-growth coastal forest, view an extensive collection of Tlingit and Haida totem poles, visit a museum and watch Native American artisans at work. See page 134.

Alaska State Museum (Juneau). Exhibits range from a Native American community house to Inuit ivory carvings and gold rush memorabilia, all illustrating Alaska's varied history. The most notable feature is a model of a towering, two-story 'eagle tree.' See page 139.

The White Pass and Yukon Route Railroad.

MONEY SAVING TIPS

Alaska is an expensive place to visit, but there are tricks you can use to mitigate the price tag of your trip without sacrificing the experience.

Train travel: Tailor your trip around the rail lines. Once in town, Seward is delightful to visit on foot, and the Hurricane Turn train allows for easy access to the backcountry.

Municipal bus: While in Anchorage, Juneau, and Fairbanks, consider the municipal bus as an alternative to costly cabs: the service may be infrequent, but it is worth the pennies saved.

Look out for passes and discounts: Many attractions offer discounts for students and retirees. Anchorage offers a culture pass that gives a discount price for admission to two museums.

Travel during the off season: Prices for lodging and transportation are lower in the spring and fall.

Take the ferry: The Alaska State Ferry travels practically the entire coastline of the state via a series of ferries, though note that in most cases there is no such thing as a quick trip. The reasonable fares come with access to on board entertainment, and the bar and cafeteria are surprisingly affordable.

THE BEST OF ALASKA: PLAN & BOOK YOUR TAILOR-MADE TRIP

Alaska is a vast state that offers stunning and varied natural beauty, a warm and welcoming culture and myriad things to do. From the urban sophistication of Alaska's cities to outdoor pursuits and wildlife spotting in the wilderness to serene cruises and farmers markets selling local produce, this magical ten-day adventure delivers it all.

△ **Day 2, Chugach State Park.** For snowy peaks, glacial lakes and alpine valleys head for Chugach State Park, which is a playground for outdoor enthusiasts, criss-crossed with 280 miles of trails. Climb Flattop Mountain and be rewarded with phenomenal views, or try a spot of biking, fishing, rafting, horseback riding or kayaking. See page 182.

△ **Day 1, Anchorage.** Anchorage may be the gateway to Alaska but do take time to explore the state's largest city. Visit the Alaska Native Heritage Centre, which offers an in-depth look at indigenous culture, art and traditions. Afterwards, hit Downtown for its buzzing restaurant scene, where fresh king crab and wild salmon are a menu favourite. See page 169.

▽ **Days 3 & 4, Denali National Park & Preserve.** Denali is North America's highest peak, surrounded by Denali National Park & Preserve. To get there from Anchorage, hop aboard the Denali Star train bound for Fairbanks (incidentally, one of the best places to see the aurora borealis) and soak up the scenery en route. Next day, take a tour bus through the park, keeping your eyes open for grizzlies, caribou, moose, wolves and more. See page 227.

△ **Days 5 & 6, Seward.** Make your way down south, via Anchorage, to the city of Seward, which nestles between the mountains and the ocean. Spend an afternoon exploring the picturesque harbour and historic downtown with its public mural collection. The Exit Glacier is one of the most popular road-accessible glaciers in the state, and well worth a visit. See page 201.

▽ **Day 7, Kenai Fjords National Park.** Resurrection Bay and the nearby Kenai Fjords National Park are said to be among the most reliable places to view marine wildlife in the world. Venture out on a day cruise and bring your binoculars to spot the sea lions, otters, porpoises, humpback whales, orcas, puffins, bald eagles and seabirds that call the region home. See page 202.

△ **Day 8, Homer.** A three-hour drive from Seward will bring you to the coastal community of Homer, with its seafood shacks, local galleries and bustling farmers' market. Fish abound in the town's surrounding waters, earning it the title of "Halibut Fishing Capital of the World"; birdwatchers should take a boat to Kachemak Bay, home to thousands of migrating shorebirds during summer. See page 207.

▽ **Days 9 & 10, Girdwood.** Heading back to Anchorage, stop at Portage Valley and take a boat trip to its crown jewel, the Portage Glacier, before spending your final night in the small mountain town of Girdwood. On your way to the airport, stop over at the Alaska Wildlife Conservation Centre, a 200-acre sanctuary dedicated to preserving local species. See page 177.

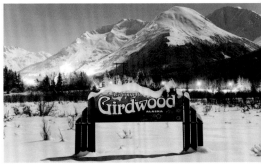

You can plan and book this trip with Insight Guides, or we can help you create your own. Whether you're after adventure or a family-friendly holiday, we have a trip for you, with all the activities you enjoy doing and the sights you want to see. All our trips are devised by local experts who get the most out of the destination. Visit **www.insightguides.com/holidays** to chat with one of our local travel experts.

A car makes its way along an icy Alaskan highway.

A grizzly bear hunts along a salmon stream in Katmai National Park.

Kayaking off Ketchikan coast.

THE LAST FRONTIER

Some people say there are no more frontiers to explore without leaving the planet. But they're forgetting about Alaska, where the wild landscape remains vastly untouched by the modern world.

The mail arrives by floatplane.

Alaska: the Great Land, the Last Frontier – more than 580,000 sq miles (1.5 million sq km) that taunted early explorers and still challenges modern-day researchers. It also provokes a fascination that attracts more and more travelers looking for something that a conventional vacation cannot give them. The hint of urban sophistication in Anchorage and Juneau rapidly gives way to the frontier, where outdoor survival skills are among the most useful attributes a resident can possess.

America's 49th state is so broad, so unpeopled, and so roadless that small airplanes are more common than cabs in other states. Men outnumber women (though women have coined the phrase 'The odds are good, but the goods are odd'). The population numbers almost 740,000, with about 40 percent living in one city, Anchorage. Nearly the entire state is raw, wondrous wilderness.

Alaska has lush rain-drenched forests and fragile windswept tundras. There are lofty mountains, spectacular glaciers, and still-active volcanoes, as well as 3 million lakes and endless swamps. Along with a handful of modern high-rise buildings, there are countless one-room log cabins. This varied land is best viewed from a small plane or surveyed from a canoe or kayak – or by foot; it cannot be seen properly from a car (though increasing numbers of people are exploring parts of the state by traveling the highways). And, although it would take forever to cover on foot, hiking is often the best way to touch the landscape, to appreciate its vastness. Alaska is an outdoor world, a wilderness, a land of many faces.

Indigenous Alaskans.

The Alaskan experience includes the sheer wonder of finding what hides beyond the horizon or over the next ridge. No one person has ever seen it all; no one person ever will. Therein lies the essence of Alaska. Its huge untamed spaces, it has been said, are the greatest gift Alaska can give to a harassed world.

WHEN TO GO

Springtime (or 'breakup') to an Alaskan is a hopeful time of dwindling snow berms, widening streets, emerging lawns and, most exciting of all, lengthening daylight hours. But to a visitor in the here-and-now of Alaska spring, it may look like dirty snow melting to reveal accumulated trash, huge puddles trapped by still-frozen drains on winter-ravaged roads and fickle weather conditions. March, April, and early May are months of renewal for Alaskans, but visitors would be wise to allow sufficient time for the state to wake up, spruce up, and set up for the tourist season.

Canoes are versatile transportation.

Before the first cruise ship arrives, store merchants bring out hanging flower baskets and the cities seem to 'bloom' overnight. Gift shops, which may have been closed over the winter, are re-opened, swept, shelves stocked and windows polished. The visitor season runs from mid-May to mid-September. During those months, all tours, parks, campgrounds, trains, buses, ferries, restaurants, hotels, B&Bs, and other service-related facilities are running at full speed. Many offer bargain rates for the 'shoulder seasons' of late May and early September. Summer in Alaska boasts mild temperatures and, in most areas, seemingly endless daylight.

If springtime is when Alaska showers and shaves, and summer is open house, fall feels like a time for getting together with a few close friends. Like spring, the timing of autumn in Alaska is a fickle business, and one can miss it altogether. Generally it begins to feel like fall in late August and continues through mid-September. The trees and grasses turn golden, the spent fireweed magenta, and the mountains, below the 'termination dust' of newly snowcapped peaks, a warm russet. Fall brings darkness back to the night sky of most of Alaska, and with it displays of the aurora borealis, or Northern Lights.

There are far fewer tourists in autumn – but fewer options, too. The favorite tourist destinations, lodgings, restaurants, transportations and other amenities taper off as suddenly as they gear up in late spring. The use of a private or rental car greatly increases sightseeing options. Careful research and planning is needed for a rewarding autumn visit to Alaska – but are well worth the effort.

If skiing, snowboarding, sled dog races, and other winter sports appeal, a wintertime visit to Alaska is an excellent option. The Fur Rendezvous, held in Anchorage in late February, is a yearly celebration that includes the Open World Championship Sled Dog Race, fireworks, art exhibits, a reindeer run through town, fur auctions, a winter outdoor carnival (dress warmly), and much more. Fairbanks also celebrates winter with Denali Winterfest, fireworks displays, sled dog races and the incredible sculptural masterpieces of the World Ice Art Championship.

The Northern Lights are best seen between late September and early April.

Lupine flowers, a native species.

THE FRAGILE WILDERNESS

It's thrilling to visit areas that have remained unchanged for a thousand years. But how can more people enjoy the experience without endangering that very wildness?

You don't really know what wild means until you've been to Alaska. With one-fifth of the land area of the contiguous United States and more shoreline than all the other states combined, Alaska includes 150 million acres (60 million hectares) of national parks and forests, wildlife refuges and other designated preserves. Its 38 mountain ranges, 3,000 rivers and 3 million lakes fall within climate ranges from temperate rainforest to arid Arctic. Much of this territory is barely charted, let alone touched by the human foot.

Of Alaska's 15 national parks, preserves and monuments, only five can be accessed by road. Glacier Bay National Park (3.3 million acres/1.3 million hectares), for example, can be reached only by boat or floatplane. North America's premier mountain wilderness and its largest national park, Wrangell-St Elias National Park and Preserve (13.2 million acres/5.3 million hectares), is home to nine peaks of more than 14,000ft (4,270 meters), including the 18,010ft (5,490-meter) Mount St Elias, the continent's fourth-highest peak (and the second-tallest in the United States). The park also has the largest collection of glaciers in North America, the Bagley Icefield, numerous wild rivers, and multitudes of wildlife. Yet only two roads penetrate the park boundaries, one of which is unpaved and best negotiated by four-wheel-drive vehicles.

NATURAL WONDERS

For those eager to explore the Arctic, Gates of the Arctic National Park, the northernmost of all the state's parks, is a remote and undeveloped 8.4 million acres (3.4 million hectares) of crags, fragile alpine meadows, crystal clear mountain streams, and sweeping Arctic valleys. Without roads or trails, backpacking, mountaineering, river floating,

Do not feed the animals; maintaining the balance between tourism and nature.

and dogsled excursions are the best ways in which visitors can explore these Arctic expanses.

Besides its federal parks and refuges, Alaska has state-managed parks and sanctuaries that are among the nation's finest, from 1.55-million-acre (630,000-hectare) Wood-Tikchik – the country's largest state park – to the Alaska Chilkat Bald Eagle Preserve and McNeil River State Game Sanctuary, where dozens of brown bears, some weighing 1,000 pounds (450kg) or more, gather each summer to fish for salmon.

Whether it's animals in the sea, air or on land, wildlife is abundant throughout much of the state's wilderness. Hundreds of thousands of caribou roam across sweeping tundra, Dall sheep graze in high alpine basins, seals sun themselves on ice floes, wolves howl from the tops of ridges, golden eagles spiral through blue skies and clouds, whales ply turquoise fjords.

Alaska has approximately 100,000 glaciers and more than 3 million lakes. The largest of these, Lake Iliamna, in southwest Alaska, encompasses 1,100 sq miles (2,850 sq km).

---

road (such as Portage Glacier, Denali National Park and Preserve, and cities such as Anchorage, Juneau, and Fairbanks) but rarely step into untouched wilderness. Only one road goes into 6-million-acre (2.4-million-hectare) Denali National Park – a 90-mile (145km) strip that bars most private vehicles. While this road channels more and more visitors into the park each year via bus tours – which cause minimum disturbance to the landscape and wildlife – only a fraction register for back-country permits.

A bus stops for a grizzly sow and her cubs to cross the road, Denali National Park.

When federal geographer Henry Gannett, a founder of the National Geographic Society, surveyed Alaska's expanse in 1904, he set the tone for today's ecotourism: 'Its grandeur is more valuable than the gold or the fish or the timber, for it will never be exhausted.' Alaska is a land where inhabitants and travelers sense that they can do no better.

LOW-IMPACT TOURISM

Unfortunately, the traditional tourist industry in the state often bypasses its great wilderness areas in favor of organized tours that take visitors by bus, train or airplane to cities, towns and developed parks. The majority of tourists see sights that are reached by

Furthermore, the Alaska Travel Industry Association reports that in one recent summer around 1.9 million non-resident visitors spent a little more than $2 billion, or about $1,060 a person. About half of these visitors said they did some wildlife viewing – although only an estimated 10 percent strike out away from traditional tourist areas into the pristine wilderness.

Guides such as Bob Jacobs, founder of St Elias Alpine Guides based in Anchorage, feel that visitors to Alaska should see a lot more, but, at the same time, the land should be protected. 'Alaska is a wonderful classroom,' Bob says. But, unlike school, 'you don't need a schedule. In summer you can hike until 2am and sleep until noon.'

On Jacobs' trips into the heart of the Wrangell-St Elias National Park you climb unnamed peaks, raft down swift, milky rivers and backpack for weeks at a time. Jacobs helped pioneer ecotourism in this state, which comprises environmentally friendly outdoor adventures such as sea kayaking, mountaineering and wildlife watching. Though the great majority of travelers continue to see Alaska by car, tour bus, or cruise ship, ecotourism has helped a growing number of people see wild and pristine areas of Alaska inaccessible to the masses.

By opening its doors to travelers in summer and to parties of schoolchildren in spring and fall, it works to foster responsible human interaction with their natural surroundings and to generate knowledge of the marine and coastal ecosystems of Kachemak Bay through its environmental education and research programs.

Ecotourism in Alaska was initiated by a handful of small, independent operators and outfitters that led groups into the outback, while the mainstream industry concentrated on marketing developed resort areas.

Heading back to camp after a trek.

PROTECTING THE LAND

According to the UN Environmental Programme, ecotourism not only falls under the umbrella of the UN's definition of 'sustainable tourism,' but it goes one step beyond by actively contributing to the betterment of local natural and human communities.

Visitors become better educated about an area and the issues facing it, while encouraged to practice low-impact measures that avoid disturbing ecosystems. Ecotourism also means that tourist dollars get filtered back through to the local community and to preservation organizations.

Alaskans place a high value on being in balance with nature. The Center for Alaskan Coastal Studies offers naturalist-led tours and experiences.

⊘ GEOLOGICAL YOUTH

Alaska is a young country, geologically speaking. Composed of fragments of the earth's crust that rafted from the Pacific area on the backs of crustal plates and then 'docked' together, the entire region is still in the process of coming together. Tracing the ridgeline along the Aleutians and Alaska Range, it is easy to see where the Pacific plate rammed into the North American. Its youth and place on the globe are responsible for much of Alaska's diversity and largesse. Its mountain ranges include active volcanoes with peaks, 19 of which are over 14,000ft (4,270 meters), and 17 that are among the 20 highest mountains in the United States.

Now some large-scale organizations have developed policies and principles that depart significantly from traditional commercial concerns and lean toward low-impact tourism. Nevertheless, ecotourism largely remains the domain of smaller businesses that emphasize small groups.

ECO-FRIENDLY OPTIONS

Dozens of outfitters offer river rafting, tundra trekking, mountain climbing, birdwatching, whale cruising, wildlife photography safaris, and sea-kayaking adventures, ranging from easy-going to incredibly strenuous. Some tour operators specialize in ecotours geared specifically toward senior citizens. Although some of these trips hark back to the days of the pioneers, they are usually made comfortable enough. Visitors can take advantage of experienced guides without having to acquire all the necessary skills themselves; and many of the backcountry meals approach gourmet quality.

Wildlife viewing is a major draw, especially for those hoping to see the monarchs of the

A humpback whale makes a splash.

⊘ TRAVELING GREEN

There are a number of ways to make your stay in Alaska more eco-friendly. Purchasing carbon credits for the long flight to Alaska as well as for any inner state air travel is a great way to offset your greenhouse gas emissions. Travel by train and ferry is also lower impact than by car. Follow the guidelines that come with backcountry permits and query wilderness lodges on their environmental practices. Opting for smaller, locally owned hotels, restaurants, and adventure outfitters keeps money within the community and is often the more ecological choice. For a list of green travel businesses, visit www.adventuregreenalaska.org.

land: the grizzly and its coastal cousin, the brown bear. One of the most notable areas is the McNeil River State Game Sanctuary, but visitors are strictly regulated by permit; only a limited number of people a day, accompanied by sanctuary staff, can visit the bear-viewing areas. This close supervision means that visitors have to apply in advance, and names are randomly drawn by computer. You have a better chance of getting to Brooks Camp, another top bear-viewing area, within Katmai National Park.

Other renowned bear-viewing areas include Denali National Park and Preserve, home to 200 to 300 bears; many can be seen grazing on plants or digging for ground squirrels near the Park Road. Kodiak National Wildlife Refuge, designated a refuge by President Franklin D. Roosevelt in 1941, is home to the largest bears on earth (they can reach 1,200lbs/540kg). As much as 10 percent of Alaska's grizzlies live on Kodiak Island. 'Big bears fill big hotels,' said the controversial grizzly activist Timothy Treadwell, who was mauled to death by a bear in Katmai National Park in 2003. 'People go to Alaska to see wilderness, to be part of what Earth used to be like. That's good for tourism. If you protect

your homework. Look for organizations that go beyond making money. Talk to them. Get a feeling for their philosophy. Ask for references. That's the best policy.'

Following some guidelines will help make your trip ecologically friendly. Check to see if an operator limits the number of people it takes into fragile areas. Does the company practice low-impact camping and hiking and vary the location of campsites from trip to trip in order to avoid scarring the ground in certain areas? Does it supply a reading list about

A photographer's paradise.

grizzly habitat, you protect your bread and butter.'

Besides bears, people come from around the world to see other wildlife: Dall sheep, moose, caribou, wolves, bald and golden eagles, and all manner of songbirds, shorebirds, and seabirds, as well as marine mammals (see page 75).

ETHICAL GUIDELINES

Although ecotourism industry operators generally follow environmental ethics, they don't all abide equally by the unwritten code of minimal impact. Bob Jacobs has some suggestions to enable would-be visitors to pick the right company with which to travel. 'Do

the area and the type of activities you will be pursuing?

Top ecotourism companies are staffed by experienced naturalists who accompany their guests on journeys and offer extensive information along the way. Such specialists help minimize impact on wildlife by keeping groups at unobtrusive, safe distances. The companies should also be committed to energy conservation and recycling, as this helps preserve the environment that you have come here to enjoy.

Even if you're traveling on your own, you can do your part by making low-impact and eco-friendly choices. It makes sense to preserve the grandeur of Alaska's wilderness for the benefit of future generations.

A hunter carries trophy moose antlers in the Chugach Mountains.

AN INDEPENDENT PEOPLE

As Alaska continues to draw more and more people from around the world, its population is slowly approaching the one-million mark. So how do you define a 'typical' Alaskan?

Before Alyson Rigby Ronningen, who grew up in England, traveled to Alaska for the first time, she thought she had a pretty clear idea of what Alaskans were like: 'They all wore flannel shirts, had big bushy beards, and they owned guns and big dogs,' she recalled. Alyson eventually married an Alaskan and moved to the Far North. Once there, she looked around at her Fairbanks neighbors and smugly told a friend, 'I was right.'

But Alyson was not a 'typical' visitor, or even a run-of-the-mill new Alaskan. She spent her first winter living in a wall tent with her husband and new baby. While her husband worked as a carpenter nearby, she used a tiny wood stove for both warmth and cooking. Temperatures plummeted as low as –30° or –40°F (–34° to –40°C) but Alyson stayed toasty by baking on her trusty wood stove. She conformed to what many believe to be an unspoken code of the north: be independent and self-sufficient.

In that way she was a 'typical' Alaskan, yet it is difficult to generalize about what is typical, because it depends so much on where you choose to settle and under what circumstances you live. Alaska is so huge and the various parts of the state are so different from each other that the residents are bound to differ widely as well.

The hand tram across Winner Creek Gorge.

ANCHORED DOWN IN ANCHORAGE

The hub of the state is its largest (although not its capital) city, Anchorage. Rural Alaskans often joke that Anchorage is only 20 minutes from the real Alaska. That may well be true, but many urban Alaskans make the best possible use of those 20 minutes.

In a state where the median age is 34, Anchorage (with around 42 percent of the population) is a city of young – but aging – professionals (the population's average age is increasing). They include active outdoor-sports lovers, such as rock climbers, mountain bikers, whitewater kayakers, and runners. Many people bring their outdoor toys to work with them, and at the end of the day, they head for the hills, the city's biking trails and parks, or nearby streams. In summer they don't have to worry about running out of daylight, either, because from late May through early August the sky never fully darkens.

People in Anchorage also spend a lot of time getting out of town. Lake Hood, a floatplane base in the city, is the largest and busiest such base in the world, with more than 1,000 takeoffs and landings recorded on a peak summer day.

Where do they all go? Just peek out of a plane window as you fly into Anchorage and you will see hundreds of little getaway cabins tucked into the surrounding wilderness and the more remote areas. Those without their own cabins may fly to public-use cabins, developed campgrounds, or backcountry destinations where they set up their own campsites.

BACKCOUNTRY LIFESTYLE

John Power, a long-time Alaskan who became a 'big city' resident in his early 40s, thought about getting one of those backcountry cabins when he first moved to Anchorage, but instead bought a 30ft (9-meter) sailboat, which he keeps in Prince William Sound. Power, a geophysicist with the Alaska Volcano Observatory, moved to Anchorage from Fairbanks, where for many years he had lived on the town's outskirts in a little cabin with no running water and, like Alyson, just a wood stove for heating.

'I liked it,' he says. 'I liked living in a place where I didn't really have any neighbors. I liked not having to worry about it when I left in winter, which I

Fishermen proud of their catch.

⊘ PAYBACK FOR THE PEOPLE

Because Alaska depends to such an extent on its natural resources, its citizens argued they should benefit directly from the exploitation of those riches rather than trust politicians to spend the money. In 1976, voters passed a constitutional amendment creating the Alaska Permanent Fund. This trust fund invests a proportion of revenues from mineral sales and each October pays out a dividend to every qualified Alaskan resident. The sum has varied from $331.29 per person in 1984 to to a high of $2,072 in 2015. It is valued income, particularly for the poor, and it tends to lessen local opposition to further oil drilling in wilderness areas.

frequently did when I was traveling. It was inexpensive. I first got into that lifestyle when I was a student and I never really changed. I didn't have to worry about housesitters, or about the plumbing freezing or the heat being on when I was gone.' He misses his reliable little wood stove most of all. 'I used to like getting up in the morning, building my fire, and cooking pancakes in the kitchen with the wood stove roaring away,' he says nostalgically.

There are several thousand Fairbanks-area residents who still embrace the wood-stove, no-running-water lifestyle with enthusiasm. These people usually fill 5-gallon (22-liter) water jugs at the laundromats in town, or at their places of employment. Showers are also available for use at the laundromats of many communities.

When winter settles in and the mercury begins to drop, conversation generally revolves around the weather, particularly the frigid temperatures endured in the Interior and Arctic regions. Eventually, someone will complain about water pipes freezing and bursting, and those who have no running water try not to look too self-satisfied.

In Kodiak and other fishing communities, XtraTuf rubber boots and heavy-duty raingear are the fashion *du jour*. Since many students and some teachers fish, the school calendar is based on fishing openings and closures. The

languages are spoken today with 22 different dialects. Like their non-indigenous neighbors, Alaskan Native Americans have an intimate relationship with the landscape, prize their independence, and celebrate their history.

Other Alaskans came here as visitors and decided to stay on. Typical among them are the descendants of Russian immigrants in the Kenai Peninsula, Kodiak, and Sitka. The first Russians came to Alaska in the late 18th century (see page 47) and established communities first in Kodiak, then in present-day Sitka, which

A husky and friend.

population swells in the summer when people arrive to fish, then contracts when they leave again at the end of the season.

ALASKA NATIVES

Making up nearly 15 percent of the population, Alaskan Native Americans play an important cultural and economic role in the state. While many live in traditional villages far off the road system, indigenous Alaskans can be found as university students in the biggest cities or as commercial fishermen in outlying communities. Some of Alaska's biggest corporations are owned by Native Americans, and the Alaska Native Medical Center is the most cutting-edge hospital in the state. Eleven different cultural

⦿ JACK LONDON AND THE YUKON

The prolific San Francisco-born novelist Jack London (1876–1916) joined the fortune hunters in 1897's Klondike Gold Rush and later created a romantically adventurous portrait of Alaska in such novels as *White Fang* and *The Call of the Wild*. In both books, sled dogs fight to survive in Alaska's unforgiving wilderness. London developed scurvy from a lack of fresh food in winter, and, having failed to strike it rich, worked as a laborer back in San Francisco until a newspaper published his account of his trip down the Yukon. Today a log cabin in Dawson City, Canada, is a Jack London Museum (tel: 867-993-5575).

became the headquarters of the fur trading Russian-American Company.

Both towns retain strong Russian influences, but it is on the Kenai Peninsula that a strict Russian Orthodox community survives, based around their 'Island of Faith' near Anchor Point. Survivors of persecution by the Orthodox Church, the government, and later the Stalinist purges, they call themselves "the Old Believers."

Today they work in local businesses, or operate companies of their own, and manage their own fishing fleet. But their lives revolve around

of uninhabited landscape by counting rivers and mountain ridges; land on bays, glaciers, lakes, river bars or tundra; and brave weather that would

> *In communities along the Alaskan coast, life revolves not only around the weather, but around the fishing season. When the fishing is poor, the whole town suffers and the economy of the whole community is in trouble.*

Sea planes are used by residents and visitors alike to access remote back country areas around Alaska.

their religious beliefs. The study of holy books is mandatory during periods of fasting before Christmas and Lent. They wear traditional clothes: the women and girls always cover their heads with scarves, and men dress conservatively, often sporting close-trimmed beards.

Yet they are no less Alaskan than the man who lives in the bush and calls the Lower 48 states 'America,' as if he inhabited a separate country; or the Anchorage college graduate, rushing from his downtown office to the mountaintops at weekends.

BUSH PILOTS

Connecting Alaska's far-flung populace is the intrepid bush pilot. Not easily daunted, Alaska's special breed of flyer can navigate mile upon mile

daunt a seasoned commercial airline pilot. They transport passengers and supplies into the remote backcountry and to tiny villages where people still rely on them to turn up in emergencies, and to deliver the mail, if not – they hope – the babies.

There is no doubt that the best way to describe the relationship between Alaska and her bush pilots is complicated bliss; they are a rugged and colorful bunch. Their courageous, comic, and sometimes tragic stories are the stuff of legend. Paul Claus, one of Alaska's most celebrated bush pilots, has been known to land on a glacier so steep that he had to anchor the plane with an ice screw to keep it from sliding off the edge. To take off, he leaned out the window, cut the tether with a knife, and throttled off the slope.

A TRAPPER'S LIFE

Fur for fashion's sake is out, but Alaskans still consider trapping a part of their heritage and a way of life in the far north.

For many, fur is an integral and critical part of life in the Alaskan bush. Not only does it provide more warmth than wool or other synthetic material, trapping is one of the few ways for those living off the land to make money to pay for their most basic provisions.

Life in the bush has changed little over the years. Most trappers maintain two or three traplines, each about 40 to 60 miles (65 to 95km) long. Checking them on a routine basis is essential to ensure that no animal is caught for long periods of time, causing excessive pain and suffering. While nearly all Alaska's small mammals, from the Arctic fox to the tiny weasel, are valued for their fur, lynx and beaver are particularly prized.

WORKING WITH DOGS

Some have started to use snow-machines, but for many, dogsleds are essential to a trapper's life. Not only do they provide companionship, dogs do not break down like machines, a factor in these remote areas that can mean the difference between life and death. Still, a trapper must be able to control a sled drawn by a dozen huskies, capable of doing some 60 miles (100km) a day on a good trail, in temperatures dipping as low as –50°F (–45°C). Many things can go wrong on a trip: a sled could clip a sapling in its careening descent of a slope; there could be a dog fight, or a threat from runaway dogs; a last-minute repair job might be needed, or the towline can disconnect from the sled, sending the dogs flying in formation without their driver; and sometimes a 1,500-pound (700kg) bull moose can challenge the team's right to use the trail.

Because there's always something to watch out for, the trapper must work in close unison with the team. The dogs are guided verbally, with commands to tell a leader which trail to take, to order slack dogs to speed up, or to encourage the team as a whole when they begin to tire. By watching the dogs' ears, eyes and attitudes, an experienced trapper can determine whether the team scent a moose or an animal in a trap ahead, if they want to fight or balk, if they're happy, discouraged, or overtired.

The seasons are important in the remote Alaskan bush – for those working with machines as much as for those still using dog teams. In the summer, many trappers concentrate on fishing, picking berries and cultivating gardens. Fishnets must be run daily and the dogs fed with cooked whitefish or salmon and rice. Any extra fish are cut and dried for next winter.

In the summer months, trappers may take the opportunity to build dog houses and sleds, sew sled bags, dog booties and harnesses. Some trappers tan and sew furs from the winter's catch, making hats and mitts that they can sell for extra cash.

Furs hang awaiting bidders during the Alaska Trappers Association's annual fur auction.

When fall arrives, there are cranberries to be picked, jam to be made, and, when the annual fish run begins, whitefish are netted and frozen whole for the dogs' food. With winter comes the trapping season, and the truly hard work: snowshoeing through deep snow, skiing miles to set trails, and cutting cord after cord of firewood.

So it goes, the yearly cycle of putting food up in summer and fall, and trapping and woodcutting in winter and spring. The weekly cycle, measured by the mail plane and the trapline rounds, and the daily cycle of mushing dogs, maintaining equipment and feeding fires. It's a hard life but, for many, a happy and fulfilled one.

Caribou crossing, near Paxson.

DECISIVE DATES

THE EARLY ALASKANS

30–10,000 BC
The migration of tribes from Asia occurs across a land bridge, which at the time linked Siberia and Alaska.

10,000 BC
The Aleuts settle in the Aleutian Islands. The name Alaska derived from their word 'Alaxsxag' meaning 'the object toward which the action of the sea is directed.' Other tribes disperse throughout North and South America but the Aleuts, the Eskimos (Inupiats and Yup'iks) and the Indians, which include the Athabascans and the coastal Tlingits and Haidas, settle in Alaska.

THE RUSSIAN INVASION

1741
First Russian ships arrive. Vitus Bering turns back after his crew made one brief

Performing a war dance.

landing in what is now called Prince William Sound, and dies before he could reach home, while Alexei Chirikof lands on Prince of Wales Island, where some of his crew mysteriously vanish. The fur trade is established, and the indigenous people forced to hunt on the Russians' behalf.

1778
Captain James Cook visits the Aleutian Islands. His brief visit prompts English interest in the fur trade the Russians have developed.

1784
Grigor Ivanovich Shelikof arrives on Kodiak Island. He enslaves and ill-treats the tribal residents, then sets up the first permanent Russian settlement on Three Saints Bay where he builds a school and introduces the Russian Orthodox religion.

An Aleutian couple wearing traditional clothes.

1790
Alexander Baranof takes over the fur enterprise. He treats the workers more humanely than his predecessors, and moves the Russian colony to the site of the present city of Kodiak.

1799
The Russian-American Company is formed.

1802
The Tlingits raze to the ground the Russian town of Mikhailovsk, built near the site of present-day Sitka, on land they had sold to Baranof. Later, the Russians destroy the Tlingit village and establish the town of New Archangel, capital of Russian America.

1812
Russia finally reaches a settlement with America over

hunting rights in Alaska, but the agreement doesn't last.

1833
The British Hudson's Bay Company establishes a fur-trading outpost in Alaska.

Mid-19th century
Russian power diminishes. British and Americans undermine the fur monopoly and the Tlingits wage guerrilla war.

1866
A Western Union expedition under William H. Dall produces the first scientific studies of Alaska and the first map of the Yukon River.

AMERICA TAKES OVER

1867
US Congress, at the instigation of Secretary of State William Seward, buys Alaska from the Russians for $7.2 million.

1870s–80s
Fish canneries established around Nushagak Bay to exploit the huge runs of salmon. In the Aleutians, fur seals and otters are slaughtered ruthlessly. Whalers pursue their quarries to the high Arctic.

THE GOLD RUSH

1880
Gold is discovered at Silver Bow Basin, and the town of Juneau is founded.

1882
The Treadwell Mine, across the Gastineau Channel from Juneau, flourishes.

1896
Gold is discovered in the Klondike, a tributary of the Yukon, and the easiest route to it is by ship to Skagway. The White Pass and Chikoot Trail to the gold fields are tackled by thousands and Skagway becomes a thriving center.

1899
Gold is discovered at Nome in the far northwest. Many prospectors who had been unsuccessful in the Yukon move west to try again.

1902
Felix Pedro strikes gold in the Tanana Hills.

1903
The town of Fairbanks, near Pedro's strike, is founded on the site of a trading post set up by entrepreneur E.T. Barnette and named for a senator who had given him financial support.

Early 1900s
Prospectors flock to Alaska from all over North America and Europe.

1910
Kennecott, the richest copper mine in the world, starts operations in the Wrangell-St Elias mountains.

A large cruise ship making its way through the fjords.

1913

The first airplane is flown in Alaska, inaugurating the state's love affair with flying.

WORLD WAR II

1942

The Alaska Highway – the Alcan – is built in under nine months as both a means of defense and an overland supply route to America's Russian allies, after sea routes are cut off following the Japanese attack on Pearl Harbor. The Japanese land on the islands of Kiska and Attu. The villagers are interned in Japan for the remainder of the war. Aleuts living in the Pribilofs and Aleutian Islands villages are evacuated.

1943

After a two-week battle the Americans re-take Attu and Kiska and the Japanese begin their retreat.

STATEHOOD AND OIL

1957

Oil is discovered at the Swanson River on the Kenai Peninsula.

1959

Alaska becomes the 49th US state in January, and is welcomed into the union by President Dwight D. Eisenhower. Sitka pulp mill opens.

1964

The Good Friday earthquake hits Southcentral Alaska. Over 100 people are killed, mostly by tidal waves. Valdez, Seward, Cordova, Kodiak, and several small villages suffer the worst effects.

1968

Oil is found at Prudhoe Bay.

1971

The Alaska Native Claims Settlement Act (ANCSA) gives Native Americans title to 44 million acres (18 million hectares) of land, and $963 million, distributed among specially formed native corporations.

1971–77

The construction of the trans-Alaska pipeline to Valdez creates thousands of jobs and transforms Anchorage and Fairbanks into bright, modern cities.

1976

The Alaska Permanent Fund is created to ensure there are long-term benefits from oil revenues.

1977

The trans-Alaska pipeline is finally completed. Oil begins to flow and the state economy booms.

1980

In one of the 20th century's landmark conservation successes, President Jimmy Carter signs the Alaska National Interest Lands Conservation Act (ANILCA), which adds 104 million acres (42 million hectares) of conservation lands in national parks, wildlife refuges, and forests.

1989

The Exxon Valdez tanker hits Bligh Reef and spills 11 million gallons (42 million liters) of oil into Prince William Sound. A huge clean-up operation is launched. Thousands of miles of coastline are inundated by oil and thousands of birds

An otter covered in oil after the Exxon Valdez disaster, 1989.

and mammals are killed. Litigation follows.

1990

A new decade sees the logging and fishing industries in steady decline but the cruise industry starts to boom.

1995

Canadian fishermen stage protests about access to Southeast Alaska's troll king salmon fishery.

1996

A fierce debate begins over the question of whether rural residents – particularly those of indigenous cultures – should be granted a subsistence priority for the harvest of Alaska's fish and wildlife.

1998

The moose is adopted as the state's official land mammal.

1999

The Alaska Native Heritage Center opens in Anchorage.

2000

A census puts the population at 626,932, a rise of 14 percent in just 10 years.

An example of the destruction caused by the earthquake in Anchorage, 1964.

2003
Bears maul to death author Timothy Treadwell, famous for approaching them up-close, in Katmai National Park. The state initiates its controversial predator control program by issuing permits to hunters to shoot wolves from airplanes.

2004
A record 708 fires burn more than 6.7 million acres (2.7 million hectares).

2006
An oil leak in August results in a shutoff of the Prudhoe Bay Oil Field for several months.

2008
Governor Sarah Palin becomes the first Alaskan to appear on the ticket of a major political party for the presidential race. The last full-blooded Eyak dies.

2009
Mount Redoubt, a volcano 100 miles (160km) southwest of Anchorage, erupts, spreading ash over Southcentral Alaska.

2010
Ted Stevens, the longest-serving US Senator until he was convicted of corruption charges in 2008, dies in a plane crash.

2012
Cordovoa gets a record amount of snow, 15ft (4.5meters) in two months. The National Guard is called out and locals dub the event 'Snowpocalypse 2012.'

2013
A 7.5 tremor strikes off the coast of Southeast Alaska near Prince Wales Island. A tsunami warning is issued, but no big waves land.

2015
Falling oil prices trigger a fiscal crisis in Alaska. Consequently, the state governor proposes the introduction of personal income tax for the first time in 35 years. President Barack Obama visits the state to highlight the dangers of the climate change. Recreational use of marihuana legalised.

2019
The hottest year in Alaska on record. March is overall 20 degrees warmer than usual, reaching 42 degrees Fahrenheit in Kotzebue.

2020
The COVID-19 pandemic reaches Alaska. On 11 March, Governor Mike Dunleavy's office declares a state of emergency; the next day, the first confirmed case, a foreign national in Anchorage, is announced to the public.

Miners at the Anvil Creek gold mine.

Native Alaskans have a long history.

BEGINNINGS

Alaska was inhabited for thousands of years by various indigenous groups, each with their own culture and language. But the discovery that the territory was rich in furs attracted the attention of Russian traders, and changed the lives of the people forever.

Who were the people who first thrived in such an unforgiving environment? Anthropologists believe the ancestors of the Alaskan natives migrated in several waves over a land bridge that joined Siberia and Alaska thousands of years ago. In 2011, the discovery of the remains a cremated child near the Tanana River puts this date back to 11,500 years ago.

When Europeans first encountered them in the early 18th century, there were dozens of tribes and language groups throughout the region, from the Inupiat Eskimos in the Arctic region to the Tlingits in the Southeast. Today, these first Alaskans are divided into several main groups: the southeastern Coastal Indians (the Tlingits and Haidas), the Athabascans (Interior Indians), the Aleuts, the Alutiiqs, the Eyak, and the two groups of Eskimos: Inupiat and Yup'ik.

THE COASTAL INDIANS

These were probably in the first wave of immigrants to cross the land bridge, although many initially settled in Canada. The Tlingits were the most numerous; they claimed most of the coastal Panhandle, leaving only a small southern portion to the less populous Haidas. (In the late 1800s they were joined by the Tsimshian, Coastal Indians who emigrated from Canada to Annette Island off the southeastern coast. The Tsimshian live on the only federally recognized Indian reservation in Alaska.)

The Tlingits were excellent navigators, and were known to travel more than 1,000 miles (1,600km) south to trade with native peoples in the Pacific Northwest. The standard of currency was 'blanket value,' based on blankets made of cedar bark and dog or goat hair.

A Tlingit man.

⊙ HARDY ANCESTORS

An archeological find at Barrow uncovered the remains of five members of an unfortunate Eskimo (Inupiat) family in their wood and sod house. The family apparently had been crushed to death hundreds of years ago by an enormous piece of ice that must have rafted in from a stormy sea. Autopsies performed on the bodies revealed the effects of seasonal starvation and the amount of soot that accumulated in the dwellings was immediately noticeable. One of the five, a 42-year-old woman, had survived bacterial pneumonia, an infection of the heart valves, arthritis, trichinosis and blood poisoning. She had also recently given birth.

The Coastal Indians had great respect for the natural world, which provided them with all they needed. They believed that fish and animals gave themselves willingly to humans, and strove to acknowledge and honor that sacrifice. A bear killed for meat might be brought to the house, greeted with a welcome speech and placed in a seat of honor for a day or two. The bones of a consumed salmon were always returned to the river where it had been caught, to allow for reincarnation.

The Coastal Indians lived in a capitalist society that allowed private ownership. Each house-

THE ATHABASCANS

The Athabascan Indians of Alaska's harsh Interior were hunters and inland fishermen. Most lived in small nomadic bands along the region's rivers. If game was scarce, they might travel for days without food; in deepest winter they survived temperatures of –50°F (–45°C) or less, sometimes without shelter or fire. Endurance and physical strength were prized; game was often run down on foot over difficult terrain.

Athabascans hunted salmon, hares, birds, caribou, moose, and bear with the help of snares,

Young natives pose with their dogs.

hold owned economic goods, such as weapons, utensils, and clothing – anything they had made themselves – while the clan owned religious titles and objects, for example, the right to perform a certain dance or practice a profession such as seal hunting.

In the social organization of the Tlingits and Haidas, status was determined by wealth. To maintain position, a person of power demonstrated wealth by giving a ceremonial 'potlatch' when he would give away, destroy or invite guests to consume all his food and possessions. Those who received goods at one potlatch had to reciprocate and better their host in the future. Another important feature of the potlatch was the recitation of family histories and bloodlines

clubs, and bows and arrows. Because they were semi-nomadic and hunted on foot, footwear was very important, and the Athabascans designed efficient snowshoes made of birch.

Some Athabascan groups inhabited permanent winter villages and summer fishing camps. Most bands consisted of a few nuclear families, and had limited internal organization. Leadership was acquired by great warriors or hunters.

Athabascans also gave potlatches for a variety of reasons: to mark a death, to celebrate a child's first successful hunt, as a prelude to marriage. Those who aspired to leadership were expected to host especially memorable potlatches, at which the would-be leader would give away all his possessions then prove his prowess by providing for himself and his family for an entire year without outside help.

THE ALEUTS

This group settled the windswept islands of the Aleutian chain 10,000 years ago. Although their location allowed them to harvest the sea's bounty, they also had to contend with harsh and often unpredictable weather, as well as earthquakes and volcanic eruptions.

Aleut fishing technology included fish spears, weirs, nets, hooks, and lines. Various darts

that they could even hold water. Mats and some kinds of clothing were also made in this way.

THE ALUTIIQS

Close relatives of the Aleuts, Alutiiq peoples settled on the Alaska Peninsula, Kodiak Archipelago, and parts of the Kenai Peninsula and Prince William Sound. Sites dating back 7,000 years suggest the Alutiiqs were skilled maritime hunters and fishers. They paddled *bidarkas* while hunting sea lions, seals, sea otters, and whales. They fished for halibut, cod, and

Aleuts standing near their huts.

and nets were used to obtain sea lions and sea otters. Whales were usually killed with a poisoned, stone-bladed lance. The job of women and children was to gather shellfish at low tide.

Aleut society was divided into three categories: honorables (usually respected whalers), common people, and slaves. At death the body of an honorable was mummified, and sometimes slaves were killed to honor the deceased.

In winter Aleuts wore hoodless, knee-length parkas; in colder weather they added knee-length skin boots. Waterproof overgarments made from the intestines of sea lions were also worn.

Because of a ready supply of grass in the summer, Aleut women became skillful at basketry – their baskets were so closely woven

salmon and harvested seabirds and their eggs. Occasionally, they hunted bears and caribou.

The people collected all manner of items to make their clothes and build their homes and tools: animal skins, feathers, bones, sod, driftwood, and grasses. Most houses were made of sod and dug partly into the ground; these semi-subterranean dwellings were often reinforced with whalebones or driftwood. Seal oil was used as a fuel to light their lamps.

THE EYAK

The tribe's oral history suggests that the Eyak people traveled south through Alaska's Interior, then down the Copper River, to the Gulf of Alaska coast, where they finally settled. Though their language has links to both Athabascan and Tlingit, linguists believe it began to develop as a separate language some 3,500 years ago.

A relatively small group, the Eyak were sometimes raided by other coastal tribes, particularly the Alutiiq residents of Prince William Sound. They had friendlier relations with the Tlingit tribes of Southeast Alaska, who had similar social structures. The two groups regularly traded goods and even intermarried. Over time, much of the Eyak population was assimilated by the Tlingit's larger and more dominant society.

Today the Eyak tribe is Alaska's smallest tribal group, with a little more than 100 survivors. The Eyak, like other coastal tribes, depended heavily on the ocean's abundance.

THE ESKIMOS

Eskimos, the indigenous group most familiar to non-Alaskans, were originally divided into two sub-groups. The Inupiat Eskimos settled in Alaska's Arctic region, while the Yup'ik lived in the west. Life was a constant struggle against hunger and the cold. Seasonal food was stored

Eskimo women beside their storage platforms.

⊘ THE RISE AND FALL OF RUSSIA'S TRADE

In 1795, Alexander Baranov, the managing officer of the Russian-American Company, established Mikhailovsk 6 miles (10km) north of present-day Sitka to get a toehold in the growing fur trade of the Southeast. For a while, the Russians and Tlingits peacefully co-existed. But in 1802, while Baranov was away, Tlingits from a neighboring settlement attacked and destroyed Mikhailovsk. Intent on revenge, Baranov returned in 1804 with a Russian warship and razed the Tlingit village. He then built the settlement of New Archangel, which became the capital of Russian America.

Meanwhile, as Baranov secured the Russians' physical presence in Alaska, back in Russia the Shelikof family

continued to seek control of Alaska's fur trade. In 1799, Shelikof's son-in-law, had acquired a monopoly on the American fur trade. Rezanov then formed the Russian-American Company. As part of the deal, the Tsar expected the company first to establish new settlements in Alaska and then carry out an expanded colonization program.

By 1804, Alexander Baranov had consolidated the company's hold on fur trade activities in the Americas. But despite all these efforts, the Russians never fully colonized Alaska; for the most part they clung to the coast, shunning the rugged inland. By the 1830s their monopoly on trade in the region was weak enough to allow the Hudson's Bay Company to gain a foothold.

against future shortage and for the long dark winter; and even though his own family might be wanting, a hunter always divided a fresh kill evenly throughout the community. Status was determined by hunting ability.

The Eskimos used boats called *umiaks* to hunt larger sea animals. They also used smaller, one-man craft, called kayaks. Both were made of a frame of wood covered with skins or hides. Sleds and dog teams were used for winter travel, and in summer dogs were used as pack animals.

Women were skilled in basketry and sewing. They stitched and fitted waterproof garments made of animal intestine and fish skins. The Eskimos' everyday clothing of trousers, boots, and coats were sewn from skins and fur, sometimes in complex geometric designs. The coats (parkas) featured an attached hood and ruff.

Eskimos are renowned for their fine carving, especially their small ivory pieces. In early times household utensils and weapons were beautifully ornamented. Using wood, bone, baleen (bony plates that line the mouths of baleen whales), walrus ivory, and fossil mammoth tusks, Eskimos crafted dishes and knives, oil lamps, small sculptures and game pieces, and goggles to protect their eyes from the glare of snow and ice. The *ulu*, or woman's knife, is found in tourist shops today and is appreciated for both its beauty and its utility.

THE RUSSIAN INVASION

The story of Russia's invasion of the land begins in 1741, when two tiny vessels, the *St Peter* and the *St Paul*, captained respectively by a Dane, Vitus Bering, and a Russian, Alexei Chirikof, set sail from Russia.

When Chirikof sighted land, it was probably the west side of Prince of Wales Island in Southeast Alaska. He sent a group of men ashore in a long boat. When the first group failed to return, he sent a second. Eerily, that group also vanished. Most likely, the men drowned or were killed by Indians. Chirikof pulled anchor and moved on.

In the meantime, and the crew of the *St Peter* sighted a towering peak on the Alaska mainland – Mount St Elias, which at 18,000ft (5,500 meters) is second only to Denali among Alaska's highest mountains. Turning westward, Bering

anchored his vessel off Kayak Island, in Prince William Sound, while crew members went ashore to explore and find water.

Alerted by these explorers to the riches represented by the fur-bearing marine life and mammals, Russia threw itself wholeheartedly into setting up hunting and trading outposts.

For the native populations, the coming of the Russians was an unprecedented disaster. Rather than hunting the marine life for themselves, the Russians forced the Aleut people to do the work for them. Hostages were taken,

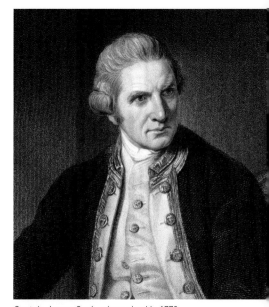

Captain James Cook, who arrived in 1778.

☉ COASTAL CULTURE

The mild climate and plentiful resources of the Panhandle allowed the Coastal Indians to develop a rich culture over many years. They enjoyed ceremony and drama, and the traditional recitation of family histories and bloodlines kept an accurate account of the generations. The painted designs developed by the Coastal tribes feature fish and animals, often in bold patterns of black and red. They decorated their crafted goods: domestic utensils, clothing, masks, canoes, ritual objects, and the characteristic totems that marked family residences. Meanwhile, the Aleuts made ingenious skis by drying hair-seal skins over wooden frames.

families split up, individuals forced to leave their villages and settle elsewhere. Eighty percent of the Aleut population was destroyed by violence

> *Eskimo villages were sited near food sources. The Arctic coast people depended on seal, walrus, and whale, while the inland Eskimos – known as the Nunamiut – lived on a diet of caribou, birds and other small game animals.*

US Secretary of State, William Henry Seward.

and European diseases, against which they had no defenses, during the first two generations of Russian contact.

THE EUROPEANS

About this time, the British were continuing their search for the Northwest Passage, the fabled water route between the Atlantic and the Pacific. In 1778 Captain James Cook sailed north from Vancouver Island, through the Inside Passage and then along the Gulf Coast, to the Aleutians. Along the way, he explored a narrow embayment that would later be given his name: Cook Inlet. The Russians tried to impress him with the extent of their control over the region, but Cook saw

how tenuous was the position of this ragtag group of hunters and traders stationed 3,000 miles (4,800km) from home.

Although Cook died in Hawaii after visiting Alaska, his crew continued on to Canton, China, where they sold their Alaskan sea otter pelts for outlandishly high prices. Britain became interested and increased its sailings along the northwest coast. Then came the Spanish, already well established on the coast of California, who founded the towns of Valdez and Cordova.

GAINING A FOOTHOLD

The Russians were determined to dig in and keep Alaska's fur wealth for themselves. One particularly ruthless individual, Grigor Ivanovich Shelikof, arrived in Three Saints Bay on Kodiak Island in 1784 with two ships, the *Three Saints* and the *St Simon*. Fearing the foreigners, the island's Alutiiq residents tried to drive off the Russians, but failed. Shelikof responded by killing hundreds and taking hostages to enforce the obedience of the rest.

Having established his authority on Kodiak Island, Shelikof founded the first permanent Russian settlement in Alaska on the island's Three Saints Bay, built a school to teach the Alutiiq to read and write Russian, and introduced the Russian Orthodox religion.

In 1790, Shelikof, back in Russia, hired Alexander Baranov to manage his Alaskan fur enterprise. Baranov moved the colony to the northeast end of Kodiak Island, where timber was available; the site is now the city of Kodiak. Russian members of the colony took Alutiiq wives and started families whose names survive today.

COLONIAL POWERS

The Hudson's Bay Company, formed by the British in 1821, set up a post on the southern edge of Russian America in 1833. The British firm, which was more organized and better run than the Russian, began siphoning off trade. Baranov began to depend heavily on American supply ships, since they came much more frequently than Russian ones. Also, Americans could sell furs in Canton (then closed to the Russians).

The downside of the US presence was that American hunters and trappers encroached on territory the Russians considered theirs.

In 1812 a settlement was reached giving the Russians exclusive rights to the fur trade above 55°N latitude, the Americans to that below. The agreement didn't settle matters, however, and with Baranov's retirement in 1818 the Russian hold on Alaska was further weakened.

When the Russian-American Company's charter was renewed in 1821, it stipulated that the chief managers from then on be naval officers. But most naval officers did not have any experience in the fur trade, so the com-

Alaska tribes who had survived contact – primarily the Aleuts, Alutiiqs, and Tlingits – conditions improved, if only slightly.

The Tlingits were never conquered, and continued to wage guerrilla warfare on the Russians into the 1850s. The Aleuts, many of whom had been removed from their home islands and sent as far south as California to hunt sea otter for the Russians, continued to decline in population during the 1840s. For them, the naval officers of the Russian-American Company were a blessing: they established schools and hospi-

The Russian-American Company headquarters at Sitka, Alaska.

pany suffered under a string of incompetent 'governors.'

The second charter also tried to cut off all contact with foreigners, especially the competitive Americans. But this strategy backfired, since the Russian colony had become used to relying on American supply ships, and the United States had become a valued customer for furs. Eventually the Russian-American Company entered into an agreement with the Hudson's Bay Company, which gave the British rights to sail through Russian territory. Pacts were also signed in the mid-1820s that allowed both British and US vessels to land at Russian ports.

Although the mid-1800s were not a good time for the Russians in Alaska, for those coastal

tals for the Aleuts, and gave them jobs. Russian Orthodox clergy moved into the Aleutian Islands. Slowly, the Aleut population began to increase.

AN AMERICAN BUY-OUT

By the 1860s the Russians were considering ridding themselves of Russian America. Overhunting had severely reduced the fur-bearing animal population, and the difficulties of supplying and protecting such a distant colony caused interest to wane.

A Russian emissary approached the US Secretary of State, William Henry Seward, about a possible sale, and in 1867 the US Congress, at Seward's urging, agreed to buy Russian America for $7.2 million – just under 2 cents an acre.

THE MAKING OF MODERN ALASKA

People regarded the new possession as a wild land, producing nothing but furs, until the discovery of gold in 1896 made the world sit up and take notice. In the 20th century the discovery of oil would change Alaska's fortunes yet again.

America wasn't sure what, exactly, it had acquired when it bought Alaska. The interior had been little touched by the Russians, who had stayed in the coastal areas. US exploration, too, had been limited. In 1865, Western Union had decided to lay a telegraph line through Alaska across the Bering Strait to Siberia, where it would connect with an Asian line. William H. Dall took charge of the Western Union expedition, conducting the first scientific studies of the region and producing the first map of the entire Yukon River.

That same year (1866), workers finally succeeded in laying an Atlantic undersea telegraph cable, and the Alaskan overland project was abandoned. Dall returned to Alaska many times, recording many geographical features. A breed of sheep and a type of porpoise bear his name.

The Alaska Commercial Company also contributed to the growing exploration of Alaska in the last decades of the 1800s, building trading posts along the Interior's many rivers. Small parties of trappers and traders entered the Interior.

Troughs were constructed to separate gold from soil during the Klondike Gold Rush.

EXPLORING THE INTERIOR

Army officers sometimes undertook their own explorations. In a four-month journey, Lt Frederick Schwatka and his party rafted the Yukon from Lake Lindeman in Canada to Saint Michael near the river's mouth on the Bering Sea. Lt Henry T. Allen made an even more remarkable journey. In 1885 Allen and four others left the Gulf of Alaska, followed the Copper River to its headwaters, crossed the Alaska range and traveled down the Tanana River to the Yukon, portaged to the Kanuti and then the Koyukuk rivers. Allen went up the Koyukuk, then back down to the Yukon, crossed over to the coastal village of Unalakleet, and then made his way to Saint Michael. In all, his team explored about 1,500 miles (2,400km) of Interior Alaska.

Whether the US knew what it had or not, the territory still needed to be governed. Unfortunately, back in Washington, DC, legislators had their hands full with post-Civil War reconstruction issues. As a result, a US Army officer, General Jefferson C. Davis, was put in charge.

THE GOLD STRIKE

It was the discovery of gold in the Yukon in 1896 that finally made the world sit up and take notice of America's northern possession. A wave of fortune hunters clamored for passage to the Klondike.

The Klondike was in Canada's Yukon Territory, not in Alaska, but the easiest route was by ship to Skagway, in Southeast Alaska. Once in Skagway, miners had the choice of two brutal passes across the mountains to the Yukon gold fields: White Pass, also called Dead Horse Trail, because it was littered with corpses of pack animals, or the Chilkoot Trail, a route used by the indigenous people.

Alaska, in fact, had plenty of gold of its own, and many who didn't make their fortunes in the Klondike strike came back to look for it. An earlier strike had established Juneau in Southeast Alaska, and

walk to Circle City, and Barnette was equally delighted to see his first customers walking out of the wilderness. Replenished with supplies, Pedro resumed prospecting and finally struck gold in July 1902. Shortly afterwards Barnette's

Many Americans thought that even at its low purchase price, the territory of Alaska was a waste of money, and dubbed it 'Seward's Folly.'

The Miners and Merchants Bank.

gold was found in Nome in 1899. A combination of fortune and misfortune led to a gold strike and the birth of Fairbanks in the early 1900s. For several years a prospector called Felix Pedro had been searching the Tanana Hills of Alaska's Interior for a gold-rich creek he had stumbled upon years earlier but had been forced to abandon. As the summer of 1901 drew to a close, Pedro and his partner prepared to embark on a 165-mile (265km) walk to Circle City for supplies. Plans changed when the men met E.T. Barnette, who had been forced to disembark from the steamer *Lavelle Young* with his entire load of supplies – some of which he was happy to sell to Pedro.

It was a match made in heaven: Pedro and his partner were delighted to be spared the long

☉ JUNEAU'S STRIKE

Before the Klondike strike, prospectors were pulling gold out of the rivers and streams in Alaska's Panhandle. Gold was first discovered in 1872 near Sitka; gold fever moved south eight years later when prospectors Richard Harris and Joe Juneau found 'large pieces of quartz... all spangled with gold.' The town that sprang around the strike was eventually named Juneau and became the state capital in 1906. But it is the Treadwell Mine on Douglas Island that became the most lucrative strike in the southeast. Pulling out 5,000 tons daily and employing 2,000 people, the mine was once the largest in the world, operating from 1881 to 1922.

outpost was transformed into a booming town. Named Fairbanks in honor of a US senator, the settlement grew as more miners and new businesses arrived. Fairbanks had shanties on the fringes, but the center offered many of the conveniences to be found in more 'civilized' settings. Traffic came and went on the river, and an overland route to Valdez cut days off a trip to the Lower 48.

Eventually the Tanana Mining District became a huge gold producer, and a powerful magnet for Americans and Europeans alike.

Of course, not everyone in Alaska was a gold miner. Many more found ways to profit from the gold rushes without actually panning for the metal themselves. At Ruby Creek, for example, gold strikes in 1907 and 1910 brought the predictable rush of miners to the area, giving birth to the town of Ruby. Newcomers arrived, some by small riverboats, others on large paddle wheelers. The steamers required large quantities of wood to keep them moving, and locals along the river bank were only too happy to sell them the wood.

A salmon cannery south of Ketchikan.

⊘ THE THREAT FROM OVERHUNTING

Whaling, a traditional marine occupation, continued well into the 20th century with no regard for overhunting. Bowhead whales, the awesome behemoths of northern seas, attracted a parade of whale hunters to the high Arctic. Following routes they had used since the end of the Pleistocene Age, the bowheads migrated twice yearly through the Bering Strait on their run from the southwestern Bering Sea to summer feeding areas in the Beaufort Sea. Weighing a ton per foot and reaching lengths of 60ft (18 meters), bowheads carry huge quantities of oil in their tissue.

Whalers seeking the oil pursued the bowhead to the edge of extinction, but their numbers have now recovered to the point that tribal whale hunters are able to harvest a limited number each year for subsistence purposes without affecting the population.

The American fishing, canning and whaling operations, as well as walrus hunting, were as unchecked as the Russians' hunting. The Aleuts soon suffered severe problems due to the depletion of the fur seals and sea otters, which they needed for survival. As well as requiring the flesh for food, they also used seal skins to cover their boats, without which they couldn't hunt. The American newcomers also expanded into Interior and Arctic Alaska, exploiting the furbearers, fish and other game on which indigenous cultures depended.

Ruby grew from a tent city in 1911 to a bus-tling river port. With running water in summer, a theater, shops and cafés, it sought to provide all the amenities of its rival, Fairbanks. By 1917, at the height of the rush, creeks south of Ruby had yielded $875,000 worth of gold.

THE COMING OF CANNERIES

The more traditional ways of life – fishing, in particular – also provided a livelihood for many Alaskans, particularly after canning was intro-duced. In 1878 the first two canneries were built in Southeast Alaska. In 1883 the Arctic Pack Company established a cannery at Nushagak Bay in Southwest Alaska, where they were able to exploit the immense runs of salmon.

Two years later the Alaska Packing Com-pany opened a cannery across the bay, and by 1908, ten canneries ringed Nushagak Bay. Kodiak's first canneries were built in the late 1800s, when word of phenomenal fish runs became widespread.

By the turn of the 20th century, commercial fishing had gained a foothold in the Aleutian Islands. But, before long, overfishing became a serious threat.

WORLD WAR II

On June 3, 1942, the Japanese launched an air attack on Dutch Harbor, a US naval base on Unalaska Island, in the Aleutians. US forces held off the planes, and the base survived this attack, and a second one, with minor damage. But on June 7 the Japanese landed on the islands of Kiska and Attu, overwhelming Attu villagers. The villagers were taken to Japan and interned for the rest of the war. Aleuts from the Pribilofs and Aleutian villages were forcibly evacuated by the United States to Southeast Alaska, where they too were interned.

In the fall of 1942, the US Navy began con-structing a base on Adak, and on May 11, 1943, American troops landed on Attu, determined to retake the island. The bloody battle wore on for more than two weeks. The Japanese, who had no hope of rescue because their fleet of trans-port submarines had been turned back by US destroyers, fought to the last man.

The end finally came on May 29 when the Americans repelled a banzai charge. Some Japanese remained in hiding on the small island months after their defeat. When discovered, they killed themselves rather than surrender.

The taking of Attu was the second bloodiest battle of the Pacific theater; only Iwo Jima was more costly in terms of human lives. The US then bombed the other occupied island, Kiska. But the Japanese, under cover of thick Aleutian fog, escaped via transport ships. After the war, the Attuans who had survived internment in Japan were resettled to Atka by the federal gov-ernment, which considered their home villages too remote to defend.

Soldiers arrive by boat at Massacre Bay.

World War II affected Alaska in unexpected ways. One was the construction of the Alaska–Canada Military Highway (Alcan), which was completed in 1942 at great speed (nine months) and great cost ($20 million) to form an overland supply route to America's 'last frontier' – and northwesternmost line of defense. Running from Great Falls, Montana, to Fairbanks, the 1,420-mile (2,280km) road – the work of 9,000 soldiers and 12,000 civilians – was the first sta-ble link between Alaska and the rest of America.

New military bases also contributed to the growth of some cities. Anchorage almost dou-bled in size, from 4,200 people in 1940 to 8,000 in 1945. And two other catalysts were just around the corner: statehood and oil.

THE PUSH FOR STATEHOOD

After its purchase by the US in 1867 Alaska was governed by the US Army, the US Treasury Department and the US Navy. Finally, in 1884, the federal government declared the territory the District of Alaska, and a civil government was created.

By the turn of the 20th century, a movement pushing for Alaska statehood had begun. But in the Lower 48, legislators were worried that Alaska's population was too sparse, its location too distant and isolated, and its economy too unstable for the territory to become a state.

A man ponders a fracture after the earthquake.

World War II and the Japanese invasion of Attu and Kiska highlighted Alaska's strategic importance, and the issue of statehood was taken more seriously. Anticipating their home would eventually become a state, residents organized a constitutional convention in 1955. After 75 days, the participants drafted and approved a 14,400-word document that the National Municipal League called 'one of the best, if not the best, state constitutions ever.' That same year, a poll showed that 82 percent of Americans favored Alaska's becoming a state.

The discovery of oil at Swanson River on the Kenai Peninsula in 1957 helped the statehood movement, because it made Alaska less dependent on federal assistance. On January 3, 1959, President Dwight D. Eisenhower formally admitted Alaska to the union as the 49th state. William A. Egan was sworn in as the first governor, and Juneau continued to be the capital.

DISASTER STRIKES

It was not long before the young state underwent its first trial. On March 27, 1964, the Good Friday earthquake struck Southcentral Alaska, churning the earth for four minutes. At an estimated 8.7 on the Richter scale – later revised upward to 9.2, under the current scale used to measure earthquake intensities – the Good Friday quake is the most powerful ever recorded in North America. The earthquake and its aftermath killed 131 people, including 115 Alaskans; most were drowned by the tidal waves (tsunamis) that tore apart the towns of Valdez and Chenega.

OIL AND LAND

Despite the extent of the earthquake catastrophe, Alaskans rebuilt many of the devastated communities. Four years later, the state experienced a different sort of upheaval. In the mid-1960s Alaskan Native Americans had begun participating in state and local government and flexing their electoral muscles. More than 200 years after the arrival of the first Europeans, indigenous people from all ethnic groups united to claim title to the lands wrested from them. The government responded slowly until, in 1968, the Atlantic-Richfield Company discovered oil at Prudhoe Bay, and catapulted the ownership issue into the headlines.

Prudhoe Bay is on Alaska's Arctic coast, along the Beaufort Sea. Drilling at such a remote location would be difficult enough – but transporting the resulting crude to refineries in the Lower 48 seemed impossible. The answer appeared to be to build a pipeline to carry the oil hundreds of miles to the port of Valdez (rebuilt a few miles from the ruins of the previous town). At Valdez the oil would be loaded onto tanker ships and sent by water to the Lower 48. The plan was approved – but a permit to construct the pipeline, which would cross lands involved in the native land claims dispute, depended on those claims being settled.

With major petroleum dollars on the line, there was new urgency for an agreement, and in 1971 the Alaska Native Claims Settlement Act (ANCSA) was signed, under which the indigenous peoples relinquished aboriginal claims to their lands. In return they received title to 44 million acres (nearly 18 million hectares) of land and were paid $963 million. The land and money were divided among regional, urban and village corporations. Some have handled their funds wisely; others have not.

THE PIPELINE

After ANCSA was signed, there remained the challenge of building a pipeline that would stretch from Arctic Alaska to Valdez. Between the two points were three mountain ranges, active fault lines, miles and miles of unstable *muskeg* (boggy ground underlain with permafrost) and the migration paths of wildlife, particularly caribou.

The pipeline was designed with all these factors in mind. To counteract the unstable ground and allow animal crossings, half the 800-mile (1,280km) pipeline is elevated on supports. The supports hold the pipe – and its cargo of hot oil – high enough to keep it from melting the permafrost and destroying the natural terrain. To help the pipeline survive an earthquake, it was laid out in a zigzag pattern, so that it would roll with the

The partially collapsed Million Dollar Bridge.

⊙ THE 1964 EARTHQUAKE

One cannot understate the damage done by the Good Friday Earthquake of 1964. Throughout the Prince William Sound region towns and ports were destroyed, land uplifted or shoved downward, islands tilted. Salmon could no longer negotiate the upset and displaced streams to reach their spawning grounds. Ports at Valdez and Cordova were beyond repair – what land and mudslides didn't claim, ensuing fires did.

At Valdez, an Alaska Steamship Company ship was lifted by a huge wave over the docks and out to sea. Amazingly, most hands survived. Witnesses on shore swore that at one point they could see daylight all the way under the ship. There were very few witnesses, however,

because most of those who had been waiting on the dockside to greet the ship were swept to their deaths.

Along Turnagain Arm, off Cook Inlet, the incoming water destroyed trees and caused cabins to sink into the mud. In Anchorage, huge chunks of road asphalt piled on top of each other like shingles and many buildings were destroyed. At Seldovia, near the junction of Kachemak Bay and Cook Inlet, fish processing facilities and a fishing fleet were laid waste, along with Seldovia's harbor.

On Kodiak, a tidal wave wiped out the villages of Afognak, Old Harbor, and Kaguyak, and damaged other communities. Seward, a thriving port town at the southern terminus of the Alaska Railroad, also lost its harbor.

earth instead of breaking up. That construction was tested on November 3, 2002, when a magnitude 7.9 quake struck Alaska and the ground ruptured along a fault that ran beneath the pipeline.

Many of the supports collapsed and the pipeline was temporarily shut down, but it withstood fierce shaking without any serious damage or leakage of oil.

The first oil arrived at Valdez in July, 1977. The cost of the pipeline and related projects, including the tanker terminal at Valdez, 12 pumping stations and the Yukon River Bridge, was $8 billion.

Pipeline technology in Alaska.

During the years of pipeline construction, Anchorage and Fairbanks blossomed into bright, modern cities. As the oil bonanza took shape, per capita incomes rose throughout the state, with virtually every community benefitting. State leaders were determined that this boom would not end like the fur and gold booms – in an economic bust as soon as the resource had disappeared.

To this end, the Alaska Permanent Fund was created in 1976. Into the fund is deposited 25 percent of all mineral lease proceeds (including oil and gas). Income from the fund is divided in three ways: it pays annual dividends to all residents who apply and qualify; it adds money to the principal account to hedge against inflation; and it provides funds to the state legislature.

The fund, worth nearly $40 billion, is the largest pool of public money in the US, and a major source of income to Alaska's state government. Since 1993, the fund has produced more revenue than the Prudhoe Bay oil fields, where production has halved from its peak in the late 1980s. Prudhoe Bay oil may dry up, but the fund should continue to benefit the state.

TOURISM AS A MONEY SPINNER

In the second half of the 20th century, Alaska discovered another important source of revenue. Although visitors had been lured north by Alaska's natural wonders since at least the late 19th century, tourism got a big boost after World War II when men stationed in the region returned home praising its amazing natural splendor.

The Alcan Highway, built during the war, and the Alaska Marine Highway System, completed in 1963, made the state more accessible than before. The major cruise lines arriving in the 1970s also added to the tourist boom.

Tourism is now very big business in Alaska, with a steadily climbing arrival rate. As of 2018, a record 2 million people visited during the May toSeptember peak season (a figure set to grow as more cruise liners add Alaska to their itineraries). Once there, they flocked to the top attractions: Denali National Park, Katmai, Glacier Bay, and other destinations within the Inside Passage, and the Kenai Peninsula. Wildlife watching is a main attraction, although only a small proportion of visitors go deep into the wilderness.

ENVIRONMENTALISM

With tourism ever more vital to the economy, environmentalism has also risen in importance (see page 61). Alaskans are working to balance the needs of their remarkable land with the needs of its residents.

Much is already well protected – the Alaska National Interest Lands Conservation Act (ANILCA) of 1980 added 53.7 million acres (22 million hectares) to the national wildlife refuge system, parts of 25 rivers to the national wild and scenic rivers system, 3.3 million acres (1.3 million hectares) to national forest lands, and 43.6 million acres (17.5 million hectares) to national park land. As a result of the lands act, Alaska now contains two-thirds of all American national parklands.

THE OIL SPILL

Nothing better illustrates Alaska's struggle to protect the environment, and to benefit from the state's natural resources, than the *Exxon Valdez* disaster. The huge tanker ran aground on March 24 1989, in Prince William Sound, releasing 11 million gallons (42 million liters) of crude oil into the water. The oil eventually spread along 1,100 miles (1,760km) of formerly pristine shoreline.

It was an ecological disaster of unprecedented proportions. At least 300,000 seabirds, 2,000 otters and countless other marine animals died as a result of the spill. Exxon spent $2 billion on cleaning up in the first year alone.

The 1971 Alaska Native Claims Settlement Act (ANCSA) officially compensated Native Americans for the invasion of their lands. It also opened the way for all Alaskans to profit from the state's tremendous natural resource – oil.

Sailboat cruises by Prince William Sound.

Cleaning the beach after the Exxon Valdez oil spill.

⊘ THE BRIDGES THAT WENT NOWHERE

In Alaska, the saying goes, corruption flows like crude oil. Federal conspiracy, bribery, tax evasion, influence-peddling, and self-dealing... all these charges and more have been leveled against Alaska's senators, congressmen and government officials, and the frequency of scandals encourage Senate committees in faraway Washington, DC, to regard it as one of the most ethically challenged states.

At the heart of many federal investigations have been the close ties between Alaska lawmakers and the powerful oil industry. Oil money doesn't talk, say cynics, it shouts. But the state's relatively small population and its remoteness from the rest of the nation can all too easily tempt vote-hungry politicians into all manner of pork-barrel spending. One notorious example was the 2005 saga of the 'bridge to nowhere,' a proposed $230 million span higher than the Brooklyn Bridge intended to connect Ketchikan (population 7,400) with Gravina Island (population 50). Another envisaged a bridge connecting Anchorage to the town of Knik (population 22) that would cost the taxpayers $1.5 billion.

Congress torpedoed both schemes, though it didn't keep legislators from dreaming. In 2010, a road to Nome (population 3,600) was proposed. The estimated cost, $2.7 billion (or $5 million per mile), has caused many to roll their eyes and say, 'Here we go again!'

TODAY'S ISSUES

Over the past 15 years there has been a steady shift from complete dependence on resource extraction (and government employment) to service industries. Oil fields on Alaska's North Slope continue to be the primary fuel (literally and figuratively) that drives Alaska's economy and state government programs, but even oil production has slipped dramatically, to half of what it was during Prudhoe Bay's late 1980s peak. The timber and commercial fisheries industries have suffered even greater losses.

Visitors to the Independence Mine State Historical Park.

⊘ TWO WORLDS

Alaska's indigenous culture continues to be confronted with the challenge of living in two worlds – their traditional one, which stretches back generations, and the modern, Western way of life. Few native Alaskans would choose to return to live without electricity, modern plumbing, computers, and TV; but technological advances have also disrupted the family and community lives in many villages. As a result, leaders are fervently seeking a way to balance old and new. A cultural revival begun in the late 20th century has continued to flourish as more people celebrate their roots and long-lived cultural values, art, dance, and storytelling.

Centered in the Panhandle's Tongass National Forest, Alaska's timber industry has been on the skids since the 1980s; its two largest mills (one in Ketchikan, the other in Sitka) shut down in the 1990s due to changing Forest Service policies and decreased demand for wood pulp, causing hardships for many Southeast Alaska communities.

Nowadays timber cutting and milling is done on a much smaller scale, but the widespread economic crisis predicted by many in the timber industry hasn't been realized, largely because there's been something of a tourism boom in the Panhandle.

Increased numbers of cruise ships travel the Inside Passage, bringing thousands of visitors to spend money in Southeast communities and sparking an industry of ecotourism and visitor services. Much of the area's fishing industry, however, has been struggling to stay in business.

HARD TIMES FOR FISHERMEN

Commercial fishing has been steadily declining – in some areas, precipitously – since the early 1990s. The fisheries most in trouble are those that harvest salmon. Declining numbers of fish, particularly in western Alaska waters, have severely hurt rural residents who depend on commercial (and in some cases, subsistence) fishing for their livelihood. Several years in a row, the governor declared a state of emergency for parts of the state, because the salmon returns were so poor that people in many villages didn't earn enough money for necessities such as food and fuel. Nevertheless, the strictly enforced fishing limits have resulted in replenishment of the stocks and Alaskan salmon currently accounts for around 80 percent of the total North American wild salmon harvest.

Some areas, most notably Bristol Bay, have been hard hit by a double whammy: smaller numbers of fish and lower prices, brought on by a worldwide glut of salmon attributed to the rise of farmed salmon in countries like Chile, Canada, and Norway. Though Bristol Bay remains Alaska's biggest salmon fishery, its fishing fleet has had some disastrous seasons.

Recently, the commercial fishermen who ply the Gulf of Alaska and Bering Sea for bottom fish have also been plagued with dwindling numbers and reduced fish size.

While it has been a traditionally thriving fishery, several years ago new limits were installed on the number of halibut fishermen could pull in. Amounting to nearly a 20 percent reduction from the previous year, the regulations have sent shock waves through the fishing community. There is reason for optimism, however: the aggressive legislative action has been proving effective, causing an across-the-board catch increase. In order to protect the halibut stocks, strictly enforced limits are also imposed every year on recreational anglers. For more information, visit www.adfg.alaska.gov.

GREEN ALTERNATIVES

Many Alaskans know that the boom times created by their timber, fisheries, and oil reserves are largely a thing of the past. Talk remains about a natural gas pipeline to the Lower 48, but the effort continues to stall. Even tourism, once viewed as a panacea, has proven fickle, especially during the recent economic downturn.

The declining number of fish has put a strain on the region's fishermen.

⊙ CLIMATE CHANGE

The average duration of the ice-melt season has increased by 36 days since the late 1990s and many researchers estimte that summer sea ice could be a thing of the past by 2030. It's not just the Arctic where climate change is being felt. Elsewhere in Alaska change is evident: suddenly trees grow where they never did before, permafrost is melting, causing summertime bogs and foundations to crumble; glaciers melt at an accelerated rate, and warming waters are blamed for vanishing fish and marine mammal populations. Polar bears are especially struggling; in one study, a collared female polar bear embarked on a marathon, 426-mile swim over nine days without finding a resting place.

Villages like Shishmaref are moving inland because retreating sea ice leaves them exposed to the pounding surf of an encroaching sea. Today, it is not uncommon to hear longtime Alaskans talk about when winter was cold.

Coming decades are likely to see bigger storm surges as sea ice melts, more frequent and extensive wildfires, deteriorating glaciers, and ever increasing shoreline erosion in the world. At the same time, global warming will soon open the North Passage for both tourist and commercial ships providing a boost to the state's economy. Maintaining the right balance between economic needs and protecting the environment will present a significant challenge for the state's authorities.

All this has caused many to return to the ethos that made this state famous: self-reliance. A small but growing effort has been made to revive Alaska's agricultural tradition that at its height had over 500 farms when Alaska's population was just 138,000. Today, farmers' markets, dairies, meat producers, and small farms are popping up in a state that imports 98 percent of its food.

Alaskans continue to invest in renewable energy across the state. Solar panels can be seen on office buildings in Anchorage, tidal

Native Alaskans maintain much of their ancient culture and traditions, but there is an acceptance of some elements of modern life.

power generation is being studied in the Cook Inlet, and wind farms have sprouted up in communities along the western coast and the Interior. One of the largest is located on Fire Island near Anchorage, where 11 turbines generate enough electricity to power 4,000 homes. Overall, the green economy in Alaska has grown ten percent every year for the past ten years and provides a growing opportunity for employment. Investing in the green economy has particular importance in tribal villages where diesel must be flown or barged in at a premium cost. Nearly a dozen villages now have wind turbines, while others are investing in small

hydroelectric turbines. In 2010, the community of Eagle installed a floating hydrokinetic turbine, making it the first community in the US to be powered solely by this type of turbine. That is, until the Yukon froze. Experts are now considering geothermal power as a way to power homes and businesses in Nome. The Pilgrim Hot Springs, 50 miles (80km) northeast of the city, offer sufficient resources to provide geothermal energy for a variety of uses including power generation.

A CULTURAL CLASH

Though it centers on the harvest of animals and plants, subsistence is about more than hunting, fishing, and gathering; it's a way of life that has spiritual and emotional importance to tribal residents, particularly in rural areas beyond the road system. For more than 15 years, there's been a cultural clash over native subsistence rights:. Some Alaskans – mostly white, urban sportsmen – insist that all residents must have equal access to fish and wildlife resources. However, most Alaskans – of all backgrounds – agree that some sort of subsistence priority must be recognized if indigenous culture is to thrive.

There's been a strong push to change the Alaska Constitution, so that it guarantees a rural subsistence preference, but the Alaska Legislature has so far resisted enacting legislation that would allow a statewide vote. The federal government, meanwhile, has recognized a rural subsistence priority since the passage of ANILCA in 1980. Because the policies differ, the US government took over fish and wildlife management on Alaska's federally managed lands and waters during the 1990s. This dual management system is unique to Alaska and complicates hunting and fishing regulations throughout the state. Extremely low cod numbers lead feds to close the Gulf of Alaska fishery for the first time ever.

Most Alaskans seek to heal urban versus rural and tribal versus non-tribal tensions. They also seek to find new sources of revenue to improve their lifestyles, while also protecting the magnificent wildness and scenic splendor that makes Alaska such a unique place to live in – and to visit.

Almost every dollar that flows through Alaska's economy originates from its land or water – or from the pocketbooks of the nearly 2 million tourists who come here each year.

Natural resources are the primary fuels that drive Alaska's economy. The oil and mining industries extract vast wealth from underground, fishermen harvest much of the nation's seafood from the water, and loggers and tourism operators exploit the landscape itself.

Oil is by far the largest industry. Due to dwindling fish populations and competition from fish-farming operations in other parts of the world, tourism has replaced fishing as the second-largest private sector employer. The logging industry has shrunk under the pressure of new environmental concerns. The government employs more people than any other industry, and state government is largely funded by oil.

It's not surprising that most Alaskans support more resource development. Every new oil field discovered on the North Slope creates jobs and new revenue that affect every citizen. When the salmon season is good, coastal towns thrive. And the flow of summer visitors employs thousands.

Many Alaskans also advocate environmental protection, and not only because they tend to be young and to spend time outdoors enjoying the beauty of the place. Fishermen know that oil spills damage the waters from which they draw their livelihood. Tourism operators know their clients aren't interested in visiting areas that have been clear-cut for logging.

While the oil and logging industries have long caused environmental concerns, tourism and fishing, if unchecked, can also harm the environment. In Glacier Bay National Park, environmental groups sued the National Park Service to stop it granting more permits for cruise ships to enter the bay, contending that they are scaring away the humpback whales. Cruise ship companies have also drawn criticism – and large fines – for polluting southeast Alaska.

Environmentalists blame large-scale factory trawlers operating in the Bering Sea for reducing marine mammal populations by taking too many fish from the food chain. There are also concerns that bottom-fishing trawlers wreak havoc on the ocean bottom.

Resistance to environmental protection remains stiff, particularly when it conflicts with potential profits. The overwhelming support for drilling in the Arctic National Wildlife Refuge is one example. The state suing the federal government over its polar bear listing on the Endangered Species List is

A fracturing tower, used for excavating oil.

another. There was a similar fight over the listing of two species of ice seals and the Pacific walrus. The ice seals made it to the list, but the Pacific walrus did not. Despite clear evidence of global warming in Alaska, Juneau has yet to enact any legislation based on the legislature's 2006 panel investigation.

In some cases, Federal authorities seem more determined to protect Alaska's natural wonders. In 2014, President Obama took steps to protect millions of hectares of Alaskan coastline and wilderness; he also put a stop to drilling in Bristol Bay. However, later administrations, more concerned with development than conservation, have tried to circumvent legal protections, though those attempts have largely been invalidated by the courts.

A striking view at one of Alaska's ski resorts.

A Yupik man and his fish trap on frozen Kuskokwim River.

VISITING ALASKA'S NATIVES

Tourists are a useful source of income as they experience Alaskan native cultures, but the people don't want to be treated simply as a visitor attractions.

Many native Alaskans live a subsistence lifestyle that still depends upon collecting meat and fish during the abundant summer months and preparing it for storage to sustain them over the long winter. In the southern part of the state, they depend upon deer, salmon and other food from the sea. In the Interior, the Athabascans fish on the rivers and hunt caribou, moose, black bears, and waterfowl. Farther north, Eskimos hunt whales and seals, caribou and polar bears, geese, and seabirds.

VILLAGES WELCOME VISITORS

An international fascination with indigenous people has spread to Alaska, and village residents from Saxman Native Village in Southeast Alaska to Gambell on St Lawrence Island in the Bering Sea are cautiously opening their doors to visitors. Visiting an Alaskan native village can be a great adventure for people who are both flexible and open-minded. Organized tours are now offered to more than a dozen villages.

In these encounters, both the visitors and the visited learn from each other. Visitors learn how descendants of the 'first peoples' live in various parts of the state and along the way, they discard stereotypes about igloos, wardrobes of animal skins and rubbing noses. 'Visitors come with an expectation that they're going to go back in time,' says the American Indian Alaska Tourism Association (www.aianta. org), an organization that formed in 1999 to promote rural tourism and to help local groups who operate tours. The culture and life of the people haven't changed a lot. Value systems are still deeply rooted in the past and in their culture.'

Inupiaq children at a hunting camp along the Arctic Coast.

In recent years, as an increasing number of young people leave villages for life in the cities, indigenous tribes have worked to keep their culture and their language alive. Tourism now provides an impetus for them to do so. Young people learn the dances and stories of old, passing them on to their own children and to the rest of the world.

SELLING ANCIENT RIGHTS

The 20th century brought numerous changes to these communities. Thirteen regional, four urban and 200 native village corporations were formed to manage money and land received from the government as a result of the 1971 Alaska Native Claims Settlement Act. The measure approved the transfer of 44 million acres (nearly 18 million hectares) and

Until the early 1990s, about the only outsiders who spent any time in Alaska's remote native villages were friends, relatives, healthcare workers or teachers. Now the list is growing.

$963 million to corporations in exchange for giving up their aboriginal rights to the land.

Some of these corporations have been phenomenally successful, parlaying the oil, mineral and other natural resource wealth of their lands into large annual dividends for members. Others made bad investments, and some were tainted by corruption. There has been increased debate as to whether the corporations serve the best interests of Alaska's indigenous peoples.

Although snowmachines have largely replaced sled dog teams as a means of winter

An Inuit child.

⊙ THE BEST WAY TO VIEW NATIVE VILLAGES

Some villages, like Anatuvuk Pass located within Gates of the Arctic National Park, are used to visitors, while others, far off the beaten path, are not. Therefore, it is a good idea to contact the village council of where you wish to visit before you show up. Finding a tour operator that includes native villages on its customized itineraries is another good option.

In the Southeast, Jilkaat Kwaan Cultural Tours combines wildlife viewing along the Chilkat Trail and a visit to a traditional Tlingit village; tel: 907-767-5505; www.chilkat-nsn.gov/.

The Northern Alaska Tour Company offers Arctic Circle adventures with trips to Fort Yukon and Anaktuvuk

Pass; tel: 907-474-8600 or 800-474-1986; www.northernalaska.com. Warbelow's Air Ventures (tel: 907-474-0518; www.warbelows.com) also takes day trips to Anaktuvuk Pass and Fort Yukon. For a complete listing of Alaskan native villages, corporations, or education organizations, visit www.fairbanks-alaska.com/alaska-native-corporations.htm

Some residents worry about tourists walking into their houses unannounced, as if they were strolling into a Disneyland attraction, or indiscriminately snapping photographs. It is common courtesy to ask before taking pictures of people. Some villages, such as Gambell, prefer that you ask before taking any photographs at all, others prohibit the use of video cameras entirely.

travel and boats with motors are preferred to the skin boats that their ancestors used for fishing and hunting, the people still follow traditional ways. Now, however, they must have money to buy gasoline for their snowmachines and bullets for their guns. Their subsistence way of life requires modern tools. It's a delicate balance.

The modern world has also brought its share of ills to the communities and many struggle to overcome high rates of alcoholism, suicide, and domestic strife. A number of

closed, the Tlingit community of Hoonah nearly bottomed out, but when it turned its attention towards tourism, things turned around. Now, its Icy Straight attraction has earned a coveted spot on many cruise ships' itineraries.

Interior villages have not seen the same boom of those in the Southeast. Fort Yukon and Anaktuvuk Pass are the most popular villages. Still, these villages only see a few dozen visitors a year, making tourism less an economic boom that many anticipated and hoped for.

A woman prepares fish by hanging them up to dry at a fishing camp.

villages have voted to stay dry, with no alcohol allowed.

Yet modern conveniences have also made life a little easier. Under her fur parka, an Eskimo woman may be wearing a dress bought through a mail-order catalog. Her whaler husband and friends stay in touch with shortwave radio as they track movements of their prey through ocean waters, and when the meat is consumed raw, as in the old days, they may supplement that meat with store-bought foods.

MIXED RESULTS

For many remote communities, welcoming tourists is a step prompted by an increasingly gloomy economic outlook. After its cannery

⊘ TIPS FOR TRAVELERS

A big hurdle for villagers is the fear of losing their privacy. Indeed, outsiders who show up unescorted in some villages may receive a chilly reception. Whether you are visiting as part of an organized tour or on your own, remember that what happens in these villages is real life, not a tourist attraction: day-to-day community life takes precedence over visitors' needs. Read up on the people and their culture and learn as much as you can about their values before you reach a village. Show your respect for native culture by the way you behave. Don't ask personal questions. Observe first, then ask a question respectfully.

A skier showing off on the slopes.

LIFE IN WINTER

Sled dog racing, alpine and Nordic skiing, energetic seasonal festivals, and the Northern Lights all help Alaskans get through the long, cold winters.

Winter is Alaska's longest season, and its quietest – at least from a tourism perspective. Most visitors explore the state between the end of May and the beginning of September, when daylight hours are long and temperatures warm – though, in some parts, warm may mean only 50 or 60°F (10 or 15°C).

By mid-September, most tourists have gone south with the waterfowl and locals have begun preparing for the winter, which in most of the state will last seven or eight months. Yet Alaska is not a frozen wasteland, and unlike bears, its human residents do not go into hibernation.

A growing number of Alaskans run dog teams purely for recreation, and several companies now offer sled dog rides and trips that range from a few hours in urban Alaska to a week or more in the state's remote wilderness.

Wrapped up warm for a journey in the snow.

THE LOWEST TEMPERATURE

As would be expected, Alaska's Interior and Arctic regions experience the most severe and prolonged winter conditions.

Temperatures bottom out in February, which has average daily lows of –25°F (–32°C) and highs of –12°F (–24°C). But Barrow isn't just frigid in winter – it's also very dark. The long winter polar night begins at noon on November 18 and lasts through January 24. The duration of darkness is 67 days from sunset until the next sunrise.

WINTER IN ANCHORAGE

By comparison, Anchorage is downright bright and balmy. The city's shortest day (the winter solstice, December 21) has 5 hours and 28 minutes of daylight, plus a couple of hours of twilight. Its coldest month, December, has average daily highs and lows of 20° and 6°F (–7° and –15°C). Even more moderate conditions are experienced in Southeast Alaska. Ketchikan, near the Panhandle's southern tip, has 7 hours, 6 minutes of daylight on the winter solstice and even its coldest month, January, averages above-freezing temperatures of 34°F (1°C).

For further evidence of Alaska's winter extremes, consider that the state's record snowfall for one season is 974.5 inches (2,475cm), at Thompson Pass (near Valdez) during the winter of 1952–3; nearly 300 inches (760cm) fell in a single month, February. The one-day record, also at Thompson

Pass, is 62 inches (160cm) in December 1955. Barrow holds the state record for the least snowfall in one season: 3 inches (7.5cm), in 1935–6.

The coldest temperature ever recorded in Alaska was –80°F (–62°C), at Prospect Creek Camp in January 1971. Barrow, the nation's northernmost outpost, averages sub-zero temperatures from December through March.

The darkness and cold produce a variety of malaises, from cabin fever to seasonal affective disorder (SAD). To combat winter woes, residents around the state participate in a variety of activities and special events – some strenuous and skillful, others just plain enjoyable.

SLED DOG RACING

Among the most popular cures for seasonal blues is sled dog racing, Alaska's official winter sport. And the best known of the mushing events is the incredible Iditarod Trail Sled

Alaska's official winter sport – dogsled racing.

⊘ THE NORTHERN LIGHTS

Alaska is the best place in the USA to view the aurora borealis, or Northern Lights. Literally meaning 'dawn of the north,' this is a solar-powered light show that occurs in the earth's upper atmosphere when charged particles from the sun collide with gas molecules.

The Northern Lights occur most intensely in an oval band that stretches across Alaska (as well as Canada, Greenland, Iceland, Norway and Siberia). All the state, except parts of the southwest and the Aleutian Chain, are within the 'auroral zone,' with the best light shows visible north of the Alaska Range. One of the best views to be had is in Fairbanks, which calls itself an 'auroral destination,' in an attempt to lure winter visitors.

The aurora occurs throughout the year, but can be seen only on clear nights when the sky has darkened. In Alaska that means from fall through spring, with peak viewing in winter. Colors vary from pale yellowish green – the most common shade – to red, blue and purplish-red. Northern Lights often begin as long, uniform bands, stretching along the horizon, but may develop vertical bars or rays, that give the appearance of waving curtains.

Some people claim they can not only see the aurora but can hear it as well. Scientists at the University of Alaska, Fairbanks, who have been studying the Northern Lights for years, have yet to confirm these reports.

Dog Race, also known as 'The Last Great Race' (see page 306).

The Iditarod is billed as a 1,150-mile (1,850km) race but in reality mushers and dogs often travel much further. The race celebrates the 'mushers' who helped open up the state in the early 1900s and also commemorates a frantic dash in 1925 to get diphtheria vaccine to Nome, which was on the verge of an epidemic. The trail follows a historic freight-and-mail route established during the gold rush of the early 1900s. It crosses two mountain ranges, runs along the Yukon River for about 150 miles and the top contenders are household names. But many would agree that the dogs are the true heroes, the athletic stars, of this and other mushing events. They're specially bred, raised, trained, and conditioned to race.

SPEED AND STAMINA

While the Iditarod is unquestionably Alaska's best-known sled dog race, dozens – perhaps hundreds – of other competitions are staged around the state. Another major long-distance event is the 1,000-mile (1,600km) Yukon Quest,

A camp provides shelter for the dogs.

(240km) and crosses the pack ice of Norton Sound. From its ceremonial (and noisy) start in Anchorage – the first Saturday in March – until the final musher has reached the finish line in Nome, the Iditarod is given center stage throughout Alaska.

A contest in which men and women compete as equals – four titles were won by the late Susan Butcher, another by Libby Riddles – the Iditarod not only pits competitors against each other, but also against the raw wilderness and brutal winter weather. But most importantly, the Iditarod celebrates Alaska's frontier past. The first Iditarod took place in 1967, as a two-day event that covered 50 miles (80km). Six years later the inaugural race from Anchorage to Nome was staged. The mushers are the glamour figures in sled dog racing

⊘ WINTER FESTIVALS

Many communities host festivals to chase away winter doldrums. In December, there's the Barrow Christmas Games, followed in January by Kodiak's Russian New Year and Masquerade Ball celebration. Things begin to pick up in February, with the Anchorage Fur Rendezvous, the Wrangell Tent City Days, Cordova Ice Worm Festival and the Sitka Jazz Festival. March brings the North Pole and Fairbanks winter carnivals and the Bering Sea Ice Golf Classic tournament in Nome. For more details of winter events, contact the Alaska Travel Industry Association, tel: 907-929-2842 or 800-862-5275; www.travelalaska.com.

staged each February between Fairbanks and Whitehorse, in Canada's Yukon Territory. At the other end of the mushing spectrum are the so-called 'speed races,' or sprints.

The two most prestigious speed races are the Open North American Championship, a three-day event staged each March in Fairbanks, and the Fur Rendezvous World Championship, another three-day affair (teams run 25 miles/40km each day), and the main attraction of Anchorage's late-February winter festival. While Iditarod champions such as Butcher, five-time champion Rick Swenson, and four-time winner Doug Swingley of Montana (the first 'outsider' to win the Iditarod) have achieved far greater acclaim outside Alaska, several of the premier speed racers – Blayne Streeper, George Attla, and Roxy Wright-Champaine among them – are every bit as famous within the state.

NORDIC AND ALPINE SKIING

Skiing is especially popular in and around the main towns. Anchorage has one of the nation's premier cross-country ski-trail systems: more than 100 miles (160km) of lit trails wind through

A snowmobile scales the slopes with ease.

⊘ IS SLED DOG RACING CRUEL?

Sled dog races, especially the Iditarod, have come under pressure from animal rights organizations who claim that, although most dogs are treated well, too many die or are injured. Figures are hard to come by, but causes of death include strangulation in towlines, internal hemorrhaging after being gouged by a sled and pneumonia. Some mushers are alleged to abuse their dogs, while others, intent on crossing the finish line, bypass veterinary checkpoints. The high number of deaths in the 2009 Iditarod once again forced the issue, prompting organizers to tighten their safety rules. However, subsequent dog deaths have added to calls for the race to be permanently banned.

a variety of terrain, with opportunities for both traditional diagonal striders and skate skiers.

The city's best-known Nordic center, at Kincaid Park, has hosted several national championship races, as well as the Olympic Trials. For those who want backcountry solitude, Chugach State Park – Anchorage's 'backyard wilderness' – has dozens of valleys and ridges to explore.

Other popular Nordic backcountry destinations within a half-day's drive of Anchorage include the Talkeetna Mountains, Chugach National Forest on the Kenai Peninsula, and the Peters Hills, the foothills of the Alaska Range.

While most lodges shut down for winter, a few cater to cross-country skiers. The three most popular Nordic retreats are Hatcher Pass Lodge, in the

Talkeetna Mountains; Sheep Mountain Lodge along the Glenn Highway; and Denali View Chalet – also known as Sepp Weber's Cabin after its builder and owner – in the Alaska Range foothills. Each of the lodges offers groomed trails, wood-fired saunas, heated rooms, home-cooked meals and other amenities. Hatcher Pass and Sheep Mountain are accessible by road, while Denali View is about 2 miles (3.2km) from the nearest road.

Though not known as a magnet for alpine ski-ers, Alaska nonetheless offers a wide variety of downhill ski areas. They range from Alyeska's world-class facility in Girdwood, about 40 miles (65km) south of Anchorage, to Moose Mountain, whose ski lift consists of buses with ski racks climbing up the mountain.

The most unusual of Alaska's eight downhill sites (which include three in the Anchorage area, two near Fairbanks and one on Douglas Island, 12 miles/20km from Juneau) is the Eyak Ski Area, near Cordova. The tiny, single-seat Prince lift here used to operate at Sun Valley until it was replaced in 1969. Eventually the lift made its way to Cordova, where it has been in operation since 1974.

The Northern Lights on a clear night.

⊘ RIDING THE IRON DOGS

While some Alaskans choose to explore the winter land-scape behind a team of sled dogs, many others prefer 'iron dogs.' Snowmobiles, also locally known as snow-machines and sno-gos, have replaced sled dogs as the primary means of winter transportation in most of rural Alaska, where roads are minimal. Though commonly used by bush residents for work, or simply 'getting from here to there,' snow-machines are also popular for rec-reation and racing in both urban and rural Alaska.

The most challenging snowmobile race by far is the Iron Dog Gold Rush Classic, a long-distance event along the Iditarod Trail from Wasilla to Nome, then on to Fairbanks (a distance of nearly 2,000 miles/3,200km).

Another intriguing race is the Arctic Man Ski & Sno-Go Classic ('The Ultimate Adrenaline Rush'), which is staged in April in the Hoodoo Mountains near Paxson; on uphill stretches, a snowmobile pulls a skier at speeds of up to 86mph (138kmh).

It's relatively rare to see skiers and snowmachiners enjoying each other's company in the backcountry. Some recreational areas popular with both user groups – for instance, Chugach State Park in the mountains just east of Anchorage, Hatcher Pass in the Talkeetna Mountains and Turnagain Pass on the Kenai Peninsula – have desig-nated snowmobile corridors, to minimize conflicts between these motorized and 'quiet' activities.

A young billy goat on a mountain trail.

ALASKAN WILDLIFE

Far from being a wasteland permanently covered with snow and ice, Alaska is a world teeming with wildlife, from birds to bears, living as they did a millennium ago.

More than 400 different species of birds have been officially documented in Alaska. With few exceptions, these species inhabit the state only during spring and summer and then migrate south. They come north to take advantage of the eruption of life which occurs on the tundra each spring, when a multicolored explosion of flowers covers the ground and clouds of insects fill the air. The tundra offers an almost unlimited banquet of foodstuffs – plants, insects, and small animals – for birds attempting to raise their hungry young.

LONG-DISTANCE FLYERS

The Arctic tern is the world's record holder for migration distances. These gull-like birds breed and nest on the shores of Alaskan tundra ponds. In late summer, the terns and their young start a migration that will eventually take them all the way to the Antarctic. Summer is just beginning in the Southern Hemisphere as the terns arrive. The round-trip flight from Alaska to the Antarctic and back is approximately 25,000 miles (40,000km).

Other long-distance commuters include the American golden plover, the surfbird, the long-tailed jaeger, and the Arctic warbler. Along with its close relatives, the rock ptarmigan and the white-tailed ptarmigan, the willow ptarmigan lives in Alaska year-round. A ptarmigan is brown in summer and white in winter, changing to blend with the surroundings, and is usually found on high ground: look for them in willow thickets and on the open tundra.

While near tundra ponds, look for loons, grebes, geese, ducks, phalaropes, yellowlegs, and sandpipers. On the tundra, watch for long-tailed jaegers, golden plovers, whimbrels, snow buntings, wheatears, sparrows, and water pipits. Owls, woodpeckers, gray jays, and

A bald eagle enjoying a salmon lunch.

Alaska's state bird, the willow ptarmigan, was chosen by a vote of the state's schoolchildren. During extremely cold weather, ptarmigans keep warm by burrowing into snow drifts.

chickadees are common in forested areas, as are goshawks – the large, handsome birds of prey which swoop down through the trees and catch their prey completely unawares. Gulls, terns, murrelets, auklets, shearwaters (known for their highly developed powers of navigation), cormorants, and puffins are found along the coastlines.

MAMMALS

The premier wildlife-viewing area in Alaska is Denali National Park (see page 227). Grizzly bears, moose, Dall sheep, caribou, red foxes, snowshoe hares, beavers, Arctic ground squirrels, and hoary marmots are seen by almost everyone who visits Denali. The park's shuttle bus system is designed to maximize wildlife sightings. The only vehicles allowed in the park are the buses, which cause comparatively little disturbance, and many animals, including grizzlies, can be photographed within 300ft (90 meters) of the road.

If you are lucky, you may also spot wolves in Denali. Ranging from black to white, but more commonly gray in color, they are usually not fond of human company and are more likely to be heard than seen. At Denali they have become habituated to the presence of vehicles and are sometimes spotted near the Park Road – or even trotting along it.

Denali and other Alaskan national parks are textbook examples of what wilderness parks were meant to be. A half-dozen or more protect entire ecosystems in a condition nearly identical to their

A red fox, one of Alaska's natural predators.

⊘ WHERE EAGLES DARE

Alaska is the stronghold of the bald eagle, the national bird of the United States. More of them live in Alaska than in the other 49 states combined. White heads, white tails and 8ft (2.4-meter) wing-spans make them easily identifiable, even at a great distance. They are most often seen where fish are common, especially along the coastal areas of southern Alaska, from the Aleutians to the southernmost Panhandle.

The best place to see large gatherings of bald eagles is near Haines, during October and November. A late run of chum salmon into the Chilkat River, just north of town, attracts thousands of bald eagles, which feed on the dead or spent salmon. A single tree may contain dozens of

roosting eagles – an extraordinary sight. Because fish are available throughout the winter in coastal areas, these bald eagles have no need to migrate from Alaska. You can visit the American Bald Eagle Foundation in Haines (see page 151) for attractive displays and useful information about the birds, which are no longer classified as an endangered species.

Golden eagles, the darker cousins of the bald eagle, are normally found in Alaska's Interior and Arctic regions, soaring above tundra and mountainous areas. They hunt rodents, such as the Arctic ground squirrel, rather than fish. The Polychrome Pass area of Denali National Park is an excellent place to see golden eagles.

original state. The population levels of wildlife such as Dall sheep, moose, caribou, hares, and marmots are controlled not by human interven-

Confusingly, black bears are sometimes brown in color; and brown bears can appear black. The best way to distinguish them is by looking for the hump which the brown/grizzly variety has at the back of its neck.

Partly because of the almost unlimited supply of salmon, adult male brown bears can grow to weights of more than 1,200lbs (540kg).

The best place to see them is at Brooks River and Camp, in Katmai, and the best time is in July, the peak of the sockeye salmon run. The McNeil River State Game Sanctuary, just outside the park, provides the ultimate bear-watching experience, but you literally have to enter a lottery to get in. A third option is to do guided day trips from Anchorage, Soldotna, or Homer to view bears on the west side of Cook Inlet. Another excellent region to

A grizzly bear forages in the colorful autumn tundra of Denali National Park.

tion, but by the area's natural predators: grizzly and black bears, lynx, wolverines, foxes, wolves, and raptors. If you are lucky enough to see a grizzly dig out a ground squirrel from its burrow or a wolf pack chase a caribou herd, you will be witnessing a scene which could have taken place during the last Ice Age.

ALASKA'S BEARS

Katmai National Park (see page 330) is the most popular place to closely observe brown bears. At one time, grizzlies and browns were classified as different species but they are now known to be the same animal (*Ursus arctos*). Grizzlies are residents of Alaska's inland regions, while brown bears inhabit the coast.

see brown bears is the Tongass National Forest in Southeast Alaska, especially Admiralty Island where there's a bear-viewing program at Pack Creek. Admiralty's original tribal name is Kootsnoowoo, which translates to 'fortress of the bears.' Much of Kodiak Island (see page 315) is home to a particularly large variety of brown bear, which has long tantalized trophy hunters. Black bears also inhabit much of Alaska. Smaller and more timid than grizzlies and brown bears, they tend to prefer forested areas.

Polar bears live along the Arctic coastline. They are among the largest land carnivores in the world, with some of the older males weighing over 1,500lbs (680kg). Spending most of their lives on the ice floes of the Arctic Ocean, they can swim long distances in these frigid waters and survive on a diet of seals and other marine mammals. Because they live in the remote Arctic, they are seldom seen by visitors, although polar bear-viewing tours are becoming more and more popular.

MOOSE AND OTHER SPECIES OF DEER

It is sometimes said that a camel is a horse designed by a committee, and much the same could be said of the moose: its legs are too long and its nose is too big. But if you watch these lumbering creatures running or swimming you will realize that nature got it right after all. The best places to see them are in Denali Park and the Kenai National Wildlife Refuge. The Athabascan Indians once relied on the moose for their survival, eating the meat and using the skins for clothing, blankets and boat making. The animals are still hunted extensively in the fall.

Denali is, again, the best – or at least the most accessible – place to see caribou, though its herd is among the state's smallest, with just a couple thousand animals. In all, more than half a million caribou migrate through the state, including two

Polar bears make their home along the Arctic coast.

A caribou in the tundra.

⊘ PRESERVING THE WILDLIFE

It's easy to assume that within Alaska's wide-open spaces its wildlife is safely protected. Sadly, this is not the case. Chief among the threats is climate change. Retreating sea ice is endangering the polar bear, walrus, and bearded and ringed seal. Further complications related to climate change include the introduction of invasive species and shifts in habitat vegetation. Warming ocean temperatures are partially blamed, along with overfishing, for declining fish and marine mammal populations. But it is not all bad news. In 2009, blue whales, once on the verge of extinction, began to return to Alaskan waters for the first time in 40 years.

huge herds (the Porcupine and Western Arctic herds) each with more than 100,000 members. Like other varieties of deer, caribou are herbivores and will eat the available grasses and berries as they travel the very long distances between their calving grounds and their over-wintering areas.

Reindeer, the domesticated version of caribou, were introduced into northern Alaska in 1892 as a dependable source of food and clothing. Today, there are approximately 30,000 reindeer in Alaska. The largest herd lives near Nome on the Seward Peninsula. A small herd can be seen at the Reindeer Farm in Palmer.

Sitka black-tail deer are distributed throughout the Southeast and also on the Kodiak Archipelago, southwest of Anchorage: these small, rusty-brown animals (their coats turn gray in the winter) are most likely to be seen in Misty Fiords National Monument (see page 118), Admiralty Island National Monument (see page 116), and on Kodiak Island. Other island residents are the Roosevelt elk and mountain goats.

THE MUSK OX

Nunivak Island, off Alaska's Southwest coast, is inhabited by a most extraordinary native animal: the musk ox, a stout, shaggy, creature which appears to be the result of an amorous

in the past decade, Cook Inlet's beluga population is believed to be stabilized.

A state-managed walrus-viewing program has been established at Round Island, in Bristol Bay, where thousands of bull walrus haul out every summer. Large numbers of walrus can also be seen in the Togiak National Wildlife Refuge and other northern communities. Harbor seals, sea otters, and sea lions are frequently sighted in the Gulf of Alaska and Prince William Sound. In fact, Alaska's coasts offer opportunities for wildlife watching that are difficult to match.

A young humpback whale breaches spectacularly near Juneau.

encounter between a prehistoric ox and a mountain sheep. Musk oxen are rare but small herds roam the Arctic and some are held captive in research stations, particularly in the Large Animal Research Station, part of the University of Alaska-Fairbanks.

SEA CREATURES

Alaska is rich in marine life: humpback, killer and minke whales can be seen in Glacier Bay and Kenai Fjords national parks, as well as other coastal regions. Belugas – small, white whales – inhabit Cook Inlet and can sometimes be seen from Anchorage's coastal fringes, or the Seward Highway, as it winds along Turnagain Arm south of the city. Though their numbers have declined

⊘ STREAMS OF SALMON

The lives of brown bears and salmon are inextricably linked, since salmon are the bears' favorite food. The fish come in five varieties (sockeye, king, chum, coho, and humpback) and are as popular with fishermen as with bears – understandably so, since their flesh has more flavor than the farmed variety. Witnessing a salmon run (from June to mid-September), when thousands of the fish cram the streams and leap the waterfalls, as they swim upstream to spawn, is a wonderful experience, as is watching the bears who come to prey on them, though access to prime venues such as McNeil River State Game Sanctuary is limited.

A glacier cave – camping in
extreme conditions requires the
services of an experienced guide.

SURVIVING IN THE WILDERNESS

Whether you are planning a leisurely stroll on a trail outside of Anchorage or Juneau or climbing Alaska's highest peak, taking sensible precautions is essential for any outside or wilderness adventure.

Sean Penn's 2007 movie *Into the Wild* captured Alaska's breathtaking beauty – and its deadliness. The film was based on the story of a 24-year-old Virginian, Christopher McCandless, who in 1992 starved to death near the Teklanika River, at the eastern edge of Denali National Park, after living in the wilderness for four months in an abandoned bus. Opinions vary about whether McCandless was mentally unstable or a victim of circumstances, but it is beyond argument that Alaska is an unforgiving environment unless proper precautions are taken.

Due to the latitude and varying weather conditions, travelers must have the appropriate equipment and be physically prepared for the activities they wish to pursue. Because there are so few roads and distances are so great, clear and precise communication is also vital.

VARIATIONS IN WEATHER

Coastal and Southcentral Alaska: The word to remember when selecting equipment for coastal Alaska is rain. Some of this area receives up to 200 inches (508cm) annually. If you plan to be outside for long periods, a waterproof suit (jacket, pants, and hat) and a synthetic pile or fleece jacket will be used frequently. Tents must be able to withstand long wet spells. Sleeping bags filled with synthetic materials are better than down because they retain more of their insulating qualities when wet.

The Interior: The Interior has dramatic seasonal contrasts. Summer temperatures are pleasantly warm while in winter the mercury can dip below –40°F (–40°C).

Even in summer, visitors should expect nighttime temperatures sometimes to dip below 40°F (4°C). A hat and gloves and at least one heavy long-sleeved shirt, plus the usual jacket and rain gear

Hiking towards Spencer Glacier.

⊘ THE THREAT FROM TIDES

There are large tidal variations in Southeastern Alaska, Prince William Sound, Cook Inlet, and Bristol Bay. The extreme diurnal variation occurs in spring in Cook Inlet near Anchorage, where high tide can be 38ft (11.5 meters) above low tide. Such tides present two dangers for those traveling through or near the water: swift incoming tides and strong currents, which are intensified in island areas. Obtain a tide book from a fishing tackle shop, hardware store, bar or gas station. All too frequently, the fisherman standing on a rock working the incoming tide waits too long to retreat, and this situation can become life-threatening.

will be useful, as will a mosquito head net, which takes up little luggage space.

The extreme cold of winter demands the best quality equipment. A good down jacket, a hat, mittens, and warm boots are essential. Camping in winter requires a sleeping bag that is comfortable at −40°F (−40°C) or colder.

Spring is the finest time, by far, to ski in the mountains. Temperatures may allow people to ski without shirts – although the sensible ones cover themselves in sunblock. But snow-blindness is a painful reality for unprotected eyes; mirrored sun-

and communities, and this will save you a lot of money. But if you are bound for the wilderness, a charter flight is necessary.

Before departure, be sure someone knows where you are going. If you have no alternative, inform the Alaska State Troopers and land managers of your destination and expected return date. Make firm arrangements to be picked up. Be certain that someone besides the pilot knows where you are going.

What happens if the plane crashes while you are in it? There is a legal requirement for all planes

Glacier-walking courtesy of a helicopter.

glasses are best, but dark sunglasses will suffice. And there's always the chance of springtime blizzards and avalanches.

The North Slope: If the key word for coastal Alaska is rain, the equivalent for the North Slope is wind. The area is technically an Arctic desert with less than 5 inches (13cm) of annual precipitation. But this meager amount should not be disregarded as it may fall as snow or freezing rain and be driven by gale force winds. Travelers to the North Slope need clothes that are windproof and warm, and camping equipment that can withstand heavy winds.

GETTING THERE

Charter flights: Check first to see if there is a regular air service – there is for some small villages

to carry emergency equipment. The required list includes food for each person for two weeks, an ax, first-aid kit, a knife, matches, mosquito head nets, gillnet, fishing tackle, and a pistol or rifle with ammunition. A sleeping bag, snowshoes, and a wool blanket are added to the list for winter travel.

It's a good idea to check the survival gear before taking off. If you decide to bring your own, keep as much of it on your person as possible. In winter fill your pockets; in summer, use a small waist pack.

Every plane in Alaska is also required to carry a downed aircraft transmitting device (Emergency Location Transmitter, or ELT). Learn how to operate this device before you set off. If the pilot becomes incapacitated, you can activate the ELT and be rescued more quickly. Don't be deterred by these dire warnings: these precautions pertain only to the 0.5 percent of flights during which an inflight problem does occur.

Automobile travel: There is no Alaska law which governs what survival equipment should be kept in a motor vehicle, yet far more cars than planes break down while traveling. In sub-freezing weather, a breakdown can be inconvenient as well as life-threatening. The Alaska State Troopers recommend the following survival kit: down coat, boots, mittens, hat, snow-pants, sleeping bag, flare, candles, extra spark plugs,

driving on gravel roads – and many road-accessible destinations require some driving on gravel.

ENCOUNTERING BEARS

'Bearanoia' is a term commonly applied to people with an unreasonable fear of bears. Others, usually inexperienced in the ways of the Alaskan wilderness, sometimes lack a healthy respect for these powerful, if generally shy, animals. Treading a middle ground, seasoned bear-country trekkers use common sense and a basic understanding of bear behavior to avoid close encounters. Most

On the beach in Homer with all the gear.

extra belts, shovel, chain, flashlight, and high-energy food.

Automobile maintenance is vitally important. Even if you come to no real harm, it is expensive and time-consuming to break down on the road – towing charges can be very costly, especially in remote areas. Check the car carefully before leaving the city, and remember winter essentials: snow tires or studded tires, an operating engine heater, and ample electrical cord to reach a power source.

When renting a car, inform the rental agency of your proposed route and confirm that maintenance is available along the way. Anticipating problems before traveling will avoid misunderstandings later. Most agencies have stringent rules about

⊘ LEARNING THE RULES

Taking the trouble to learn a few basics could save your life if you were stranded in the wilderness. There is a record of one man in a desperate situation who spotted an Alaska State Troopers airplane flying over his campsite. He frantically waved both his arms over his head. When the plane flew over a second time, he waved again. The plane flew off. It was only much later that the man realized his mistake; when he studied his hunting license, he saw that he had signaled, 'Everything OK, don't wait.' Sadly there was no happy ending: this information was recorded in a diary found when the man's body was discovered.

bears turn tail and run upon seeing people, but in some instances the bear will stand its ground, or charge.

If you do meet a bear, stay as calm as possible. Talk to the bear, to identify yourself as a human, but don't yell, and definitely *don't run*. Running is usually the worst possible strategy, because it will likely trigger the bear's predatory instincts. Back away slowly and give the bear an escape route. Avoid getting between a female and her cubs. Some experts suggest that you raise your arms above your head and wave them

important to avoid surprise encounters, which lead to the vast majority of bear attacks. Make plenty of noise while walking in the wilderness. Some people tie 'bear bells' to their shoes or pack, but talking or singing is better. Human voices carry farther than tinkling bells. If bears hear your approach, there's less chance they'll be surprised and they're likely to leave.

Stay alert and look for signs of bear, such as tracks, scat, partially eaten salmon. Choose your tent site carefully and avoid trails, streams with spawning salmon, and berry patches. Don't

Grizzly bears investigating a camp site – all food should be kept in bear-proof containers.

slowly. If you're in a group, stand side by side, to increase your apparent size.

Should a bear attack and make contact with you, it's usually best to fall to the ground and 'play dead.' Protect your head and neck and try to lie on your stomach, but do not struggle. If you're wearing a pack, leave it on. Once a bear feels there's no longer a threat, it will likely end its attack. The exception to this rule is when a bear shows predatory behavior. Instead of charging in a rush, such a bear will show intense interest and may circle or stalk you. If you think a bear is treating you as prey, fight it off. Such behavior is extremely rare and almost always involves black bears.

Some important strategies should be used to minimize chance meetings with bears. It's most

attract bears with your food and cook well away from your tents and store food far from your campsite. Keep all food and garbage in airtight, bear-proof containers. These can be purchased at any outdoor store and are often available at park visitors centers for a small deposit.

Finally, carry a firearm only if you know how to use it. (Guns are forbidden in some wilderness areas.) Pepper spray is another option, but it is only effective if the bear is close enough to make contact, which is certainly something you want to avoid. Air horns are the best protection against an unwanted bear encounter. Bears have extremely sensitive ears and a quick blast of the horn will deter a curious or approaching animal.

HIKING WITH MOOSE

More dangerous than bears are moose, and, unlike bears, a moose never bluffs. Killing more people

> *Wolf encounters aren't uncommon in Alaska, particularly in Denali National Park. Should a wolf approach, it's likely out of curiosity as they are not known to attack people. Nonetheless, try to discourage it by shouting and waving your hands.*

The following suggestions may help prevent an emergency:

Try to stay dry. Wet clothing loses most of its insulating value. Functional rain gear is vitally important. Ponchos are almost useless.

Avoid the wind. Wind carries body heat away much faster than still air; it also refrigerates wet clothing by evaporation. If you feel yourself getting chilled, look for shelter from the wind.

Understand the cold. Most people die of hypothermia when the temperature is between 30° and 50°F (–1° and 10°C). The majority of hikers

A reminder that climbing can be dangerous.

annually, moose can charge, kick, and stomp anyone too close to them or their young. Therefore, always give moose a wide berth. If one does charge, run and quickly get behind something, like a tree. If you are about to be stomped, curl into a ball, protecting your head with your hands.

AVOIDING HYPOTHERMIA

Beware of hypothermia, the sub-normal lowering of the body temperature. It is caused by exposure to cold, but aggravated by exhaustion, wind, and wet clothing. Left untreated, a person suffering from hypothermia may become disoriented, incoherent, then unconscious, and may finally die. The time to prevent hypothermia is during the initial period of exposure.

underestimate the severity of being wet in Alaskan waters. Many rivers are fed by glaciers and their temperatures, even in mid-summer, aren't much above the freezing mark. Getting soaked can be fatal, and first-aid measures must be taken immediately.

End the exposure. If someone shows any signs of hypothermia, or if it becomes impossible to keep dry, make camp or end the trip.

Avoid over-tiredness. Don't be too ambitious. Make camp before you get exhausted, and bring high-energy food to replenish your reserves.

SURVIVING AVALANCHES

These pose a serious threat to winter mountain adventurers. Research has shown that most avalanches involving humans are triggered by people traveling through avalanche-prone terrain.

A snow-covered slope is especially prone to sliding when its gradient ranges between 27 and 45 degrees. On steeper slopes, the snow usually won't accumulate, and on shallower slopes, the angle is usually not sufficient to release snow. Avoid disaster by careful route selection and trip planning.

Spring is an especially dangerous season for avalanches, as the snow melts and the weight of the snowpack increases. If possible, take an avalanche-awareness class to learn more about safe winter travel in the mountains.

Alaska may have been spared snakes, but the mosquito more than makes up for it. Thick clothing will reduce the number of bites, but sometimes a head net is the only means of relief.

Heed the signs.

⊘ DIAGNOSING AND TREATING HYPOTHERMIA

One of the first signs of hypothermia is violent and uncontrollable shivering. As the core body temperature drops, shivering diminishes and muscles become rigid. The chief symptoms at this stage are what one outdoor writer calls 'the umbles': stumbling, mumbling, fumbling, bumbling. Speech is slurred, coordination poor, and comprehension dull. If not properly treated the victim quickly becomes irrational, drifts into a stupor, and loses consciousness. Sufferers often don't realize they're in danger and may even deny it. It only takes a few minutes to slip into the condition, and, if untreated, death can follow in less than two hours.

If you suspect a member of your party is suffering from hypothermia, immediately try to find shelter. Put the victim into dry clothes, wrap him in blankets or sleeping bags, keep him off the ground, provide whatever heat may be available, and warm the core area of the body with hot liquids. If the condition worsens, put the victim in a sleeping bag with another person. Alone, the victim will be unable to produce enough heat to warm the bag, much less his own body.

Avoid rapidly warming the extremities, as it takes much-needed blood away from the core area and can result in unconsciousness. Do not give a victim any alcohol, as this could prove fatal; forget stories about a sip of brandy being restorative. It can speed up hypothermia and can cause dehydration.

PUBLIC-USE CABINS

Between luxury wilderness lodges and tent camping, there's a third way for travelers to spend the night in Alaska's backcountry that is surprisingly comfortable and affordable.

Given Alaska's often cool and wet weather, it can make all the difference to return to a roomy, dry, and heated shelter at the end of a day's explorations. Public-use cabins provide an economical way of doing this. For as little as $25 a night, you can spread out your soaked clothing, pull up a chair, and read a book beside an oil- or wood-burning stove while your hiking or paddling partner grabs fresh greens from the cooler and prepares a gourmet meal on your camp stove.

ESSENTIALS TO BRING

You don't have to worry about crowding, leaky tents, or a wild animal getting into your food supplies, which can be safely stored inside the cabin. All public-use cabins include heating stove, bunks or other platforms for sleeping, table, chairs, counter tops or shelves, and outhouse. Some also include propane-fueled lights, burner plates, stainless steel sinks, picnic tables with benches, wash area, and more. Prepare to bring your own food, heating and cooking fuel, utensils, water, cook stove, and bedding.

Frontier etiquette demands that, where possible, you attempt to leave cabins in better condition than you found them. You are encouraged to restock firewood, sweep and wipe down surfaces, and leave any extra canned goods for the next occupants. There may be additional instructions with regards to propane, water, and other amenities.

WHERE TO FIND THEM

Balancing these 'comforts of home' is the wildness and solitude to be found outside your shelter. Many public-use cabins are located in remote wilderness areas that can be reached only by boat or plane. Others can be easily reached from the road system. Rugged and well worn, they add the beauty of refuge to the surrounding wilderness.

More than 300 such cabins are available for rent throughout much of the state, in state and national parks, wildlife refuges, Bureau of Land Management lands, and Alaska's two national forests. Some are along trails, others are on lakes, rivers, forested coastlines, or alpine meadows.

Their nightly costs range from around $25 to $75 – a bargain for those seeking dependable protection from Alaska's unpredictable weather as well as some degree of comfort. Some can be rented only in summer, while others can be used year-round.

Hiking up to a cabin near Beaver Creek in the White Mountains National Recreation Area.

HOW TO RESERVE A CABIN

Most cabins are available on a first-come, first-served reservation system and can be reserved up to six months in advance. However, some agencies incorporate a lottery system in the booking of some of the more sought after locations. In nearly all cases, the length of stay is limited.

Check for specifics, as details vary by agency. These include the National Park Service, Alaska State Parks, the US Fish and Wildlife Service, the US Forest Service, and the Bureau of Land Management (BLM).

Information on public-use cabins throughout Alaska is available from Alaska Public Lands Information Center, tel: 907-644-3661; www.alaskacenters.gov/trip-planning/lodging-permits/cabins, with the exception of the Alaska State Parks cabin, which must be booked on their website, www.dnr.alaska.gov/parks/aspcabins.

The Oosterdam approaches Hubbard Glacier.

CRUISING AND TOURING

From tidewater glaciers to North America's highest peak, there is a lot to see in Alaska. To squeeze it all in, many travelers opt for all-inclusive cruises or tours on the Alaska Railroad.

Taking a cruise up through Alaska's Panhandle or riding the Alaska Railroad from Seward to Fairbanks are popular ways to see Alaska. The adage, 'focus on the journey, not the destination' rings especially true in this vast state. Fortunately, there are plenty of options for both the independent traveler and those seeking maximum luxury on the state's railroad and high seas.

Alaska's cruise season is short, from May to September, and it can be misty, wet, and chilly in both early and late summer. But the lure of the state's dramatic wilderness scenery, invigorating clean air, wildlife, and fascinating shore excursions have led to a phenomenal growth in cruise traffic. Indeed, more than 58 percent of Alaska's summer visitors are now cruise passengers, served by more than 27 vessels.

THE EARLY DAYS

The first organized cruises to Alaska took place when a young Chuck West, originally a bush pilot, formed a travel company called Westours. In 1954, he pioneered Alaska cruising using two small ships, the 1,835-ton *Yukon Star* and sister ship, the 1,833-ton *Glacier Queen*. Both ships carried 148 passengers in a one-class arrangement.

Eventually, the major cruise lines got wise, and started offering Alaska cruises in addition to their Caribbean trips. Discovering a goldmine, they soon added longer trips, more luxurious boats, and elaborate shore excursions along with Interior treks.

ECONOMIC BENEFITS

Alaska cruising has evolved into a big money-maker for the cruise companies, and provides income and work for local Alaskans who operate some of the land-based tourism infrastructure

On-board dining is an elegant affair.

⊘ CANADIAN DEPARTURES

The US Passenger Services Act of 1886 requires that only US-flag and US-built vessels can be used to carry passengers between two US ports, but it allows foreign-flag vessels to pick up or drop off passengers while calling at a single US port. Since most large cruise ships are registered not in the US but with a foreign-flag nation (such as the Bahamas, Bermuda, Liberia, Panama, and the UK), many cruises to Alaska start and end in Vancouver, British Columbia. An increasing number of seven- and 12-day cruises also run from Seattle and San Francisco. However, passengers on trip such as these will have less time for tours and excursions.

and cruise-related services. The government is happy too, as it collects taxes not only from visiting cruise ships, but also from every passenger carried, and through certain services on shore.

Alaskan cruises were the most-booked domestic vacation among North Americans for three years running as of 2019, with an estimated 1.3 million cruise passengers arriving at Alaska's shores for the year ahead.. For Alaska's port cities, revenue from cruise ships represents a significant part of their income. In Juneau alone, it amounts to roughly $200 mil-

In Glacier Bay National Park.

lion each year. The impact the cruise industry has on the local economy is immense and cannot be understated.

ENVIRONMENTAL CONCERNS

The cruise industry has plenty of critics. It is estimated that a 3,000-passenger ship produces 50 tons of trash, generates and releases 210,000 gallons of untreated sewage every week, and emits diesel exhaust equal to thousands of automobiles, a third of which is given off while idling in port.

Large vessels also pose a threat to the wildlife they are trying to showcase. In addition to impacting the solitude of important breeding and feeding grounds, there have been three incidents

when large cruise ships have struck whales since 2001. The most recent occurred in 2017 when an adult female humpback was pinned to a ship's bow, which protrudes from the bowline to increase the stability of these large vessels.

For these reasons locations like Glacier Bay, a critical feeding ground for the endangered humpback whale, restricts the number of vessels entering its waters each day. To do so, a cruise line needs an entry permit from the Glacier Bay National Park and Preserve. A limited number of permits are issued for the 'prime season' (June 1–August 31). Only two cruise ships (over 100 gross tons) are allowed in each day, plus three ships of under 100 gross tons (such as the ships of Alaskan Dream Cruises, Lindblad Expeditions, and Un-Cruise Adventures).

In a typical summer season, the National Park Service issues more than 220 cruise-ship permits to enter Glacier Bay. Although these are spread around the industry, Holland America and Princess Cruises receive the greatest number.

PLAYING HARDBALL

Over the years, the state has worked to lessen the impact of these floating cities. Today, cruise ships use power from Alaska's grid instead of idling in port, and can only release sewage, waste, or graywater 3 miles (5km) offshore or away from ecologically sensitive areas. Despite attempts to lessen the effects of large cruise ships, their sheer size and copious number of amenities (pools, patios, restaurants, barbers, stores, and theaters) keep cruising from being a low impact way to travel.

The cruise industry also plays hardball when it comes to any new regulations. In 2010, when Alaskans voted to instate a $46 'head tax' for each cruise-ship passenger to upgrade port infrastructure, the industry sued, and slashed its Alaska sailings by 10 percent. In response, the state legislature reduced the tax to $34.50 per passenger. The cruise industry thanked the state by adding more ships in later seasons, but it continued to pressure the legislature to relax its stringent wastewater treatment and discharge regulations. In line with new, stricter regulations introduced by the Obama administration, large ships were forced to reduce the highly polluting sulfur content in their fuel.

CRUISE TOURS

Over the past decade, the cruise companies have extended their reach and have begun offering multi-day land extensions to their seafaring

While cruise ships provide an opportunity to see wild Alaska landscapes for those who might not otherwise, the ships themselves have a significant environmental impact.

trips. Cruise tours have become an increasingly popular way to see more of Alaska, particularly by those who have limited time and may only visit it once. These tours usually involve a cruise plus land-stay in a hotel, or a cruise plus an extended trip, usually via train. Although the most popular cruises to Alaska last for seven days, extending a vacation by taking a cruise plus an escorted land tour can stretch to 18 days.

The most popular destinations are Denali National Park and the Yukon, but tours of Wrangell-St Elias and Kenai Fjords are

The GTS Summit gets close to the Mendenhall Glacier near Juneau.

⊘ THE BEST SHORE EXCURSIONS

Shore excursions have increased in number (and cost) over the years; Holland America Line alone offers more than 100 optional excursions. These include flightseeing (by floatplane or helicopter), salmon fishing, glacial ice treks, mountain biking, jeep safaris, and whale watching.

On cruises to Skagway, a trip on the White Pass & Yukon Route Railroad is recommended. This narrow-gauge track, built in 1898, now provides Alaska's most popular shore excursion. The railroad operates 20 diesel locomotives and two steam locomotive.

Flightseeing excursions depart from Juneau and land on Mendenhall Glacier, which has signed trails and interpretive panels. Most floatplanes fly at around 2,000ft (600

meters), and all passengers have window seats.

Tours to Denali National Park can be made by plane or bus. Wildlife includes moose, caribou and brown bears.

Prudhoe Bay provides close-ups of the trans-Alaska oil pipeline and sightseeing along the Dalton Highway. A ride on the Mount Roberts tramway above Juneau offers great views across Gastineau Channel.

There is top-class salmon fishing to be had on expeditions to the Ninilchik River and Deep Creek, plus deep-sea charters for halibut.

A walking tour of historic Ketchikan, a trip to nearby Saxman Totem Park, and a trip through the rainforest's canopy on a zipline tour are also recommended.

becoming increasingly popular. All trips are neatly packaged by the cruise lines, include a variety of luxurious amenities, and some lines, like Princess, own a network of hotels and lodges, so that travelers never have to sleep in a bed not made by a cruise-line staffer. They also almost always include a leg in their special domed railroad cars. Part of the Alaska Railroad, trains such as the McKinley Explorer owned by Holland America or Princess's Midnight Sun Express provide spectacular views and first-class service.

Smaller cruise lines also offer a variety of land extension tours. These depend on local transportation and accommodations, but provide a more intimate look at the state.

RAIL TOURS

The Alaska Railroad is a great way to tour Alaska, whether you take one of its packaged tours or just ride the rails. Completed in 1923, the railway extends northward, from Seward through Anchorage to Fairbanks, a distance of 470 miles (756km). It is operated by the state

The specially constructed domed railcars of cruise trains offer fine paroramic views.

⊘ POPULAR CRUISE ROUTES

The Inside Passage Route from Vancouver to Skagway, with visits to tidewater glaciers, such as those found in Glacier Bay's Hubbard Glacier or Tracy Arm (just two of the 15 active glaciers along the 60-mile/100km Glacier Bay coastline). Ports of call might include Juneau, Ketchikan, Skagway and/or Haines. The Glacier Route, which usually includes the Gulf of Alaska during a one-way cruise between Vancouver and Seward, Whittier or Anchorage. Typical ports of call might include Haines, Sitka, and Valdez. Of special interest is the marine life of Hubbard Glacier and Prince William Sound.

of Alaska and is one of the few railroads in the country where trains carry both passengers and commercial freight. Spurs run to Whittier and the Anchorage Airport.

In the summer, trains run daily from Anchorage to Seward and Whittier, and include stops at Girdwood and Portage. Also leaving daily is the Denali Star, which travels to Fairbanks with stops to Talkeetna and Denali National Park along the way. Like those owned by the cruise companies, the railroad features a number of domed luxury cars, to take in the surrounding scenery fully. These, in addition to onboard dining facilities and open-air decks, make a trip along the Turnagain Arm or through the Alaska Range a sightseeing tour in itself. The

Hurricane Turn running from Talkeetna to Hurricane along the Chulitna River operates Thursday through Monday. One of the last flag-stop trains in the US, it is, however, a great way to jump off into the Alaskan wilderness for an afternoon of hiking, fishing, or river rafting. Winter service is only available from Anchorage to Fairbanks on the weekends.

To compete with the cruise lines, the railroad offers tour packages of its own. Guests may opt for the daylong Spencer Lake and Grandview Tour aboard the Glacier Discovery Train, or the all-inclusive Deluxe Alaska Sampler, a seven-night journey from the Kenai Fjords to the Denali backcountry.

Another popular trip is the 10-day Glaciers, Rails and Trails tour package which features whitewater rafting, glacier hiking, and a 130-mile (210km) jet boat ride, from the Kenai Fjords to Denali National Park and Talkeetna. All destinations are connected by the rail line. Whether one day or several, tour packages include lodging, meals, and specialty tour arrangements. For more information visit www.alaskarailroad.com.

Shore excursions include dogsledding.

⊙ CROWDS AND CONGESTION

With almost 1 million cruise passengers a year visiting Alaska and several large resort ships likely to be in port on any given day, there is so much congestion in many small ports that avoiding crowded streets can be difficult. With more people around, wildlife is harder to spot.

These high volume bursts of tourists have also been blamed for the 'Disneyfication' of many towns in the Southeast. Often filled with over-priced trinket shops, lots of fudge hawkers, and diamond jewelry stores (many of which are also found in Caribbean destinations), they can feel like brightly painted parodies of the downtowns frequented by locals, which are usually only a couple of blocks away.

Sitka is the one city in Alaska to prohibit cruise ships docking in town and it shows, but places like Ketchikan and Juneau can feel as if the real and imagined versions of the city sit side-by-side. However, a quick stroll will take you beyond these sometimes-tacky tourist zones into the sloped residential neighborhoods, where narrow streets yield to lush staircases, giving you a sense of daily life in the Southeast.

The more adventurous might consider one of the more unusual Alaska cruises to the far north, around the Pribilof Islands (superb for bird watching) and into the Bering Sea. Or you can create your own cruise tour by taking to the ferries.

BIG SHIPS VS SMALL SHIPS

Choosing a ship is a lot like buying a car. Big or small? Classic or modern? Luxurious or functional? Assess what you really want.

The difference between so-called 'big ships' and 'small ships' could hardly be more stark, and it isn't simply a matter of tonnage or floor space, but what they have to offer. These days, large mainstream ships tend to be very big indeed, carrying 3,000 passengers or more, soaring 14 stories above the water, and stretching to lengths of nearly 1,000ft (300 meters).

By contrast, small ships in Alaska tend to be very small, measuring around 100ft (30 meters) in length and carrying between 12 and 140 passengers. Some are closer to yachts in size and appearance, others have the utilitarian feel of expedition ships, and still others look like the miniaturized cruise ships that they are.

A CHOICE OF ENTERTAINMENT

In examining whether a big or small ship would best suit your needs, you need to consider three main variables: the onboard experience you should expect during your cruise, the kinds of itineraries and ports of call offered by each, and the cost.

By design, most big ships are busy places, with activities, entertainment, and meals programmed so that, if you cared to, you could be occupied during every waking moment you were on board. As such, they're ideal for families, allowing parents and children to pursue their own interests and stay out of each other's hair. They're also the better choice for people who, although they want to see the natural wonders of the 49th state, don't expect that glaciers, whales, and mountains will be able to hold their interest every minute of the day.

These people want a show in the evening, multiple restaurants for dinner, sports options (of both the active and couch-potato varieties), maybe a casino, and they might even like to take a dip in the ship's pool – if only for the kick of doing so within sight of an iceberg. For these people, Norwegian Cruise Line and Carnival are the top choices.

Those looking for a slightly more refined version of this same experience should check out tradition-minded Holland America, while those with the money to go with their refinement should opt for the luxury lines Crystal and Seabourn, which feature much enhanced service, cuisine, and facilities.

ACCOMMODATIONS

Accommodations run the gamut from smallish inside cabins to outside ones with private balconies, to palatial suites with butler service. Balcony cabins offer the pleasant option of landscape- and wildlife-viewing in the privacy of your own room, but if you're

Princess Cruises get as close as they can.

just as happy watching from public areas you can save by opting for an inside cabin (if you're not claustrophobic) or an exterior one with a small window.

EATING AT SEA

Dining is another area of great choice on the big ships. Whereas a decade ago the most you could expect to find would have been a main restaurant with two seatings and a buffet option at breakfast and lunch, today's mega-ships are being built with multiple main dining rooms, casual options for every meal, specialty coffee-and-pastry cafés, and multiple reservations-only restaurants serving Asian, Italian, French, steakhouse, and other menus, at an extra cost of up to $40 per person per meal.

And if you want to work off the calories you are likely to pack away at those restaurants, the megaships all have sprawling gym complexes, jogging tracks, and varying sports amenities, from the almost ubiquitous golf-driving nets and basketball/volleyball courts to rock-climbing walls. In essence, sailing aboard a mega-ship in Alaskan waters is like checking into a smart, big-city hotel and then taking that hotel with you to the wilderness.

SMALL SHIPS FOR WATCHING WILDLIFE

Across the board, small ships offer exactly the opposite kind of experience, with onboard dining, activities, and entertainment taking a backseat to the natural world outside. All meals are served in a single, simple

Alaska, which is the main reason people choose this type of cruise. Typically, the range of accommodations on these vessels is limited, tending toward cozy outside cabins with few amenities.

PORTS OF CALL

Itinerary-wise, ships both large and small tend to visit the popular Alaska ports of Juneau, Ketchikan, and Skagway, where all passengers get exactly the same experience, although big ships tend to offer a wider range of shore-excursion options. One advantage small ships do have here is that, with fewer passengers, it takes less time to get on and off the ship, so you have more time in port and less frustrating waiting time. Small ships also have the advantage when it comes to visiting smaller port towns like Petersburg and Metlakatla and sailing narrow wilderness passages like Misty Fiords

dining room (with a small buffet also set out in a lounge at lunch and dinner times), while the only entertainment you might expect is, perhaps, a crew talent show or an informal lecture by the ship's onboard naturalist.

Instead of inside-oriented activities, passengers spend their time out on deck with binoculars scanning for whales, bears, sea otters, and other wildlife – which they're much more likely to see from these ships than from the big ones, since small vessels are less obtrusive, can therefore sail closer to shore, and have passenger decks that begin only a few yards above the waterline. These same factors also mean you get a more intimate experience of

National Monument – places from which the big ships are barred by their sheer bulk.

COUNTING THE COST

Small ships, which cost more to operate, are more expensive than the big mainstream lines. Consider your priorities and your budget. For the same cost, you could sail with a mainstream line and take all the best optional shore excursions (helicopter glacier treks, sportfishing, dogsledding); sail with a luxury line and find your own way around ports of call; or sail with a small-ship adventure line, where most off-ship wilderness activities are included in the cost. In the end, it's all a matter of taste.

ALASKA FROM THE AIR

Even long-time Alaskans are awestruck by the view from the air. Flightseeing, a growing industry, provides two guarantees: the view will be incomparable, and there's not a bad seat in the house.

Flying through the Knik Valley in Southcentral Alaska, a Cessna 185 descends into the Gorge, a canyon with a glacier on one side and a sheer rock face on the other. The landscape dwarfs the buzzing aircraft, giving passengers the sense that they're riding inside the hull of a fragile flying insect. They drink in the astonishing view. Pastel-blue cracks on the face of the glacier are deep enough to swallow a 17-story building. No one speaks. It's a wondrous sight.

Wild places stretch from horizon to horizon, untouched by human hands. From the lush rain forest of the southeastern Panhandle to the delta wetlands of the western coast and the tapestry of the far northern tundra, much of Alaska is accessible only by air. And it may never look more spectacular than it does from above.

TRAVEL BY AIRPLANE

A plane trip in Alaska is almost always a breathtaking journey, but it's also a crucial mode of

Floatplane on Lake Hood.

⊘ A CHECKLIST FOR PASSENGERS

Before you plan to fly into the wilderness, there are a few things you should keep in mind. First, air taxis aren't cheap. Cost varies widely depending on the destination, amount of gear, and the number of passengers, and is usually based on flight hours. Even a relatively short hop in the outback can cost as much as a flight from the Lower 48 states to Alaska.

Second, patience is a virtue. Bad weather and mechanical problems often delay flights for hours or days, so bring extra provisions, a deck of cards, and a sense of humor. Impatience, known by some pilots as 'get-home-itis,' is a leading factor in small aircraft accidents.

Finally, put safety first. Do ask your pilot if he or she

has insurance and a commercial license, which requires a higher standard of training and aircraft maintenance than a private license. And be sure the plane has life vests, an emergency locator transmitter (ELT), and other essential safety equipment.

Never challenge a pilot's decision to cancel a flight; the sun may be shining where you are, but the weather at your destination could be dramatically different – and unsafe. Nor should you pressure a pilot to carry more people or gear than the aircraft can handle. Weight and balance are critical for safe flying.

Taking to the air in Alaska should be enjoyable. The experience is routine here, but it is very seldom boring.

transportation. Beyond the cities and towns, many communities can't be reached by road. Most bush villages appear on the map like disconnected specks without the usual web of asphalt connecting them to the outside world. Almost everything that goes in or comes out – people, mail, groceries, medicine – travels by air.

Given the importance of air travel, Alaska has been dubbed the 'flyingest' state in the Union. More than one percent of the population has some flight training, with one out of 71 Alaskans a registered pilot of some sort –and the percent

can be found just about anywhere. Once in the air, it often feels as though the pilot is having just as much fun as the passengers.

HOW TO ARRANGE A FLIGHT

This is a fairly straightforward matter. Some companies offer a regular schedule of flights and destinations. Others operate on a charter basis and will take you just about anywhere you want to go. Still others specialize in flightseeing tours of the region's most scenic places. Want to spend a day or two fishing in complete solitude at a remote

A Cessna floatplane negotiates the Neacola Mountains above Lake Clark National Park.

of state residents who own aircraft is six times the national rate. Lake Hood in Anchorage is the largest and busiest seaplane base in the world, averaging 234 landings and take-offs a day; 800 per day are not uncommon in summer. Merrill Field, also in Anchorage, is also home to hundreds of small aircraft.

FLIGHT TOURS

Nothing compares to taking to the skies to experience Alaska's grandeur. Helicopter and hot-air balloon tours are available in many destinations, but jumping on board an idling fixed-wing plane feels particularly Alaskan. Many tour operators moonlight as bush pilots or run commuter trips to remote communities, so a willing tour guide

mountain lake, or perhaps spend a few hours trekking across an otherwise inaccessible glacier? If so, these are the people you need to see.

Bush planes range in size from a two-person Piper Super Cub to a 20-passenger DeHavilland Twin Otter. They are remarkably versatile aircraft designed to operate in the most rugged settings. Depending on season and terrain, they may be equipped with pontoons, skis, or tundra tires. Pontoons on an aircraft make convenient landing strips of coves, lakes, and streams; skis are used on ice and snow; and tundra tires, like big rubber donuts, cushion landings on gravel bars or soft, spongy tundra. Helicopters are also an option for backcountry travel, especially for close-up views of the terrain and extremely tight landings.

Denali National Park.

Traversing nearly-bare ice on the way to the finish line in Nome, Alaska, during the Iditarod Trail Sled Dog Race.

The White Pass and Yukon Route Railroad.

A snowy scene in the Copper River Valley.

INTRODUCTION

A detailed guide to the entire state, arranged by region and with main sites clearly cross-referenced by number to the maps.

Remote wintry stream.

Given that its landmass amounts to one-fifth the size of the combined Lower 48 states, it's not surprising that Alaska has six distinct geographic areas.

Southeast Alaska (also known as the Panhandle) is a narrow, 400-mile (640km) strip of land sandwiched between the Pacific Ocean and Canada, and cut off from the rest of Alaska by the towering St Elias range. It is covered by huge temperate rainforests nurtured by a mild climate: readings of 60° or 70°F (15° or 21°C) are not uncommon in the summer, and winter temperatures don't often dip much below freezing.

Southcentral Alaska lies along the Gulf of Alaska. A region of mountains, fjords, tidewater glaciers, and forested lowlands, it includes Prince William Sound, the Kenai Peninsula, Cook Inlet, and Kodiak Island, as well as the fertile Matanuska Valley. Temperatures vary from –20°F (–29°C) in winter to 60 to 70°F (15 to 21°C) in summer. In the summer of 2019, the temperature of 90°F (32°C) set an all-time record in Anchorage.

Alaska's Interior is a broad lowland cradled between the Brooks and Alaska mountain ranges. It encompasses the mighty Yukon, Tanana and Kuskokwim rivers. In some areas, birch and spruce thrive; others support only vast reaches of tundra. Temperatures can fall to below –50°F (–45°C) in winter and climb to 70 to 80°F (21 to 26°C) or higher in the summer.

Arctic Alaska stretches north from the southern edge of the Brooks Range to the Arctic Ocean. Huge stretches of tundra flower spectacularly in the nightless summer. Mid-summer temperatures sometimes exceed 80°F (26°C), while mid-winter temperatures can sink to –40°F (–40°C) or below. The minimal rainfall of 5 inches (13cm) a year qualifies it as a desert.

Pine trees in the foreground of the Mendenhall Glacier in Juneau.

Southwest Alaska is the home of the Alaska Peninsula and Aleutian Islands, which stretch 200 miles (320km) west into the Bering Sea. A warm current from Japan meets the icy northern air over the Aleutians, creating the rain and fog that enshroud them. Temperature range: 0°F (–17°C) to 50 to 60°F (10 to 15°C).

Western Alaska and the Bering Sea coast stretch from the Arctic Circle to Bristol Bay. Much of the land is treeless tundra underlain with permafrost. Temperature range: 0°F (–17°C; with wind-chill) to 60°F (15°C).

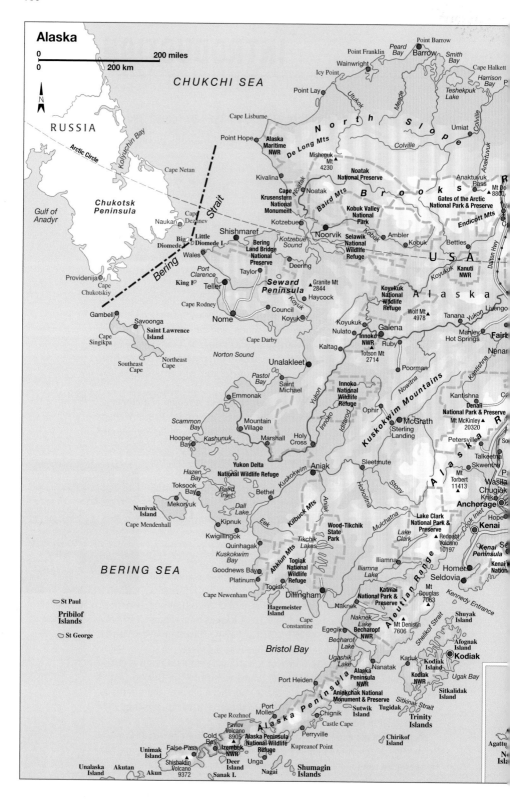

Alaska

0 ————— 200 miles
0 ————— 200 km

N

CHUKCHI SEA

RUSSIA

Arctic Circle

Kolyuchin Bay

Cape Netan

Gulf of
Anadyr

Chukotsk
Peninsula

Providenija
Cape
Chukotskiy

Naukan
Cape
Dezhnev

Bering Strait

Big Diomede
Little Diomede I

Cape Prince of Wales
Wales

Providenija

Point Barrow
Barrow
Peard Bay
Smith Bay
Point Franklin
Wainwright
Cape Halkett
Harrison Bay
Teshekpuk Lake
Icy Point
Point Lay
Umiat
Colville

Cape Lisburne

North Slope

Point Hope
Alaska Maritime NWR
De Long Mts
Misheguk Mt 4230
Anaktuvuk Pass
Mt Do 8800

Kivalina
Noatak National Preserve
Gates of the Arctic National Park & Preserve

Cape Krusenstern National Monument
Noatak
Baird Mts
B r o o k s

Endicott Mts

Kotzebue
Kobuk Valley National Park
Ambler
Kobuk
Bettles

Shishmaref
Kotzebue Sound
Noorvik
Selawik National Wildlife Refuge

Dalton Hwy

U S A

Bering Land Bridge National Preserve
Deering
Koyukuk Kanuti NWR

Port Clarence
Taylor
Seward Peninsula
Granite Mt 2844
A l a s k a

King I
Teller
Council
Koyuk
Haycock
Koyukuk National Wildlife Refuge
Wolf Mt 4978
Tanana
Manley Hot Springs
Yukon
Livengo
Fairb

Cape Rodney
Nome
Kaltag
Koyukuk
Nulato
Galena
Innoko NWR
Ruby
Totson Mt 2714
Nenan

Gambell
Savoonga
Saint Lawrence Island
Cape Darby
Poorman
Kantishna

Cape Singikpa
Southeast Cape
Northeast Cape
Norton Sound
Unalakleet
Innoko National Wildlife Refuge
Ophir
Kantishna Mts
Denali National Park & Preserve
Mt McKinley 20320

Pastol Bay
Saint Michael
Ophir
McGrath
Sterling Landing
Petersville

Scammon Bay
Mountain Village
Marshall
Holy Cross
Sleetmute
Talkeetna
Skwentna

Hooper Bay
Kashunuk
Aniak
Mt Torbert 11413
Wasill
Chugiak
Knik

Hazen Bay
Yukon Delta National Wildlife Refuge
Lake Clark National Park & Preserve
Anchorage
Hope
Kenai

Toksook Bay
Baird Inlet
Bethel
Wood-Tikchik State Park
Hononitna
Lake Clark
Redoubt Volcano 10197
Kenai Peninsula

Mekoryuk
Dall Lake
Kilbuck Mts
Iliamna
Homer
Kenai Nation
Seldovia

Nunivak Island
Cape Mendenhall
Kipnuk
Kwigillingok
Quinhagak
Ahklun Mts
Tikchik Mts
Tikchik Lakes
Iliamna Lake
Mt Douglas 7063
Kennedy Entrance

Kuskokwim Bay
Goodnews Bay
Platinum
Togiak National Wildlife Refuge
Katmai National Park & Preserve
Mt Denison 7606
Shuyak Island

Cape Newenham
Togiak
Dillingham
Naknek
Becharof NWR
Afognak Island

BERING SEA
Hagemeister Island
Cape Constantine
Egegik
Becharof Lake
Karluk
Kodiak Island
Kodiak

St Paul
Pribilof Islands
St George
Bristol Bay
Ugashik Lake
Nanatak
Kodiak NWR
Ugak Bay

Port Heiden
Alaska Peninsula NWR
Sitkalidak Island

Port Moller
Aniakchak National Monument & Preserve
Chignik
Sutwik Island
Tugidak
Trinity Islands

Cape Rozhnof
Pavlov Volcano 8905
Alaska Peninsula National Wildlife Refuge
Perryville
Castle Cape
Kupreanof Point
Chirikof Island
Agattu
Ne
Isl

Cold Bay
Izembek NWR
Deer Island
Unga
Shumagin Islands

Unimak Island
False Pass
Shishaldin Volcano 9372
Sanak I.
Nagai

Unalaska Island
Akutan
Akun

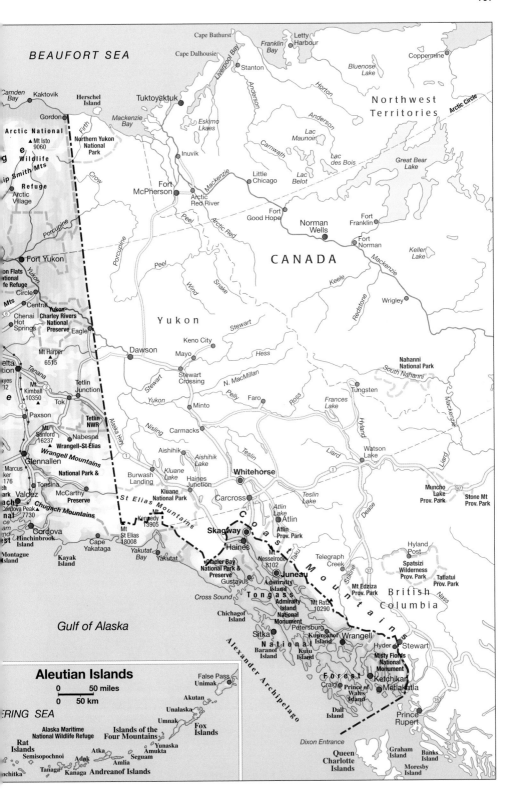

BEAUFORT SEA

NORTHWEST Territories
Arctic Circle

CANADA

Cape Bathurst
Cape Dalhousie
Franklin Bay
Letty Harbour
Coppermine
Liverpool Bay
Stanton
Bluenose Lake
Camden Bay
Kaktovik
Herschel Island
Tuktoyaktuk
Gordon
Mackenzie Bay
Eskimo Lakes
Arctic National
▲ Mt Isto 9060
Northern Yukon National Park
Inuvik
Anderson
Lac Maunoir
Carnwath
Wildlife
Lac des Bois
Great Bear Lake
ip Smith Mts
Crow
Fort McPherson
Arctic Red River
Little Chicago
Mackenzie
Lac Belot
Refuge
Arctic Village
Peel
Fort Good Hope
Fort Norman Wells
Fort Franklin
Porcupine
Arctic Red
Fort Norman
Keller Lake
Fort Yukon
Porcupine
Yukon
Peel
Wind
Snake
Keele
Redstone
Mackenzie
Wrigley
on Flats ational fe Refuge
Circle
Central
Yukon Charley Rivers National Preserve
Eagle
Yukon
Keno City
Stewart
Hess
N. MacMillan
Nahanni National Park
South Nahanni
Mts
Chenai Hot Springs
Mt Harper 6515
Dawson
Mayo
Stewart Crossing
Tungsten
elta tion
Tanana
Mt Kimball 10350
Tetlin Junction
Stewart
Yukon
Pelly
Faro
Frances Lake
Ross
Hyland
Mackenzie
e
hayes 32
Tok
Paxson
Tetlin NWR
Minto
Carmacks
Nisling
Mt Sanford 16237
Nabesna
Wrangell-St Elias
Aishihik
Aishihik Lake
Teslin
Watson Lake
Glennallen
Wrangell Mountains
Burwash Landing
Kluane Lake
Whitehorse
Liard
Muncho Lake Prov. Park
Stone Mt Prov. Park
Marcus ker 176
National Park &
Haines Junction
Carcross
Teslin Lake
Dease
Valdez
Tonsina
McCarthy
Preserve
St Elias Mountains
Atlin Lake
Atlin
Cordova Peak 7730
Chugach Mountains
Kennedy 15905
Skagway
Atlin Prov. Park
Hyland Post
nal
Mt St Elias 18008
Haines
Telegraph Creek
Spatsizi Wilderness Prov. Park
Tatlatui Prov. Park
Cordova
Hinchinbrook Island
Cape Yakataga
Yakutat Bay
Yakutat
Mt Nesselrode 8102
Mt Edziza Prov. Park
BRITISH Columbia
Montague Island
Kayak Island
Glacier Bay National Park & Preserve
Juneau
Gustavus
Admiralty Island
Cross Sound
Tongass
Admiralty Island National Monument
Mt Ratz 10290
Petersburg
Chichagof Island
National
Kupreanof Island
Wrangell
Hyder
Stewart
Gulf of Alaska
Sitka
Baranof Island
Kuiu Island
Misty Fiords National Monument
Forest
Ketchikan
Metlakatla
Craig
Prince of Wales Island
Alexander Archipelago
Dall Island
Prince Rupert
Dixon Entrance
Queen Charlotte Islands
Graham Island
Banks Island
Moresby Island

Aleutian Islands

0 — 50 miles
0 — 50 km

RING SEA

Alaska Maritime National Wildlife Refuge
Rat Islands
Semisopochnoi
chitka
Tanaga
Adak
Kanaga
Amlia
Andreanof Islands
Atka
Seguam
Amukta
Yunaska
Islands of the Four Mountains
Umnak
Unalaska
Akutan
Unimak
False Pass
Fox Islands

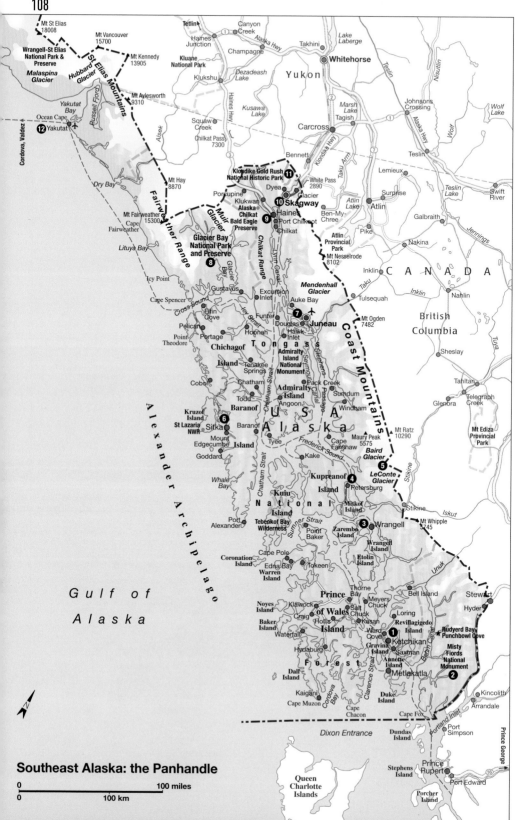

Southeast Alaska: the Panhandle

0	100 miles
0	100 km

TOURING THE SOUTHEAST PANHANDLE

A cruise or ferry tour of the Panhandle is a good introduction to Alaska, giving the visitor a taste of the scenery and the culture.

A pair appreciate a glacier.

Ever since it emerged from the melting of the last great Ice Age 15,000 years ago, the great island-studded, 1,000-mile (1,600km) passage of water that stretches from present-day lower British Columbia to the top of the Southeast Alaska Panhandle has been one of Earth's treasures. The first Europeans to visit a portion of what is now called the Inside Passage did not get a friendly reception from the locals, however. In 1741 Alexei Chirikof, captain of the *St Paul*, set sail from Russia. With his commander, Vitus Bering (who also was captain of the vessel *St Peter*), he left the Kamchatkan Peninsula in Siberia and headed east on a voyage of exploration and discovery.

The two captains were separated in a storm that struck soon after leaving port, and never saw each other again. Bering died after being shipwrecked on his voyage home. Chirikof and his crew sighted the high wooded mountains of what is now called Prince of Wales Island in Southeast Alaska on July 15, 1741. Two days later they dropped anchor near the present-day city of Sitka. It was there that tragedy struck, when two boatloads of sailors put ashore to reconnoiter disappeared without trace.

These days, it is not often that visitors to the Panhandle fail to return to ship. When it does happen, it is probably because they lose track of time while hiking to the top of Deer Mountain in Ketchikan, get carried away in the pursuit of pleasure at the Red Dog Saloon in Juneau, or simply decide the fishing is too good to be hurried.

Fishing boats in Ketchikan harbor.

THE INSIDE PASSAGE

The sights along the Inside Passage are surprisingly varied and seldom boring. There are two capital cities, one Canadian (Victoria) and one American (Juneau), where life and lifestyle revolve largely around politics and bureaucracy. And there are tiny Native villages where the food on most residents' tables still depends on the skills of the hunters and fishermen.

The geography and the geology of the Inside Passage vary greatly as well. At its southernmost end, the passage is protected by Vancouver Island, a large, elongated landmass that begins near the northern border of the continental United States and stretches almost 300 miles (480km) northwest, nearly half the distance up the British Columbia coast to Southeast Alaska. Then comes the seaward protection of the Haida Gwaii (Queen Charlotte Islands), none of them as large as Vancouver Island but a number of them – especially Graham and Moresby islands – quite sizeable nonetheless.

And finally, about where US jurisdiction resumes and Southeast Alaska begins, there's the Alexander Archipelago, a 400-mile (645km) -long maze of 1,000 islands which, along with a 30-mile (48km) -wide sliver of mainland, make up the Southeast Alaska Panhandle.

If the size and national colors of the islands of the Inside Passage vary, there is this commonality all along the way: lush green forests of spruce, hemlock, cedar, fir, and other conifers cover whole islands and mountains except for snow-capped peaks, ice fields feeding glaciers, and gravel beaches. Generous bays and exquisite little coves rival one another for attention, and major rivers course through great glacier-carved valleys, while waterfalls plunge from mountainside cliffs to the sea.

THE ISLANDS' ALLURE

Float plane in Skagway.

Everywhere along the way are watercraft: seine-haul fishing boats with crews of half a dozen or more; small trawlers and gillnet fishing craft with a skipper and, maybe, a single helper; tugs pulling rafts of logs or barges of commercial goods; exotic yachts and simple open boats; cruise ships; state ferries; freighters; even sailboats and kayaks. To be protected is why this concentration of watercraft end up here: thesame islands that provide evergreen beauty to visitors along the way provide buffers from North Pacific winds and weather that could otherwise threaten all but the toughest vessels.

SPOTTING WILDLIFE

The islands also protect and nurture a wide variety of wild creatures. Ashore, and beyond the gaze of spectators, numerous animals make their homes within the forests and even atop the mountains of the Southeast Alaska Panhandle. Charter a light aircraft at Yakutat, near the very top of the Panhandle, and you are likely to see moose and perhaps brown bear as well. Near Juneau or Ketchikan or any of the other cities in the region, there is a good opportunity to spot groups of white mountain goats.

A totem.

Humpback and killer whales, cavorting porpoises in twos and fours, and sea lions, seals and sea otters by the dozen are frequent sights on boat trips, much appreciated by vessel-borne visitors along the Inside Passage.

Eagles are everywhere – the white-headed, white-tailed bald eagle, symbol of the United States. You see them diving and swooping from the heights to grab unwary fish swimming near the water's surface and high in the spruce trees, standing guard over heavy nests lodged in the forks of great branches.

The fishing here is world-class. Perhaps your goal is to haul in a lunker king salmon of 50lbs (23kg) or more. Or maybe you want to test your skill against diving, dancing, and frothing steelhead trout. Whatever your heart's desire, the fishing in this region is simply unbeatable anywhere else.

With this concentration of fish, wildlife, and scenic beauty, it's easy to see why increasing numbers of people choose to settle in this region.

Snow in the Chilcat Valley.

A tribal totem pole in Ketchikan.

KETCHIKAN

Creek Street's brothels have turned into restaurants and boutiques, but the area's frontier past is commemorated in shows and exhibitions highlighting totems, eagles, and lumberjack skills.

The city of **Ketchikan ❶** tumbles down the densely forested, mountainous, southwestern side of Revillagigedo Island until it reaches its distinctive angle of repose: stacks of steep-roofed houses cling to the wooded slope, while the business district, apparently unable to halt the momentum, surges forward onto pilings in the Tongass Narrows. Located near the southernmost boundary of Alaska, Ketchikan is a major port of entry for Southeast Alaska and is generally the first stop for Alaska-bound cruise ships and Alaska Marine Highway System ferries.

SALMON CAPITAL

The 'First City', or the 'Salmon Capitol of the World' as it is referred to by locals, has adapted through several economic 'boom-and-bust' cycles. Many of the 8,300 (in 2017) residents (14,000, counting the surrounding areas) work in commercial fishing, fish processing, tourism, or logging.

The earliest inhabitants of the area were Tongass and Cape Fox Tlingit Native Americans who established a fish camp by Ketchikan Creek and called it 'kitschk-hin,' or 'thundering wings of an eagle.' The region's mild, maritime climate and rich natural resources, primarily timber and fish, eventually drew non-native adventurers. As more settlers moved into the

area, the majority of the Tlingit population relocated to nearby Saxman.

In 1885, a founder of Ketchikan, Mike Martin, bought 160 acres of land from Tlingit Chief Kyan – a parcel that later became the town site. The first cannery was soon built along the creek and, by 1936, a total of seven canneries were operating in the area.

Following the discovery of gold and copper in the region, the City of Ketchikan (incorporated in 1900) became an important mining supply center. As the city grew, so did the demand for lumber.

Main attractions

Creek Street
Admiralty Island National
  Monument
Dolly's House
Southeast Alaska
  Discovery Center
Tongass Historical
  Museum
Potlatch Park
Saxman
Totem Heritage Center

**Maps on pages
108, 115**

Ketchikan.

Welcome sign.

Ketchikan Spruce Mills opened its doors in 1903, and the city became the hub for logging activities and supplies. In 1954, the Ward Cove pulp mill was constructed nearby, and the operation provided many years of economic growth and stability for Ketchikan residents. The US Forest Service eventually canceled its 50-year contract with the company, however, and the pulp mill closed in 1997.

There were other reasons for fishermen, miners and loggers to flock to Ketchikan in the early 1900s. The town's infamous **Creek Street** Ⓐ enjoyed a booming alcohol trade at the time of the territory's Bone Dry Law of 1917, the subsequent National Prohibition Act of 1920 and for many years after. Rowdy crowds gathered for the music, dancing, and 'social opportunities' of the notorious Star dancehall and the several houses of prostitution nearby. In 1953, this era ended as city officials permanently closed the doors of the brothels.

FROM BROTHEL TO MUSEUM

Today the wooden walkway of a chastened Creek Street leads tourists through a colorful array of gift shops, galleries, restaurants, coffee shops (featuring a delicious, locally roasted brew) and **Dolly's House** (24 Creek Street; tel: 907-225-6329;; daily 8am–5pm May–Oct) a popular brothel-turned-museum. While in the Creek Street area, take a ride on the **funicular tram**, which travels up the steep mountainside to the lobby of the beautiful Cape Fox Lodge Hotel (www.capefoxlodge.com). The brief ride will afford a good view of the city and a chance to enjoy fine dining at the hotel restaurant.

Stop at the **Ketchikan Visitors Bureau** Ⓑ (131 Front Street; tel: 800-770-3300 or 907-225-6166; www. visit-ketchikan.com; Mon–Fri 8am–5pm, Sat–Sun 6am–6pm), located on the cruise-ship dock at Berth 2 (open year-round), or at its satellite station situated two blocks down at Berth 3 (seasonal). At either location, the staff will help you plan your visit and hand you a walking tour map as well as a free *Ketchikan Tour Planner* pamphlet.

The Bureau's **tour center**, located in the same building as the main office, provides public restrooms, pay phones, an ATM (cash machine), and a phone card dispenser. You may also purchase tickets at the center for local attractions (like the popular **Great Alaskan Lumberjack Show**; www.alaskanlumberjackshow.com) or to tour Ketchikan and surrounding areas via horse-drawn trolley, motorcycle, all-terrain vehicle, tour boat, kayak, or amphibious craft, aerial zipline, or floatplane (to name a few). The tour center can also help you arrange for a fishing charter from one of many local operators. Public transportation and taxi stands are close by for those who prefer to strike out on their own.

Be sure to visit the **Southeast Alaska Discovery Center** Ⓒ (50 Main Street; tel: 907-228-6220; www.alaskacenters.gov/visitors-centers/ketchikan; May–Sept daily 8am–4pm, Oct–Apr Fri 10am–7pm; free Oct–Apr.). This excellent interpretive facility, operated by the US Forest Service, will give you an overview of the Tongass National Forest, its history, wildlife, and various recreational opportunities including hiking, boating, kayaking, fishing, camping, and remote cabin rentals. The center also features authentic totems, Native artists in residence, cultural exhibits, and a gift shop.

The small, but interesting **Tongass Historical Museum** Ⓓ is also nearby (629 Dock Street; tel: 907-225-5600; www.ktn-ak.us/tongass-historical-museum; May–Sept daily 8am–5pm, Oct–Apr Tues–Sat 1–5pm; $6, free Oct–Apr). Its photographic collection is particularly strong.

A pretty window box in Ketchikan.

POTLATCH PARK

Among the indigenous peoples of North America's northwest coastal communities, a potlatch is a ceremony that includes not only a sumptuous feast of traditional Native dishes, but also the giving of gifts (often lavish) by the potlatch host. **Potlatch Park** Ⓔ (9809 Totem Bight Road; tel: 907-225-4445; daily 7.30am–approximately 6pm) is dedicated to the major tribal ancestors of the Native villages of the

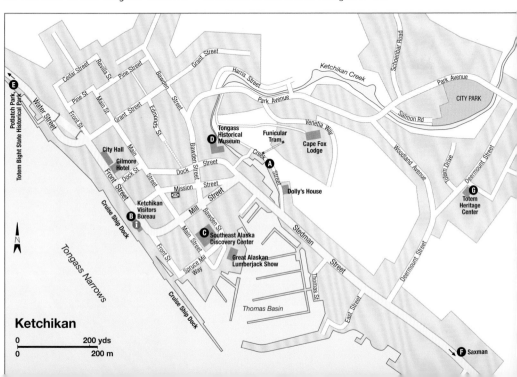

Ketchikan

0   200 yds
0   200 m

Traditional totems – a pole's height was often an indication of wealth and power.

The funicular tram to Cape Fox Lodge Hotel.

Ketchikan area. The 5-acre (2-hectare) park, located 10 miles (16km) north of Downtown, is situated in a wooded area facing the Tongass Narrows – the site of ancient Tlingit fishing grounds. It features 12 full-sized totems (the tallest measuring 42ft/12.8 meters in height), five intricately carved tribal houses, a busy carving center, an antique car museum, an antique Alaskan firearm museum, interesting Native art displays, an expansive gift shop, and free coffee.

The main tribal house is an exact re-creation of a 19th-century dwelling, which would have housed up to 50 people, and is held together by gravity, as opposed to nails and bolts.

Inside the nearby carving center, master carvers are busy chiseling family stories into elaborate totems made from 36ft (11-meter) cedar logs. Potlatch Park, owned by Kanoe Zantua, of the Eagle Frog Clan of the Haida Nation of Ketchikan is well worth visiting by those interested in native culture, as it '... stands in tribute to the souls of Alaska coastal communities.'

SAXMAN

Just 2 miles (3km) south of Ketchikan is the Native village of **Saxman** Ⓕ (actually an incorporated city, with a population of about 410 – primarily Tlingit – residents). The Cape Fox Corporation (www.capefoxtours.com; tel: 907-225-4421) offers the interesting **Saxman Native Village Tour**, which features a tribal house with a presentation of the Cape Fox Dance group and a carving center where you can watch native artisans at work.

More totems are on show at the **Totem Heritage Center** Ⓖ (601 Deermount Street; tel: 907-225-5900; www. ktn-ak.us/totem-heritage-center; May–Sept daily 8am–5pm, Oct–Apr Tues–Sat 1–5pm), at the **Totem Bight State Historical Park** (10 miles/16km north of town on North Tongass Highway; http://dnr.alaska.gov/parks/aspunits/south east/totembigshp.htm; free, donation requested). Ketchikan is also the jumping-off point for **Misty Fiords National Monument Wilderness**. The monument, 40 miles (64km) south of Ketchikan, is accessible by boat or floatplane.

⊘ REMOTE ADVENTURING

In addition to the major communities along the Inside Passage, there are countless other settlements worth a day's or a week's visit. **Angoon** is the only settlement in **Admiralty Island National Monument**, a wilderness preserve that can be reached by air or sea from Sitka or Juneau, and which is famous for its salmon and large number of brown bears (see page 77). **Kake**, which has what is rumored to be the tallest totem pole in the world at 132ft (40m), is the jumping-off point for trips to **Tebenkof Bay Wilderness** where experienced kayakers can spend days paddling the waters around the bays and coves of many tiny islands. **Hoonah**, the largest Tlingit village in Southeast Alaska, has some good hiking trails, as well as an old cannery on Icy Strait that has been converted to a tourist attraction.

Tenakee Springs is known for its thermal baths. The lodge (www.tenakeespringsak.com) offers home-cooked meals and arrangements for fishing and whale watching. If you are eager for a soak, hot springs are scattered throughout the Southeast. Baranof Island has a number of them, including the **Goddard Hot Springs** and the **Baranof Warm Springs**. The least visited are the **Trocadero Soda Springs** on Prince of Wales Island, whose carbonated waters allow for a unique experience.

GETTING AROUND BY FERRY

Founded in 1949, the Alaska Marine Highway System (AMHS) is the main means of travel around this region, but you need to plan ahead in the summer months.

For independent travelers with the luxury of time, cruising the Inside Passage aboard one of the 13 state-run Alaska Marine Highway System (AMHS) ferries is a relaxing, comfortable and reasonably convenient option for seeing the coastal communities of Southeast, Southcentral, and Southwest Alaska. Since driving between these communities is not an option, locals rely on ferry travel as a primary mode of transportation. The fleet covers an astounding 3,500 miles and stops at 35 ports covering its routes, which extend from Bellingham, Washington to the Aleutian Islands.

CONNECTING REMOTE COMMUNITIES

If you're traveling in spring or fall, you'll likely see school athletes, debate teams or spelling bee contestants bound for competitions in neighboring (or far-flung) coastal communities. Residents of more remote towns travel for doctor visits, shopping, business, and countless other reasons. In fact, 70 percent of the Marine Highway's passengers are Alaskan.

But that doesn't mean that the ferries ignore their role as tour guide for their out-of-state guests. US Forest Service interpreters are onboard the ferries during the summer months to give informative lectures and to point out the interesting sights along the way. Additionally, visitors generally have no problem getting Alaskans onboard to talk about their state.

The AMHS ferries offer clean, comfortable staterooms (for most ships, advance reservations are important), tasty, reasonably priced cafeteria-style food service, a bar, clean restrooms, hot showers (towel rental available), and various lounges (some with recliners) featuring large windows for easy viewing of the passing landscape. Should the captain see a whale (or other notable wildlife) en route, he'll usually make a public announcement and try to maneuver the ship to allow for a good view.

FAMILY-FRIENDLY

Traveling aboard the Alaska ferries is also a great option for families with children. There's plenty of wiggle room, and most ferries have a play area for toddlers, a video game room, a movie room and, if you pay extra for a stateroom, a good place to nap. Those without staterooms spread out sleeping bags onto the carpeted floors at night, stretch out in one of the many recliners, or pitch a tent up on the top deck near the solarium. Each of the 11 ferries (all named for Alaskan glaciers) has different sleeping and camping options.

The downside of ferry travel is that if you bring a vehicle aboard the cost jumps considerably. You must make reservations early because the car decks fill up quickly for the summer months. The price for traveling non-stop from one end of Southeast to the other is not hugely different from that of breaking up your trip with stopovers at various communities along the way. But it may be a day or two before another ferry traveling in the desired direction comes along. Information, routes, ship descriptions, fares, scheduling information and reservations are all available online at www.dot.state.ak.us/amhs, or tel: 800-642-0066/907-465-3941.

A ferry crossing Kachemak Bay.

MISTY FIORDS NATIONAL MONUMENT

The southernmost of Alaska's national monuments is a magical place, carved out by the steady progress of gigantic glaciers, colored by pristine forests and towering waterfalls, and animated by abundant wildlife.

Map on page 108

Misty Fjords was designated by the US Congress as a national wilderness as well as a national monument, and within the 3,570 sq miles (9,240 sq km) of its largely untouched coast and backcountry lie three major rivers, hundreds of small streams and creeks, icefields, glaciers, old-growth rainforest, snowcapped mountains, and mountain-top lakes.

GLACIAL SCENERY

Eons ago, great glaciers thousands of feet deep filled what are now Southeast Alaska bays and valleys. Slowly but relentlessly they ground their way seaward from mountaintop heights. In the process they carved and scoured great steep-walled cliffs that now plunge from mountain summits to considerable depths below sea level. The effect of this carving and scouring has never been more beautifully evident than it is in **Misty Fiords National Monument ❷**.

It is the southernmost of Alaska's four national monuments and one of two in the Tongass National Forest (the other is Admiralty Island). Visitors to this 2.2-million-acre (890,000-hectare) wilderness experience every major ecosystem of Southeast Alaska, from the ocean swells on the outer coast to the high alpine lakes and icefields. There are tiny coves, great bays, and forest groves so thick you can barely see daylight through them.

Misty Fiords wildlife includes brown and black bears, Sitka blacktail deer, wolves, mountain goats, beavers, mink, marten, foxes, and river otters. But it is not only a place of scenery and wildlife on a grand scale, it also has tremendous commercial value. Some of Alaska's most productive fish-rearing streams are located here.

There are very few marks of human activity inside Misty Fiords. The area's

A bird's-eye view of Misty Fiords.

first human inhabitants, the Native Tlingits and Haidas, are believed to have settled here many thousands of years ago, after crossing the land bridge from Siberia, but there is very little evidence of their passing.

TOURING MISTY FIORDS

No roads lead to Misty Fiords, and visitors can reach the monument only by water or by air. Some travelers opt for a combination cruise/fly tour – going in by water and out by air, or vice versa. Some cruise ships visit the monument as part of an Inside Passage experience (see page 92). You can fly there with one of several Ketchikan air charter companies; you can cruise there by charter boat; or you can sign up on a flight tour (with water landing) offered by Taquan Air (tel: 907-225-8800), a local air service.

These excursions, aboard one of the company's smooth riding catamarans, typically last 4.5 hours, and can be done either round trip or one way, with one part of the journey – either coming or going – completed by air. Round-trip cruises last about 6.5 hours, while combination cruise-flightseeing trips are 4.5 hours long. On a typical cruise/fly tour, the boat will depart from near downtown Ketchikan in early to mid-morning, but coffee is always ready on the galley stove and donuts are on the serving table for passengers who arrive on the ship early. These boats are wide, beamy, comfortable cruisers with plenty of walking-around room, big view windows, and table seating for 32. When the weather is good, you can arrange yourself on the open-air deck above the cabin. At one point or another during the cruise, most passengers will crowd into the vessel's little wheelhouse and talk to the skipper. On Allen Marine Tours (https://allenmarinetours.com), you are likely to learn about culture and history presented by a native story-teller and artist.

SALMON ROUTE

The sightseeing begins as soon as the boat's lines are cast off and the

No permit is needed for camping in Misty Fiords, but visitors are advised to discuss plans with rangers before arriving. For details, contact the US Forest Service, tel: 907-225-2148.

Fishing boat, Ketchikan.

⊘ DRESSING FOR THE SOUTHEAST

The temperate rainforest of Southeast Alaska features a mild, wet, maritime climate. Average winter temperatures range from 29° to 39°F (–2° to 4°C) in Ketchikan (southernmost city) to 18° to 31° (–8° to –1°C) in Yakutat (northernmost community). Summers average 51° to 65°F (11° to 18°C) and 47° to 60°F (8° to 16°C) respectively. The entire Panhandle experiences heavy precipitation (13.5ft/4.1 meters per year average in Ketchikan; 11ft/3.3 meters in Yakutat), which creates the ideal environment for the unique flora and fauna of the area.

These conditions also create the need for summertime visitors to bring along excellent protection from wind and rain. Plan to dress in layers (to allow for warmth and comfort in a variable climate), and make sure the outermost layer is waterproof. A quality-constructed, hooded rain jacket (with a drawstring to pull the hood close to your face), a lightweight, knitted hat, gloves, waterproof pants, and comfortable, waterproof footwear are ideal. Umbrellas, on the other hand, are difficult to manage, block your view and tend to turn inside out easily in a sudden gust of wind... which provides no end of amusement for the locals.

Wintertime travelers should add winter-weight hooded coats, warm knit hats, mittens, and insulated boots to their clothing list.

vessel begins its southeasterly path toward the lower end of Revilla-gigedo Island (the locals abbreviate it to Revilla Island), on which Ketchikan is located. Passing dockside fish processors, supply houses and the town's main business district, the vessel soon cruises past the entrance to **Ketchikan Creek**.

Late in the summer, thousands of salmon assemble at this spot before ascending the creek – and formidable waterfalls – to spawn in the upstream shallows and then die. Shortly after Creek Street, the boat goes past **Saxman** (see page 116), a traditional village containing one of the largest collections of totems in the state.

Next is **Bold Island**, where passengers line the port (left-hand) rails and windows of the vessel in the hope of seeing bald eagles perched in the island spruce trees. For Southeast Alaskans, such sightings are commonplace, though they never become dull. For visitors, the sight of America's national bird is a highlight of the trip.

A waterfall, Misty Fiords National Monument.

At one point or another during the morning's cruise, most passengers will crowd into the vessel's little wheelhouse and talk to the skipper.

PORPOISE COMPANIONS

As the boat cruises toward the fjords, the on-board guide and naturalist may announce that there are porpoises both fore and aft of the vessel, and the passengers – half going in each direction in order to keep an even kilter – scramble for a view of the small marine mammals. The porpoises swimming behind the catamaran are too far away for a close look – they are visible only as leaping, playing creatures 300ft (0.9 meters) or more astern. But the ones in front are only a few feet away, clearly visible, and just as clearly having a wonderful time pacing the boat. It's obvious they could easily outdistance the vessel, but they prefer to stay and play.

By noon the vessel is inside the monument boundaries and the skipper guides it through a narrow channel into an exquisite tree-shrouded cove on **Rudyerd Island**. Here you can see the steep granite rock formations on the shore and the occasional jet black vertical streaks, a few inches to a couple of feet or more wide, that appear among the brown granite walls. These were formed 60 million years ago when earthquakes cracked the granite, and hot molten magma came up from below the earth's surface to fill the cracks. The black streaks that you see are the magma.

NEW EDDYSTONE ROCK

A little later, **New Eddystone Rock** comes into view. Depending upon the time of day when you see it and the angle from which you approach it, the rock can resemble several things: sometimes it looks like a man-made building, at others, a ship under sail, or it can look exactly what it is – a high-rising volcano 'plug' from millennia past. It was called Eddystone Rock by the British navigator Captain George Vancouver (1758–98) – after whom the Canadian city is named – because he thought it looked very much like Eddystone Lighthouse off the shore of his native Plymouth, England.

RUDYERD BAY AND PUNCHBOWL COVE

Overnight campers and kayakers who want to go into the fjords often travel with the day visitors on Alaska cruise trips, and now leave the ship to paddle the waters off Winstanley Island. There's a US Forest Service cabin there, one of relatively few located on saltwater sites in Southeast Alaska.

The comfortable, weather-tight shelter is popular with campers who paddle around **Rudyerd Bay** during the day. On entering the bay, the cruiser often meets a welcoming committee of at least 20 seals, which

lie basking on the rocks of an island to port. Minutes later, within the bay, the boat approaches the towering vertical walls of **Punchbowl Cove**. And it is here that you really begin to feel the magical, mystical effect of the place.

It can be truly eerie hereabouts, especially when – as the monument's name suggests – there is mist or cloud or fog in the air. Steep, stark granite walls descend from heights hidden in clouds. Waterfalls, which range from torrents to trickles, plunge from unseen sources just as high. Trees cling tenaciously to many of the cliff-sides, on surfaces that don't seem to have enough soil to support a house plant.

The waters around and beneath the boat are a cold, slate gray, and they descend to depths of 750ft (230 meters) or more. There have, as yet, been no sightings of sea monsters reported in these waters – but it's exactly the right kind of place for them.

On board, thoughts turn to more practical matters: it is time for a

A floatplane lands in Rudyerd Bay.

A kayaker explores Misty Fiords.

lunch of seafood chowder, rolls, and tossed green salad. After lunch, the vessel leaves Punchbowl Cove and cruises toward the head of Rudyerd Bay.

Along the shoreline that now replaces the steep cliffs, you may look out for bears, wolves, and other wild creatures.

CREEKS AND WATERFALLS

The boat stops again an hour later, this time at **Nooya Creek** where, in season, 1,000 or more pink salmon descend to salt water each year from Nooya Lake in the high country. Here a trail leads to the uplands – although it is not as steep as the one that takes off, and up, from the Punchbowl Cove area. Camping and trout-fishing opportunities at the ends of the trails are outstanding.

Then, if you are lucky, it might be time for yet another memorable experience. On some trips the skipper will edge his boat right up to the bottom of a large plummeting waterfall, and passengers are given

paper cups that they can fill with the icy water. By mid-afternoon, it is time for those who fly back to Ketchikan to disembark and board the floatplane which taxis gently up to the boarding platform.

FROM THE AIR

Fifteen minutes later, goodbyes are yelled to those remaining and the pilot drifts his plane away from the vessel. He then gives the aircraft full throttle, and within a minute it is fully airborne. Within three or four minutes more the airborne passengers may well be spotting white, furry mountain goats, usually nannies and their youngsters, negotiating seemingly impossible cliff faces to the right of the plane. The flight back through the fjords makes for dramatic viewing, and the wildlife is only part of the excitement as the dark granite walls seem to be just inches away from the plane's wing tips – a little bit too close for comfort, some may think, but passengers are in very safe hands.

NATIONAL FORESTS

Alaska is home to the nation's two largest national forests, the Tongass and the Chugach. Spanning the Southeast and Southcentral regions, they are home to a wide diversity of ecosystems.

At nearly 17 million acres (6.9 million hectares), the **Tongass National Forest** (tel: 907-225-3101; www.fs.fed.us/r10/tongass) is by far America's biggest. Stretching the entire length of Alaska's Inside Passage, it encompasses three-fourths of the Panhandle. The Tongass was created in 1907 by President Roosevelt to protect the region's timber resources, wildlife, and fisheries; its name is taken from the Tlingit Native tribe's Tongass clan.

Within the Tongass boundaries are huge expanses of old-growth coastal rainforest – about 32 percent of the total acreage. Over the years, a little more than 6 percent of this old-growth forest area has been harvested, mostly by clear-cut methods. The remaining expanse, comprising approximately 97 percent of the total old-growth area, remains today as it was 100 years ago, providing critical habitat for all sorts of animals, from brown and black bears to Sitka blacktail deer, moose, mink, river otters, beavers, and five species of Pacific salmon. Birds range from eagles and owls to loons and songbirds.

One of the forest's prime wildlife areas is Admiralty Island, near Juneau, with one of the world's densest populations of brown bears; some 1,500 to 1,700 inhabit Admiralty, or about one per square mile. It is also has one of the world's largest concentrations of nesting bald eagles; biologists have identified more than 800 nests along Admiralty's 700 miles (1,100km) of coastline. To protect its wildlife habitat, more than 90 percent of the island is protected as wilderness within Admiralty Island National Monument.

Besides its famed coastal forest, the Tongass includes a wide range of habitat, from coastal waters to high alpine tundra and huge icefields that feed hundreds of glaciers. Forest lands and waters are used for all sorts of recreation, from fishing to wildlife viewing.

THE CHUGACH

Alaska's second vast forest, the **Chugach National Forest**, includes nearly 6 million acres (2.4 million hectares) within its borders. Centered around Southcentral Alaska's coastal area, it spans three geographic regions: the northeastern Kenai Peninsula, Prince William Sound, and the Copper River Delta. Within its borders are Kayak Island, where Europeans first stepped foot on Alaskan soil; Columbia Glacier, one of the world's largest tidewater glaciers; and the Copper River Delta's rich wetlands, which serve as a critical staging and breeding area for North American waterfowl and shorebirds during their yearly migrations.

The Chugach encompasses many types of habitat, from lush forests and rugged coastline to high mountains, jagged ridges, ice fields and glaciers. It is a playground for all types of outdoor enthusiasts. One of the Chugach's most popular destinations is the Begich Boggs Visitor Center (open late May to early Sept; tel: May–Sept 907-754-2326, Oct–Apr 907-754-3242) near Portage Glacier, less than an hour's drive south of Anchorage. Additional information on Chugach National Forest is available from the US Forest Service in Anchorage (tel: 907-743-9500; www.fs.fed.us/r10/chugach).

A bald eagle, national bird of the United States.

WRANGELL

This was the only town in Alaska to fly the Russian, British, and American flags. Today it is known for sportsfishing and petroglyph spotting.

⊙ Main attractions
Garnet Ledge
Chief Shakes island
Petroglyph Beach
Muskeg Meadows
Stikine River
Anan Bear and Wildlife
  Observatory

Maps on pages 108, 125

When you visit the heavily forested island community of **Wrangell ❸**, located 89 miles (143km) north of Ketchikan on Wrangell Island, what you see is pretty much what you get. There won't be any semi-submersible or zipline tours like in Ketchikan; no streets lined with restored (or, as in Skagway, recreated), gold rush-styled false-front saloons or dance halls to amaze and amuse.

What you can look forward to is an authentic, working town of about 2,500 people, many of whom, for generations, have fed their families by logging in the Tongass, working in local saw-mills or commercial fishing. National forest management policies, respond-ing to environmental concerns, have curtailed much of the Tongass logging, and Wrangell's lumberjacks have done what their grandfathers and great-grandfathers before them did: adapt. Their city is changing to a broader-based economy that includes seafood processing, value-added timber prod-ucts and tourism.

Wrangell is one of the oldest settle-ments in Alaska. It has the distinction of having been ruled by four nations: Tlingit, Russia, England, and the US.

TLINGIT HERITAGE

Ancient Tlingit stories tell of a migra-tion to the area through 'the hole in the ice,' a possible reference to a river (flowing beneath the glacier ice) that led from interior Canada through the Stikine River corridor to the lush, coastal forests. The milder climate, protected coastal waterway and rich resources of the Stikine River delta must have seemed like paradise to the Tlingits, and they fiercely defended their newfound home against the Haida and Tsimshian who arrived later. These same Tlingit warriors were also skilled traders, and their area of commerce extended into interior Canada, up the Copper River and beyond.

Wrangell's shoreline.

Russian fur trade with the Stikine Tlingit began as early as 1811. Wrangell Island was named in honor of the manager of the Russian American Company, Ferdinand von Wrangel, around 1830. In 1834, the Russians built a stockade, Redoubt St Dionysius, in the same general location as today's community of Wrangell. Recognizing the benefit of Russian protection and trade, Chief Shakes decided to relocate the nearby Tlingit village to a small island in the harbor near the stockade. In 1840, the British Hudson's Bay Company leased the stockade from the Russians, and the name was changed to Fort Stikine.

The Tlingit, while protesting the Hudson's Bay Company's use of their traditional trade routes, were already facing a new, more deadly battle. Two outbreaks of smallpox, in 1836 and 1840, resulted in the deaths of half of their population. By 1849, the hypercompetitive fur trade had dwindled, and both Russian and British interest in the area began to wane.

In 1861, an employee of the Hudson's Bay Company, Buck Choquette, found gold on the Stikine River and started the first of three gold rushes that shaped much of Wrangell's (and the rest of Southeast's) history.

One year after the US purchase of the Alaska Territory in 1867, the Fort Wrangell military post was built, and a second gold rush arrived in 1872, when two prospectors, Thibert and McCullough, found gold at Dease Lake (in Canada's Cassiar country). When the Klondike gold was discovered in 1897, Wrangell's population surged again as thousands of prospectors – and the attendant dance halls, gambling establishments, and suppliers – flooded the small town. Miners gathered provisions and then journeyed up the Stikine River into the gold fields.

The noted naturalist John Muir frequented the area in the 1880s. It is also rumored that the infamous Soapy Smith (see page 155) would occasionally hide out in Wrangell when the situation in Skagway became too dicey.

CANNERY CITY

Wrangell incorporated as a city in 1903. Not long afterward, the flourishing

⊙ Fact

The legendary Wyatt Earp served as Wrangell's marshal for 10 days in 1897 as he and his wife were en route to the Klondike. During these gold rush days, false-front shops lined both sides of Front Street, which was then built on pilings over the water. Two tragic fires, in 1906 and in 1952, destroyed most of these historic buildings.

Chief Shakes Tribal House.

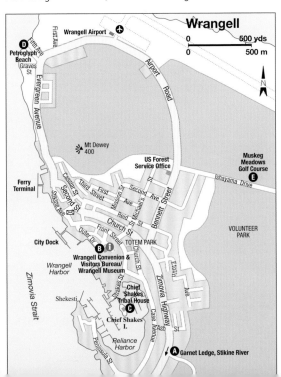

fishing industry built several canneries within Southeast Alaska. By the late 1920s, four canneries (for salmon, shrimp and crab) were operating in Wrangell. Chinese workers, who were willing to work long hours for low wages, were brought to Southeast Alaska to man the factories. **Deadman's Island**, next to the Wrangell airport, is said to be where the Chinese preserved their dead in salt-brine barrels until they could be sent home for burial.

Due to the narrow channels surrounding the island, Wrangell is off the beaten path of large cruise ships, but the community welcomes smaller cruise ships, and the business of many sportfishers, birders, and water enthusiasts headed for the Stikine River. Perhaps because the city has not experienced waves of passengers from multiple large cruise ships docking just offshore on the same day, Wrangell is less altered by tourism than many other Southeast towns.

There are many sights unique to this delightful, laid-back town, so grab your quality rain gear and explore. On

Ancient rock carvings on a beach in Wrangell.

your way past the **city dock** area, you will likely see young merchants selling garnets dug from Wrangell's **Garnet Ledge** Ⓐ A good place to gather Wrangell information is the **Wrangell Convention & Visitors Bureau** Ⓑ (293 Campbell Drive; tel: 800-367-9745; www.wrangellalaska.org). The center houses both the city's **visitor center** and the **Wrangell Museum** (tel: 907-874-3770; May–Sept Mon–Sat 10am–5pm, Oct–Apr Fri–Sat 1–5pm). The museum has exhibits on gold, timber, fishing, and trapping.

The visitor center's staff will connect you with the tour operators who will take you around by foot, helicopter, kayak, boat, bus, or plane.

TOTEMS AND PETROGLYPHS

Take a stroll out to **Chief Shakes Island**, accessible year-round by a walkway into Wrangell harbor. The island has intricately carved Tlingit totems and **Chief Shakes Tribal House** Ⓒ (tel: 907-874-4304; open by appointment), listed as a historic monument.

Also worth a visit is **Petroglyph Beach** Ⓓ (1 mile/1.6km from the ferry

terminal), a State Historic Park which has the Southeast's largest concentration of ancient rock carvings. The origin of the petroglyphs remains a mystery. Visitors are encouraged to search the beach, where more than 40 known carvings are located. Visitors are free to take photographs, but rubbings should be made of the replicas only, which are located on the observation deck overlooking the beach.

Wrangell also owns the distinction of having a USGA-rated, nine-hole golf course, **Muskeg Meadows** **E** (tel: 907-874-4653; www.wrangellalaskagolf.com).

BIRD-SPOTTING

The nearby **Stikine River** delta is a fabulous area for birders, hosting over 120 species of migrating birds in spring and fall. In April, as many as 1,600 eagles swoop down to feast on the local hooligan run, and thousands of snow geese stop over on their northerly trek. Other wildlife includes sea lions, otters, bears, and moose.

For the more adventurous, a jet boat tour on the Stikine is a breathtaking

opportunity for a rare glimpse of wild Alaska, or you could choose to soar over the area in a floatplane for a bird's-eye view. For a quieter and perhaps less adrenaline-soaked experience, canoes, kayaks, and rafts are locally available.

BEAR-VIEWING

A trip by boat or floatplane to the **Anan Bear and Wildlife Observatory** (located 30 miles/48km southeast of Wrangell, near the mouth of the Bradfield Canal) provides an opportunity to see brown and black bears (plus bald eagles and sea lions) feasting on one of the largest pink salmon runs in the Southeast. Bears are viewed from a covered platform overlooking a waterfall at The US Forest Service-managed observatory (Wrangell Ranger District, 525 Bennett Street; tel: 907-874-2323; July–Aug 8am–6pm). In peak season, permits are essential and the number of visitors is restricted to 60 per day. You can make a reservation at www.recreation.gov or by calling 1-877-444-6777. Outside peak season, a permit is not required.

A sow and her cubs at Anan Bear and Wildlife Observatory.

Looking over rooftops lit by morning sun on Wrangell island.

⊘ GARNET LEDGE

Garnet Ledge (www.wrangellgarnetledge.com) was well known to prospectors during the 1860 gold rush, Located a few miles from Wrangell at the mouth of the Stikine River, it was also the setting of a unique, all-woman mining company in the early 1900s. Ownership eventually transferred to Mr Fred G. Hanford, the former mayor of Wrangell. The site was given to the Southeastern Alaska Area Council of Boy Scouts of America (in 1962) for scouting purposes and to allow the children of Wrangell to continue collecting and selling the stones. Today, many Wrangell families make the 9-mile (14km) boat trip to the ledge each spring, allowing their entrepreneurial children to continue the tradition of chiseling, shoveling, and prying garnets from the rock ledge, and then returning home to sell them to summer visitors.

Crab traps on a pier in Petersburg.

PETERSBURG

The large cruise ships can't navigate the Wrangell Narrows past here, which has helped Petersburg retain its small-town charm and the atmosphere of a bustling fishing village.

Alaska has always been home to a diverse population, and the communities within the state reflect that diversity. The picturesque fishing hamlet of **Petersburg ❶**, on the northwest end of Mitkof Island, serves to illustrate that point. 'Little Norway,' as it is often called, is home to nearly 3,200 residents. They offer warm, Scandinavian-style Alaskan hospitality to visitors of their charming city, which, like Wrangell, is not a port of call for large cruise-ship traffic. Transportation to the city is provided by daily Alaska Airlines flights, air taxis, and the Alaska Marine Highway System ferries.

FREDERICK SOUND

Petersburg claims to be 'blessed by geography,' and so it is. This spic-and-span island community nestled in the heart of the Tongass, perches at the intersecting waterways of Wrangell Narrows and **Frederick Sound** – the latter being one of the best places in the world to observe the feeding behavior of humpback whales.

The area waters are also home to Steller sea lions, harbor seals, Dall's porpoise, and orcas (killer whales).

Other wildlife common to Petersburg includes wolves, black bears, deer, moose, eagles, Canada geese, trumpeter swans, and marbled murrelets. Just across the Frederick Sound

are the towering peaks and glaciers of the Coast Mountains.

The mighty **LeConte Glacier ❺**, the southernmost active tidewater glacier in the northern hemisphere, is a mere 20-minute boat ride away from Petersburg and is a good spot for seal watching.

As is the case throughout most of the Southeast Alaska communities, the Tlingits were the first ones on the scene, using the north end of Mitkof Island as a summer fish camp. In the late 1890s, Peter Buschmann, a Norwegian

⊘ Main attractions

Frederick Sound
LeConte Glacier
Hammer Slough
Sons of Norway Hall
Clausen Memorial
  Museum
Eagle Roost Park
Sandy Beach Recreation
  Area
Outlook Park

**Maps on pages
108, 130**

Girls in traditional costume at Sons of Norway Hall.

immigrant, established a cannery, a saw-mill, and by 1900, a dock on the island. The Buschmann family's homesteads eventually grew into a community known for its strong Scandinavian influence. Today's Petersburg successfully maintains both its Tlingit and its Scandinavian flavors. Primarily a fishing town, the city also serves as a supply center for area logging camps.

EXPERT INFORMATION

The **Visitor Information Center ⒶⒾ** (19 Fram St; tel: 907-772-4636; www.petersburg.org; Apr–mid-May and end Sept Mon–Fri 9am–5pm, mid-May–mid-Sept Mon–Sat 9am–5pm, Sun 10am–2pm, Oct–Mar Mon, Wed & Fri 10am–2pm) provides information on lodging and myriad guided boat, floatplane, helicopter, kayak, glacier-viewing, whale-watching, and fishing tours lasting from a few hours to a week or more. For those preferring unguided tours, boat, kayak, and equipment rentals are locally available, as are remote drop-off and pick-up flights. The center also has natural history information and trail guides.

Totem poles.

The **Petersburg Ranger District Office Ⓑ** (12 North Nordic Drive; tel: 907-772-3841; www.fs.usda.gov/tongass) offers maps, as well as information on current conditions, area trails, and remote US Forest Service cabin rentals (advance reservations essential in summer).

DOWNTOWN AND HARBOR

The city of Petersburg centers on its harbor area, and nearly all the city's attractions are within easy walking distance. Take a stroll around the town and be sure to bring a camera. Petersburg is known for its natural beauty and unique public art displays, including interesting concrete stamps along the sidewalks and the colorful Rosemaling (Norwegian folk art painting) on the homes and storefronts. You'll enjoy a variety of murals, totems, and sculptures by local artisans displayed throughout the area.

The boardwalk streets of **Hammer Slough Ⓒ**, the tidal area of a creek emptying into the waterfront, lead to an opportunity to photograph old, beautifully weathered boathouses reflecting in the slough's still water. The nearby **Sons**

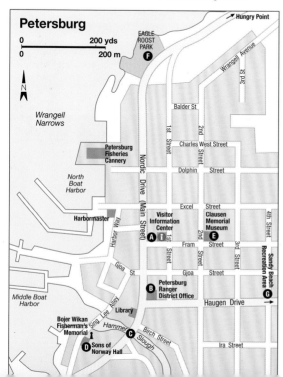

of **Norway Hall**  (www.petersburgsons.
org), dating to 1912 and recognizable by
the Viking ship in front, offers summer
visitors a buffet that includes Norwegian
pastries, fish cakes, and pickled herring
(times coincide with cruise-ship arrivals).

You may also be treated to local
storytelling and a performance of the
Leikerring Dance Group (Petersburg
children dressed in colorful Norwegian bunad costumes). It's worth stop-
ping at the **Bojer Wikan Fisherman's
Memorial** (next door), a memorial to
those who lost their lives at sea.

HISTORY OF FISHING

The small, tasteful **Clausen Memo-
rial Museum**  (203 Fram Street; tel:
907-772-3598; www.clausenmuseum.com;
Apr–Sept Mon–Sat 10am–5pm; Oct–
Dec and Feb–Mar Mon–Fri 1–5pm, Sat
noon–5pm) offers an insight into the
history and art of fishing, life in Petersburg, and Tlingit culture.

Eagles Roost Park  (www.petersburg
rec.com), on North Nordic Drive near
the town's edge, provides a platform
for viewing eagles roosting in trees. It

also has picnic tables, and a pathway to
the beach to explore tidal pools. As in
Wrangell, there are ancient petroglyphs
(rock carvings) that can be seen at low
tide 3 miles (5km) down Sandy Beach
Road at the **Sandy Beach Recreation
Area** . Along with the petroglyphs are
2,000-year-old Tlingit stone or wooden
fish traps, supposedly found only in the
40-mile (64km) area around Petersburg.

On the way to Sandy Beach, the
small **Outlook Park** (www.petersburgrec.
com) contains a covered timber-framed
shelter built by a local shipwright in
the style of a Norwegian stave church.
You can use the binoculars provided to
scan Frederick Sound for marine life.

*Houses on stilts,
Petersburg.*

*Bojer Wikan
Fisherman's Memorial.*

⊘ GLACIER SEALS

The glacier, part of the Stikine Ice Field
20 miles (32km) east of Petersburg, is
the southernmost, active, tidewater glacier in the northern hemisphere. Not only
do giant hunks of ice crack off the head of
the glacier and crash into the sea, but
because of the deep (810ft/247-meter)
waters of LeConte Bay, the glacier also
calves from underwater. Huge slabs of
icy missiles shoot up into the air, and
then splash back into the sea. These
'shooters' can reach out hundreds of
yards from the face of the glacier. The
sparkling, often deep-blue icebergs clog
a spectacular 10-mile (16km) long fjord.
Seals nonchalantly lounge on, or swim
around the floating bergs. In June, visitors to the glacier from Wrangell or
Petersburg tours are often treated to the
sight of new seal pups on the ice floes.

SITKA

Known as the 'Jewel of the Southeast,' Sitka showcases Alaska's unique and complex mix of Native, Russian, and American cultures in the only city facing out to the Pacific.

**Maps on pages
108, 133**

Situated on the western coast of Baranof Island, the historic city of **Sitka ⑥**, population 8,900, is backed by nearly 1,600 sq miles (2,472 sq km) of the most mountainous terrain in the Southeast. But it is far from just a wilderness outpost. The city's crammed and narrow streets are dotted with beautifully restored historic buildings, and it is home to Alaska's oldest National Park, which is also one of two of the state's urban parks, adding to Sitka's European feel.

Tlingit lived here for many centuries before the island was visited by Russian explorer Vitus Bering in 1741. Fifty years later, Alexander Baranov, of the Russian-American Company, built a fort and trading post, St Michael's Redoubt, a few miles to the north of Sitka's present-day location. Local Tlingits, fearing Russian domination and fur-trade enslavement, attacked the fort in 1802, killing most of the settlers. Baranov retaliated two years later by bringing a Russian warship into the harbor and bombarding the village.

The Tlingits fought bravely but after six days were driven from the area in what became known as the Battle of Sitka. The Russians then re-established the settlement and renamed it 'New Archangel.'

In 1808, Sitka became the capital of Russian America, and by the mid-1800s, the major port of the north Pacific Coast. Fur shipments to Europe and Asia were the primary commodity, though salmon, lumber, and ice were also shipped to various locations along the western coasts of North and Central America.

AMERICA TAKES OVER

Eventually, the lucrative fur trade declined and, in 1867, Alaska was sold to the United States. The transfer ceremony was held in Sitka on October 18 (now a state holiday, 'Alaska Day') and is re-enacted each year at the city's Castle Hill. Sitka remained the territorial capital

A ship in front of Mount Edgecumbe.

of Alaska until 1906, when the seat of government was transferred to Juneau.

During World War II, the US Navy built an air base on nearby Japonski Island, which housed an astonishing 30,000 military personnel plus more than 7,000 civilians. Following the end of the war, the Bureau of Indian Affairs converted some of the former military buildings into a boarding school for Alaska natives, Mount Edgecumbe High School, which is still operational today, educating more than 400 students from over 100 Alaska communities. The island is also the location for a US Coast Guard Air Station and Boat Station, the Sitka campus of the University of Alaska Southeast, a hospital and Sitka's Rocky Gutierrez Airport. The O'Connell Bridge, built in 1972, connects Japonski Island to Sitka.

CRUISING PORT OF CALL

Sitka's broad-based economy is fueled by various industries including fishing, fish processing, retail and healthcare services, government, transportation, and tourism. Alaska Airlines offers daily flights to the community (as do various local air taxi services), and the Alaska Marine Highway System provides both regular and high-speed ferry options. The city is a popular port for the cruise-ship industry, and for good reason. There are many interesting things to see and do within easy walking distance of the harbor (remember to bring adequate rain gear).

A convenient and profitable first stop is in the waterfront district at the **Harrigan Centennial Hall** Ⓐ (330 Harbor Drive; tel: 907-747-4090; www. cityofsitka.com/government/departments/centennial), housing both the **Visitors Center** and the **Sitka History Museum** (tel: 907-738-3766; www.sitkahistory. org; Mon–Fri 9am–4pm). Check the schedule for performances of Russian folk songs and dances by the **New Archangel Dancers** (tel: 907-747-5516; www.newarchangeldancers.com) and other cultural events in The Sitka Performing Arts Center (1000 Lake Street; tel: 907-747-3085).

The **Convention and Visitors Bureau** Ⓑ (104 Lake Street; tel:

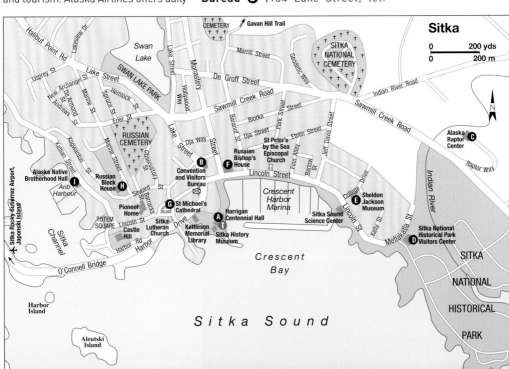

907-747-8604; www.visitsitka.org), while a bit tricky to find, is another helpful resource for visitors. They will provide you with the contacts for various tour operators wanting to show you the sights in and around Sitka via semi-submersible vessel, all-terrain vehicle (ATV), bike, bus, or on foot.

Additional exploration options include wildlife cruises, diving and snorkeling, flightseeing, and kayaking.

ALASKA RAPTOR CENTER

If a self-guided walking tour is what you have in mind, you can make an east-to-west sweep of the city by heading first to the **Alaska Raptor Center** ⒞ (1000 Raptor Way; tel: 907-747-8662 or 800-643-9425; www.alaskaraptor.org; May–Sept daily 8am–4pm, Oct–Apr Mon–Fri 10am–3pm; tours only in summer). This small but fascinating facility's mission is to educate the public concerning raptors and their environment, to provide medical treatment for injured bald eagles (and other birds), and to conduct bald eagle research. Visitors have an opportunity for close-up raptor observation. The **Fortress of the Bear** (4639 Sawmill Creek Road; tel: 907-747-3550; www.fortressofthe-bear.org; May–Sept daily 9am–5pm, Oct–Apr call for hours), a rescue center for orphan bears, located 5 miles (7km) from the city center, provides the possibility to observe them in their natural habitat from a large viewing platform.

SITKA NATIONAL HISTORICAL PARK

When leaving the Raptor Center, take a delightful stroll across Indian River and through an old-growth rainforest as you head downhill (toward the Sound) to the **Sitka National Historical Park Visitors Center** ⒟ (located at the east end of Lincoln Street; tel: 907-747-0110; www.nps.gov/sitka; May–Sept daily 8am–5pm, Oct–Apr Mon–Fri noon–3pm, Sat 9am–3pm, closed on Federal holidays during winter; park open daily 6am–10pm). Within the 100-acre (40-hectare) park are beautiful Tlingit totem poles, the remains of historic Tlingit and Russian structures, and the 1804 battleground. Inside the cultural center is a museum featuring Native American history, art and Native artist demonstrations.

On leaving the Park, head west and stop at the **Sheldon Jackson Museum** ⒠ (104 College Drive; tel: 907-747-8981; www.museums.alaska.gov/sheldon_jackson; mid-May–Sept daily 9am–4.30pm, winter Tue–Sat 10am–4pm, closed holidays). The oldest museum in Alaska, it features one of the largest collections, gathered between 1888–98, of Native cultural artifacts. At the **Sitka Sound Science Center** (834 Lincoln Street, Suite 200; tel: 907-747-8878; www.sitkascience.org; May–Sept Mon–Sat 9am–4pm, Oct–Apr Wed 10am–noon, Sat 10am–3pm), you can visit an aquarium with touch tanks, a hatchery and enjoy

Sitka Channel in summer.

a bowl of tasty chowder at Ludvig's Chowder Cart next door.

RUSSIAN BISHOP'S HOUSE

Continuing your westerly ramble, stop by the **Russian Bishop's House** **F** (103 Monastery Street; tel: 907-747-0110; www.nps.gov/sitka; daily May–Sept 9am–4.30pm, Oct–Apr,Tue–Fri by advanced appointment only). A National Historic Landmark, this 1842 example of restored Russian colonial architecture, complete with original furniture, appliances, and articles of clothing, gives you a glimpse of Sitka life during the Russian-America period.

Leaving the Bishop's House, head west again and visit **St Michael's Cathedral** **G** (240 Lincoln Street; tel: 907-747-8120; summer Mon–Fri 9am–4pm, or check posted hours on door. Sun by appointment only; donation requested). The reconstructed Orthodox cathedral replaces what was Alaska's oldest church structure from the Russian era. The earlier building was destroyed by fire in 1966, but nearly all the icons were rescued. The church was later rebuilt, strictly following the original plans.

You'll probably regret it if you don't have a look at the **Russian Block House** **H**, located behind the Pioneers' Home. It is a replica of one of the three original structures that once separated the Russian and Tlingit segments of town following the Natives' return to Sitka around 1824.

Close by is the **Alaska Native Brotherhood Hall** **I** (235 Katlian Street), and the **Sheet'ka Kwaan Naa Kahidi Tribal Community House** (456 Katlian Street; tel: 907-747-7137; www.sitka tours.com; call for performance times), both of which host colorful Native dance performances, storytelling, and other cultural events. A small gift shop features Native artwork.

Castle Hill, on the National List of Historic Places, is just south, across Lincoln Street. In addition to being the site of the 1867 Russian/US transfer ceremony, it is the former location of Baranof's Castle, built in 1837 and destroyed by fire in 1898.

OUTDOOR ACTIVITIES

To take in the sights outside Sitka, consider a wildlife cruise to see humpback whales, sea otters, sea lions, and eagles. Birders would enjoy a trip to **St Lazaria Island**, part of the Maritime National Wildlife Refuge (www.fws.gov/refuge/Alaska_Maritime), at the mouth of Sitka Sound, where you'll see thousands of seabirds, including tufted puffins.

You could also take a flight tour to peer into the volcanic crater of nearby dormant Mt Edgecumbe or view the frigid expanse of the Baranof Icefields. Charter options are available for sportfishing, and kayak enthusiasts have a variety of paddling opportunities. Hot springs around the island reward the intrepid backpacker. For tours involving any of these activities (and many more), contact Sitka's Convention and Visitors Bureau.

View of Sitka from Gavan Hill.

JUNEAU

Juneau is a small but busy capital, with narrow streets and alleys leading to museums, galleries, and bars Downtown, and a variety of hiking trails to nearby glaciers and icefields.

The delightful city of **Juneau ❼** today is a far cry from where gold was discovered by Joe Juneau and Richard Harris in 1880. On the North American mainland, across the Gastineau Channel from **Douglas Island**, Juneau is home to nearly 32,200 Alaskans, and is the only US state capital to border another country. Most Alaskans here work for the government (state, federal, or local), provide services for those that do, or are employed in the tourism industry.

But Juneau is much more than that. While its dense Downtown is a hive of business and government activity, don't be surprised to find many shops 'closed due to sunshine' on Juneau's few clear days. Locals are quick to take to the water or the mountains when the skies open up, and are more than likely to be found enjoying a play at the Perseverance Theatre on Douglas Island or sipping an espresso and relaxing at the Heritage Café (www.heritagecoffee.com) on South Franklin Street.

Lodged in natural splendor, Juneau has a touch of urban sensibility befitting a bustling capital.

GOLD FEVER

The town was first named Harrisburg – some say because Harris, unlike his partner Juneau, was able to write and recorded it that way. But the name didn't stick: after news of the gold

strike spread to Sitka and elsewhere, nearly 300 prospectors swarmed to the scene and decided to rename the place Rockwell. Shortly thereafter it became Juneau. By whatever name, the camp was bustling with gold fever and, later, gold production. It didn't take long for simple gold pans, pickaxes, and human labor to be replaced by miles-long flumes and ditches, carrying water to massive hydraulic earthmoving and sluicing operations.

Within a decade of the Juneau/Harris discovery, wagon roads penetrated

◉ Main attractions
Alaska State Museum
Marine Park
Red Dog Saloon
St Nicholas Russian
  Orthodox Church
State Capitol Building
Juneau-Douglas Museum
Governor's Mansion
Douglas Island
Mendenhall Glacier
Alaska Brewing Company

Maps on pages 108, 138

Juneau seen from Mount Roberts.

the valleys behind the camp-turned-town – roads you can still hike on.

FRONTIER LAW

Early on, politics assumed considerable importance in Juneau. The future state's first political convention was held here in the summer of 1881. The camp became a first-class municipality under the law in 1900, and in 1906 the district government of Alaska transferred there from Sitka.

In 1913, Alaska's first territorial legislature convened, in what is now the Elks Hall on Seward Street. Nearly life-size photo murals of that distinguished group can be seen today on the first floor of the State Capitol Building.

As the city grew and prospered, enterprises such as fishing, saw-milling, and trading became important. But gold powered Juneau. Miners labored daily in miles and miles of tunnels that honeycombed the mountains both on the mainland and on Douglas Island. For recreation on days off they scoured the wild country beyond the urban centers, digging, panning, hoping against hope

that they, too, might strike it rich like Juneau and Harris. Yet these two early prospectors never realized much from their discoveries. Juneau died penniless in the Canadian Yukon and a collection had to be taken up to send his body home for burial in the city he co-founded.

WARTIME BOOM

Gold remained Juneau's, and Alaska's, mainstay, until 1944 when the government closed down the massive Alaska-Juneau goldmine and milling operation for reasons of manpower and conservation. By that time, the city was experiencing something of a war boom, and with the end of World War II there came a gradual but continuous rise in territorial government activity and employment.

By 1959, when Alaska became state number 49, government had all but filled the economic void left by mining's demise. And Juneau has since grown from a waterfront community hovering beneath the skeletal remains of the old Alaska-Juneau mill sites, to a gregarious, outreaching city spreading for miles to the north and south.

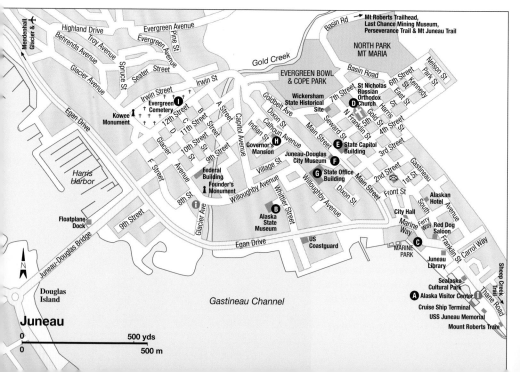

The city's size was established in the mid-1960s when Juneau and Douglas and the Greater Juneau Borough were unified by a democratic vote into the City and Borough of Juneau.

Juneau is a small town in terms of population, but in square miles it is the second-largest in the US, measuring 2,701 sq miles (6,998 sq km).

TOURING THE CAPITAL

It's a good idea to start your tour of Juneau with a visit to the **visitors center**  (800 Glacier Avenue; tel: 888-586-2201; www.traveljuneau.com; daily May–Sept 8am–5pm), opposite the cruise-ship terminal off Thane Road. Year-round visitor information is also available at the Juneau International Airport and the Alaska Marine Highway System Ferry Terminal. Summertime information sources also include the visitor information kiosk located at Marine Park. You can get a city map at any of these locations, plus information about Juneau's many points of interest and tour operators.

One of its biggest attractions, the **State Library, Archives, and Museum (SLAM)** (395 Whittier Street; tel: 907-465-2901; http://museums.alaska.gov; summer daily 9am–5.30pm, winter Tue–Sat 10am–4pm) is within walking distance of downtown hotels and shopping.

Inside, visitors are greeted by a towering spruce tree rising from ground level almost to the ceiling and a large floormap of Alaska. On the left of the lobby, will find Inuit culture is represented by small, intricate ivory carvings and a huge 40ft (12-meter) *umiak*, or skin boat, of the type that were used for whale- and walrus-hunting along the ice floes of the Arctic Ocean.

Southeast Alaska's ancient Native way of life is reflected in the re-creation of a community house, complete with totemic carvings, and the Athabascan Natives (from the Interior) are represented with displays of a birch bark canoe, weapons, and bead-decorated moose-hide garments.

There is also gold rush memorabilia, and from the Russian era there are Orthodox religious exhibits including precious coins, priests' raiments, and the first American flag to be flown at Sitka when Russian America became American territory on October 18, 1867. Looking forward, the museum also features exhibits on Alaska's natural resources and its role in the global climate. The Richard Foster Reading Room, with its soaring ceiling and high windows offering stunning mountain views is also worth a look.

MARINE PARK

Most of Juneau's other attractions can be seen in a walking tour along the docks and among its meandering, frequently narrow, streets and alleys. Go east along Egan Drive to **Marine Park** overlooking the city's dock and wharf area. It's a small, but pleasurable place of benches and shady trees situated near the ramp where cruise-ship passengers land after being lightered from

Juneau's winter temperature seldom falls below 20°F (-6°C) and it is rarely hotter than 65°F (18°C) in summer.

JUNEAU'S TRAILS

Few capital cities in the world can offer such a variety of hiking trails, suitable for the fit and the not so fit, right on its doorstep.

Juneau is a city for the outdoor type, offering a rich variety of hiking trails that can be reached easily from the city center. All of the starting points are clearly marked and you can get information about routes and the degree of skill and stamina needed from the US Forest Service, Juneau Ranger District at 8510 Mendenhall Loop Road (tel: 907-586-8800; www.fs.usda.gov/tongass).

TRAILS FROM BASIN ROAD

Among the best-known trails are Mount Roberts, Perseverance, and Mount Juneau. All three start at Basin Road. **Mount Roberts** takes off from a trailhead just past the wooden trestle bridge. It's a steep climb, but a good one, with alpine ground cover above the treeline, and splendid views. You can cheat by hopping on the Mount Roberts Tramway, which takes you from

Greenery along the Treadwell Ditch Trail.

South Franklin Street, near the dockside, up to the treeline, where you can begin your hike, browse in the visitor center, or watch a documentary in the theater.

The starting point for the gentler and most popular trail, the **Perseverance Mine Trail**, is a little further east on Basin Road. Before setting off, hop into the Last Chance Mining Museum, near the trailhead (daily in summer 9.30am–12.30pm and 3.30–6.30pm; tel: 907-586-5338), to get an idea of what life used to be like when the mines were functioning. On the Perseverance Mine Trail you have the chance to see and explore the ruins of some of the early mining sites, including the Silver Bowl Basin Mine and the Glory Hole. Or you can continue along the Granite Creek Trail, and hike as far as the creek basin.

The experienced and thoroughly fit hiker can link up with the steep **Mount Juneau Trail**, which provides the best view that can be had with two feet on the ground. Mainland Juneau and Douglas Island are laid out 3,500ft (1,100 meters) below the mountain summit, and the twisting, glistening Gastineau Channel seems to go on and on forever. This trail will bring you back full circle to join Perseverance near Ebner Falls. The less fit, or those with less time, can miss this loop, by retracing their steps from the Granite Creek Basin.

The **Sheep Creek Trail**, which starts in the southeast of the city, at Thane Road, takes you through the beautiful valley south of Mount Roberts, then up to Powerline Ridge and on to Sheep Mountain.

TRAILS STARTING FROM DOUGLAS

Several interesting trails start from Douglas, on the other side of the Gastineau Channel. The **Treadwell Ditch Trail**, which begins at E Street, is a 12-mile (20km) hike to Eagle Crest, but it can become a much easier walk by going only as far as the Dan Moller Trail, then returning on the road. Only the really experienced should try the **Mount Bradley Trail**, which sets off from Fifth Street. Mount Bradley is 3,337ft (1,017 meters) high and the going can be tough, although the scenic rewards are huge. An easier walk is 2-mile (3.5km) **Cropley Lake Trail**, which starts at Fish Creek Road out in the Eaglecrest Ski Area (www.skieaglecrest.com).

The non-profit Trail Mix has a complete listing of Juneau's trails, their level of difficulty and current condition (tel: 907-790-6406; www.trailmixinc.org).

ships at anchor offshore. This is where half of Juneau seem to eat lunch, especially on sunny summer days. Street vendors in the vicinity offer food ranging from fried halibut to hot dogs, from tacos to Vietnamese spring rolls.

You can also jump aboard the Mount Roberts Tramway (www.mountroberts tramway.com; tel: 888-461-8726), which climbs nearly 2,000ft (610 meters) in six minutes. At the top, you will be met with spectacular views, a couple gift stores, and scores of hiking trails, and you can even check out the restaurant here if the trip has piqued your appetite.

THE RED DOG SALOON

From Marine Park, cross Ferry Way to South Franklin Street, where you will find art galleries and stores that entice you with displays of Alaskan ivory, jade, totemic wood carvings, and leatherwork. Also on South Franklin (turn right from Ferry Way) is the best-known bar in the city, the fun but touristy **Red Dog Saloon** (www.reddogsaloon. com). Further up the street is the **Alaskan Hotel Bar** (www.thealaskanhotel.com), which retains its gold-rush era decor and is well worth a visit.

Continue north along Franklin Street to the tiny **St Nicholas Russian Orthodox Church ⓓ** (www.stnicholasjuneau.org; summer Mon–Thu 8.30am–4.30pm, Fri–Sun noon–4.30pm, winter Sat 6–7pm, Sun 9am–12.30pm; donation requested), one of the most picturesque houses of worship in Alaska. The onion-domed, octagon-shaped church, located on Fifth Street, was constructed in 1894 at the specific request of Ishkhanalykh, the then principal chief of the Tlingits of Juneau. It is the oldest original Orthodox church in Southeast Alaska and one of the senior parishes of the entire state.

STATE CAPITOL

Downhill on Fourth Street is the **State Capitol Building ⓔ** (mid-Jan–mid-May, daily 7am–9pm, rest of year Mon–Fri 7am–5pm; tours every half hour in summer). Built in the 1930s, many of its halls and offices have been refurbished to reflect that era. You can see where the Alaska House and Senate meet during sessions; it's worth a stop.

On the corner of Fourth and Main streets is the **Juneau-Douglas City Museum ⓕ** (tel: 907-586-3572; www. juneau.org/library/museum/index.php; May–Sept Mon–Fri 9am–6pm, Sat–Sun 10am–4.30pm, Oct–Apr Tue–Sat 10am–4pm; free in winter). It has interesting displays on the town's fishing and gold-mining history, and provides a free map of Juneau's nationally registered historic buildings and totem poles.

If you find yourself here on a Friday, bring your lunch to the **State Office Building ⓖ**, across the road on Fourth Street. There you'll find a giant old Kimball theater organ – a magnificent relic of Juneau's silent movie day. There are also concerts here on Fridays.

Two blocks beyond, on Calhoun Avenue, is the **Governor's Mansion ⓗ**, which cost $2 million to restore to the glory of its 1913 opening. You can photograph the exterior, but you are not allowed entry.

The State Capitol in Juneau; inside, clay murals from the 1930s celebrate Alaska's rich coastal waters and native hunting traditions.

Juneau's Visitor Center.

The Perseverance Mine Trail.

Tourists visit Mendenhall Glacier by helicopter.

Beyond the Governor's Mansion and across **Gold Creek** – where Joe Juneau and Dick Harris panned their first gold in the area – you come to the **Evergreen Cemetery** ❶ where the two prospectors are buried. The two founders' burial monuments are not overly impressive, but the partially wooded cemetery is a popular place for visitors and dog-walkers.

DOUGLAS ISLAND

Home to the world-famous Treadwell mine, Douglas, a tidal island, once rivaled Juneau in size and industry, but is now a 'neighborhood' within the city limits of more than 5,200 people. West of downtown Juneau and off the beaten path, it feels like a local's hideaway.

To visit the island, consider renting a bike at Cycle Alaska (www.cycleak.com) and cruise over the Douglas–Juneau Bridge on one of its bike lanes. Once there you'll find in downtown Douglas a handful of bars and restaurants, including The Island Pub (www.theisland-pub.com), known for its gourmet wood-oven baked pizzas.

There is also the Perseverance Theatre (tel: 907-463-8497; www.ptalaska.org), and on the north end is the Eaglecrest Ski Area and Sandy Beach, the only such beach around Juneau. A multitude of hiking trails crisscross the island and afford fantastic views of the channel and mountains beyond.

MENDENHALL GLACIER

From Juneau, a number of impressive glaciers can be reached by car or by trail, or viewed from the air. The best known is the **Mendenhall Glacier**, which can be seen from a US Forest Service information center about 13 miles (21km) north of town. The center sits on the edge of a frigid lake into which Mendenhall Glacier calves icebergs large and small. The face of the glacier is about 1 mile (2km) from the visitor center, while its 1,500 sq miles (3,885 sq km) of ice and snow is called the **Juneau Icefield**.

Perhaps the most exciting way to savor the glacier and its originating icefield is to take one of the flightseeing trips organized by one of several Juneau-based air charter companies, or to try one of the helicopter carriers that offer 45 minutes or so flying over the great white deserts of snow, and a landing on the surface of the icefield. Some companies supply a guide and equipment – boots, crampons, ice axes, and so forth – for a two-hour trek and even a little ice climbing.

Whatever adventure you decide on, stop by the **Alaska Brewing Company** (5364 Commercial Boulevard; summer hours 219 S Franklin St ; tel: 907-780-5866; www.alaskanbeer.com; brewery May–Sept daily 11am–7pm, Oct–Apr Mon–Sat noon–7pm, Sun noon–6pm. Giftshop and tasting room 219 S Franklin St Mon–Sat 11am–6pm, summer 9am–8pm) on your way back into town. Tours are available, as are complimentary tastings of its award-winning brews, including seasonal brews and limited edition beers. PhotoID required.

Fireweed is a common sight in open meadows.

GLACIER BAY NATIONAL PARK

Alaska
Anchorage

Both a World Heritage Site and an International Biosphere Reserve, the park offers visitors unparalleled views of tidewater glaciers and the chance to explore the rich ecosystems that surround them.

⊙ Main attractions

Gustavus
Fairweather Range
Bartlett Cove
Muir Inlet
Beardslee Islands

Map on page 108

Glacier Bay National Park and Preserve ❽ (www.nps.gov/glba) encompasses 3.3 million acres (1.3 million hectares). Located at the northern end of Alaska's Panhandle, the park's center lies approximately 90 miles (145km) northwest of Juneau and 600 miles (965km) southeast of Anchorage.

Most visitors arrive at Glacier Bay on large cruise ships or package tours, but you can reach **Gustavus** on the Alaska Marine Highway or by air and boat charters from Juneau. This village of just 450 year-round residents has an attractive beach and the 9-hole **Mount Fairweather Golf Course** (www.gustavus.com/activities/golf.html), which early summer golfers share with flocks of Canada geese.

In a land comprising three climatic zones – marine to Arctic – seven different ecosystems support a wide variety of plant and animal life. From the endangered humpback whale and Arctic peregrine falcon to the common harbor seal, black and brown bears, marmots, and eagles, Glacier Bay provides a rich overview of Alaska's wildlife.

Glacier Bay's physical environment is as diverse as any found in Alaska. Sixteen massive tidewater glaciers flowing from the snowcapped mountain peaks of the **Fairweather Range** (reaching 15,300ft/4,663 meters) plunge into the icy waters of the fjords. Besides the jagged icebergs, the ice-scoured walls of rock lining the waterways, the saltwater beaches, and protected coves, numerous freshwater lakes and thick forests of western hemlock and Sitka spruce are also found in the area.

HISTORY AND EXPLORATION

Evidence of human habitation in the Glacier Bay region dates back 10,000 years. Researchers have outlined seasonal patterns of hunting, fishing, and

A chance to explore inside a glacier.

gathering from semi-permanent villages. Native Tlingit folklore includes tales of periodic village destruction from earthquakes, tsunamis, and other natural forces.

European exploration of the area began in July 1741, when Russian ships sailed the outer coast. Other explorers followed, such as Captain George Vancouver, who charted the waters of the Inside Passage in the 1790s. But it was the widespread publicity soon after naturalist John Muir's first reconnaissance of the area in 1879 that stimulated extensive scientific investigations and early tourism. Where early explorers had found only a massive wall of ice, Muir paddled in waters newly released from glacial ice, which had begun to retreat up the fjords it had carved.

Today's visitors see views very different from those that were observed in Muir's day, as glaciers – and their steady retreat – have further changed the landscape in the past century. In Muir's time, the network of fjords had not yet been established; a huge glacier extended into areas which are now open water.

THE GLACIERS RETREAT

These glaciers have, over time, retreated and advanced due to severe climatic fluctuations. De la Perouse and Vancouver both observed glacier ice at the mouth of the bay in 1786 and 1794. By the time of Muir's trip to Glacier Bay in 1879, however, the ice had retreated 32 miles (51km) to a point near what is now the mouth of **Muir Inlet**. Ninety years later, the Muir Glacier had receded another 24 miles (39km). Today the bay is more than 65 miles (105km) long.

Glacier Bay visitors can often watch entire sections of glacier ice calve from 150ft (46-meter) walls. The cracking ice produces a thundering roar, easily heard by those on the water. Huge bergs are set adrift, and waves sweep across sandbars outward from the glacier's tidewater base.

Kayakers are warned to keep a safe distance from the glacier faces. Those on the water, close to ice chunks slowly

Getting close to a humpback whale.

Cruise ship passengers admire a glacier.

⊘ Fact

Commercial whaling in the 20th century reduced the world population of humpback whales from an estimated 125,000 to just 5,000. Today the population is something like 21,000 in the North Pacific (or around 80,000 the world over). Princess Cruise Lines paid a $200,000 fine and $550,000 to the National Park Foundation after one of its ships hit and killed a pregnant humpback whale in Glacier Bay.

A good vantage point for appreciating Glacier Bay.

melting in the salty bay, may hear a crackling sound similar to breakfast cereal or champagne, which comes from the release of thousands of air bubbles that became trapped in the ice from high pressure during its formation. From the air, the sound cannot be heard above the drone of an aircraft engine, but the perspective of shimmering ice flowing from mountaintop to sea is a dramatic one.

PLANT AND ANIMAL LIFE

Two hundred years ago, when a glacier filled what is now a network of inlets in Glacier Bay, only a small number of plant and animal species inhabited the region. Since the retreat of the ice, life has flourished. Today, the nutrient-rich waters of the fjords are important feeding grounds for large marine mammals, and even the windswept, insect-free upper slopes of the glaciers provide welcome refuge for mountain goats and other animals.

The four land and three marine ecosystems in Glacier Bay support life forms adapted to the environment.

Near Gustavus, an ecosystem of sandy grassland, thick coniferous forests and damp marshes provides habitat for sandhill cranes, river otters, wolves, bears, coyotes, and moose. **Bartlett Cove**, the park's only developed area, lies within a region dominated by coastal western hemlock and Sitka spruce; watch for bald eagles flying overhead.

In the magnificent backcountry, you may climb to elevations of 2,500ft (760 meters), or much higher if you're an experienced mountaineer. Here, in the alpine tundra ecosystem, the thick vegetation of lower elevations is replaced by shrubby plants – alpine grasses and dwarf blueberry.

The many delicate flowering plants and lichens should be respected, for regeneration in this environment is extremely slow; glacial history can be computed by studying the steady rate of lichen growth.

Although few visitors venture onto the higher snowfields and glaciers, life in this seemingly barren, mountainous environment does exist. The ice

worm, the only earthworm known to live on snow and ice, feeds on a red-pigmented green algae and organic debris swept onto the frozen surface. The glacier flea, a vegetarian insect, also lives above the treeline.

Possibly the most threatened species here is the humpback whale. Wintering near Hawaii or Mexico, humpbacks feed in the icy waters of southeastern Alaska and Glacier Bay in the summer. Killer and minke whales are sometimes spotted in the bay as well. Environmentalists fear that excessive numbers of cruise ships may drive out the whales. Besides small intertidal creatures, Glacier Bay is also home to many varieties of fish and shorebirds. Sea lions and otters, harbor seals and porpoises are frequently sighted.

PARK ATTRACTIONS

Despite its isolation, there are a number of ways to experience Glacier Bay, either for the day or on longer stays. Whale-watching cruises and flight-seeing tours depart from Gustavus and Juneau daily in the summer, but kayaking is perhaps the best way to experience the park's marine life. Off limits to motorized boats in the summer, the **Muir Inlet** is especially tranquil, and the **Beardslee Islands** are an easy day excursion from Bartlett Cove and provide some excellent bear-watching opportunities. There are a number of outfitters in Gustavus where you can rent kayaks, arrange a tour, or get tips for adventuring around the bay.

For those eager to explore on foot, Bartlett Cove, near the mouth of the bay, is the best place to start. In addition to the full-service Glacier Bay Lodge (with a visitor center inside, tel: 907-697-2661), there is a campground, a number of maintained trails, and a ranger station at the public dock (tel: 907-697-2627; www.nps.gov/glba) to help you plan longer expeditions. Free ranger-led nature and walking tours occur daily in the summer.

There are also excellent rafting, boating, mountaineering, and bird-watching opportunities. For more information about local tour operators, visit www.gustavus.com.

A colony of sea lions.

HAINES

This quirky southeastern seaside town is hemmed in by majestic glacier-laden mountains under the watchful eyes of thousands of bald eagles.

**Maps on pages
108, 149**

Most motorists traveling through **Haines ⑨** are anxiously looking forward to only one of two things. If southbound, the main focus is *not missing the ferry*. They're intent on getting in line at the Alaska Marine Highway terminal, driving their car onboard, grabbing a bite to eat at the ship's cafeteria and then finally making their way to a recliner (or, better yet, a comfortable stateroom) to recover from a marathon drive.

If they're headed north, they're consumed with making it 40 miles (65km) beyond Haines to the Canadian border (appropriate paperwork in hand) *during the hours of operation*, then getting on with their all-day or all-night drive to Interior Alaska or Canada. Haines is a town most Alaskans have traveled *through*, but seldom *to*. And that's a shame, because this little city, in many ways, exemplifies the very best that Alaska has to offer.

With the exception of Holland America Line (www.hollandamerica.com), most of the major cruise lines bypass Haines, choosing to dock at Skagway instead. The townspeople are divided over whether this fact constitutes a slight or a blessing. It certainly makes for less summertime congestion as the 2,500 local residents go about earning their living, primarily through commercial fishing, government, tourism, and transportation.

THE ROAD CONNECTION

The city is one of only three Southeast cities (Haines, Skagway, and Hyder) connected to the state's (or Canada's) road system. Air taxi service from Anchorage and various Southeast cities is available – there is no major commercial airline service to Haines – and the Alaska Marine Highway Service provides regular ferry transport throughout the year.

For visitors who are clever enough to actually plan a trip *to* Haines, the opportunity to experience a genuine, small, quirky seaside Alaska town,

Haines as seen from above.

hemmed in by glacier-laden mountains and under the constant, watchful eyes of literally thousands of bald eagles, is its own great reward.

ANCIENT TRADE ROUTE

Like most of Southeast Alaska, the first inhabitants of the Haines area were two tribes of Tlingit Indians, the Chilkat and the Chilkoot. The natives called their home 'Dei-Shu' or 'End of the Trail.' The ancient Tlingit trade route, up the Chilkat Valley into interior Canada, later became the Dalton Trail used by prospectors to access distant gold fields.

Today, parts of this long-used trail have become the Haines Highway, connecting Haines to the Canadian and Alaska road systems.

The noted naturalist John Muir visited Haines in 1879. Muir's traveling companion and friend, S. Hall Young, was the first missionary to arrive in the area. Muir and Young successfully petitioned the Chilkat for permission, and the Presbyterian Women's Executive Society of Home Missions for funds, to build the Willard Mission and School.

The name of the mission was later changed to Haines in honor of the Society's secretary, Mrs F.E. Haines, who raised the necessary building funds for the project. As the gold rush frenzy accelerated in the late 1890s, the area became a mining supply center. The fishing industry was also booming at that time, and by the turn of the century four canneries were in full operation.

FORT SEWARD

In 1904, responding to border issues with Canada, the first US government military post in Alaska (and the only one prior to World War II) was built just south of Haines and named **Fort William H. Seward Ⓐ**. The fort, in rather stark contrast to Haines' rustic frontier motif, was a collection of stately, white clapboard buildings surrounding the central parade grounds. The fort was decommissioned in 1947, and listed as a Historic Landmark in 1972. Today, these same white buildings serve as private homes, accommodations establishments, art galleries, and restaurants. A Tlingit clan house in

A good chance to experience a small Alaskan town.

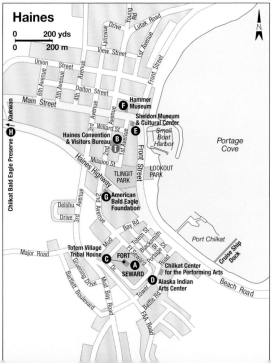

the center of the Parade Field makes Haines' housing juxtaposition complete.

A walking tour brochure for Fort Seward is available at the **Haines Convention and Visitors Bureau B** (122 Second Avenue; tel: 907-766-6418; www.visithaines.com; summer Mon–Fri 8am–5pm, Sat–Sun 8am–4pm, winter Mon–Fri 8am–5pm).

The staff will also connect you with local tour operators eager to show you the sights (in and around Haines) in a number of creative ways: kayak or bike rentals, rafting trips, day cruises, flightseeing, landings on glaciers, cultural tours, fishing charters, and birding or photography treks. The center also offers a bear-viewing guide, a birding checklist, area tide books, and a list of ten nearby totem pole locations, plus maps and lots of helpful advice.

Regardless of whether you opt for a tour or take off on your own, you'll want to stroll over to Fort Seward and check out **Totem Village Tribal House C** at the center of the parade grounds. Outside stands a collection of totem poles representing the blending of clans, the tallest

measuring a height of 35ft (10 meters). Across the green you can see this artistic tradition in action at the **Alaska Indian Arts Center D** (located in the old fort hospital building on the south side of parade grounds; tel: 907-766-2160; www.alaskaindianarts.com; Mon–Fri 9am–5pm), where local carvers, silversmiths, and other artisans work.

PIONEER MUSEUMS

In the Small Boat Harbor area, visit the **Sheldon Museum and Cultural Center E** (11 Main Street; tel: 907-766-2366; www.sheldonmuseum.org; summer Mon–Fri 9am–5pm, Sat–Sun 1–4pm, winter Mon–Sat 1–4pm). The museum has Haines' pioneer history exhibits as well as those of early native Tlingit culture.

For an even more unique collection, check out the one-of-a-kind **Hammer Museum F** (108 Main Street; tel: 907-766-2374; www.hammermuseum.org; May–Sept Mon–Fri 10am–5pm, Sat 10am–2pm). In this interesting, though admittedly oddball museum you'll find exhibits of over 1,500 historic (and new)

A bald eagle surveys the territory.

hammers used throughout the world for a dizzying array of purposes.

BALD EAGLES PRESERVATION

To view some regal wildlife up close, visit the **American Bald Eagle Foundation**  (113 Haines Highway at 2nd Street; tel: 907-766-3094; www.baldeagles.org; summer Mon–Fri 9am–5pm, Sat 11am–3pm, winter Mon–Fri 10am–2pm). This natural history museum features unique natural history dioramas, along with live bald eagle displays. Outside are nine enclosures housing a variety of raptors. The center is a non-profit educational foundation dedicated to the protection and preservation of bald eagle habitats and presents daily live bird presentations in the summer.

If you travel 18 miles (29km) out the Haines Highway, you will find roadside pullouts for eagle viewing in the **Chilkat Bald Eagle Preserve** , created in 1982 by the State of Alaska, and probably the best spot in the world to view bald eagles. This is especially true from early October until February each year, when thousands of eagles congregate in the Chilkat Valley in order to feed on the late run of salmon spawning in the Chilkat River. The preserve also provides interpretive displays, trails and shelters. The prime viewing areas are from mile 18 to 21, but the eagles often disregard those boundaries and can be seen, sometimes a dozen or more to a single cottonwood tree, maintaining a constant surveillance on salmon swimming upstream.

At Mile 22 is the Native village of **Klukwan**. With a cultural museum and 66 residents, it is the last remaining Tlingit village in the area. For visiting information, contact Jilkaat Kwaan Cultural Tours (tel: 907-767-5505; www.chilkat-nsn.gov).

Located even further north is the **Kroschel Films Wildlife Center** (1.8 Mile Mosquito Lake Road; tel: 907-767-5464; www.kroschelfilms.com). Although somewhat difficult to find, it is worth the journey for the opportunity to get close to animals such as lynx, mink, caribou, grizzly bears, and wolverines in their natural environment.

Chilkat dancers perform in Haines. The highly stylized blankets, depicting clan symbols and animals in abstract geometric patterns, could take a year to weave and were very valuable, selling for $30 (a huge sum) in the mid-19th century. A few weavers keep the tradition alive.

The road to Haines Pass.

SKAGWAY

The town was founded on gold and dreams, and its brief period of glory is re-created – in a suitably sanitized way, of course – for the enjoyment of today's cruise-ship tourists.

⊙ Main attractions

Klondike Gold Rush
  National Historic Park
Mascot Saloon
Eagle's Hall
Gold Rush Cemetery
Chilkoot Trail

Maps on pages 108, 153

Familiar sounds resonate in **Skagway ❿**, where the rollicking past has been preserved. On a calm midsummer night when the sun has just skipped behind the last peak, you can't help but hear them coming from behind those false fronts as you walk up the boardwalk on Broadway Street. They are the sounds of a not-too-distant era: ragtime pianos, whooping cancan girls, ringing cash registers, songs, and raucous laughter; the happy sounds of gold fever run rampant at the start of the trail. Re-created for the tourist market, they give visitors a taste of the past and boost the local economy.

There's no town in Alaska quite like Skagway when it comes to blending history with natural beauty. Situated at the northern end of Southeast Alaska's Inside Passage, Skagway is the natural jumping-off point for anyone taking the shortcut over the coastal mountains into Canada's Yukon. In 1897–98 stampeders took to the trail, and a town of 10,000 to 20,000 people sprouted. Today, many of the old buildings still stand, and the town's 1,000 or so residents cater to the crowds of tourists.

FINDING THE PASS

When you approach Skagway from the south – by Alaska Ferry, cruise ship, or air taxi – you see a tiny town at the base of a river valley surrounded by mountains ranging from 5,000 to 7,000ft (1,500 to 2,100 meters) above sea level, rising almost straight out of the saltwater fjord. You would not expect to find a pass to the closed-in valley, but there is one – the White Pass.

The first white man to discover it was Captain William Moore, a member of an 1887 Canadian survey party, a 65-year-old dreamer who had captained steamboats on rivers all over the western hemisphere. The big strike in the Yukon did not occur until August 1896, and by October 1897 Skagway's

Arctic Brotherhood Hall.

first newspaper reported 15 general stores, 19 restaurants, four meat markets, three wharves, 11 saloons, six lumber yards, eight pack trains, and nine hotels. Three other newspapers were established within a year.

DYEA

Skagway was not alone in its quest to become the 'Metropolis of the North.' **Dyea**, a city on the bay 10 miles (16km) to the west, sprang up as well. It sat at the foot of the Chilkoot Trail, an established Native route that was shorter but steeper than the White Pass Trail.

Fewer prospectors used the the White Pass Trail, nicknamed 'Dead Horse Trail' because of the 3,000 pack animals that perished in the canyon, but Skagway won the battle for survival. The White Pass and Yukon Route Railroad laid its first tracks up the middle of Broadway Street on May 28, 1898, and by 1900 the narrow-gauge line was completed, 100 miles (160km) to Whitehorse, future capital of the Yukon Territory. By providing an easy route to the gold fields, it turned Dyea into a ghost

town. Today, its sparse remains can be seen at the start of the Chilkoot Trail.

The White Pass and Yukon Route Railroad (www.wpyr.com) was Alaska's first railroad and still has an international reputation as a first-class feat of engineering. It is, to this day, something to marvel at.

The Klondike Rush had subsided by 1900, but Skagway was set up solidly as the port for the Yukon. Its population has fluctuated between 400 and 3,000 in the years since, due to a continuous boom-and-bust cycle. Food, fuel, war supplies, minerals, and tourists have all been hauled by the railroad in various volumes and numbers. In the early 1980s the railroad went through a bad patch and closed down, but was reopened in 1988.

RIDING THE RAILROAD

Riding the narrow-gauge train over the White Pass is the best way to get a feel of what the gold rush was like. You travel in turn-of-the-20th-century parlor cars, pulled by steam or diesel engines, which seem to cling to the

The White Pass and Yukon Route Railway.

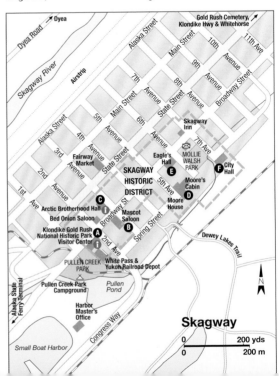

Skagway

small cut in the mountainside. Hundreds of feet below are the still visible remains of the old trails. Excursions are available to White Pass Summit (2,890ft/880 meters) or passengers may book a one-way ticket from Skagway to Fraser, British Columbia, where they can continue to Whitehorse by bus. Visitors can also drive the Klondike Highway, which climbs the opposite side of the canyon from the railroad. The three-hour drive gives you much the same splendid scenery as is seen from the railroad: Skagway River Gorge, Pitchfork Falls, White Pass Summit, and the beautiful lake country of British Columbia and the Yukon, while the road continues all the way to Dawson City, BC.

KLONDIKE GOLD RUSH NATIONAL HISTORIC PARK

The center of activity in Skagway is along Broadway Street, which starts at the dock and ferry terminal, where more than 60 gold rush-era buildings still stand. The **Klondike Gold Rush National Historic Park** , created in 1977, took over

Skagway's architecture recalls the gold rush era.

ownership of many of these buildings and has since spent millions of dollars on their restoration. Private restoration has also taken place. Restaurants, saloons, hotels, art galleries, ice-cream parlors, and other businesses are here, many of them staffed by people in gold rush period dress.

Start a tour of the town with a visit to the **Klondike Gold Rush National Historic Park Visitor Center Ⓐ** (tel: 907-983-9200; www.nps.gov/klgo; daily May–Sept 8.30am–5.30pm, Oct–Apr Mon–Fri 8am–5pm) on the corner of Second Avenue and Broadway Street. The center contains a small museum offers informative talks, shows an atmospheric movie about the gold rush days, and conducts free walking tours of the district May–Sept at 9am, 10am, 11am, 2pm, and 3pm.

Nearby, on the corner of Third Avenue and Broadway Street, and also under the egis of the National Historic Park, is the **Mascot Saloon Ⓑ** (daily May–Sept 8.30am–5.30pm; free) Built in 1898, when it was one of many barrooms designed to slake the miners' thirst, it has some well-displayed exhibits which conjure up the rough, tough atmosphere of the saloon's heyday.

The **Arctic Brotherhood Hall Ⓒ** (www. alaska.org/detail/arctic-brotherhood-hall) is just across the street. Its exterior covered with thousands of pieces of driftwood, it is now the home of Skagway's **Convention and Visitors Bureau** (tel: 907-983-2854; www.skagway.com; Mon–Fri 8am–5pm).

At the corner of Fourth and Broadway is the restored **Pantheon Saloon**, which houses the **Junior Ranger Activity Center** (May–Sept Mon–Fri 10am–noon, 1–3pm) with hands-on activities for children that document the gold rush.

Walk up Broadway Street and turn right on Fifth Avenue to **Moore's Cabin Ⓓ** (May–Sept 10am–4.30pm) built by the city's neglected founder and his son in 1887 and transferred to this spot when stampeders trampled over their land.

This, too, has been renovated by the National Historic Park Service.

On the corner of Broadway Street and Sixth is **Eagles Hall ⓔ**, where the 'Skagway in the Days of '98' show re-creates the Soapy Smith story nightly (www.thedaysof98show.com). This one-hour melodrama follows an hour of live ragtime music and gambling. The dealers are cast members, the money is phoney, and some of the tables date back to the gold rush. The show's popularity has kept it going since 1925.

At the end of Seventh Avenue (turn right off Broadway Street just past the post office) is the **City Hall ⓕ**, a century-old building that has been both a place of learning (the McCabe College, which is why it is often known locally as the 'McCabe Building') and a courthouse. The building now houses **the Skagway Museum and Archives** (tel: 907-983-2420; summer Mon–Sat 9am–5pm, Sun 9am–4pm; call for winter hours) with an array of artifacts related to the local history, such as a Portland Cutter sleigh and a Bering Sea kayak. Outside, you will find a display of historic railcars.

GOLD RUSH CEMETERY

Running parallel with Broadway Street is State Street; follow this northeast for just over 2 miles (3km) and you will come to the **Gold Rush Cemetery**, where Soapy Smith and Frank Reid were laid to rest after reaching their violent mutual end.

FUN AND FESTIVITIES

Skagway has the reputation for being a party town, above all in summer: ask any Yukoner who bolts for the coast on weekends. There are two saloons which are usually hopping, especially on days when the cruise ships are in town.

Jazz musicians working on the cruise vessels sometimes jump ship in Skagway for a few hours to attend jam sessions, because, they say, it's the only day that they don't have to play 'old folks' music.' If business is good, the bars will stay open right through until 5am, the official closing time.

Visitors are welcome to join locals in the town-wide parties. The Summer Solstice Party, held on June 21 – the longest day of the year – is a rollicking

The Visitor Center, once the White Pass and Yukon Route Railroad Station.

Skagway became a boom town during the gold rush.

Downtown Skagway.

event, with bands performing in city parks throughout the night.

A traditional gold rush style Independence Day is celebrated on July 4, complete with parades, races, and jovial contests of all kinds. Four days later, on July 8, is Soapy Smith's Wake (www.soapysmith.net), a party and a champagne toast to Skagway's notorious con man, which is held at the Eagles Hall.

The Klondike Trail of '98 Road Relay is held in early September. About 100 10-person teams run a distance of 110 miles (176km) from Skagway to Whitehorse, ending, naturally enough, with a party.

THE CHILKOOT TRAIL

Around Skagway, there is much to be seen. Hiking the **Chilkoot Trail**, also part of the Klondike Gold Rush National Historic Park, is the most adventurous option for tracing the route of the gold seekers. The trail was established by Tlingit people as a trade route before the gold rush. The trail extends nearly 35 miles (53km) from old Dyea to Lake Bennett, British Columbia. Most hikers allow three to five days to capture the scenery and explore the thousands of gold rush relics left behind during the stampede. A limited number of permits (about 50; fee charged) are available daily to cross the pass.

Contact the National Park Service (tel: 907-983-2900; www.nps.gov/klgo) or Parks Canada (tel: 1-867-667-3910/800-661-0486; www.pc.gc.ca/eng/index.aspx).

As you approach the base of the Chilkoot Pass, you can't help but visualize the scenes of more than a century ago, when men went out, full of high hopes, to seek their fortunes, and so many returned empty-handed.

Edwin Tappan Adney recorded the scene for *Harper's Weekly* in September 1897: 'Look more closely. The eye catches movement. There is a continuous moving train; they are perceptible only by their movement, just as ants are. The moving train is zigzagging across the towering face of the precipice, up, up into the sky, even at the very top. See! They are going against the sky! They are human beings, but never did men look so small.'

OTHER HIKING TRAILS

There are several other trails, most described in a booklet obtainable from the National Park Service Visitor Center, where you can also find information on campsites and cabins.

The **Dewey Lake Trail System** comprises various trails, the shortest (about half an hour each way) being to Lower Dewey Lake, where pink and silver salmon run in August and September, and which has picnic spots and camp spaces. From here you can continue up to the Upper Dewey Lake and the Devil's Punchbowl. For a tougher hike, try the **Skyline Trail**, officially called the AB Mountain Trail, which starts on Dyea Road, just over 1 mile (2km) out of town, and takes a whole day from start to finish. The **Denver Glacier Trail** is another option.

The trailhead is located 6 miles (9km) out of town along the White Pass and Yukon Railroad. Trains offer flag-stop service here from May through September.

The best weather for exploring the area is in spring. Skies are clear, the sun is hot, and the snow is still deep on White Pass until mid-May. Later in the summer, after the snow has melted, hundreds of small ponds form on the moon-like terrain. But keep in mind that spring snow can obscure glacier crevasses, and the warmer temperatures increase the risk of avalanches, especially on the Skyline Trail.

KLONDIKE HIGHWAY

Since the opening of the **Klondike Highway** out of Skagway, more and more travelers drive the 360-mile (580km) 'Golden Circle' route to include both Skagway and Haines on their way to or from the Interior.

Driving up the Alaska Highway from the south, you can cut off to Skagway, put your car on the ferry for the short ride to Haines, and then proceed north along the Chilkoot River on the Haines Cut-Off till you meet the Alaska Highway again at Haines Junction. This is the most direct road route to Alaska's interior from the Panhandle.

A steam engine on the White Pass and Yukon Route Railroad.

📷 THE GREAT KLONDIKE GOLD RUSH

Gold was discovered in the Klondike in a period of economic depression, attracting the penniless, the adventurous, and the unscrupulous to this vast and unforgiving wilderness.

During 1897–98, 100,000 people poured into Dawson in the Klondike in search of gold. Although Dawson is in Canada, the best way to reach it was by ship, 600 miles (960km) from Seattle to Skagway, then overland, across one of two treacherous passes – the White Pass from Skagway or the Chilkoot from Dyea. The former was believed to be slightly easier, but it was controlled by 'Soapy' Smith – a villain who virtually ran Skagway during the gold boom (see page 155) – and stories of men being robbed and murdered were rife.

On the Chilkoot Pass it was the elements that were the killers, particularly avalanches and winter's extreme cold. The journey was made more difficult by the fact that, after some of the early prospectors died of starvation, the Canadian government insisted that each man should take a year's supplies – which weighed roughly a ton.

DREAMS AND DESOLATION

While some people became rich, and others found just enough to give them security, many of the so-called stampeders, having sunk everything they owned into the enterprise, were ruined. It's estimated that fewer than 100 of the gold rushers retained or built on their wealth in the long term.

The idea of heading off in search of gold lent itself to storytellers; Heart of the Klondike written by Scott Marble (c.1897), became very popular.

Miners came to Alaska during the Klondike Gold Rush.

A photograph of recently-arrived miners near Dyea in the Klondike, in 1897.

Mary's Hotel in Bonanza Creek was one of many roadhouses which sprang up along the Klondike creeks for the mutual benefit of the owners and the gold diggers. These hostelries provided a few home comforts, and gave the lucky ones somewhere to spend their money, distributing the rewards of the gold fields.

Dishing the Dirt in Dawson

Mining was a laborious business and those who went to the gold fields thinking the precious metal was there for the taking were soon disillusioned. The early prospectors had been lucky, striking gold near the surface, but by the time the great influx of hopefuls reached Dawson they were digging for gold which could be some 50ft (15 meters) beneath the surface. To reach it, they had to force their way through permafrost, burning fires to soften the land, then sinking shafts which might, or might not, hit the right spot.

Once the 'pay dirt' – the mixture of earth and gold – had been extracted it had to be separated and cleaned, and this was done in a primitive sluice. When the streams began to thaw in spring, water channeled through the sluice separated the precious dust from the dirt. The more sophisticated hydraulic sluicing methods introduced in Silver Bow could not be used in Dawson because of the difficulty of getting equipment across the passes.

The sluice pictured above is 'Long Tom' in Nome, where gold was discovered in late 1899.

A group of pioneers make portage in treacherous conditions at Devil's Bluff, the canyon near Sheep Camp, Klondike.

Prospectors eye the scales and weigh the gold that has been gleaned during a long winter's work. By 1900, more than $250 million of gold had been found.

YAKUTAT

The tiny, superlative-worthy community of Yakutat is far off the beaten path of just about everybody. It is the northernmost town of Southeast Alaska, located on Monti Bay, the only sheltered, deep-water port in the Gulf of Alaska.

⊙ **Main attractions**

Malaspina Glacier
Hubbard Glacier
Situk River
Harlequin Lake

📍
Map on page 108

The majestic 18,008ft (5,489-meter) spire of Mount St Elias, the second-tallest mountain in North America, dominates the northwestern skyline of **Yakutat ⑫** (about 635 residents). Providing a formidable backup is the rest of the St Elias Mountain Range, the highest coastal range in the world (exceeding the Himalayas in vertical relief). The area also contains the greatest number of glaciers in North America – giant ones – surrounding the town on three sides. In fact, the 45-mile (72km) -wide **Malaspina Glacier**, a few miles west of Yakutat, is North America's largest piedmont glacier and covers more area than the state of Rhode Island.

The **Hubbard Glacier**, to the north, is the longest tidewater glacier in Alaska. Twice in recent history (in 1986 and again in 2002), this galloping glacier has built suspense among the world's glaciologists (and among *everyone* in Yakutat) by surging forward, damming the mouth of Russell Fjord, and creating an ominous, rapidly rising freshwater lake. In both instances the ice dam eventually gave way allowing the water to flow into Yakutat Bay, the trapped marine mammals to escape to the sea, and the residents of Yakutat to breathe a sigh of relief.

Commercial fishing, fish processing, and government form the primary economic base for the community. Most residents live a subsistence lifestyle, hunting and fishing to provide for their families, as they have for many generations.

THE FIRST SETTLERS

Eyak-speaking people, driven from the Copper River area by Tlingit warriors, were probably the first settlers of Yakutat (the name means 'the place where canoes rest'). Throughout the 18th and 19th centuries, explorers from Russia, Spain, France, and England made their way to the area's protected harbor. In

Lake house, Yakutat Bay.

1805, the Russian-American Company built a fort in Yakutat to advance the sea otter trade. Tlingit warriors, having been denied access to their traditional fishing grounds by the Russians, eventually attacked and destroyed the fort. Gold was mined from the black-sand beaches of the area in 1886. The Swedish Free Mission Church built a sawmill and school in Yakutat in 1889, and by the early 1900s a railroad, store and cannery were constructed nearby. Like much of Alaska, Yakutat gained a sudden surge of military population during World War II.

Yakutat is one of the smallest communities in the US to enjoy daily jet service (from both Seattle and Anchorage). Other options for travel include air taxis and floatplane services. In summer, the Alaska Marine Highway provides a scheduled ferry service, but only two or three times a month.

Popular activities include beach-combing, birding, kayaking, and surfing. But Yakutat is probably best known for its world-class sport fishing. The **Situk River**, 11 miles (17km) from town, has the largest run of steelheads in the state. All five species of Pacific salmon may be found in the area. Other species include halibut, rainbow and cutthroat trout, and northern pike. But bring your quality rain gear: This area receives some of the heaviest precipitation in the state, averaging 160in (407cm) per year.

OUTDOOR ACTIVITIES

Local lodges offer fishing packages, glacier and wildlife viewing, hunting trips, kayak or river-running support, boat rentals, and a host of other services. If you are eager to strike out on your own, consider renting a car and kayak and drive to **Harlequin Lake**, 30 miles (50km) from town, to paddle among the lake's icebergs. The area also offers a forest service cabin, a campground, and excellent hiking and wildlife viewing opportunities. The office of the **Yakutat Ranger District** (712 Ocean Cape Road; tel: 907-784-3359; www.fs.fed.us/r10/tongass) is a good source of information, as is the **Greater Yakutat Chamber of Commerce** (www.yakutatalaska.com).

⊙ **Tip**

If the idea of catching a glassy wave beneath Mount Elias appeals, visit Icy Waves Surf Shop (635 Haida Street; tel: 907-784-3226; www.icywaves.com) where the owner will get you outfitted. Armchair surfers may want to watch Yakutat surfers rush past bewildered black bears in *Endless Summer 2*, the 1994 sequel to the 1966 surf classic.

A cruise ship near Hubbard Glacier.

Anchorage from above.

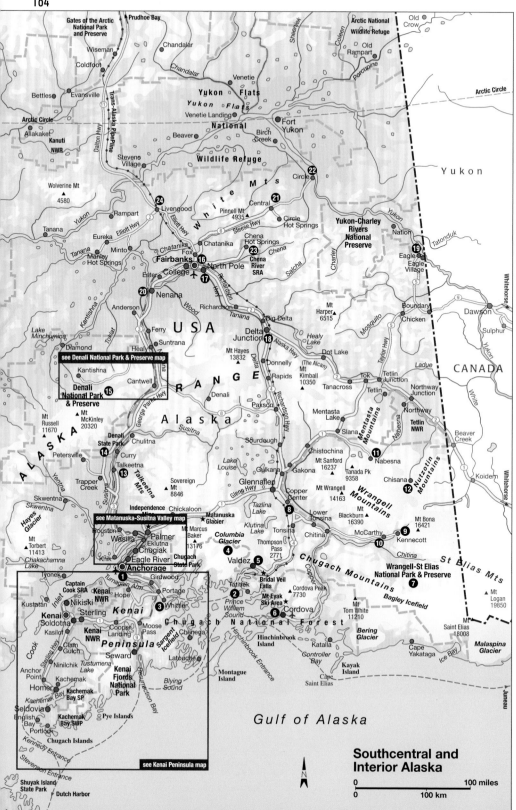

Gates of the Arctic
National Park
and Preserve
Prudhoe Bay

Wiseman
Coldfoot

Chandalar

Arctic National
Wildlife Refuge

Old
Crow

Old
Rampart

Coleen

Porcupine

Arctic Circle

Bettles
Evansville

Venetie

Yukon   Flats

Yukon

Arctic Circle
Allakaket
Kanuti
NWR

Stevens
Village

Beaver

Birch
Creek

Fort
Yukon

Venetie Landing

National

Wildlife Refuge

Circle

22

Yukon

Wolverine Mt
4580

Rampart

Livengood

24

Pinnell Mt
4935

Central

21

Circle
Hot Springs

Yukon-Charley
Rivers
National
Preserve

Nation

Tatonduk

Tanana

Eureka

Minto

Chatanika

Chatanika

23

Chena
Hot Springs

Chena

Eagle

19

Eagle
Village

Whitehorse

Manley
Hot Springs

Fox
Fairbanks

16

North Pole

College

17

Chena
River
SRA

Salcha

Boundary

Dawson

Ester

20

Nenana

Anderson

Richardson

Big Delta

Mt
Harper
6515

Chicken

Sulphur

Lake
Minchumina

Ferry

Suntrana

Tanana

Delta
Junction

18

Healy
Lake

Ladue

Taylor Hwy

CANADA

Diamond

see Denali National Park & Preserve map

Healy

Kantishna

Cantwell

Denali
National Park
& Preserve

15

Mt Hayes
13832

Donnelly

Rapids

Dot Lake

(The Alcan)
Mt
Kimball
10350

Tanacross

Tok

Tetlin
Junction

Northway
Junction

Northway

Beaver
Creek

Whitehorse

Koidern

Mt
Russell
11670

Mt
McKinley
20320

Denali

Paxson

Mentasta
Lake

Mentasta
Mountains

Slana

Tetlin
NWR

Petersville

Denali
State Park

14

Chulitna

Curry

Sourdough

Chistochina

Mt Sanford
16237

Nabesna

11

Chisana

Nutzotin
Mountains

Talkeetna

13

Trapper
Creek

Talkeetna
Mts

Sovereign
Mt
8846

Lake
Louise

Gulkana

Gakona

Tanada Pk
9358

12

Skwentna

Hayes
Glacier

Mt
Torbert
11413

Yentna

Independence
Mine

Chickaloon

Glennallen

Copper
Center

Mt Wrangell
14163

Wrangell
Mountains

Mt Blackburn
16390

Mt Bona
16421

Kennecott

9

St Elias Mts

Chakachamna
Lake

see Matanuska-Susitna Valley map

Hogston

Wasilla

Palmer
Eklutna

Chugiak

Mt Marcus
Baker
13176

Tazlina
Lake

Lower
Tonsina

Chitina

10

McCarthy

Chitina

Mt
Logan
19850

Knik

Eagle River

Chugach
State Park

Columbia
Glacier

Klutina
Lake

Tonsina

Wrangell-St Elias
National Park & Preserve

7

Tyonek

Anchorage

1

Girdwood

Matanuska
Glacier

Thompson
Pass
2771

Chugach   Mountains

Mt Bona
16421

Saint Elias
18008

Mt
Torbert

Captain
Cook SRA

Kenai
NWR

Hope

Portage

Valdez

5

Bridal Veil
Falls

Cordova Peak
7730

Bagley Icefield

Bering
Glacier

Cape
Yakataga

Ice Bay

Malaspina
Glacier

Kustatan

Nikiski

Sterling

Kenai

Soldotna

Kasilof

Kenai

Whittier

3

Moose
Pass

Cooper
Landing

Tatitlek

Prince
William
Sound

Mt Eyak
Ski Area

6

Cordova

Mt
Tom White
11210

Chugach   National   Forest

Cook

Clam
Gulch

Kenai

NWR

Peninsula

Chenega

Seward

Sargent
Icefield

Hinchinbrook
Island

Katalla

Controller
Bay

Kayak
Island

Ninilchik

Tustumena
Lake

Latouche

Hinchinbrook Entrance

Anchor
Point

Homer

Kachemak

Kachemak Bay

Kachemak
Bay SP

Kenai
Fjords
National
Park

Blying
Sound

Montague
Island

Cape
Saint Elias

Seldovia

English
Bay

Portlock

Kachemak
Bay SWP

Pye Islands

Resurrection Bay

Chugach Islands

Kennedy Entrance

Stevenson Entrance

Shuyak Island
State Park

Dutch Harbor

see Kenai Peninsula map

Gulf of Alaska

N

Southcentral and
Interior Alaska

0   100 miles

0   100 km

SOUTHCENTRAL ALASKA

This awe-inspiring region includes Anchorage, Matanuska-Susitna Valley, Prince William Sound, Copper River Valley, and the Kenai Peninsula, and is where mountains, rivers, and fjords meet Alaska's urban center.

A floatplane on Lake Hood.

Southcentral Alaska extends from the coastal fjords, glaciers and forests of the Kenai Peninsula and Prince William Sound areas, northeast through the remote Copper River Valley, or northwest through Anchorage (Alaska's largest city, in terms of population), then past the picturesque farmlands and sobering mountain ranges of the Matanuska-Susitna Valley, and finally to the wild, southern boundary of the alluring Denali National Park and Preserve.

The various communities that contributed to the development of Southcentral are as diverse as the land itself. Athabascans were the first inhabitants of much of the area, though Alutiiq and Eyak peoples populated the area now called Cordova. Intrepid explorers from Russia traveled to the mainland of Alaska beginning in 1741, and were soon followed by other adventurers from Britain, Spain, and America.

The discovery of valuable minerals, primarily copper and gold, drew boatloads of prospectors to the area, prompted the construction of two railroad systems in the early 1900s, and spawned many of the communities of both the Copper River Valley and Prince William Sound, as well as Seward, Anchorage, Palmer/Wasilla, and Talkeetna. From 1939 to 1957, US military construction created new roads, airports and harbors throughout the region.

Anchorage's Saturday market.

ACHIEVABLE ADVENTURES

Because of the mind-boggling size and scope of the state, today's visitors to Alaska are faced with a difficult choice: which area should one explore during the typical two-week vacation? In many ways, it could be argued that Southcentral Alaska, because of the climate, location, availability of goods and services, road system and transportation options, may well provide the greatest number (and variety) of easily accessible adventure options.

Anchorage is not Alaska's capital, but has many of the attributes of a capital city. Approximately 42 percent of Alaska's total population lives here. Most visitors to Southcentral arrive via commercial airlines into Anchorage, by cruise ship (through Whittier, Seward, and the Anchorage cruise-ship terminal), or by Alaska Marine Highway System ferry (through Whittier). Southcentral's towns and points of interest are well connected by road, and thus easily accessible by car, RV, or bus.

FLIGHTSEEING OPPORTUNITIES

Every town in Alaska, regardless of size, has some sort of airport, ranging from the modern Ted Stevens Anchorage International Airport, to unpaved strips in the bush. Pilots also land on beaches, gravel bars, and lakes

where no constructed facilities exist. Air taxis can be chartered in most communities to take you to outlying villages, on day trips for dramatic flightseeing opportunities, or they will drop you off in remote areas for a backcountry experience, and return to pick you up at a pre-arranged time and location.

In addition to traveling to and within Southcentral by air, sea or road, there is also the delightful and scenic option of 'riding the rails.' While no US nor Canadian rail system provides rail service to Alaska, the Alaska Railroad (www.alaskarailroad.com) provides excellent (though not inexpensive) opportunities to see Southcen-

Moose in Chugach State Park.

tral Alaska during the summer months, connecting the Kenai Peninsula city of Seward with Anchorage, Wasilla, and Talkeetna as it travels north, and ending up in the interior city of Fairbanks.

THE CLIMATE

Summer temperatures in Southcentral Alaska are generally pleasant. Anchorage's July temperatures average from 51° to 65°F (10 to 18°C), and average yearly precipitation is 15ins (38cm) – compared to 162ins (411cm) in Ketchikan, and 5ins (13cm) in Barrow. While some summers in Southcentral may well be cool and rainy, the rain comes mostly in a constant sort of drizzle; you may yearn for sunshine, but your vacation plans will likely be unaffected. And when the sun does shine, it hardly knows when to stop. Anchorage enjoys more than 19 hours of daylight at the summer solstice (June 20 or 21).

Plan to dress in layers for a visit to Southcentral Alaska. Long pants (although the locals, especially the younger ones, will likely be wearing shorts in the summer),

An indigenous drummer.

a short-sleeved T-shirt, a light rain- and wind-resistant hooded jacket, and comfortable, casual walking shoes would be perfect for a summer visit. Add a fleece jacket, a knit hat, and gloves if you plan to go out on the water for a day cruise. If it's overcast or rainy, with even a slight wind, you'll be glad for the extra warmth.

Unusually strong fall colors on the Seward Highway.

Fur Rondy fireworks over downtown Anchorage.

ANCHORAGE

Anchorage is a good jumping-off point for many parts of the state, but it has a lot more to offer, from interesting museums to lively nightlife, and ski slopes right on the doorstep.

Imagine you're a passenger aboard one of the many domestic and international air carriers serving **Anchorage ❶** daily. About three hours out of Seattle, the pilot announces you'll be landing in Anchorage in a few minutes – but, as you peer out of the window, you can see few signs of civilization.

Just as you're beginning to wonder if the pilot has lost his way, you spot Anchorage. Sitting on a roughly triangular piece of land that sticks out into Cook Inlet, with Turnagain Arm bordering the southwest shore and Knik Arm the northwest one, the city sprawls out over a 10-mile (16km) length, seeming to spread over most of the available land between the inlet and the Chugach Mountains to the east.

COMMERCIAL CENTER

With almost 300,000 residents, Anchorage is the state's largest metropolis and its commercial center. This port city developed from a railroad tent camp to a city of high-rise offices, ethnic restaurants, and world-class trail systems for biking, hiking, and skiing.

Captain James Cook, the British explorer, sailed into Cook Inlet in 1778, while looking for a Northwest Passage to the Atlantic. Trading furs and fish with the Dena'ina Natives, he noticed that they carried iron and

copper weapons, the first evidence of trade with the Russians who had set up trading posts in lower Cook Inlet and at Kodiak.

Russian influences can still be seen today at Eklutna, a Dena'ina village inside the northern boundary of the municipality of Anchorage.

When Cook found no way out of the arm of Cook Inlet to the south of Anchorage, he ordered his ships, the *Resolution* and the *Discovery*, to turn around, hence the name 'Turnagain.' Knik Arm gets its name from the Inuit

⚓ Main attractions
Ship Creek
Imaginarium Discovery Center
Alaska Native Heritage Center
Alaska Zoo
Girdwood
Eagle River Nature Center
Eklutna Village Historical Park
Alyeska Resort and Ski Area

📍
Maps on pages 164, 170, 174

In the Port of Anchorage.

word for fire, knik, which was used in reference to the Dena'ina people and their villages.

THE GOLD RUSH

After Alaska was purchased from the Russians in 1867, gold seekers worked the land along Turnagain Arm and at Crow Creek and Girdwood, which is now the southern boundary of the municipality. The gold rush rapidly spread north and across Knik Arm. The old mining supply center of Knik is located across the inlet from downtown Anchorage.

During its short history, Anchorage has reverberated with the sounds of several major construction booms: laying track for the Alaska Railroad, building two adjacent military bases during World War II, the discovery and development of the Cook Inlet and Kenai Peninsula oil fields, and, in the 1970s, the construction of the 800-mile (1,285km) trans-Alaska oil pipeline from Prudhoe Bay to Valdez. The most recent boom has been of the retail variety: several national chains

have opened stores in Anchorage in the mid-1990s.

RUGGED INDIVIDUALISM

The Good Friday earthquake of 1964, measuring 9.2 on the Richter scale, was the most powerful earthquake ever recorded in North America, and it brought Alaskans together to work for a common cause. While the quake devastated many homes and businesses in Anchorage and in other communities, the reconstruction generated a mini-boom and Anchorage emerged a new city. Quakes still shake Anchorage and Southcentral Alaska occasionally, including a 7.9 tremor in 2002 and a 5.8 quake in 2012. In 2018, a 7.1-magnitude earthquake hit Anchorage, injuring 117 people.

During the past decade Anchorage has begun to overcome the consequences of its boom-and-bust economy – unemployment, out-migration, poverty, to name a few. While the record high fuel prices of 2008 kept Alaska's economy relatively strong through the beginning of the most

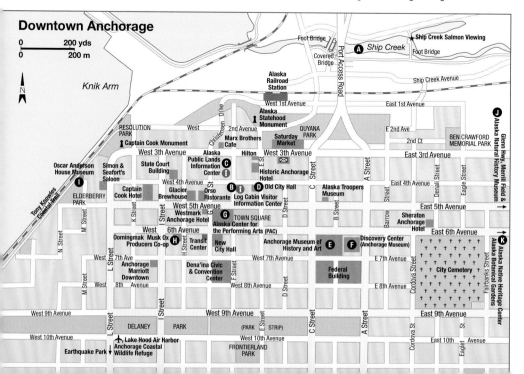

recent economic downturn, its growing reliance on tourist dollars keeps the majority of Alaskans working in the service sector on edge. In 2010, the major cruise lines added the port of Anchorage to their itineraries, keeping the tourist dollars flowing.

BACKYARD WILDERNESS

Some people move to Anchorage from other parts of the USA because they are attracted by the idea of adventurous living at the 'last frontier.' This is a city where one needs only to walk out of the back door to see – and, in some cases, step into – the wilderness.

Although some residents take off on weekends to pursue various outdoor activities, many others find no need to get away. Not surprising, perhaps, when it is quite common to see a moose outside the living room window, or a bald eagle flying overhead, and when you can share city parks with lynx, owls, and bears. Even wolf packs sometimes prowl the city's edges. Wildlife is so ubiquitous that no one who lives here blinks when they

see a moose along the Glenn Highway. An estimated 1,500 moose, 2,400 Dall sheep, and 250 black bears live in the metropolitan Anchorage area and nearby foothills.

Fishing enthusiasts have to go no further than **Ship Creek Ⓐ**, on the north side of downtown, to have the chance of catching a 40lb (18kg) salmon. The king salmon run lasts from May to early July, and the silver salmon (also known as Coho) run from late July until later October. For regulations, check www.adfg.alaska.gov.

DISCOVERING THE CITY

Anchorage is an air crossroads, with several major airlines offering direct flights, primarily from Seattle, but also from other US cities, Tokyo, and the Russian Far East. It is as close to London or Tokyo as it is to Houston. More than 200 flights arrive daily at the Anchorage International Airport.

If you are staying Downtown, you can easily explore this section of the city on foot. Start at the **Log Cabin Visitor Information Center Ⓑ** (tel:

Flowers in Anchorage.

Cyclists on the Bird Point to Girdwood trail.

907-257-2363; daily mid Sept–mid-May 9am–4pm, June–Aug 8am–7pm, until 6pm second half of May and first half of Sept) on the corner of Fourth Avenue and F Street. The center is housed in a log cabin built in 1954, which is surrounded by flowering foliage in the summer. Note the 5,145lb (2,333kg) block of solid jade, the state's official gemstone, outside the cabin. Here you can pick up maps and brochures, including a booklet outlining a suggested walking tour; or you could walk a block down the street and take one of the local trolley tours.

From here, you can cross the road diagonally to reach the **Alaska Public Lands Information Center ⓒ** (tel: 907-644-3661; www.alaskacenters.gov; summer daily 9am–5pm, winter Tue–Fri 10am–5pm). You can see wildlife exhibits, watch videos on the regions and activities available, and generally pick up all the information you'll need.

Armed with this information, you can then continue your urban tour. First go back to the **Old City Hall ⓓ**, a classic 1930s construction next door to the log cabin, where the lobby holds a display of photographs and other exhibits that trace the city's history.

Continue your walking tour by heading east along Fourth Avenue. You will pass many T-shirt shops and stores offering Native art, including carved walrus ivory, soapstone, and baskets. Genuine Native American crafts are identified by a tag, either showing a silver hand or stating 'Authentic Native Handicraft.'

Three blocks past the mall (and the main post office), turn right down C Street to the glass and steel **Anchorage Museum** at **Rasmuson Center ⓔ** (tel: 907-929-9200; www.anchoragemuseum.org; summer daily 9am–6pm, winter Tue–Sat 10am–6pm, Sun noon–6pm). Among the museum's permanent collections are the Alaska Gallery, with historical exhibits, and a fine selection of native art and works by travelers, explorers and early residents, displayed in sky-lit galleries.

The museum houses the **Imaginarium Discovery Center ⓕ** (tel: 907-929-9200; summer daily 9am–6pm, winter Tue–Sat 10am–6pm, Sun noon–6pm). While aimed primarily at children, this award-winning science center has a wealth of exhibits and hands-on experiences that are also popular with adults. If you want to know more about marine life, wetlands and the solar system, this is a good place to explore. Also found at the museum is the Smithsonian Arctic Studies Center, a planetarium, and the Muse Restaurant, which serves lunch and dinner throughout the week and brunch on the weekends. Buy an Alaska Cultural Pass and save 30 percent of the entry fee to both the museum and the Alaska Native Heritage Center in summer.

ARTS CENTER

A few blocks west is the **Alaska Center for the Performing Arts ⓖ** (tel: 907-263-2787; www.myalaska

⊘ FUR RONDY

Fur Rendezvous ('Fur Rondy') is a 10-day celebration (late Feb–early Mar) featuring more than 150 events, ranging from sled dog races to the annual snowshoe softball tournament between 9th and 10th avenues on the Delaney Park Strip. Competitions are held for the best snow sculpture (which draws competitors from as far away as Japan) and the hardiest feet in the Frostbite Footrace. Other events include the traditional Eskimo blanket toss and the largest outdoor public fur auction in the United States. The highlight of the carnival is the World Championship Sled Dog Race. For three days competitors run heats totaling 75 miles (120km). Participants start on Fourth Avenue and continue to the outskirts of town where they circle back. Dog mushing is the official state sport.

On the last Saturday of Fur Rondy (usually in early March), the Miners' and Trappers' Ball is held. Everyone in the city is invited, although tickets must be purchased in advance. It is held in a huge warehouse and people arrive in every conceivable attire, some hoping to win the contest for the most unusual costume. Fur Rondy is when Alaskans let down their hair and celebrate all that is original about their state.

As the event is becoming more popular, it is best to book well in advance. Contact Greater Anchorage Inc. for the exact dates of the festival and travel deals (400 D Street; tel: 907-274-1177; www.furrondy.net).

center.com). Some view this building (locally referred to as 'the PAC') as a monstrosity, while others consider it to be architecturally innovative, but its lush flower garden beds certainly add to the beauty of the downtown area.

Alaskan artists have designed much of the interior, including the carpets and upholstery, and the center is decorated with numerous Native masks. Tours are available, but by appointment only. There is no set charge, but a donation is appreciated.

Also, while you're there, those who long to see a display of the Northern Lights may do so, virtually speaking, via a 40-minute digital show set to music. Twenty-five years worth of nature's light shows may be seen within the PAC, at the Sidney Laurence Theater (tel: 907-263-2787; www. thealaskacollection.com; end May–early Sept, call for schedule). The PAC is also a hub of activities for the arts. Check local newspapers, especially the Anchorage Daily News, and visitors' guides for events.

One block further west, on the corner of Sixth Avenue and H Street, you will find the **Oomingmak Musk Ox Producers' Co-op** ❶ (tel: 907-272-9225; www.qiviut.com) where you can buy, or just admire, distinctive garments made of musk ox wool, called qiviut (pronounced *kee-vee-ute*). These are made in Inuit villages.

Continue west a few blocks along Fifth Avenue to M Street, to the **Oscar Anderson House Museum** ❶ (tel: 907-929-9870; www.aahp-online.net/oscar-anderson-house-museum.html; summer tours Tue–Thur and Sat noon–4pm, Fri by appointment), set in the attractive little Elderberry Park. Listed on the National Register of Historic Places, this is Anchorage's first wood-frame house, built by Swedish immigrant Anderson in 1915.

If you find yourself in Anchorage in the summer, the Anchorage Market and Festival (May–Sept Sat 10am–6pm, Sun 10am–5pm) is worth a stop. Filling up the large parking lot on West Third Street between C and E streets, hundreds of vendors hawk fresh

The Anchorage Museum of History and Art.

A child enjoying the exhibits at the Imaginarium.

Drummers at the Alaska Native Heritage Center.

Alaska produce, local tribal crafts, and a wide variety of takeaway food that range from espresso drinks and pizza to gyros and smoked fish. Live music keeps things festive, and it seems as if all of Anchorage shows up, particularly on sunny days.

LEAVING DOWNTOWN BEHIND

Outside the downtown area, but worth seeing, especially if you have dinosaur enthusiasts in tow is the **Alaska Museum of Natural History J** (201 North Bragaw Street, tel: 907-274-2400, www.alaskamuseum.org, Tue–Fri 10am–5pm, Sat 11am–4pm). Full of

hands-on displays and artifacts from Alaska's prehistoric past, visitors learn about the amazing variety of polar dinosaurs and ice age animals that once roamed Alaska.

Travel the Glenn Highway to the Muldoon Road Exit to reach the **Alaska Native Heritage Center K** (tel: 907-330-8000; www.alaskanative.net; summer daily 9am–5pm), a gathering place for all of Alaska's native cultures where you can learn about traditional customs and see master artists at work.

Turning south on Muldoon Road will take you to the Alaska Botanical Garden (4601 Campbell Airstrip Road;

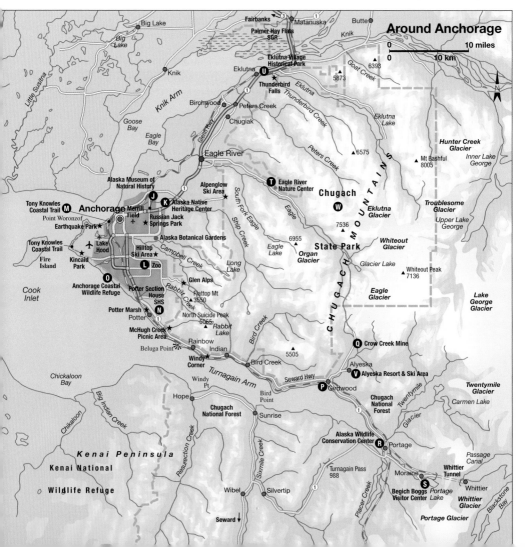

tel: 907-770-3692; mid-May–mid-Sept daily 9am–7pm). Filling the 110-acre (44.5-hectare) garden are over 1,000 species of native plants carefully tended and arranged into themed gardens. There is a mile-long interpretive trail to guide you through.

ALASKA ZOO

Visitors unable to see a bear in the wild can see several (polar, brown, and black) at the **Alaska Zoo ❶** (4731 O'Malley Road; tel: 907-346-2133; www.alaskazoo.org; summer daily 9am–9pm, winter 10am–4pm). A shuttle bus operates from the Hilton, Captain Cook, and Sheraton hotels.

The 25-acre (62-hectare) zoo houses approximately 100 birds and mammals, including natives such as moose, musk oxen, caribou, seals and otters, but also such non-natives as alpacas, Amur tigers, and a Bactrian camel. The zoo had its genesis in 1966 when a local grocer, Jack Snyder, won a contest offering as a prize $3,000 or a baby Asian elephant, Annabelle. He chose the elephant and the idea of a zoo took shape.

TONY KNOWLES COASTAL TRAIL

Anchorage is a great place for cyclists, with more than 120 miles (190km) of paved paths, and plenty of bikes for rent (ask at the Visitor Information Center log cabin).

The best-known and most scenic route is the **Tony Knowles Coastal Trail ⓜ**, which starts near Elderberry Park on Second Avenue. The trail (www.alaska.org/detail/tony-knowles-coastal-trail) – which bicyclists share with walkers, joggers, rollerbladers, and stroller-pushing parents, and the occasional moose – is 11 miles (19km) long and parallels Cook Inlet, continuing past Westchester Lagoon and Point Woronzof, and ending at Kincaid Park.

Along the way, it passes through Earthquake Park, founded on the spot where, during the 1964 earthquake, 130 acres (52 hectares) of land fell into the inlet and 75 houses were destroyed. If you are not on a bike, you can reach the park by driving to the end of Northern Lights Boulevard toward the inlet. A walking trail and interpretive signs and monuments make it worth the stop, and there are good views of the city and Denali.

In winter, the Tony Knowles Trail becomes a cross-country ski trail. There are other bike routes in town. Trail maps are also available from the Parks and Recreation department, as well as at the Visitors Information Center. Bicycling is an ideal way to get around, and offers great views of the city and the waters of the inlet, where migrating beluga whales are sometimes seen on the surface.

Another popular excursion is to Flattop Mountain, which is arguably the most climbed peak in Alaska. At 3,510ft (1,070 meters) high, the mountain offers incredible views over Anchorage, the Alaska Range, Chugach Range,

⊙ WHAT TO DO AFTER DARK

The Crow's Nest at the top of the Captain Cook Hotel (on the corner of Fifth Avenue and K Street; tel: 907-276-6000.www.captaincook.com/dining/crows-nest) has gourmet cuisine and a formal atmosphere, together with great views. But if you fancy a taste of nightlife in the last frontier, complete with sawdust on the floor, you won't do much better than Chilkoot Charlie's (www.koots.com) on Spenard Road. Don't bother with a coat and tie; this is where Alaskans go in their boots and jeans to dance, drink, and be entertained.

The Bear Tooth Theaterpub and Grill (www.beartooththeatre.net), just off Spenard Road, offers second-run movies on a big-screen, tasty food and draft beer or wine. Humpy's (www.humpysalaska.com), across from the PAC (Performing Arts Center), serves their proprietary brew, plus others from the region, along with quality food; they also host live music performances. Anchorage has several cinemas and theaters, as well as events that take place at the PAC – see the local press for listings.

One popular award-winning theater is Cyrano's (3800 Debarr Rd; for schedule and fee information visit www.cyranos.org or call 907-274-2599). This theater/coffeehouse/bookstore entertains locals and visitors with live theater, comedy improv, poetry readings, and more. Customers may enjoy beer and wine along with a selection of appetizers and desserts.

On the Tony Knowles Coastal Trail.

Girdwood ski station.

and the Cook Inlet. In summer, Flattop Mountain Shuttle provides transportation from downtown Anchorage to the Glen Alps Trailhead. For more information, visit www.hike-anchorage-alaska.com.

AROUND ANCHORAGE

If you want to experience the Alaska outdoor life, try a flightseeing trip. Excursions can easily be arranged by flight operators at Lake Hood or at Merrill Field. Not far from Downtown near the international airport is **Lake Hood Air Harbor**, the busiest seaplane base in the world.

Channels on Lake Hood and Lake Spenard provide the runways for these seaplanes. Merrill Field (800 Merrill Field Drive), located one mile east of downtown Anchorage just off the Glenn Highway, was the first real airport in Anchorage and still today serves as a commercial service airport for the general aviation community. Alaskans fly into the bush for fishing, hunting, hiking, and myriad other activities. Flight operators at Lake Hood or at Merrill

Field can easily arrange flightseeing excursions.

At Anchorage's gateway to the east is **Chugach State Park**; the park headquarters are located on Seward Highway milepost 115 across from Potter Marsh in the **Potter Section House State Historic Site** (tel: 907-345-5014; Mon–Fri 10am–noon 1–4.30pm). Here you will find a railroad museum and an old rotary snowplow on the track behind the house. Chugach State Park covers 495,000 acres (200,500 hectares) and offers visitors a wide variety of opportunities to experience the Alaska outdoors without being too far away from civilization.

SOUTH OF THE CITY

With only one main road leading in and out of Anchorage, selecting a day trip is easy: you go north or south. Heading south on Seward Highway, visit Girdwood, Crow Creek Mine and Portage Glacier. The drive parallels the Turnagain Arm, an extension of Cook Inlet, and offers breathtaking

views and wildlife viewing opportunities. For those with sturdy legs and time to spare, there is a bike trail flanking the highway all the way down to Portage.

Beginning at the southern edge of town, you can see a variety of waterfowl at **Potter Marsh**, part of the **Anchorage Coastal Wildlife Refuge O**. This 2,300-acre (920-hectare) wetland area is the nesting ground for migratory birds during the summer. Bald eagles, Arctic terns, trumpeter swans, sandhill cranes, shorebirds, and many species of geese and ducks are commonly spotted; Canada geese and mallards raise their young here. From the boardwalk that borders Potter Marsh's western edge, salmon are visible from mid-July to September as they return to spawn in nearby Rabbit Creek.

Not far from Potter Marsh, down the Seward Highway, visitors have a chance to see larger wildlife. During spring and summer it is common to see Dall sheep peering over the rocks of the adjacent cliffs at passing motorists; the best viewing is at **Windy Corner**, near Mile 107. Several spots on this road allow visitors to pull over and watch the waters for belugas, the small white whales that chase salmon up the Turnagain Arm. Stop at **Beluga Point Interpretive Site**, where you will find spotting 'scopes, benches and information about the area.

If you just want to contemplate the beauty and mammoth size of Alaska, you can grab a take-out lunch in town and picnic at nearby **McHugh Creek Picnic Area**, just a few miles down the road from Potter Marsh. Here you can see miles down the inlet, look at the majestic mountains on the other shore, and take a short hike along the 9.5-mile (15km) long Turnagain Arm Trail.

Off Mile 90 of the Seward Highway, the Alyeska Highway will take you into the forested town of **Girdwood P**. A quaint community, it sees an influx of tourists in the summer and skiers in the winter. A ride on the Alyeska Ski Resort tram on a clear day provides

You can view various types of waterfowl at Potter Marsh.

Contestants at the World Beard and Moustache Competition.

Children examine owl pellets to learn about owl ecology.

an incredible view of the surrounding mountains and the inlet.

Outside Girdwood, 3 miles (5km) up Crow Creek Road, is **Crow Creek Mine** (tel: 907-229-3105; www.crowcreekmine.com summer daily 9am–6pm). The placer mine and its eight original buildings, listed on the National Register of Historic Sites, represent the first non-native settlement in the area. Visitors can pan for gold in this scenic setting, and for the robust, nearby **Crow Pass Trail** climbs through beautiful mountain valleys.

Continuing down the Seward Highway, at **Twentymile River**, visitors may often see Arctic terns, bald eagles, mew gulls, and moose from the observation platform. Plaques on the platform have information on the various species.

Just beyond is the **Alaska Wildlife Conservation Center** (Mile 79, Seward Highway; tel: 907-783-2025; www.alaskawildlife.org; Jan & Dec Fri–Mon 10am–3pm, Feb 10am–4pm, Mar, Apr and Oct 10am–5pm, May–Aug 8.30am–7pm, Sept 9am–6pm,

Nov Fri–Mon 10am–4pm) is a 140-acre (57-hectare) drive-through animal park that is dedicated to the rehabilitation of orphaned and injured animals. Get a close-up look at Alaska's wildlife, and visit its new bear interpretive center, the only one of its kind in North America.

Mile 78.9 is the turn-off for **Portage Glacier**. Following your turn, look on the right-hand side of the road to see Explorer Glacier (there's an excellent vantage point for photographers). Stop at the bridge over Williwaw Creek to see salmon spawning from late July to mid-September. Sadly, Portage Glacier is rapidly retreating, and with it the once dramatic view of Portage Lake with its huge blue icebergs.

At the end of the road is the **Begich Boggs Visitor Center** (tel: summer 907-783-2326, winter 907-783-3242; www.fs.usda.gov; summer daily 9am–6pm). The center's state-of-the-art displays cover the natural history of Chugach National Forest. Don't miss an award-winning documentary film,

Voices from the Ice, shown hourly during the summer (charge).

BLACK BEAR TERRITORY

There are several impressive glaciers in Portage Valley with a number of trails where visitors can view glacial features, including a profusion of wildflowers and plant life. Take the short walk to **Byron Glacier**. Signs near Portage Glacier Lodge mark the road to the trailhead. Black bears, smaller cousins of the grizzly, are commonly seen in this area. If you wish to continue south to the Prince William Sound community of Whittier (see page 186), Portage Glacier Road connects to the Portage Glacier Highway where for a toll of $13, you can pass through North America's longest combined railroad and vehicle tunnel. Call 877-611-2586 for further details on road and tunnel opening information.

HEADING NORTH

Traveling on the Glenn Highway north of Anchorage on a day trip, visitors have an opportunity to observe the cultural remnants of Alaska's past and to enjoy several scenic areas in the fertile Matanuska-Susitna Valley.

In Eagle River, stop at the **Eagle River Nature Center ❶** (tel: 907-694-2108; www.ernc.org; May–Sept Wed–Sun 10am–5pm, Oct–Apr Fri–Sun 10am–5pm), 14 miles (20km) out of town in Chugach State Park. At the end of the 12-mile (19km) -long Eagle River Road, it is 15 to 20 minutes from downtown Eagle River. The drive through the lake-dotted valley is worth the trip in itself, and once at the center there are displays, nature videos, and several hiking trails, from easy to rigorous. During August the berries are plentiful, and cross-country skiing is a popular winter activity. Continuing on the Glenn Highway, you will see beautiful **Mirror Lake** wayside area on the right. Here, if you're brave, you can swim in the icy water on a warm day, or ice fish in the winter. A mile further takes you to the entrance of **Thunderbird Falls Trailhead**, also in Chugach State Park. This is a pleasant 1-mile (2km) walk to the rushing falls.

Switchbacks on the way to Crow Pass.

Spectacular **Eklutna Lake** is Anchorage's largest lake. There is a state park campground and a wide, multi-use trail to **Eklutna Glacier**, whose waters feed the lake, good wildlife viewing and berry picking.

The Anchorage area's oldest building may well be the **St Nicholas Russian Orthodox Church**, which is part of **Eklutna Village Historical Park**  (www.eklutnahistoricalpark.org; mid-May–mid-Sep Mon–Fri 10am–5pm; services held Thu and Sat 5pm, Sun 9am) on the Eklutna turn-off, off the Glenn Highway. It was constructed with hand-hewn logs, and the surrounding spirit houses represent the interaction between the Natives and the Russians.

This was the site of the first Dena'ina Indian settlement east of the Knik Arm, in around 1650. The 'spirit' houses show how Native beliefs were mixed with Russian orthodoxy. Spirit houses were placed over traditional graves and contained personal items thought to help the spirit in the afterlife. A three-bar Orthodox cross was placed at the foot of the grave.

A skier skins up a slope in the Hatcher Pass backcountry.

Small spirit houses indicate the resting place of a child and a large house with a smaller one inside means a mother and child were buried together. A picket fence around a spirit house means that the deceased was not a Dena'ina.

WINTER ACTIVITIES

Winters are long in Alaska, but Alaskans have found ways of coping with the season: from competitions to festivals. After the Christmas holiday season, Anchorage residents prepare for their own 10-day carnival in February – **Fur Rendezvous** (see box).

SKI AREAS

Downhill and cross-country skiing in Anchorage can be found in at the **Hilltop Ski Area** (www.hilltopskiarea.org), which boasts a chairlift and is an excellent facility for novice skiers. It also has night skiing and is accessible by public bus. For advanced skiers, **Arctic Valley** (www.skiarctic.net) offers slightly more challenging slopes. Two chairlifts, a T-bar and three rope tows service the area, which has a 1,000ft (300-meter) drop. Runs can be very steep and maintenance is sometimes questionable.

Alaska's largest and most popular ski area – **Alyeska Resort**  (www.alyeskaresort.com) is 40 miles (64km) southeast of Anchorage in Girdwood. With a vertical drop of 2,500ft (760 meters), it caters to all levels of skiers and is a full-service resort with both day and night skiing. The area has six lifts, including a quad chairlift and four doubles, and a high-speed gondola, which operates in the summer months, taking visitors to a restaurant on the mountaintop.

CROSS-COUNTRY TRAILS

Anchorage offers more than 140 miles (225km) of cross-country trails. **Russian Jack Springs Park** offers 8 miles (13km) of trails, while **Kincaid Park** on Raspberry Road has 34 miles (55km) of Nordic ski trails, nine of them illuminated. Near Service High School and Hilltop Ski Area, another trail is lit for skiers. In Chugach State Park, just east of the city, there are dozens of hiking trails, which in winter are frequently used by cross-country skiers. The **Glen Alps** area at the top of Upper Huffman Road offers breathtaking views of the city and is manageable for skiers of any level. To get to it, take the Seward Highway to the O'Malley turn-off going east, continue toward the mountains, turning on to Hillside Drive, and making a left on Upper Huffman, then follow signs to the trailhead.

An hour's drive north of Anchorage lies an excellent cross-country ski area with a historical flavor. **Hatcher Pass** is at the heart of the majestic Talkeetna Mountains off the Glenn Highway on Fishhook Road. At the turn of the 20th century, Independence Mine was a hub of gold-mining activity. Today it is a state historic park and its abandoned buildings and machinery have become landmarks of the past.

The area has miles of groomed ski trails that pass through treeless alpine bowls and on a clear day you can see all the way down the valley to the city of **Palmer** (20 miles/32km). At the lodge, grab a cup of steaming cocoa to warm up. Cozy accommodations are also available.

Skiing from Alyeska Resort.

CHUGACH STATE PARK

Established in 1970, Anchorage's 'backyard wilderness' offers all sorts of recreational opportunities for residents and visitors within a short distance of Alaska's urban center.

◉ Main attractions

Mount Bashful
Flattop Mountain
Eagle River Nature Center
Windy Corner
Turnagain Arm
Glen Alps

Map on page 174 ◉

Just to the east of Anchorage is a rugged chain of peaks; these are the **Chugach Mountains**. Stretching 300 miles (480km) across Alaska's Southcentral region, the range arcs from Cook Inlet almost to the Canadian border. The westernmost portion, touching the edges of Alaska's largest city, is encompassed by **Chugach State Park ⓦ**, 495,000 acres (200,000 hectares) that make up the third largest state park in the United States, and that many locals consider to be their 'backyard wilderness.'

Among the oldest and largest of Alaska's state parks, Chugach was established in 1970, thanks to the determined efforts of a few Anchorage residents who wanted to protect the neighboring alpine wilderness. Their passion ignited a grassroots movement of the sort rarely seen in Alaska, before or since.

Various recreational groups – hunters, horseback riders, skiers, hikers – had tried to get the western Chugach Range preserved as parkland since the 1950s, to no avail. Then, in 1969, the state announced it would open two of the range's forested valleys to commercial logging. Appalled by the plans, four Anchorage residents – Sharon Cissna, Art Davidson, Ted Schultz, and Skip Matthews – filed a lawsuit and forced the state to cancel the sale.

CREATING A JEWEL

Though satisfying, the court victory left the foursome wanting more. In August 1969, a group of about 20 activists began a campaign to establish a wilderness park, nearly a half-million acres (200,000 hectares) in size. Within a few months, they gained the support of nearly all of Anchorage's recreational organizations. They also garnered the backing of local politicians, who pushed

Trail runners traverse tundra on Indian Peak.

a bill in the Alaska Legislature to establish a new park. Legislation to create Chugach State Park passed both the state senate and house in May 1970 and Governor Keith Miller signed it into law in August of that year. Cissna, now a state representative herself and known in some quarters as the 'mother of Chugach State Park,' still marvels at the speed and ease of the effort, more than 30 years later. 'I think it was meant to happen,' she says. 'It was a moment in time when the right people and the right idea came together at exactly the right time. And so we created a jewel.'

THE LURE OF FLATTOP

Though it is little known outside Alaska, Chugach is a wild and pristine wilderness on a par with many of America's national parklands. Within its boundaries are more than 150 peaks, dozens of glaciers, and beautiful alpine valleys that in summer are brightened by dozens of wildflower species, and crystalline mountain streams. The mountains within Chugach park are modest by Alaska standards; the highest, **Mount Bashful**, rises only to 8,005ft (2,440 meters). Yet many are steep, jagged peaks with substantial vertical relief, as they rise thousands of feet from sea level.

Still, the most popular of the Chugach's mountains is Flattop, a humble hill that looks as if its top has been sliced off. Standing only 3,550ft (1,082 meters) above Cook Inlet at its summit, **Flattop Mountain** has a special pull on locals. Less than 15 miles (24km) from downtown Anchorage, Flattop is visible throughout the city. And city roads approach to within a mile or so of its base. Easy to find and easy to reach, Flattop is also easy to climb: from the main trailhead, the mountain's summit is only

half a mile and 1,350 vertical ft away (412 meters).

The ascent is more of a strenuous hike than a climb, though some rock scrambling is necessary near the top. (That's not to say the mountain can't pose dangers: over the years, a handful of people have died on its slopes.) Most people can be up and back to the trailhead within two or three hours. All sorts take the trail to Flattop's summit, from preschoolers to senior citizens, and from hill runners to curious tourists.

Flattop is easily the most climbed peak in all of Alaska. Shuttle service to Flattop is available from downtown Anchorage at the Downtown Bicycle Rental shop (tel: 907-279-5293; www.alaska-bike-rentals.com).

For those who are more experienced and ambitious, there are dozens of peaks within a few hours of Chugach park's many trailheads. Hikers headed to Flattop may share the trail with dozens, but go a few miles beyond, and you can have an entire mountain or alpine basin to yourself.

⊘ CHUGACH TIPS

Chugach State Park is easy to reach from Anchorage. Several of its most popular trailheads can be reached from city streets, while other trails and park facilities are accessible from either the Seward or Glenn highways. Maps showing trail routes and campgrounds are available from Chugach State Park headquarters, located at Mile 115 of the Seward Highway in the Potter Section House (tel: 907-345-5014; dnr.alaska.gov/parks/aspunits/chugach/chugachindex.htm) or the Alaska Public Lands Information Center in downtown Anchorage (tel: 907-644-3680; www.alaskacenters.gov). Some three dozen trails crisscross the park, totaling nearly 200 miles (320km). This size of the park as well as its proximity to Anchorage makes it perfect for day hikes or extended backpacking trips. To make it even easier, many trailheads have parking, information displays, and latrines.

The prime visitor season is June to September, but locals frequent the park year-round. Summers tend to be cool, with overcast skies and frequent rain, often as drizzle. Summer daytime temperatures normally range from the 50s into the 60s Fahrenheit (12° to 18°C), though temperatures occasionally rise above 70°F (21°C) or sink below freezing at night. Snowstorms may occur throughout the year at higher elevations, so always be prepared, and bring extra food and clothing when undertaking any long hikes.

Parts of the park are most easily reached by helicopter.

A moose in Chugach State Park.

ABUNDANT WILDLIFE

Though it's on the perimeter of Alaska's urban center, Chugach is rich in wildlife. The park's alpine tundra, forested valley bottoms, and coastal waters are inhabited by nearly 50 species of mammals – from orca and beluga whales to little brown bats and porcupines – 100 species of birds, nine species of fish, and one amphibian, the wood frog. An estimated 2,000 Dall sheep live here, as well as some 500 mountain goats, 400 black bears, two dozen grizzlies, at least two wolf packs, and a handful of lynx.

This diversity is one reason that one of the park's most popular facilities is the **Eagle River Nature Center**, at the end of Eagle River Road off the Glenn Highway. There, visitors enjoy natural history displays, Dall sheep-spotting scopes, as well as nearby trails into the park. The center also provides year-round naturalist activities for adults and children; they range from guided hikes to bear-awareness talks, a winter astronomy program, plant and mushroom identification, and butterfly identification.

Wildlife is abundant, and therefore easy to spot elsewhere in the park. Some of the best Dall sheep-viewing in Alaska occurs along Chugach's southern edge, at a place called **Windy Corner**. From April through August, ewes and lambs and young rams inhabit steep cliffs and grassy meadows above the Seward Highway and **Turnagain Arm**, between mileposts 106 and 107.

Peak viewing occurs in June and July, after the ewes have given birth. Only rarely are the older, full-curl rams seen; they prefer backcountry solitude, away from the highway crowds.

Moose are also seen along the park's fringes. In late September, during the rutting season, large congregations of moose gather near the **Glen Alps** area. It's an amazing sight made all the more incredible when the moose let out their haunting, low-range bugle.

STATE PARKS

Alaska is famous for its national parks. The wild gems protected by the Division of Parks and Outdoor Recreation are less well known but equally breathtaking and accessible.

Established in 1970 by the Alaska Legislature, the Alaska State Parks system has become the nation's largest and grandest; its 130 or so units encompass 3.2 million acres (1.3 million hectares), while stretching more than 1,100 miles (1,770km) across Alaska. Their numbers include recreation sites and areas, historic sites and parks, marine parks, wilderness parks, state trails, and a world-famous preserve: the Alaska Chilkat Bald Eagle Preserve, which each winter attracts between 1,000 and 4,000 eagles.

While many are small and located along the road system, a handful rank among America's premier wilderness parks: Chugach, Kachemak Bay, Wood-Tikchik, Shuyak Island, and Denali.

UNSPOILED WILDERNESS

Three of those parklands – Denali, Kachemak Bay, and Wood-Tikchik – include lands and waters once proposed for national park status. Within their boundaries are rugged mountains, glaciers fed by large ice-fields, centuries-old coastal forests, high alpine meadows that grow bright with wildflowers in summer. Here too there are salmon-rich streams, enormous river-and-lake systems, and all manner of northern wildlife, from grizzlies and wolves, to Dall sheep, wolverines, little brown bats, whales, bald and golden eagles, loons and owls, and scores of songbird, shorebird, and seabird species.

Though these parks protect large expanses of unspoiled wilderness, they are, by Alaska standards, surprisingly easy to reach – and in most cases, easy to explore. Even the wildest, remotest state parks are within 325 miles (520km) of Anchorage. Chugach and Denali state parks are connected to Alaska's road system, while Kachemak Bay is a short boat ride from Homer, an end-of-the-road tourist town 220 highway miles (350km) south of Anchorage. None of the three requires air service to reach the backcountry. While Wood-Tikchik's wilderness is most easily reached by plane, the park's lowermost lake is only 20 road miles (32km) from Dillingham, the largest city in the Bristol Bay region. The most remote wilderness park, Shuyak, is less than 100 air miles (160km) from Homer.

By contrast, wilderness within Alaska's national parks in many cases is remote and expensive to reach, with a third of them within the state's Arctic region. Backcountry trips in most national parks require the use of air taxis.

Less rugged day adventures can be found at parks like the historic Independence Mine at Hatcher Pass or the Nancy Lake Recreation Area, both in the Matanuska-Sustina area. It is in parks like these where most Alaskans spend their off days hiking, picnicking, cross country skiing, snowmobiling, powerboating, or fishing. Most parks, even those with a deep backcountry are user-friendly. Many have campgrounds, public-use cabins, and trail systems and most require a small fee for parking ($5 to $10 per vehicle) or camping ($15 to $30 per night). Cabins must be reserved in advance and cost from $45 to about $90 per night.

For more details, contact Alaska's Department of Natural Resources Public Information Center, 550 West Seventh Avenue, Suite 1360, Anchorage, AK 99501-3557 (tel: 907-269-8400; dnr.alaska.gov/parks).

Flyfishing in the middle of Symphony Lake.

PRINCE WILLIAM SOUND

Glaciers, birds, and marine life are the highlights of the wild country southeast of Anchorage, yet its towns – Whittier, Valdez, and Cordova – are reminders that nature has its harsher side.

⊙ **Main attractions**

Whittier
Columbia Glacier
Montague Island
Valdez
Cordova
Copper River Delta

📍 Map on page 164

Few slide shows or promotional clips present pictures of rain in **Prince William Sound** ❷. Usually, it's sunshine flickering on water cascading from the flukes of a breaching humpback whale. Or kayakers wearing T-shirts silhouetted in front of a brilliant blue-white glacier. Or sea otters munching on crab plucked from the ocean floor. All such images are taken on the Sound's few clear days.

Each year those photographs, along with the stories told by the travelers who took them, draw more people to see the Sound's wonderful natural displays of flora and fauna, ice, forests, and mountains. Few are disappointed, yet it is wise to remember that, as in much of coastal Alaska, it rains a lot here. Often it pours.

GETTING THERE

You can savor the atmosphere of Prince William Sound most simply on a ferry or tour boat. **Whittier** ❸ (population 208) is where many people begin a tour of the Sound. It is easily reached by road from Anchorage through a tunnel in the Chugach Mountains. A road connecting Whittier to the Seward Highway opened in 2000. Historically, the site where Whittier stands was a resting place for native and Russian traders carrying their wares between the Sound and Cook Inlet. Later, gold miners and mail carriers crossed Portage Pass to reach the Iditarod Trail, which led to Alaska's far-northwest gold fields (now better known for Alaska's biggest sled dog race). But Whittier didn't really develop until World War II, when the army used its ice-free harbor for a strategic fuel dump and the town became an important military port. Troops blasted two tunnels through the Chugach Mountains to connect Whittier with the Alaska Railroad depot at Portage.

Prince William Sound.

In the 1964 earthquake (see page 55), Whittier was hit by three successive tidal waves, one of which crested at 104ft (32 meters), and a huge amount of damage was done to the town and its harbor. Now, there's not a lot to see in Whittier, a town of two tall concrete apartment blocks built by the military, one of which houses all Whittier's residents, while the other is abandoned. If you have some time to spare, there are hiking trails, a campground, and a museum located at the bottom floor of the Anchor Inn (tel: 907-472-2354; www.anchorinnwhittier. com), Whittier's lone hotel. At the dock you can also find plenty of charter fishermen and wildlife tours happy to take you out on a day cruise. Kayak tours and rentals are also available. It is best to plan your trip to Whittier ahead of time. For more information contact the Whittier Chamber of Commerce (www. whittieralaskachamber.org).

COLUMBIA GLACIER

Passengers traveling by boat between Whittier and Valdez sometimes see bears and, occasionally, goats balanced on cliffs above them. Humpback and killer whales frequent the route, and Dall porpoises surf the bow wake. Sea lions haul out on rocks, and harbor seals rest on chunks of ice that drift with the wind and tide away from the glaciers. There are dozens of glaciers in the Sound, and some calve huge chunks of ice into the ocean in spectacular explosions of spray. **Columbia Glacier** ❹ is the largest among the many that drop down from the Chugach Mountains into the northerly fjords of Prince William Sound.

Fed each year by enough snow to bury a five-story building, Columbia Glacier covers an area the size of Los Angeles. It flows more than 40 miles (64km) from the mountains to Columbia Bay, where its 4-mile (7km) -wide face daily drops hundreds of thousands of tons of pristine ice into the sound.

The glacier's output of ice increased in 1983, when it began a rapid retreat. Now, glaciologists estimate that 50 cubic miles (210 cubic km) of

Kayaking in Prince William Sound.

The Alaska Railroad connects Chugach Mountains to Whittier.

icebergs could possibly be released during the next half century. So much ice has filled the bay in recent years that boats can't approach the glacier as closely as they could in the past, when passengers were provided with a close-up view of massive flakes peeling from the 300ft (90-meter) wall. When the flakes come down, the harbor seals resting on bergs in the bay are rocked by the resulting swells. They don't even look up.

Meanwhile, gulls and other birds swarm around the glacier face; the plunging ice stirs the seafood-rich water, bringing shrimp and other delicacies to the surface for their consumption. Thus, the glaciers are an intrinsic part of the life cycle of Prince William Sound.

QUAKES AND TIDAL WAVES

Forces other than slow-moving glaciers also shape the land. Earthquakes cause sudden, dramatic changes in the lay of the country. On March 27, 1964 – Good Friday – bedrock shifted just west of Columbia

Glacier in the Prince William Sound.

Glacier. The shock waves, believed to have registered 9.2 on the Richter scale, were the most intense ever recorded in North America. In just a few minutes, extensive new beach lines emerged as the land rose in some areas; in other places the ground sank, killing large stands of trees. The most dramatic geological adjustment occurred at the southern end of **Montague Island**, which tilted upward 38ft (11.5 meters).

But tsunamis did the most damage. Whittier suffered badly, but among the worst human disasters was that at **Chenega**, a village of 82 on an island south of Whittier near the western edge of the sound. A wave enveloped all the buildings but the school and one house, and swept away 26 residents. The village was rebuilt on another site 25 years later.

VALDEZ

Valdez ❺, the next port of call for ferry and tour boats after Whittier and situated to the east of the earthquake epicenter, was completely

⊘ PRINCE WILLIAM SOUND SIGHTS

Various tour companies offer day trips into the many fjords surrounding Whittier. Tidewater glaciers thrill visitors and seasoned boat captains alike with their sudden, percussive, cracking sounds followed by thunderous roars as massive chunks of ice break loose and crash down into the sea. Larger companies, like Phillips Cruises and Tours (800-544-0529/907-276-8023; www.phillipscruises.com), will arrange transportation from Anchorage via motorcoach or train, and a day cruise into western Prince William Sound.

Exciting glacier tours operate out of Valdez as well. Stan Stevens Cruises (tel: 866-867-1297; www.stephenscruises.com), for example, offers comfortable six-hour tours to visit the magnificent Columbia Glacier (the largest tidewater glacier in Southcentral Alaska), or a nine-hour cruise to witness the active calving of Meares Glacier in the eastern area of the Sound.

The surrounding coastal areas provide rich habitat for whales, sea lions, puffins, seals, sea otters, bears, goats, and eagles (and much more), and multiple sightings are common. For a complete listing of tour options for both Whittier and Valdez, contact the Whittier Chamber of Commerce (www.whittieralaskachamber.org) or the Valdez Convention and Visitors Bureau (tel: 907-835-2984; www.valdezalaska.org).

destroyed, and had to be rebuilt on a different site. The tsunami that wiped out the waterfront also killed 32 people. Consequently there are no buildings of historic interest in Valdez, but it's a lively town of just under 4,000 residents, which grew to prosperity as the terminus of the trans-Alaska pipeline. The setting, between the Sound and the Chugach Mountains, is splendid.

For more information, drop in at the **Valdez Convention and Visitors Bureau** on 309 Fairbanks Drive (tel: 907-835-2984; www.valdezalaska. org; summer Mon–Sat 8am–8pm, Sun noon–5pm, winter Mon–Fri 10am–4pm). Next, drop by the **Valdez Museum and Historical Archive** (tel: 907-835-2764; www.valdezmuseum.org; daily 9am–5pm) on Egan Drive a block away. It is worth a visit to see a variety of exhibits, including one on the *Exxon Valdez* oil spill. Don't pass up a trip to the harbor, where you can watch fishermen unload their catch while enjoying a halibut sandwich at one of many harborside joints.

In addition to the ferry, Valdez can be reached by air from Anchorage (there are numerous daily flights). You can also rent a car here and drive along the **Richardson Highway** through the scenic Copper River Valley toward **Glennallen** and the Wrangell-St Elias National Park (see page 192).

It's a beautiful stretch of road. Leaving Valdez, you pass the site of the original, pre-1964 town, although there's not much to see except a commemorative plaque.

Some 12 miles (20km) further on, you come to the **Keystone Canyon** and the lovely **Bridal Veil Falls**. Drive on for another 7 miles (11km) or so and the trans-Alaska pipeline comes into view. Nearby is an attractive camping spot with good trout fishing.

Now you carry on up to **Thompson Pass**, perhaps Alaska's most spectacular mountain road. Passing the Edgerton Highway junction (82 miles/132km from Valdez), you will reach **Copper Center**, a village that was an early mining camp and is well worth a stop

Art on display at Copper River Delta Shorebird Festival.

A sight to behold – the Columbia Glacier.

Valdez harbor and town.

(accommodations are available) before visiting the national park.

CORDOVA

Cordova ❻ became a transportation center in the early 20th century. The important mineral was copper, and the deposit, the richest in the world, was at **Kennecott**, 200 miles (320km) up the Copper and Chitina rivers (see page 192). Cordova, an attractive community of wood-framed houses, was born a railroad town with the arrival of a shipload of men and equipment on April 1, 1906. The railroad was the brainchild of Michael J. Heney, an engineer who had also pushed the White Pass & Yukon Route Railroad through the White Pass from Skagway to Whitehorse in Southeast Alaska in 1900.

ENGINEERING ACHIEVEMENT

For the next five years, Cordova was the operations center for the Copper River & Northwestern Railroad construction project. Along with the oil pipeline, this ranks among the greatest engineering feats of its time. Heney had to contend with temperatures of −60°F (−50°C), a ferocious wind that knocked boxcars off the tracks, and drifting snow that buried his locomotives.

The ore transported was almost pure copper, and it added to the fortunes of the railroad backers, a syndicate led by J.P. Morgan. But by the mid-1930s the price of copper had fallen and all the high-grade ores had been mined; in 1938 the railroad was abandoned.

Cordova today is a pretty little fishing town where not much happens. You can't reach it by road. Whittier–Valdez ferries stop here, and a new dock has brought some of the cruise ship operators to town. Otherwise, it is reached by a short flight from Anchorage, and airport buses run you into town. The **Chamber of Commerce** (tel: 907-424-7260; www.cordova chamber.com) on First Street will fill you in on current activities.

For historical and marine exhibits, including many evocative old photographs, visit the nearby **Cordova Historical Museum** (tel: 907-424-6665; summer Mon–Fri 10am–6pm, Sat 10am–5pm, Sun 2–4pm, other months

Tue–Fri 10am–5pm, Sat noon–5pm; $1 donation recommended), also on First Street. Nearby, the **small-boat harbor** is a lively spot and the heart and soul of the town.

If you are eager to get the lay of the land, take a trek up to the **Mount Eyak** ski area (www.mteyak.org), which boasts unbeatable views of the town and the surrounding Sound.

But the main attractions of the area are out on the 50-mile (80km) Copper River Highway, which traces the railroad line across the biologically rich **Copper River Delta** to the spectacular Child's Glacier. The delta is a birdwatcher's paradise and home to the world's entire nesting population of Dusky Canada geese. It is also a refueling spot for swarms of migrating waterfowl.

INDUSTRIES IN FLUX

The Sound is still rich in copper and gold, molybdenum, tungsten, and silver, but low mineral prices mean those resources will be left in the ground for the immediate future. The timber industry has also been doing poorly, and fur harvesting has long been abandoned.

The long-term ecological consequences of these industries, including the disastrous oil spill in 1989, are unknown. Still, the Sound continues to heal, and wildlife officials have reported seeing animals return to the area. Commercial fishing remains a major source of income for the 7,500 people who live along the Sound. While fishing runs have been erratic in recent years, 2010 set a new record when fishermen hauled 67 million pink salmon out of the Sound. Nonetheless, increased competition from other parts of the world remains high while prices stay low, tempering any optimism.

The most promising resources in the Sound are its wilderness. Every year a growing number of kayakers can be found pitching tents on beaches, park officials answer inquiries for cabin-use permits, and visitors book boat tours with hopes of seeing a glacier calve or catching a glimpse of the Sound's spectacular wildlife.

Bird-watchers flock to the Area during the Shorebird Festival.

Dusky Canada geese.

WRANGELL-ST ELIAS NATIONAL PARK

America's largest national park has emerged from obscurity to become a jewel of the park system, complete with the historic landmarks, a quirky frontier town, and stunning natural beauty.

Map on page 164

Until the late-1980s, **Wrangell-St Elias National Park and Preserve ➐** was an overlooked and undervalued mountain wilderness. Created in 1980, America's largest park – at 13.2 million acres (5.3 million hectares), the size of six Yellowstones – was also one of its least known and least visited. Then, Wrangell-St Elias was 'discovered.' And, though it hasn't yet become 'the next Denali' as some in the tourism industry had predicted, the park's use has grown significantly in the past few decades from an average of 25,000 visitors over the course of the 1980s to a peak of 80,000 in 2015. Before visiting the park, stop off at the headquarters and visitor center at **Copper Center ➑** (www.nps.gov/wrst; tel: 907-822-7250) on the Richardson Highway, some 200 road miles (320km) east of Anchorage, for maps, publications, and advice.

A MOUNTAIN OF COPPER

At the turn of the 20th century, a couple of prospectors named Jack Smith and Clarence Warner spotted a large green spot in the Wrangell Mountains, on the ridge between the Kennicott Glacier and McCarthy Creek which proved to be mineral staining from a fantastically rich copper deposit.

Mining engineer Stephen Birch bought the copper claims and won the backing of the Guggenheim brothers and J.P. Morgan. Known collectively as the Alaska Syndicate, the investors formed the (misspelled) Kennecott Mines Co., which later became the Kennecott Copper Corp.

The copper discovery sparked the construction of the 200-mile (320km) Copper River & Northwestern Railroad, connecting the mining camp to the coastal town of Cordova. When the mine closed in 1938 it had produced over 4.5 million tons of ore, worth $200 million. At its peak, around 600 people lived at **Kennecott ➒**.

Wrangell-St Elias National Park.

The main settlement included all the operations needed to mill the ore, as well as houses, offices and stores, a school, hospital, post office, dairy, and recreation hall. Just down the road, a second community, eventually named McCarthy, sprang up around 1908.

In a perfect complement to staid, regimented Kennecott, **McCarthy** ⑩ played the role of sin city. Among its most successful businesses were several saloons, pool halls, gambling rooms, and back-alley brothels. In its heyday, 100 to 150 people lived in McCarthy. But after the mine shut down, only a few people stayed on.

For decades after the mine's closure, McCarthy-Kennecott served as the quintessential haven for Alaska recluses. But more recently the region has become a major tourist draw, complete with lodges, a hotel, bed-and-breakfast inns, ice-cream parlor, air taxi operators, wilderness guide operations, museum, and an espresso bar – impressive for a community whose year-round 'hard core' population numbers a couple of dozen people.

ACCESS TO THE PARK

The northern entry to the park is the 45-mile (72km) Nabesna Road, which connects the state's highway system with the tiny mining community of **Nabesna** ⑪ (population about 5). The road's first 5 miles (8km) are paved; the remainder is gravel. Four-wheel-drive vehicles are recommended for the final 5 miles, which cross several creeks and are not regularly maintained by the state.

Motorists should check for updated road conditions before making the drive, as sections of it are occasionally washed out during summer rainstorms; call ahead to park headquarters and check in at the ranger station, at Mile 0.2.

Although some gold, silver, copper, iron, and molybdenum were discovered in the Nabesna area early in the 20th century, a much bigger attraction now is the wildlife. Caribou, moose, and even grizzlies may be spotted in the open countryside bordering Nabesna Road, and large populations of Dall sheep are found in the hills surrounding the 9,360ft (2,850-meter) Tanada Peak,

The abandoned Kennecott Mine.

⊙ Tip

Wrangell-Elias National Park is open year-round, but peak visits occur in August. Wildflowers and mosquitoes peak in June and July. The prime mountaineering season is from mid-March to early June. Snow is possible at any season in the high country.

about 15 miles (24km) southwest of the road's end. Also calling the park home are two herds of bison that were introduced at the behest of hunters nearly 100 years ago. (Trophy hunting for sheep and other species is allowed in the preserve, which encompasses about 37 percent of the unit's total area.)

The principal avenue into Wrangell-St Elias is **McCarthy Road**; at 60 miles (95km) long and unpaved, it stretches from Chitina, at the park's western boundary (where it connects with the Edgerton Highway) to the gateway community of **McCarthy**, located deep within one of America's most spectacular wildlands.

Once known as the worst road in Alaska, the McCarthy Road has benefited from state money. It has been widened and re-graded, making for a much smoother (albeit still slow) ride. One still needs to carry a spare, but stories of getting two and three flats in one trip are of the past.

Only a small percentage of those who drive the McCarthy Road actually visit the park's awesome backcountry. Most

The old hardware store in McCarthy.

are content to hang out in McCarthy, take hikes to the nearby **Kennicott Glacier** and **Root Glacier**, or travel some 4 miles (7km) to the abandoned Kennecott copper mining camp (the original company misspelled the name). Until 1997 visitors could reach McCarthy-Kennecott only by crossing the glacially fed Kennicott River on hand-pulled trams. These historic trams have been replaced by a footbridge that makes the crossing considerably easier. Locals have resisted a vehicular bridge fearing it might open up their community to large-scale 'industrial' tourism. Recently, however, a privately owned and gate-locked vehicle bridge was built down river. To obtain a key to the gate, whether for a day or an entire summer season, locals must pay a $300-a-year fee to the Rollin family, who own the property and equipment responsible for supporting the bridge.

GLACIERS AND RUGGED PEAKS

The park's real treasures lie in a wild and magnificent alpine world that wilderness guides call 'North America's

mountain kingdom.' It's a kingdom that includes four major mountain ranges – the St Elias, Chugach, Alaska, and Wrangells – and six of the continent's 10 highest peaks, including 18,008ft (5,490-meter) **Mount St Elias**, fourth-highest in North America.

Here, too, is North America's largest subpolar icefield, the **Bagley**, which feeds a system of gigantic glaciers; one of those, the Malaspina Glacier, covers an area of more than 1,500 sq miles (4,075 sq km) – larger than Rhode Island. Hubbard Glacier, which flows out of the St Elias Mountains into Disenchantment Bay, is one of the continent's most active glaciers; in 1986, Hubbard was nicknamed the Galloping Glacier when it surged more than a mile and sealed off Russell Fjord. The ice dam later broke and the glacier retreated, but it advanced again in 2002 to create yet another temporary ice dam and scientists say it's only a matter of time before the Hubbard closes off the fjord permanently.

The glaciers have carved dozens of canyons; some, like the Chitistone and Nizina, are bordered by rock walls thousands of feet high. Rugged, remote coastline is bounded by tidewater glaciers and jagged peaks. The park's alpine superlatives, along with those of neighboring Kluane National Park in Canada, have prompted their combined designation as a Unesco World Heritage Site.

Much of what's been 'discovered' in Wrangell-St Elias by modern-day explorers was known to local residents centuries ago. This is especially true of the **Skolai Creek-Chitistone River** area, the most popular of the park's backcountry destinations.

Less recently, both the Chitistone and Skolai Pass routes were used by stampeders traveling from McCarthy to **Chisana** ⑫, the site of Alaska's last major gold rush. Chisana's boom times lasted only a few years, from 1913 to 1915. But during that short period, as many as 10,000 people may have traveled through the mountains.

MODERN EXPLORERS

Nine decades later, people attracted by wilderness values rather than gold are

A hike to the Root Glacier.

Sunset in the Wrangell Mountain range.

A lake in the Wrangell-St Elias National Park.

retracing the footsteps of the Chisana stampeders. This newest rush into the Wrangell-St Elias backcountry is, so far, much smaller and more benign. Most modern explorers lured into this vast mountain landscape are curious adventurers, and they bring a minimum-impact ethic and leave little or no trace of their visit. Still, there's no question that they are having a cumulative effect.

In the first four years that he explored the Skolai–Chitistone area, wilderness guide Bob Jacobs saw only one set of footprints not made by his own parties. A quarter-century later, it's difficult to go more than a day or two without seeing signs of other backpackers, or at least hearing aircraft traffic. The increased use has taken a toll; there's been some trampling of vegetation, littering, crowding, and a growing potential problem with bears that have learned to associate humans with food.

It was only natural that the Skolai–Chitistone area became Wrangell-St Elias' heaviest-used backcountry area. It is one of the park's premier wilderness spots, ruggedly spectacular country in the heart of the mountains. Yet despite its vast, primeval richness, the area is easily accessible by plane, located less than 30 miles (48km) from McCarthy – a short hop by Alaska bush pilot standards.

This is 'big country' in the truest sense of the word. The scale of things is immense. In every direction are stark, jagged, ice-carved peaks, most of them unnamed and unclimbed. Here, too, are massive, near-vertical rock faces thousands of feet high, hanging glaciers and waterfalls by the dozen.

Yet for all the rock and snow and ice, this is not a barren or alien world. In the valley bottoms are alder groves and tundra meadows brightened with legions of rainbow-hued flowers: blue forget-me-nots, lupin and Jacob's ladder, purple monkshood, yellow paint brush, white mountain avens, tall pink fireweed, and wintergreen. Ptarmigan hide in the alder, clucking in the early morning like roosters. Bands of Dall sheep inhabit high rocky places, while occasional moose, wolves, and brown bears prowl valleys and hillsides. The valleys are also home to pikas, ground

⊘ MOSQUITOES

Jokingly referred to as the Alaska State Bird, mosquitoes fare extraordinarily well in Alaska's climate and are especially prevalent between mid-June and the end of July. While there are reported to be from 25 to 40 different species common to the state, there have been no reported cases of West Nile Virus, and the two mosquito species that transmit it in the Lower 48 don't live in Alaska. Visitors are encouraged to wear long sleeves and long pants made of tightly woven, light material – mosquitoes are supposedly attracted to darker colors – while hiking in the backcountry. Mosquito repellent is helpful and can be bought in almost any store. In remote areas the use of mosquito head nets is advised. And – not that it's any consolation – the caribou are attacked just as much as humans.

squirrels, shorebirds, and robins. And overhead, eagles soar.

PRESERVING THE WILDERNESS

All these variables have dramatically boosted recreational visits to Skolai and Chitistone valleys, and park officials are keen to protect them. Their biggest concern isn't the traditional wilderness traveler, but the novice explorer. Visitor education is one solution. Another has been to spread the use to other beautiful but neglected areas – for instance, to **Tebay Lakes**, which are similar to California's High Sierras, with beautiful granite peaks, excellent fishing and hiking.

Other areas that haven't been used as heavily include **Goat Creek**, which offers good hiking, and the wide-open, wildlife-rich upper Chitina Valley.

TRAILS AND COMMERCIAL FACILITIES

Many of Wrangell-St Elias' natural wonders are inaccessible to those who remain along the road system. Only in recent years have a small number of trails been established to parts of the backcountry. From Nabesna Road, the **Skookum Volcanic Trail** leads to a tundra area with interesting volcanic dikes and basalt flows, and is ideal for day hikers.

Two other trails begin along the McCarthy Road; one leads to the Crystalline Hills, which offer superb views of the surrounding mountains and the Chitina River valley. A longer, more challenging backcountry route, the **Dixie Pass Trail**, follows a path used by prospectors and miners.

Air taxi services provide transportation into the park and several guide outfits offer river rafting, climbing, and trekking opportunities. Increasingly popular are flightseeing tours, out of McCarthy, Chitina, Gulkana, and Nabesna.

There's a fairly primitive campground along the McCarthy Road and several public-use cabins (built by miners, hunters or trappers) in the backcountry, available on a first-come first-served basis. A list of facilities and services is available from park HQ (PO Box 439, Copper Center, AK 99573; tel: 907-822-5234; www.nps.gov/wrst).

⊙ Tip

In the backcountry, assistance may be miles or days away, so travelers must be self-sufficient and schooled in wilderness survival skills. Even in summer the weather can change suddenly and storm systems may delay pick-ups by several days, so bring extra provisions, rain gear, and warm clothing.

A bush plane takes off over the mountain range.

Catch of the day.

KENAI PENINSULA

This is Alaska in a nutshell: glaciers, salmon fishing, skiing, hiking trails, stunning scenery, and friendly towns – all within easy reach of Anchorage.

It's often said that Alaska is too big to see in a single lifetime, let alone a single vacation. But there is one place where tourists can sample most of the best of Alaska, and can do so within a few weeks: the Kenai Peninsula.

The entire peninsula is within easy driving distance of Anchorage, and people in the city like to refer to the Kenai as their backyard. But please, don't use that line. On a map of the state, the Kenai Peninsula looks deceptively small. It's worth remembering that the peninsula covers more than 16,000 sq miles (25,000 sq km), making it larger than the combined areas of Rhode Island, Connecticut, and Delaware. It is bordered by Prince William Sound and the Gulf of Alaska on the east and Cook Inlet on the west, and attached to the mainland of South-central Alaska by a narrow mountainous neck of land at the north.

TOURING THE PENINSULA

Driving out from Anchorage, you will cross into the peninsula just south of **Portage,** a town that formerly sat at the eastern end of Turnagain Arm, the thin finger of Cook Inlet that separates the peninsula from the Anchorage Bowl. Portage was completely destroyed by the 1964 earthquake, and only a few ruins remain. About 5 miles (8km) after passing the wreckage of Portage,

you begin to climb through the Kenai Mountains, with a maximum elevation of about 3,500ft (1,050 meters).

Mileage along the Seward and Sterling highways is measured from Seward. At about Mile 70 is the summit of **Turnagain Pass**, elevation 988ft (296 meters). It's popular in winter for cross-country skiing, and snowmobiling.

The pass and much of the area along the highway are part of the **Chugach National Forest** (tel: 907-743-9500; www.fs.usda.gov/chugach). Creeks, lakes, and campgrounds are scattered

Map on page 200

A nifty camp in the Kenai Peninsula.

through this area. The camps are generally open from Memorial Day through Labor Day (the last Monday in May to the first Monday in September).

Fees are charged for camp use. Facilities often include tables, fire grates, tent pads, and some type of water and sanitary facilities. While fires are usually allowed at these sites, it's a good idea to carry a small camp stove with you.

HOPE

The first town you encounter on the peninsula is **Hope** Ⓐ, a mining community of about 190, founded in 1896. A trip to Hope requires a 16-mile (25km) detour onto the Hope Cutoff, Mile 56 of the Seward Highway, but it's worth it. There you'll find the Hope-Sunrise Historical & Mining Museum (tel: 907-782-3115; Memorial Day–Labor Day daily noon–4pm) on Old Hope Road, a store, a couple of cafés, a bar, and a lodge.

An ideal site for pink salmon fishing, moose, caribou and black bear hunting, Hope also is the head of the **Resurrection Pass Trail**, one of the most popular hiking areas on the peninsula. The trailhead is located at Mile 3.5 of the Resurrection Creek Road. The entire trail is 19 miles (30km) long, and

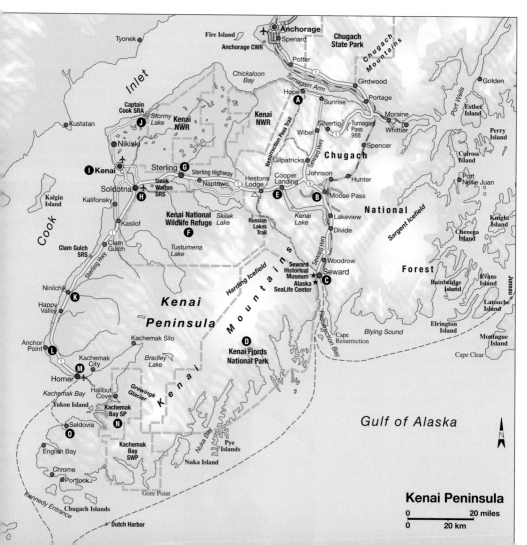

hikers emerge at **Schooner Bend**, Mile 52 on the Sterling Highway.

One option is to turn off the Resurrection Trail at Mile 20 and take the 10-mile (16km) **Devil's Pass Trail**, which emerges at Mile 39 of the Seward Highway. The Resurrection Pass Trail connects, via the **Russian Lakes Trail**, with the Resurrection River Trail to form the 72-mile (116km) Resurrection Trail from Hope to Seward.

The Forest Service operates some cabins along the Resurrection Trail. Campers must bring their own food, utensils, and sleeping bags. Because of the route's popularity, it is wise to make cabin reservations well ahead; they can be made up to six months in advance.

The Resurrection Pass Trail can take between two and six days to cover, while the entire route may take a week or more. Trout fishing is possible in several lakes. The trail also provides spectacular scenery for photography.

THE SEWARD HIGHWAY

On leaving Hope and rejoining the Seward Highway, the first decision is whether to go west or head south at the Seward Junction at Mile 40. To the south lie Moose Pass and Seward; to the west lie Cooper Landing, Kenai, Soldotna, Anchor Point, Ninilchik, Homer, and Seldovia, which can be reached only by taking a ferry. There are several smaller towns as well, including Clam Gulch and Kasilof.

Heading south, the first community is **Moose Pass B**. This is a quiet town of approximately 225 people. Residents enjoy hiking, fishing, and biking – the town has one of Alaska's relatively few bike trails. One of the highlights of the year is the annual Summer Festival, held to celebrate the solstice. The exact date of the festival changes from year to year, but is always held on the June weekend with the most total hours of sunlight. The whole community comes together for activities that include a barbecue, carnival, softball games, and an auction.

Continuing south on the highway you come to **Seward C**, an attractive city of approximately 2,700 residents. Founded in 1903, it was for years the leading port

A mascot welcomes the guests at Moose Pass.

⊙ Fact

Most Alaskans do not know the numerical designation of the state's highways. Perhaps because there are so few roads, they are always referred to by name. Most any Alaskan knows the Seward Highway heads south from Anchorage to the Kenai Peninsula, and that the Glenn Highway heads north through Palmer to Tok. Few would be able to tell you that portions of both roads are designated as Highway 1.

⊙ ATHABASCANS AND RUSSIANS

The Kenai Peninsula was originally home to Dena'ina Indians, a branch of the Athabascan tribe, and to Alutiiqs, whose linguistic group extends as far west as Eastern Russia. Their descendants still live here, mostly in small, remote villages, but they now account for something less than 10 percent of the population. Modern ways have long since replaced those of the natives; they speak and dress very much like their white neighbors, and have a lifestyle which melds traditional and mainstream American ways.

The Russians were the first whites to establish permanent communities on the peninsula. From their base on Kodiak Island, they sent out missionaries to found churches all along the eastern shore of Cook Inlet. The town of Kenai began when a Russian settlement was established in the center of a Dena'ina village in 1791.

Other Russian-founded communities include Seldovia, which also dates to the 18th century, and Ninilchik, founded in the early 1800s. Seward didn't then exist as a town, but the area around Resurrection Bay was used as a shipbuilding site for the Russian-American Company. Early Russian influence is still to be seen in the onion-domed churches, and heard in the names of places and people in some peninsula communities.

city of Alaska. It was eventually eclipsed in that role by Anchorage, though the 1964 earthquake devastated the economy. Twenty years later, it began to regain its financial legs and is once again a thriving port. The Chamber of Commerce (2001 Seward Highway; tel: 907-224-8051; www.seward.com) is at the entrance to town, on the highway.

In the heart of town, on Third Avenue, is the **Seward Historical Museum** (tel: 907-224-3902; www.cityofseward. us/departments/library-museum/museum; mid-May–mid-Sept Tue–Sat 10am–5pm, Sun 1–5pm). The town library, on Sixth Avenue, features photographs and a film on the effects of the 1964 earthquake on Seward.

One of the main attractions of the area is **Resurrection Bay**. Charter boats for sailing, whale watching, or fishing are available at the city harbor, as are kayak rentals. The state ferry system also has a dock in Seward, offering trips to Kodiak and the Prince William Sound areas.

Fishy business: a man cleans the catch.

Seward is the northern terminus for a number of cruise ships crossing the Gulf of Alaska. These ships bring thousands of visitors through Seward on their way to or from Southcentral Alaska, usually via the train.

Another major attraction is the **Alaska SeaLife Center** (301 Railway Avenue; tel: 907-224-6300/800-224-2525; www.alaskasealife.org; call for hours), built on a 7-acre (3-hectare) site next to the Marine Education Center on the shores of Resurrection Bay. This marine science enterprise combines research on saving marine species and aiding recovery from industrial damage, with the rehabilitation of maimed or stranded birds and mammals. It also aims to provide education and entertainment for the thousands of visitors to the center each year.

KENAI FJORDS NATIONAL PARK

Seward is also the gateway to **Kenai Fjords National Park ⓓ** (tel: winter 907-422-0500, summer 907-422-0573; www.nps.gov/kefj), declared a national monument in 1978 and designated a national park two years later. As well as the rugged coastal fjords for which it is named, and the glaciers which, for many, are its chief attraction, the park is home to porpoises, sea otters, sea lions, humpback and orca whales, puffins, bald eagles, and other animals. Several local tour operators offer frequent wildlife cruises into the park, starting from Seward's Small Boat Harbor.

Most of the park is only accessible by boat: the only vehicle access is to the northwest of Seward, at Exit Glacier Road. Exit Glacier is the most easily accessible point of the **Harding Icefield**, a remnant of the Ice Age that caps a section of the Kenai Mountains 50 miles (80km) long and 30 miles (48km) wide. The glacier itself lies less than a mile (1km) past the car parking area at the end of the road; you simply head up the trail, passing a visitor cabin along the way.

It's an easy walk to the face – but visitors are warned to not get too close, because of the danger of falling ice. There are ranger-led hikes but you can go it alone, taking care not to go beyond the warning signs. A challenging hike rises along the side of the glacier to the icefield above. For further information on this and all aspects of the park, contact the Park Service Information Center on Fourth Avenue by the Small Boat Harbor in Seward (tel: 907-422-0500; summer only).

After leaving the park and initially driving north, it's time to head west on the Sterling Highway. Out toward **Cooper Landing E**, you enter an area that's been closed to Dall sheep hunting. As a result, it's often a good area to spot them. But looking for sheep while driving can be dangerous, so pull off at one of many designated stops before peering up to look for the white specks high on the peaks.

Cooper Landing is a community of fewer than 300 people, spread out along the headwaters of the Kenai River. Here the river is a beautiful turquoise color, and in winter the open stretches of water are a prime feeding ground for majestic bald eagles. Sportfishing (particularly for salmon and rainbow trout), hunting, and tourism, are the area's main industries, although the town began as a mining area.

At nearby **Kenai Lake**, you can fish for Dolly Varden, lake trout, rainbow trout, and whitefish. The Kenai River has trout and four species of salmon. Trophy rainbow trout, some weighing as much as 20lbs (9kg), are caught here by spin- and fly-fishing enthusiasts, and catch-and-release fishing is widely practiced. Rafting is another popular activity on the river, and several local businesses offer fishing and float trips.

Continuing west, just outside of the Cooper Landing area at the confluence of the Kenai and Russian rivers, is the turn-off to the **Russian River Campground** (www.fs.usda.gov/recarea/chugach/recarea/?recid=6647). The site is easy to spot in the summer, as it's usually busy. The 20-mile (32km) **Russian Lakes Trail** is a delightful and not over-demanding hike, with cabins en

◯ Tip

A scenic way to reach Seward is on board the Alaska Railroad (www.alaskarailroad.com) which runs along the coast from Anchorage. It passes the Spencer Glacier and Grandview areas, and offers opportunities for spotting bald eagles and beluga whales. Trains run daily from early May to mid-Sept.

Fishing boats moored at Seward.

Tourists cruising the Kenai Fjords National Park.

A calf amongst the fireweed.

route. Reservations are needed (www.recreation.gov or tel: 877-444-6777). The Russian River is the largest freshwater fishery in Alaska, and draws tens of thousands of fishermen each year, all hoping to catch a red salmon.

KENAI NATIONAL WILDLIFE REFUGE

Heading west on the Sterling Highway, you leave the Chugach National Forest and enter the **Kenai National Wildlife Refuge F**. Refuge regulations, as well as trail maps and information about things to do in the refuge, are available from the visitor center in Soldotna (tel: 907-262- 2820; www.kenai.fws.gov), up Ski Hill Road from the Sterling Highway south of the Kenai River Bridge. The refuge, which was established by President Franklin D. Roosevelt as a wildlife range to preserve the moose population, then later expanded, is also the habitat of coyotes, grizzlies, caribou, and wolves. It comprises the western slopes of the Kenai Mountains, and spruce and birch forested lowlands bordering Cook Inlet.

Among the major recreational areas in the refuge is the 20-mile (32km) **Skilak Lake Loop**, which intersects the Sterling Highway near the Visitor Center. This road takes you to **Skilak Lake**, and also provides access to several other smaller lakes, streams and some 200 miles (320km) of trails in the area.

The most arduous trail is the Skilak Lookout Trail, which takes you up some 700ft (213 meters) and provides stunning views.

Skilak Lake itself has a surface area of some 24,000 acres (57,600 hectares). It is prone to sudden and violent storms – warning signs should be taken very seriously. The lake offers fishing for king and red salmon and rainbow and Dolly Varden trout.

STERLING

To the west from Cooper Landing along the highway you come to **Sterling G**, a community of about 5,600, based at the confluence of the Kenai and Moose rivers. It's a very popular salmon fishing area, and is the main access point to the Swanson River oil field and an endless string of lakes that are excellent for canoeing. Another attraction of the area is the **Izaak Walton State Recreation Site**. It is believed the area was an Eskimo village more than 2,000 years ago and several depressions mark the sites of ancient houses.

SOLDOTNA

Heading on past Sterling, you come to the city of **Soldotna H**, seat of the borough government and home to around 4,200 people. With its central location at the intersection of the roads to Kenai and Homer, Soldotna has become the hub of the central peninsula. It is a popular spot to meet up with fishing guides, most of whom specialize in helping you find king salmon.

The amount of traffic on the Kenai River has become the subject of statewide controversy. Twenty-five years ago, only a handful of locals fished for

king, sockeye, and silver salmon on the river. Now the Kenai River system is the most popular sportfishing area in the state, and has been designated a Special Management Area to protect its natural resources and manage the recreational use of the river.

The most up-to-date information on river use is available from the **Visitor Center**, at the corner of the Sterling Highway and Kalifornsky Beach Road, which also houses the offices for the local Chamber of Commerce (tel: 907-262-9814; www.soldotnachamber.com; summer daily 9am–7pm, winter Mon–Fri 9am–5pm).

Soldotna's festivals include the Kenai River Festival, held in June, and a winter sports festival in late January that includes a dogsled race, ice carving, and native youth Olympics.

KENAI

Heading west from Soldotna on either the Kenai Spur Highway or Kalifornsky Beach Road, you come to **Kenai ❶**, the largest city on the peninsula with a population of just over 7,000, and also the oldest permanent settlement, founded (in the center of a Dena'ina village) by Russian fur traders and Orthodox priests during the late 18th century.

Kenai is home port to a good share of the peninsula's drift-net fishing fleet. In summer a parade of boats can be seen coming in and out of the mouth of the river in a quest for red salmon. During the spring, the flats along the mouth of the river are temporary nesting ground for thousands of snow geese. They stay in the area for about two weeks and are a popular subject for early-season photographers.

Kenai Airport (www.kenai.city/airport) it the peninsula's largest, and has the most regularly scheduled flights. Airlines also fly in and out of Soldotna, Seward, and Homer, and charter flights can take you almost anywhere else.

One of Kenai's main attractions is the **Kenai Visitors and Cultural Center** on the corner of Main Street and Kenai Spur Highway (tel: 907-283-1991; www.visitkenai.com; summer Mon–Fri

⊘ FISHING FEVER

The name 'Kenai' is synonymous with the term 'fishing,' especially during salmon season – and on the Kenai River, that's pretty much all summer long. When word spreads that the salmon are 'in' (meaning huge numbers of salmon have suddenly decided to fight their way upstream to spawn), fishers from throughout Southcentral impatiently wait until the workday is over, then drive three hours (or more) south to the Kenai River. There they stand, shoulder-to-shoulder along the banks of the river, casting their lines in a mostly friendly synchrony called 'combat fishing.' Occasionally, a bear will wander over and join the action. While no one will stop fishing, the bear is generally given plenty of room and eventually leaves without incident.

When someone actually hooks a fish and yells out 'fish on,' a time-honored code of conduct demands that all other fishers reel in their empty lines to give that angler the best chance of landing his prize. Then it all starts over again. As everyone 'limits out' or becomes exhausted with the effort (usually in the wee morning hours), they load themselves and their fish into their cars for the long drive back home.

Often there's just enough time for a quick shower and to head back to work. There's no known cure for this type of 'fishing fever.' It has to run its normal course, usually lingering from early June through mid-September.

Should you feel yourself susceptible to this particular recurrent 'malady,' Alaska State law requires both resident and non-resident anglers, 16 years of age or older, to have a valid sportfishing license in their possession while fishing. Nearly every grocery, sporting goods, or general merchandise store sells sportfishing licenses, or you can purchase them by mail or online.

Choose one of the fishing lodges that populate the entire Kenai Peninsula if you want to make a weekend of it, or you can also opt for one of the many fishing guides who happily take visitors to experience this Alaskan right of passage. Often both lodges and independent fishing guides will handle the licence and have gear available for use.

For details, contact the Alaska Division of Sport Fish (tel: 907-267-2219; www.adfg.alaska.gov) or visit the local chamber of commerce for recommendations for guides and lodges.

Sunset over the Kenai Mountains.

9am–7pm, Sat 10am–6pm, Sun noon–5pm, other months Tue–Fri 9am–5pm, Sat 10am–4pm). The center features exhibits and displays of Kenai's rich and diverse culture, from its Native and Russian history through the industries that currently fuel the area: oil and commercial fishing.

Head down Overland Avenue, where you will find Fort Kenay, although the present one is only a replica of the original 19th-century fortification. On the other side of Mission Street is the **Holy Assumption Russian Orthodox Church**, the oldest Orthodox place of worship in Alaska.

Continue down Mission Avenue and you will come to the **Beluga Whale Lookout** where, in early summer, you can watch for white whales feeding on salmon in the river.

Special events include the 4th of July parade and the Christmas Comes to Kenai celebration on the weekend following Thanksgiving; the fête includes a fireworks display, when the pyrotechnics can easily be seen against the dark late-afternoon sky.

A grizzly bear on the lookout.

NIKISKI

Continuing north of Kenai on the Spur Highway, you come to **Nikiski**. The peninsula's industrial center, it has a large chemical plant and two oil refineries. The plants aren't open to the public.

North of the refineries is the **Captain Cook State Recreation Area** ❶ (tel: 907-262-5581; http://dnr.alaska.gov/parks/aspunits/kenai/captcook.htm), a popular spot for hiking, camping, fishing, and snowmachining. There are a couple of good campsites and great views across the Cook Inlet. Much of what you see across the inlet is part of the **Lake Clark National Park** (tel: 907-644-3626; www.nps.gov/lacl; see page 324). Charter flights to the park can be arranged in Kenai – ask at the Visitor Center there for details.

SOUTH ON THE STERLING HIGHWAY

To venture south from Kenai, cross the river on Bridge Access Road and connect with Kalifornsky Beach Road to return to the Sterling Highway. Farther south, the highway begins to parallel Cook Inlet and runs past some fine clamming areas in the appropriately named Clam Gulch. Digging for clams requires patience, practice, a shovel and pail, a fishing license, and a current tide book. But for those who like to eat the molluscs – particularly the razor clams, said to be the best of all – a day in Clam Gulch could well be one of the highlights of their visit.

At Mile 135 on the highway is **Ninilchik** ❷, a fishing village founded by the Russians more than 100 years ago. Fishing is still popular here today, especially for halibut or salmon. The town's nearly 900 residents mostly live in recently constructed homes along the highway. The original village, which can be visited, is an attractive spot, sitting on the inlet at the mouth of the Ninilchik River.

On a hill above the old village is the town's Russian Orthodox Church, not open for tours but still used by the parish. The modern community of Ninilchik hosts the Kenai Peninsula State Fair on the third weekend in August. Ninilchik is another good spot for clam digging.

Continuing south, you come to **Anchor Point ⓛ**, the most westerly point in North America that is accessible by continuous road system. The population of just over 2,000 in this community hosts festivities on Memorial Day weekend and on the 4th of July, the latter featuring a parade, community potluck, beach golf, and a rubber duck race.

HOMER

Still farther south is **Homer ⓜ**, the southern terminus of the Sterling Highway. Homer sits on the shore of **Kachemak Bay**, which is known for the variety of its marine life. The Homer Spit extends 5 miles (8km) out into the bay and is home to the town's boat harbor, campgrounds, hotels, restaurants, an artificial fishing hole, and the Salty Dawg Saloon, a popular watering hole housed in one of Homer's first buildings.

Homer itself is a pleasant little town with an artistic bent. The population is very socially aware, and for every development-minded resident, you'll find another who is a card-carrying member of an environmental group. Some apparently belong to both camps, which is partly what makes Homer such a lively place.

Major attractions around here include boat tours and halibut fishing trips, but call into the **Homer Visitor and Information Center** at 201 Sterling Highway (tel: 907-235-7740; www.homeralaska.org; Mon–Sat 9am–5pm) to find out what else is offered to visitors.

Be sure to stop at the **Alaska Islands and Ocean Visitor Center** (95 Sterling Highway; tel: 907-235-6546; www.islandsandocean.org; June–Aug daily 9am–5pm, Sept Tue–Sun 10am–5pm, Oct–Apr Tue–Sat noon–5pm, May daily 10am–5pm; free). Operated as a partnership between the Alaska Maritime National Wildlife Refuge and the Kachemak Bay Research Reserve, the center offers guided walks

Exploring the landscape.

Alaska Islands and Ocean Visitor Center.

that include exploration of the slough, tide pools, and the marine discovery lab.

You will also discover the **Pratt Museum** on Bartlett Street (tel: 907-235-8635; www.prattmuseum.org; summer daily 10am–6pm, rest of year Tue–Sat noon–5pm; closed Jan), a natural history museum that focuses on marine life in Kachemak Bay. It also has an exhibit on the Exxon Valdez oil spill.

Showing off its reputation as an arts center, Homer has a number of galleries displaying local pottery, jewelry, and paintings. You will also find several good restaurants and souvenir shops, as well as a year-round amateur theater company.

The town is the jumping-off point for trips to the other side of the bay, which is dominated by **Kachemak Bay State Park** Ⓝ (http://dnr.alaska.gov/parks/aspunits/kenai/kachemakbaysp.htm; tel: 907-262-5581), with the **Grewingk Glacier**, rugged mountains, coastal rain forest, steep-walled fjords, and alpine tundra. Also across the bay are **Halibut Cove** – where there are more artists and galleries – and the pleasing little town of Seldovia. The state ferry service links Homer to Seldovia, Kodiak, and Whittier in summer.

SELDOVIA

Seldovia Ⓞ is accessible only by air and water. You can bring a vehicle on the state ferry, but it isn't necessary; the town is within easy walking distance. It is home to yet another of the peninsula's still active Russian Orthodox churches. Seldovia's Russian history predates the church, however. It was the site of one of the earliest coal mines, first worked in the late 18th century. By the 1890s, the mine had been exhausted and Seldovia had become a fishing and shipping center.

Much of the town's boardwalk area was destroyed in the 1964 earthquake. Seldovia also has a winter carnival, which brightens up the peaceful, quiet months. With most visitors gone and with nearby trails for hiking and cross-country skiing, winter is one of the nicest times to venture over to the southern shore of Kachemak Bay.

Shorebird watching in Kachemak Bay.

Kenai Fjords National Park in summer.

Woodpecker in Wasilla.

MATANUSKA-SUSITNA VALLEY

'Yahoo! Mat-Su!' is the slogan for this area, referred to locally as 'the Mat-Su,' or simply 'the Valley.' The phrase captures the spirit of cowboy enthusiasm common to those who live, farm, hike, fish, hunt, dog mush, and snowmobile here.

The stunningly beautiful and diverse Mat-Su area encompasses the Matanuska-Susitna River Drainages, over 23,000 sq miles (60,000 sq km), beginning north of Anchorage on the Glenn Highway, north along the Parks Highway to the southern border of Denali National Park and Preserve, and east along the Denali Highway as far as Lake Louise, near Glennallen.

Wildlife sightings in the area are likely to include moose, bear (brown and black), birds (bald eagles, hawks, owls, swans, and loons), and on the far northern and eastern edges of the Mat-Su, impressive caribou herds. Historically the agricultural breadbasket of Alaska, today the Mat-Su is one of the state's fastest growing residential and commercial regions.

A host of new housing developments, springing up on former farmland, are filled with people who commute daily to Anchorage, at least an hour's drive (under ideal weather and traffic conditions) south along the Glenn Highway.

THE MAKING OF THE MAT-SU

The Mat-Su Valley has an interesting history, beginning in 1935 when President Franklin D. Roosevelt – in response to the crushing economic depression and widespread drought of the times – invited 203 families from the hardest-hit states of Minnesota,

Wisconsin, and Michigan to journey to Alaska for a new start with the Matanuska Colony Project. The name of each family was drawn from a box, and 40 acres (16 hectares) of farmland per family were parceled out.

The community of **Palmer**, established in 1916 as a stop along the Alaska Railroad's track to the Chickaloon coal mines, was selected as the base of operations for this New Deal project. Housing options for the colonists were few, and barns were non-existent. Following plans drawn up

⊙ Main attractions
Palmer
Wasilla
Matanuska Glacier
Lake Louise
Independence Mine
Willow
Talkeetna
Denali State Park

⦿ Maps on pages
164, 212

The mountains at twilight.

by a government architect, the colonists began constructing homes and the area's distinctive 32-sq-ft, (3-sq-meter) gambrel-roofed barns, many of which are still standing today.

The members of Matanuska Colony faced many of the same problems common to the Valley's current-day farmers: a short growing season, high freight and labor costs, and great distances to relatively small markets. Within five years, more than half of the original 203 families had given up and left the area; by 1965, fewer than 20 of the original colonists were still farming.

Driving north from Anchorage along the Glenn Highway, just before reaching the city of Palmer, you'll come upon a broad expanse of flat, marshy grasslands of the **Palmer Hay Flats State Game Refuge A** (tel: 907-746-6300). The 45 sq miles (116 sq km) of the refuge provides nesting and feeding grounds for tens of thousands of various duck and geese species en route to and from northern breeding grounds. Trumpeter and tundra swans

also frequent the marshlands during spring and fall. Sandhill cranes may be found in the drier, more isolated regions. The area is a major calving and wintering ground for the Matanuska Valley moose population. The streams, wetlands, lakes and tide flats of the refuge are also popular recreation areas for local salmon fishers and waterfowl hunters.

An excellent place to begin your exploration of the Mat-Su is at the **Visitor Information Center B** (35.5 Parks Highway to Trunk Road Exit 610 South Bailey Street, Suite 201, tel: 907-746-5000; www.alaskavisit.com; May–Sept daily 8.30am–6.30pm). The friendly folks inside the log cabin can give you information on tours, attractions and lodging options in the area, and also have a pay phone, free Wi-Fi internet access, and a gift shop.

PALMER

After leaving the Mat-Su Visitor Information Headquarters, head a few miles farther north along the Glenn Highway to **Palmer C**, a small farming

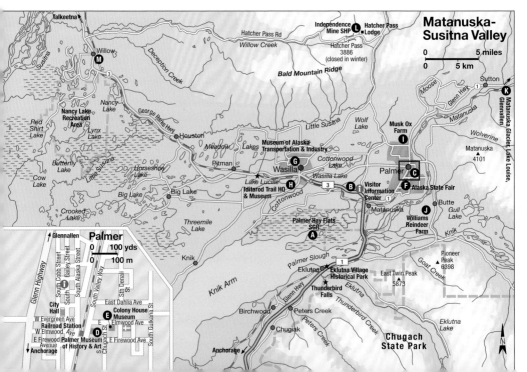

town of just over 6,500 residents happily situated in a majestic rural setting, and conforming to the image many visitors expect of Alaska. The city offers a variety of modest lodging and restaurant options, as well as an 18-hole golf course with distracting views of the surrounding mountain and glacier grandeur.

Stop in at the **Palmer Museum of History and Art** ① (723 South Valley Way; tel: 907-746-7668; www.palmer-museum.org; summer daily 9am–6pm, winter Wed–Fri 10am–5pm, second Sat of the month 10am–2pm; donations welcome), which shares its log cabin home with the town's visitor center. The museum displays colony-era household relics, farm implements, and woodworking tools, in addition to providing up-to-date information on points of interest throughout the greater Palmer area. Many local artists have their works displayed here as well, and just outside the building you can stroll through an interesting garden area featuring various local flowers and vegetables.

A short walk from the museum is the **Colony House Museum** ① (316 East Elmwood Avenue; tel: 907-745-1935; www.palmerhistoricalsociety.org; May–Aug Tue–Sat 10am–4pm, other months by appointment), a restored Colony home (c.1935), where you'll likely hear a direct descendant of an original pioneer family describe what life was like during the Matanuska Colony Project.

Palmer is best known for being the site (in late August) of the **Alaska State Fair** ① (tel: 907-745-4827; www.alaskastatefair.org), which features the famous valley produce. Grown to gigantic proportions due to proper seed selection, careful tending and 19 hours of sunlight during the growing season, the largest cabbage wins the blue ribbon – and it must weigh at least 75lbs (34kg) before it is even eligible to enter the competition. Displays also include farm animals and handmade local items. There is a colorful carnival and a host of food stalls. The two-week event, which ends on Labor Day, attracts around

A family trip across the lake.

⊘ MAT-SU BOUNTY

Although Alaska imports most of its food, the Mat-Su Valley remains Alaska's rural heartland. Many farms have given way to housing developments, but in recent years there has been an interest in reviving its agricultural heritage. Farmers' markets are blossoming, and Mat-Su farmers have been adding vegetables to their standard load of alfalfa and grains. Others are raising poultry and milking cows to produce milk and cheese. Organic farms are also sprouting up, adding apples, corn, and tomatoes to the mix. Still, what you'll find at the majority of markets and roadside farm stands are Alaska's staple crops like carrots, peas, cabbage, and potatoes. Even if you prefer a peach to a carrot, be sure to stop by a local market and take a bite out of an Alaskan carrot; it will be the sweetest you ever tasted.

⊙ Fact

Wasilla may be a small town, but former mayor,Sarah Palin fought her way to become the state's first female governor, and Alaska's first candidate on a presidential ticket. A former beauty queen, she was nicknamed Sarah Barracuda in tribute to her aggressive play as a member of her high school basketball team.

300,000 people each year and should not be missed.

WASILLA

Palmer's significantly less-quaint sister city is **Wasilla** ⓖ *(wa **sill** uh)*. North along the (George) Parks Highway, it is dominated by mile after mile of strip mall-styled commercial development, and known variously as the Home of the Iditarod, the land 'among the lakes,' and, most recently, the town where Sarah Palin began her political career. After two terms as mayor (1996–2002), Palin won the Governor's Mansion and later joined John McCain on the US Republican ticket in an unsuccessful run against Barack Obama in 2008.

Today, Wasilla (population just over 10,100) is the site of many of the large, new residential developments in the Valley. Housing and land prices are generally more reasonable here than in Anchorage; the trade-off is that most residents must then make the daily one hour-plus commute each way – in all kinds of weather

– to their Anchorage jobs. That's OK, though. In Wasilla, the folks tend to be hard drivers, hard workers and hard players; just watch out for heavy commuter traffic in the early morning and late afternoon.

Like many of the other cities and towns in Southcentral, the community of Wasilla arrived by rail. The original Dena'ina Indian residents called this area Benteh, or 'among the lakes,' sandwiched as it is between Lake Lucille and Wasilla Lake. The name Vasili' 'Wasilla' came from the highly respected local Dena'ina Indian, Chief Wasilla. Depending on whom you ask, the name means either 'breath of air,' or else it's simply a derivative of the Russian name, 'Vasili,' a variant of 'William.'

The first non-native settlers of the region lived in the nearby town of Knik, a 'boomtown' of about 500 people in 1915, providing supplies and services to the gold miners at Cache Creek and Willow Creek. In 1917, Wasilla was founded following the construction of the Alaska Railroad. The residents of Knik, realizing the advantages of living

The mountains and the Matanuska River.

near a rail service, simply packed up and moved there. Some actually dragged their houses along behind them, leaving Knik to become a ghost town. The construction of the Parks Highway in early 1970 opened up road access to the area, and made it possible to become a bedroom community for Anchorage.

THE IDITAROD'S HQ

Wasilla is the home of the world famous Iditarod Trail Sled Dog Race (see page 306). The **Iditarod Trail Headquarters and Museum**  (Mile 2.2 Knik Goose Bay Road; tel: 907-376-5155; www.iditarod.com; summer daily 8am–7pm, winter Mon–Fri 8am–5pm) is well worth a visit. Aside from the very interesting exhibits depicting the history of the Iditarod, there's a unique gift shop and, during the summer, you can go for a dogsled ride

There are two other museum options in Wasilla. The **Dorothy Page Museum** (323 North Main Street; tel: 907-373-9071; Tue–Fri 9am–5pm; free on Fri), was named in honor of

Dorothy G. Page, who joined with Joe Reddington, Sr in 1967 to organize the first Iditarod Trail Race, a 50-mile race (run in two 25-mile heats) to commemorate the 100th anniversary of US purchase of Alaska from Russia. The museum, housed in a 1931 structure, offers exhibits and lectures on the history of gold mining and dog mushing (among other things) in Wasilla. You can also visit the historic buildings of the **Old Wasilla Townsite Park** while you're there.

The **Museum of Alaska Transportation and Industry** (3800 West Museum Drive, off Mile 47 Parks Highway; tel: 907-376-1211; www.museumofalaska. org; summer daily 10am–5pm) displays interesting examples of old planes, trains, tools, vehicles and farm equipment.

REINDEER AND MUSK OX

Just north of Palmer is the **Palmer Musk Ox Farm**  (12850 East Archie Road, Palmer; tel: 907-745-4151; www. muskoxfarm.org; summer daily 10am–6pm, other months by appointment),

A musk ox bull grazing.

Sunset at Lake Lucille.

Signs point the way to the local delights.

Farmers have to cope with a short growing season.

with the world's only domesticated musk oxen. In the summer, visitors can watch the newborns romping with their parents in the pasture. The coats of these shaggy animals produce a rare type of wool known as qiviut, which is used by native Alaskans to create hand-knitted hats, mittens, gloves, and scarves in traditional patterns. The Oomingmak Musk Ox Producers' Co-op in downtown Anchorage (see page 173) sells a range of these products.

The **Williams Reindeer Farm ❿** (5561 South Bodenburg Loop Road, in the Butte area off the Old Glenn Highway; tel: 907-745-4000; www.reindeer-farm.com; summer daily 10am–6pm; winter by appointment) offers a rare chance to get a close look at the smallish creatures that are Santa's seemingly unlikely choice for worldwide air cargo transport.

MATANUSKA GLACIER

Continuing your road trip east along the Glenn Highway, you will pass the small communities of Sutton, Chickaloon, and Eureka. At Mile 101, the **Matanuska Glacier ❾** (dnr.alaska. gov/parks/aspunits/matsu/matsug-lsrs.htm) is visible on the south side of the road. At 27 miles (43km) long and 4 miles (9km) wide, it is the largest glacier accessible by car in the state. There is an interpretive nature trail along with hiking trails, and campgrounds that are open in the summer.

To visit **Lake Louise,** a popular spot among locals for trout fishing, turn left at Mile 158 and travel 19 miles (30km) down the road. The surrounding areas afford views of Tazlina Glacier, and there are private lodges, campgrounds, and, in winter, snow-machining and cross-country skiing opportunities. The Nelchina caribou herd can be seen passing through this region during spring and fall migrations, while cormorants, trumpeter swans, and ptarmigans, as well as wolves, bears, wolverine, foxes, and moose are common sightings. The Copper River Valley community of Glennallen sits just another 27 miles (43km) on the Glenn Highway.

⊙ TALKEETNA BY TRAIN

The Alaska Railroad (www.alaskarailroad.com) offers flag-stop service for a 55-mile (88km) wilderness run from Talkeetna to Hurricane and back. The train leaves Talkeetna, usually Thursday through Sunday only (Oct–May first Thu of the month only), at 1pm and returns in time for dinner. It threads its way along the Susitna River and through the Indian River Canyon. Passengers can get off the Hurricane Turn train for a fishing or river-rafting adventure along the way, and then board the train again on its return trip (or else camp overnight and flag down the next day's train). Since 1923 locals have been using this route, one of the last flag-stop services in the country, for accessing remote cabins in the area. Tickets may be purchased on board (cash only), or reserved in advance by calling 800-544-0552 or 907-265-2494.

INDEPENDENCE MINE

One of the highlights of any trip to the Mat-Su is a visit to **Hatcher Pass** and the **Independence Mine State Historical Park** ● (tel: 907-745-2827, summer only; dnr.alaska.gov/parks/units/indmine.htm; visitor center summer daily 11am–6pm; charge for parking and guided tours). Accessed just north of Palmer at Mile 49.5 Glenn Highway, turn left onto Palmer-Fishhook Road (which becomes Hatcher Pass Road), and make the scenic drive on the well-maintained, paved roadway through pleasant woodlands. The Little Susitna River runs alongside the road as you begin to climb and gradually wind your way to an elevation of 3,886ft (1,184 meters) at Hatcher Pass.

The **Hatcher Pass Lodge** is located 17 miles (27km) from the Glenn Highway turnoff. This rustic establishment, open year round, offers good food, reasonable prices, cabin rentals, and spectacular views of the Talkeetna Mountains and alpine foothills that will have you looking for Heidi and her grandfather. The area is a popular year-round recreational destination for hiking, picnicking, berry picking, camping, and, in winter, skiing, snowboarding and snowmachining (see page 181).

A mile or so beyond the lodge is the gravel parking area for Independence Mine State Historical Park. You can ramble on your own (or take a guided tour) through abandoned buildings of this 1930s gold mine operation, at that time one of the largest producers in Alaska, employing more than 200.

Hatcher Pass Road continues along, now as an old-time, un-maintained, real Alaska gravel road. During the summer you can complete the 50-mile (80km) drive (from the Glenn Highway turnoff) to **Willow** Ⓜ (located on the Parks Highway), a community of approximately 2,000 residents, many of whom are competitive mushers. The scenery of this stretch is nothing short of spectacular, but the road is steep, narrow, often rough, and switch-backed. It is not a good option for large RVs.

> **◎ Tip**
>
> Because Denali State Park is essentially a wilderness, hiking trails are not always clearly marked, and good USGS topographic maps are essential since whiteout conditions can occur in any season. Maps can be found at the Visitor Contact Station at the Alaska Veterans Memorial, Mile 147.1 Parks Highway.

Taking in the grandeur of the Matanuska Glacier.

Hatcher Pass.

Moose art.

TALKEETNA

If you turn north on the Parks Highway towards the Interior, don't pass up the opportunity to spend a few hours in **Talkeetna** ⓭ (pronounced *tal keet nuh*; turn north at Mile 98.7, then travel 14 miles/22km along the Talkeetna Spur Road), the staging area for climbers planning to summit Denali.

The Talkeetna Lodge (on the right, about a mile before Talkeetna), owned by the Cook Inlet Region, Inc. (CIRI) native corporation, is a clean, modern, beautifully rustic post-and-beam style hotel nestled in a quiet, wooded area of Talkeetna. On clear days, a fine view of Denali awaits you on the observation deck in front of the hotel.

In Talkeetna's 'downtown' area, renovated, rustic miners' cabins have been spruced up and converted into gift shops, lodgings, and restaurants. Known around the state for its quirky character, the town is home to the famous annual Moose Dropping Festival, and its beloved mayor, Stubbs, a highly regarded cat who passed away in 2017 aged 20. You can buy Stubbs T-shirts and postcards around town. Talkeetna was the inspiration for the television series *Northern Exposure*.

Talkeetna also offers fishing charters, river rafting adventures, and flightseeing tours to Denali. Contact the Talkeetna Chamber for more details (PO Box 334, Talkeetna, AK 99676; tel: 907-414-0376; www.talkeetna chamber.org).

DENALI STATE PARK

An often-overlooked option for those wanting to see Denali during their Alaska vacation is to visit **Denali State Park** ⓮, where outstanding views of the mountain are possible from a less-crowded vantage point. One of the best roadside views, weather permitting, may be enjoyed from the southern viewpoint (Mile 135.2).

You can also take a day hike to **Kesugi Ridge**, or if you're interested in backpacking adventures, a trek into the **Peters Hills** (in the western end of the park). Both options offer

stunning, panoramic views of Denali – if the weather cooperates.

Other recreation opportunities include camping, and kayaking or canoeing at the **Byers Lake Campground**. Wildlife common to the park includes moose, grizzly and black bears, wolves, lynx, coyotes, red fox, and land otters.

The area is also rich in birds, as more than 130 species use the park for breeding or during migration. Additional information is available at the visitor contact station, Mile 147.1, or contact the Denali Ranger (Alaska State Parks, Mat-Su/CB Area, 7278 East Bogard Road (HC 32, Box 6706), Wasilla 99654; tel: 907-745-3975; dnr.alaska.gov/parks/units/denali1.htm).

MAT-SU BACKCOUNTRY

Conveniently accessible from Anchorage, the backcountry opportunities of the Mat-Su are plentiful and varied. The area has the largest trail system in the Alaska State Parks network, offering over 2,000 miles (3,200km) of trails for all abilities. Prime examples include a nature walk through Denali State Park, where you can catch rare and glorious glimpses of Denali and the Tokositna Glacier.

In addition to Hatcher Pass, another excellent option is to explore some of the many trails in the **Talkeetna Mountains** – leading to alpine valleys, tundra vistas, and mountain streams.

Near Willow, the **Nancy Lake Recreation Area** (Mile 66.5 Parks Highway; tel: 907-495-6273; dnr.alaska.gov/parks/aspunits/matsu/nancylk-srs.htm) offers water enthusiasts a total of 130 interconnected lakes for their paddling pleasure – also canoe and kayak rentals, remote cabin rentals, campgrounds, and superb fishing for rainbow trout, Arctic char and northern pike.

Guided rafting adventures (whitewater or leisure floats) are available on the **Matanuska or Knik Rivers**. For details on these (and other) adventures to be experienced in the Mat-Su region, go to www.alaskavisit.com.

For those wanting to try a little solitude.

Snow-capped ridges of the Alaska Range, Denali National Park.

Family kayaking trip.

THE INTERIOR

You can follow in the footsteps of the 19th-century gold prospectors and discover the beauties, and the hardships, of Alaska's Interior. The area includes Denali National Park and Preserve, Fairbanks, outlying areas, and the Alcan highway.

Fishermen love the Interior.

The cry of 'Gold!' has lured men and women to the Interior for more than a century. That initial, passionate hunger for a handful of valuable nuggets – spawning the first of Alaska's many 'rushes' – is history now, but the spirit of the Interior still summons the adventurer.

The extraordinary wildlife-viewing, photography, and backcountry opportunities of Denali National Park and Preserve, the many historic sights and sounds of the heartland city of Fairbanks, and the scattered, outlying communities, hunkered down in the wilderness along mighty rivers, still sing out their siren call. And those who answer that call board planes, catch trains (from Southcentral Alaska), or simply pack up their cars (or RVs) and head north.

There *is* gold in the Interior, gilding every aspen leaf in the autumn explosion of color, glancing off the wingtips of geese, shimmering in the river current as it flows into a blazing sunset. It splashes across the midnight sky as the aurora and dances as moonlight over the hulking white shoulders of mountain peaks. Many who visit the Interior also find that the people have what can only be called hearts of gold. There is a longstanding tradition of caring, generosity and warm-heartedness that welcomes the traveler back again and again to the edge of the frontier.

The road to Denali.

STARK CONTRASTS

The Interior of Alaska, that one-third of the state north of the Alaska Range, south of the Brooks Range and east of Alaska's western coastal areas, is an area of stark contrasts. Denali, 20,320ft (6,195 meters) and snowcapped year-round, towers above the temperate Tanana and Yukon valleys. The Alaska Range is girdled with miles and miles of glaciers, while in the valleys, forests of white spruce, birch, and aspen fold into straggly stands of black spruce, tangles of willow, and muskeg.

If you are visiting the Interior in summer, as most people do, try conjuring up an image of what it would be like in winter, with low light reflecting blue off the snow-covered riverbed, and temperatures plummeting to –40°F (–40°C) or below. Summer weather is glorious, with nearly around-the-clock daylight and temperatures as high as 96°F (36°C). Travelers often find it hard to sleep because of all the light. The most practical advice is: don't even try to sleep until you're really tired, but enjoy the late evening light – this is the season that makes the cold dark winter worth enduring.

You will also find that the later evening is a fine time for photography. Light of this quality is experienced at lower latitudes for only a few moments around sunrise and sunset. In Alaska's Interior, the special glow hovers for hours, casting gigantic shadows and ethereal reflections.

Arctic ground squirrel.

EXPLORING THE RIVERS AND WOODS

Outdoor adventure is the glue that binds people to the land in the Interior. The mountains, rivers and valleys offer unparalleled opportunities for hiking, canoeing, hunting, and fishing. The best source of outdoors information is the **Alaska Public Lands Information Center** at 101 Dunkel Street, Fairbanks (tel: 907-459-3730; www.alaskacenters.gov; summer daily 8am–6pm, winter Mon–Sat 8am–5pm). This multi-agency information center and museum sells maps and answers questions about all categories of land.

The usually blue skies of summer coupled with hundreds of miles of wild and scenic rivers make water travel a natural pastime. Canoeing offers an idyllic opportunity to observe game animals undisturbed as the boat slips silently past. With the entire Interior river system at your paddle tip, deciding where to explore depends on ability and time. The Chena and Chatanika rivers offer a multitude of easily accessible possibilities for day trips or longer expeditions. For experienced wilderness canoeists, the more challenging clear waters of the Birch Creek can be accessed at Mile 94 Steese Highway, or consider a five-day sojourn on the broad sweep of the **Tanana River** from Delta Junction to Fairbanks. These rivers are all conveniently accessible by road.

LEGENDARY FISHING

The Interior is a freshwater fisherman's promised land, and the Arctic grayling is its manna. The flash of the strike and the fight of the silver streak on light tackle is a treasured memory for many. The Clearwater, Salcha, Chatanika and Chena rivers are superior grayling producers and are accessible by road. In fact, all clear-flowing creeks and rivers in the Interior are well stocked with grayling. Northern pike, burbot, and lake trout abound in the clear, cold waters throughout the Interior.

Sandhill cranes in flight.

A visit to the Interior presents a rare opportunity to savor the very heart of Alaska, to observe wildlife doing what they've done for thousands of years, to paddle quietly along picturesque, wild rivers, to hike rugged mountain trails to glorious panoramic vistas, to pan for gold, or to visit the area's many historic mining camps and museums to learn more about Alaska's colorful history.

View of the Richardson Highway, south of Delta Junction.

A grizzly bear forages in a blueberry patch.

DENALI NATIONAL PARK AND PRESERVE

Dominated by the magnificent mountain for which it is named, Denali National Park, which celebrated its centennial in 2017, is one of the world's greatest wildlife sanctuaries and the most visited of all Alaska's national parks.

Alaska's Athabascan people called the mountain by several names, but they all meant essentially the same thing: 'The Great One.' Denali was the most common and popular of these names. However, the mountain was first referred to as Mount McKinley by a prospector in 1896, and it became the official name in 1917. The designation stood until 2015, when President Barack Obama and US Secretary of the Interior Sally Jewell officially restored the name **Denali** for the mountain.Denali is North America's highest peak (20,320ft/6,195 meters) and is also amongst the continent's most spectacular. In one sense it is one of the highest mountains in the world: its north face rises almost 18,000ft (5,500 meters) above its base, an elevation gain that surpasses even Mount Everest.

The mountain is surrounded by one of the world's greatest wildlife sanctuaries, **Denali National Park and Preserve** ⓯ (tel: 907-683-9532; www.nps.gov/dena). A one-day trip through the park will almost certainly allow you to see grizzly bears, caribou, Dall sheep, moose, and perhaps a wolf. Denali Park is, for many, the ultimate Alaskan adventure.

GEOLOGY AND HISTORY

Denali is part of the **Alaska Range**, a 400-mile (650km) arc of mountains stretching across the state from the

Alaska Peninsula almost to the Canadian border. The oldest parts of the range are made up of slate, shale, marble, and other sedimentary deposits formed under an ancient ocean. Approximately 60 million years ago, the collision and subsequent overlapping of two tectonic plates produced such intense heat that sections of the earth's crust began to melt. A gigantic mass of molten rock deposited beneath the current location of Denali eventually solidified into granite.

Main attractions
Wilderness Access Center
Savage River
Sable Pass
Polychrome Pass
Toklat River
Highway Pass
Stony Hill Overlook
Eielson Visitor Center
Wonder Lake
Kantishna

Maps on pages 164, 228

Denali.

A hare in Denali National Park and Preserve.

The overlapping of the plates caused the whole region to rise. Granite and sedimentary rock were forced upward to form the mountain range.

As the uplift petered out, the process of erosion slowly wore down the range. As Denali is chiefly composed of erosion-resistant granite, it wore down at a slower rate than surrounding sedimentary rock. A later period of tectonic plate collision and uplift began two million years ago and continues to this day. This ongoing uplift is responsible for the towering height of Denali.

The first humans came on seasonal hunting trips to what is now Denali Park about 12,000 years ago. Later, the Athabascans followed suit, but built their villages in lower, warmer, sheltered locations, next to lakes or rivers that offered dependable fishing. However, the lack of large salmon runs limited native habitation.

The Athabascans of the Yukon and Tanana rivers gave Denali its name; one story refers to it as 'the home of the sun.' During the longest days of summer, the sun makes an almost complete circle in the local sky and drops below the horizon for only a few hours, staying light for 21 hours. From certain angles, it appears that the sun rises and sets from behind Denali.

The first recorded sighting of the mountain by a white man occurred in 1794. While sailing in Cook Inlet, the English Captain George Vancouver sighted 'distant stupendous mountains covered with snow.' Undoubtedly this was the Alaska Range. Other explorers, surveyors and adventurers in later decades commented on the mountain's great size and estimated its height.

THE NAMING PROCESS

Denali became known as Mount McKinley through a strange set of circumstances in 1896 when William Dickey went on a gold-prospecting expedition in the area. While camped within sight of the mountain, he met other miners and they argued at length whether gold or silver should back US currency. (The miners were against the gold standard while Dickey was for it.) When Dickey later returned to the Lower 48, he wrote

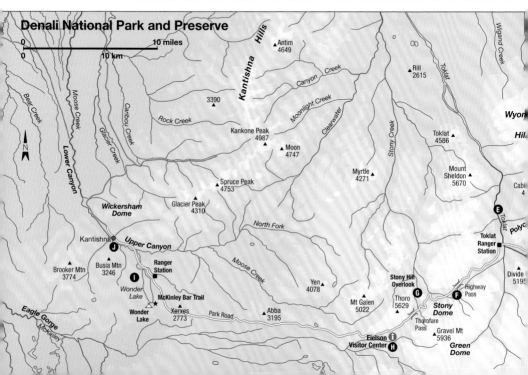

Denali National Park and Preserve

an article about his Alaskan adventures, and proposed that the highest mountain in the Alaskan Range be named after the Republican presidential candidate William McKinley, the champion of the gold standard. McKinley won the 1897 election and the name stuck.

One of the first white men to explore the Denali region was a naturalist and hunter, Charles Sheldon, who proposed that it be set aside as a national park and wildlife preserve. Sheldon made two extensive trips through the area in 1906 and 1907–08, and thought that the opportunity to see and study wildlife was the most impressive feature of the region.

After leaving Denali, Sheldon used his considerable influence to gather support for the proposed Denali National Park. Largely due to Sheldon's efforts, the park became a reality in 1917. To his disappointment however, Congress chose to call it Mount McKinley National Park.

In 1975, the Alaska Board of Geographic Names had a federal request to change the name back to Denali blocked by Ohio congressman Ralph Regula, whose constituency included McKinley's hometown. Nearly 100 years after its official naming, President Obama officially changed the name to Denali in 2015. Understandably, and after much campaigning from Alaska, the move was met with widespread praise in the state.

THE SOURDOUGH EXPEDITION

While Sheldon was campaigning for the park, others were endeavoring to make the first ascent of Denali. In late 1909, four miners (Billy Taylor, Pete Anderson, Charley McGonagall, and Tom Lloyd), not intimidated by the fact that they had never climbed a mountain before, decided to scale it. They figured if they had survived the Alaskan winters, they could do anything.

The so-called Sourdough Expedition set off from Fairbanks ('sourdough' was the nickname given to prospectors because of the yeasty mixture they brought with them to make bread) in December 1909 and spent much of the next few months establishing a series of camps. The group reached

Clouds rolling in over the mountains.

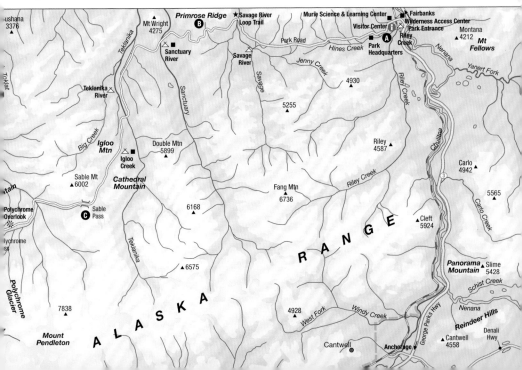

A grizzly encounter.

Denali's Muldrow Glacier in March. On the morning of April 3, 1910, McGonagall, Taylor and Anderson set out for the summit from their camp at 11,000ft (3,300 meters), carrying a 14ft (4-meter) spruce pole that they hoped would be visible from mining camps at Kantishna, and evidence of their ascent. McGonagall stopped part way up, but by mid-afternoon Taylor and Anderson stood atop Denali's North Peak: they had achieved their goal despite their total lack of experience.

Unfortunately for them, the North Peak is 850ft (260 meters) lower than the South Peak, Denali's true summit. Taylor and Anderson were never credited with being the first to the continent's top.

In 1913 Hudson Stuck and a party of three climbers mounted the first Denali expedition to actually reach the mountain's summit. Using route descriptions made by earlier parties, they ascended the Muldrow Glacier, which flows down the northeast side of Denali.

After a difficult climb, they reached Denali Pass, the saddle between the North and South Peaks, only 2,100ft (640 meters) below the summit. The high elevation, low oxygen and extreme cold made those last few hundred feet the hardest part of their climb. Walter Harper, a young Athabascan employed by Stuck and the strongest member of the team, was the first to stand on Denali's summit.

THE IMPACT OF TRAFFIC

From 1917 to the early 1970s, few people visited the park. Its remoteness and lack of direct access to Denali National Park by vehicle combined to limit tourism. In the five years prior to 1972, the average annual number of visitors was about 15,000. In 1972, the Anchorage–Fairbanks Highway was completed and it suddenly became much easier for tourists and Alaskan residents to get there. In a short time, the numbers jumped to more than 140,000 a year, almost a ten-fold increase over the previous figures. The latest estimate puts annual visitors at well over 600,000.

National Park Service rangers were concerned about the effect this dramatic rise would have on the park and

⊘ FLIGHTSEEING

If you're trying to spread limited financial resources across a very large state, here's a sound piece of free advice: go ahead and splurge by taking a flightseeing trip. No other mode of exploration will give as good an overview of all that makes this land so extraordinary. Soar over mountain peaks, swoop low over glacier-laden fjords, land on a glacier, peer down into deep, icy crevasses and get a bird's-eye-view of wildlife, rivers, forests, and scenic alpine meadows you'll otherwise only see in travel brochures. For more information, check with the Convention and Visitors Bureau in the city nearest your destination. Both Talkeetna Air Taxi (tel: 800-533-2219/907-733-2218; www.talkeetnaair.com) and Kantishna Air (tel: 907-644-8222; www.katair.com) offer spectacular tours of Denali.

the quality of visitors' experiences. One major problem was that the single dirt road that bisects the park was too narrow to handle the increased traffic. Another concern was the park's wildlife, which in the past had always been readily visible from the road.

The extra traffic and noise created by the increase in numbers was likely to drive the animals out of sight; and huge influxes of people could result in more encounters with the park's dangerous animals: grizzly bears and moose.

The creative and practical solution to these problems was the initiation of a shuttle and tour bus system: private vehicles must be parked in the entrance area and visitors board buses that run throughout the day, causing little disturbance to wildlife. However, visitors are allowed to drive their own vehicles as far as the Savage River Bridge, about 15 miles (24km) from the park entrance. That first stretch of road is paved, while the 75 miles (120km) or so beyond are gravel. The park road is closed beyond Mile 3 in winter, but a campground loop is plowed for campers.

In 1980, with the passing of the Alaska National Interest Lands Conservation Act (ANILCA), the park was expanded by 4 million acres (1.6 million hectares) and renamed the Denali National Park and Preserve,

ARRIVING IN THE PARK

The entrance to Denali Park is along the **George Parks Highway**, 240 miles (385km) north of Anchorage and 120 miles (193km) south of Fairbanks. Access to the park is also provided by the Alaska Railroad(www.alaskarailroad. com), which has a daily summer service from Anchorage and Fairbanks.

All within walking distance of each other are the train depot, the **Visitor Center Ⓐ** (tel: 907-683-2294), a bookstore and grill, the Wilderness Access Center, the Murie Science and Learning Center, the Riley Creek Campground, a post office, and a general store. Shuttle buses provide a free service between them every half hour.

Campground registration takes place at the **Wilderness Access Center.** Denali Park has six public roadside

A ranger leads dogsled demonstrations.

The view from the train up to Denali National Park.

⊙ Tip

Hiking on the tundra in Denali National Park guarantees unstable and soggy footing, and is not unlike walking on a waterlogged mattress. Many hikers wear 'gaiters,' which neatly fit over the tops of boots, to keep them dry, and extend up to the knee. A walking stick can also be helpful.

campgrounds containing a total of 275 sites. A couple of them, Igloo Creek and Sanctuary River, are very small and have no water; Riley and Savage River accommodate both tent and RV campers. Some advance reservations can be made by phone (tel: 800-622-7275) or online at www.reservedenali.com, and the rest are available on a first-come, first-served basis.

During the peak summer season (late May–early Sept), all campsites are often occupied by mid-morning. Should you arrive to find all campgrounds within the park full, you might check with the private campgrounds (located outside the boundary) that primarily cater to RV campers.

Backcountry permits are not as easy to acquire. First you must apply in person at the Backcountry Information Center adjacent to the Wilderness Access Center. Expect to watch a backcountry safety video and discuss your plans with a ranger. The park has a strict quota system for the number of campers in a given area, so you may not get your first choice of routes.

DOGSLED DEMONSTRATIONS

While in the park entrance area visit the sled dog kennel, located behind the park headquarters building at Mile 3 of the Park Road. Since the 1920s, park rangers have used sled dogs as a means of patrolling the park, as they are the most practical means of getting around Denali in the winter months. The dogs have become so popular with visitors that rangers put on several dogsledding demonstrations every day during the summer season.

THE BUS SYSTEM

The adventure of experiencing Denali National Park by road really begins when you step on a shuttle bus for an all-day trip into the park. There are several different bus trips, which all start at the **Wilderness Access Center**. The rangers can give you a bus schedule, and will explain how the system works.

The green buses, which go the whole 85 miles (136km) to Wonder Lake, do not provide a formal guided-tour program, although drivers will answer questions and help spot wildlife. Passengers can get on and off anywhere along the road, space permitting. The buses get very full in summer and should be booked well in advance, or at the Wilderness Access Center two days ahead. There are also special camper buses specifically operated for those with camping reservations or backcountry passes.

The Denali Natural History Tour bus goes to Primrose Ridge, about 17 road miles (27km) into the park, and the Tundra Wildlife Tour to the Stony Overlook at Mile 62 (in May, this tour ends at Toklat River, Mile 53). To travel the length of the park road, take the Kantishna Experience Tour, an 11 to 12 hour trip. Snacks are included in the tour bus ticket price and there are rest stops, but passengers must re-board the same bus.

Your chances of seeing wildlife, as well as Denali itself, are increased by taking as early a bus as possible (the first few depart at 6am). During

The Wilderness Access Center.

the rest of the morning they leave every half-hour. The early buses are very often in high demand. No food or drinks are available along the bus route, so be sure to take with you what you'll need for the day. Always be prepared for cool temperatures and rain regardless of what the early morning weather might be like.

The first leg of the bus route is the 14-mile (22km) stretch between the entrance and the **Savage River**. The first glimpses of Denali come into view in this area. This section of the Park Road goes through prime moose habitat; any time a moose or other animal is spotted, the bus will stop to allow passengers to watch and photograph the wildlife.

Moose are the biggest animals in the park – mature bulls can weigh as much as 1,500lbs (680kg). During the spring, watch for calves in this area. Cow moose usually have one or two calves each year. At birth, a calf weighs about 30lbs (14kg). Moose calves are one of the fastest-growing animals in the world. By their first birthday, they often weigh over 600lbs (270kg).

Each September and October this section of Denali Park becomes a rutting ground for moose. The huge bulls challenge each other over harems of cows, and they are deadly serious. A bull can kill his opponent with his sharp antler points. Rutting bulls and cow moose with calves should always be considered extremely dangerous and given a wide berth. If they are approached too closely, both cows and bulls will charge a human. If you should surprise a moose, run immediately and try to put something large, such as a tree, between you and the animal. Unlike bears, they never bluff charge.

A speckled ptarmigan making its escape.

PRIMROSE RIDGE

As your bus continues beyond the Savage River, you will pass a mountain to the north known as **Primrose Ridge B**. Dall sheep are often seen on the higher slopes of Primrose. They have pure white wool – perfect winter camouflage – but in summer, they readily stand out against the green tundra or dark rock formations. Like all wild sheep, Dall are generally found on or

A grizzly and its cubs cross the road.

⊙ Tip

A walk around the tundra ponds between Eielson and Wonder Lake will turn up many great photo compositions. Lighting on Denali is best in the early morning or late evening, when it is most likely to be cloud-free. Ansel Adams snapped his famous photo of Denali here at the aptly named Reflection Pond.

near steep cliffs, which are their security, as no predator can match their climbing speed or agility. Wolves and grizzlies can usually only catch weak or injured sheep, or those that have wandered too far from the crags.

The Dall ewes utilize the steepest cliffs in this area as lambing grounds. With luck, you may be able to spot young lambs on the higher slopes. Within a few days of birth, the lambs can match their mother's climbing ability. The lambs spend hours each day playing games of tag, king of the mountain and head-butting, which helps them develop their strength, agility and coordination.

Bands of rams may also be seen in the Primrose Ridge region. Rams are very concerned with the issue of dominance. A band will establish a pecking order based on the size of their horns, which are their most important status symbol. The older rams have horns of such size that they can easily intimidate the younger ones. Head-butting contests determine which of the mature animals will be dominant. The reward comes during the fall rutting season when the top rams are the ones who get to do most of the mating.

THE GRIZZLIES OF SABLE PASS

By the time you reach **Sable Pass ⊙** at Mile 39 you are surrounded by tundra, which is any area of plant growth above the treeline. Sable Pass has an elevation of 3,900ft (1,188 meters), well above the average local treeline of 2,400ft (730 meters). The cool temperatures and strong winds at these altitudes are too severe for trees. The low-growing tundra vegetation survives by taking advantage of the slightly warmer and less windy micro-environment at ground level.

Sable Pass is prime grizzly country. So many bears use this area that the Park Service has prohibited all off-road hiking here. Denali Park's total grizzly population is estimated at 300 to 350 bears. Grizzlies are omnivores: like humans, they eat both meat and vegetation. They would prefer to eat large animals such as moose, caribou, and Dall sheep but they are not often successful as hunters. The tundra vegetation in places like Sable Pass

Visitors traveling through Polychrome Pass.

⊙ GRIZZLY ENCOUNTERS

When it feels threatened, the grizzly is among the most dangerous animals in North America. The only visitor ever to be killed by a grizzly since the park's creation in 1917 was a backpacker in August 2012. Only a few people have been injured in bear attacks here, but clearly these large, powerful animals can kill if they are agitated or alarmed by your behavior. Visitors should do everything possible to avoid provoking a bear. Most bears will steer clear of humans if given the opportunity. The few attacks on people have almost always been provoked, for instance mothers protecting their cubs from people who get too close. The man who was mauled was photographing the bear. Park rangers can give you information on avoiding problems with grizzlies (see page 83).

offers a dependable, easily obtainable source of nutrition, while Arctic ground squirrels, nicknamed 'bear burritos' by some park naturalists, make up much of the difference. Visitors are frequently treated to an amusing show as grizzlies scramble to capture these rodents.

Grizzly cubs are born in January or February in the mother's hibernation den. The sow gives birth to between one and four cubs – the average is two – weighing about 1lb (450g) each. Sable Pass is one of the best places in the world for viewing grizzly families. You may see the cubs being nursed, or racing across the tundra, play-fighting with each other. The sow usually drives off her young when they are 2.5 years old, when they may weigh 100 to 150lbs (45 to 67kg). She then breeds again and gives birth to another litter the following winter.

Before you round the bend across the east fork of the Toklat River, keep a lookout for the cabin of famed Denali biologist Adolph Murie. Built in the 1920s, it was Murie's home as he documented his groundbreaking observations about the park's wildlife.

Next, your bus will ascend the heart-stopping **Polychrome Pass**  at Mile 45, where it will stop at summit's rest area. The visually stunning, brightly colored Polychrome cliffs are volcanic rocks formed around 50 million years ago. The spectacular view to the south includes part of the Alaska Range, as well as a vast area of tundra.

WOLF OBSERVATION

Polychrome Pass is a good place to watch for wolves. A local pack sometimes uses these flats as its hunting grounds, especially in spring when caribou are in migration. The Denali wolves range from white to black but most are gray. They may be traveling alone or in small groups.

If a pack is sighted, look for a wolf with its tail in the air. This will be the alpha wolf, the leader of the pack, although he may well be bringing up the rear. The alpha male often delegates the lead position to the beta wolf, his second in command.

In a wolf pack, the only members who normally breed are the alpha male and

A black wolf hunting for prey.

Rangers brief visitors on how to stay safe.

the alpha female. Their litter is born in the spring and all other members of the pack help to feed the young pups. Feeding a litter of five to 10 pups is a difficult job, even for the entire pack. If all its members tried to breed, the territory could not support the number of offspring. The pack is better served by limiting breeding to the dominant pair, who have proved themselves to be the fittest animals.

Much of what is now known about wolves was discovered by Murie, the first scientist extensively to study wolf behavior in the field. In 1944, Murie published *The Wolves of Mount McKinley*, one of the great classics of animal behavior. He concluded that wolves, which prey primarily on the sick and weak Dall sheep, caribou, and moose, were a necessary part of the Denali ecosystem because they ultimately helped to keep their prey species in a strong and healthy state.

CARIBOU COUNTRY

Your bus will then cross the gravelly **Toklat River ❺** to the next rest area,

Moose make their way through Denali National Park.

at Mile 53. Here you can stretch your legs and browse the Alaska Geographic bookstore. Next comes **Highway Pass ❻**, where caribou are known to frequent. In the spring, herds of several hundred pass through this area, heading toward their calving grounds to the east. Later in the season, they migrate back, moving toward their wintering grounds in the western and northern sections of the park. The herds are constantly on the move. Even as they feed, they rarely browse for more than a few moments at a time. If they spent too long in one area, they would kill off the fragile tundra vegetation.

Caribou, like moose, have antlers rather than horns. Antlers are formed of bone and are shed every year, while sheep horns consist of keratin, the same material as our fingernails, and are never shed. The caribou bulls' antlers are fully developed by September and are used to fight for harems. These matches usually occur between Highway Pass and Wonder Lake. After their rutting season is over, the antlers drop off; without their massive weight the

caribou have a better chance of surviving the winter, a stressful time.

As your bus approaches **Stony Hill Overlook** , Mile 61, be prepared for a spectacular view of Denali. From the overlook, it is 37 miles (60km) to the summit. On a cloudless day, the crystal-clear Alaskan air makes the mountain appear much closer. After a stop at Stony Hill, the bus will continue 4 miles (6km) to the **Eielson Visitor Center** . Park rangers here can answer your questions and suggest good hiking routes in the area.

If you are on a shuttle bus that continues on to **Wonder Lake** , an additional 20 miles (32km) beyond Eielson, this will add about two hours to your day. If the weather is clear, it's well worth the time, particularly in the fall when the color is brightened by reds, oranges, and yellows, and caribou frequent the area. Denali remains in full view along the entire route. On the way, many species of waterfowl are seen in tundra ponds, and in the evening, you can see beavers swimming across.

The park road ends in **Kantishna** , 5 miles (8km) beyond the turn out for the Wonder Lake campground. Once a thriving mining community, Kantishna's hills are dotted with abandoned mines, cabins, and roads that lead nowhere. Today, there are four independent backcountry lodges that were incorporated into the park when it extended its boundaries in 1980. At the Roadhouse, non-guests are welcome to sidle up to the bar and drink in the pioneer flavor.

WALKS AND HIKES

Most of Denali National Park is a true wilderness, and the best way to experience the park is by getting off the road, even if you go only a quarter mile or so. There are few official trails and these are mainly in the entrance area. Elsewhere, you are on your own. Despite the vast size of the Denali wilderness, route-making is not difficult for those who are experienced with maps. Since most of the park is open tundra, it is easy to choose a destination visually and hike straight to it, though often the distance is farther than you might expect and the terrain more rugged. You may leave the shuttle bus wherever you choose, hike for a few hours and then catch a later bus anywhere along the road.

Good areas for day hikes include the Savage River, Primrose Ridge, Polychrome and Highway Passes, the Eielson area and Wonder Lake. Before you begin a day-hike, talk to a ranger at one of the visitor centers about safety tips, and ask for a map. Permits are required for overnight trips into the park's backcountry.

National park rangers offer a wide variety of information to help you appreciate the area. Schedules of activities are posted at the Denali Visitor Center and at other locations throughout the park. The award-winning film *Heartbeats of Denali* is shown in the Denali Visitor Center's Karstens Theater (it's shown at the Murie Science and Learning Center in the off-season), and guided walks and half-day hikes are given each day in different sections of the park.

Eielson Visitor Center.

Gray wolf, Denail National Park.

THE ALCAN

They said it couldn't be built. But the Alaska–Canada Highway, conceived as a military route in World War II, now runs all the way from Seattle to Delta Junction.

⊙ Main attractions
British Columbia
Whitehorse
The Yukon
Delta Junction

Map on page 164

In 1942, while the world was at war, thousands of American soldiers drove bulldozers instead of tanks, as they spent eight months building a 1,500-mile (2,400km) highway from Dawson Creek, British Columbia, to Delta Junction, Alaska, just south of Fairbanks.

Construction of the Alaska–Canada Military Highway (the Alcan) was approved by President Franklin D. Roosevelt after the bombing of Pearl Harbor in 1941. The road linked the contiguous United States to Alaska, then still a territory, and a part of the US that many feared would be the next target. (In a propaganda broadcast, the Japanese forces thanked workers for opening a way for their own troops.)

Construction began in March 1942 and was completed by October. Soldiers battled the untracked wilderness of western Canada and eastern Alaska, along with spring mud, mosquitoes and, in fall, subfreezing temperatures. Rather than following the most direct route, the road linked existing airfields at Canada's Fort St John, Fort Nelson, Watson Lake, and Whitehorse. At the project's peak, more than 11,000 military troops and 7,000 civilians were at work on the highway.

WILDLIFE VIEWING

Today, the former military road provides a leisurely and scenic way for visitors to reach Alaska year-round. The Alaska Highway more or less follows its original path, wiggling its way northwest through British Columbia and the Yukon into Alaska's Interior. But what was once a wilderness adventure road is now a paved highway. The scenery is still breathtaking and the chances of seeing wildlife are good, but continual road improvements have eased many of the dangers that once made driving north to Alaska an ordeal.

Which is not to say the road is a Sunday drive. It's only two lanes wide, often without a centerline, and although the

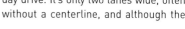
The Richardson Highway along the Delta River.

entire length is asphalt-surfaced, sections have to be repaved continually. Drivers should watch for wildlife and construction workers on the road as well as potholes, gravel breaks, and deteriorating shoulders. On the northern section of the highway, frost heaves – the result of the freezing and thawing of the ground – cause the pavement to ripple.

In addition, it's a long drive. Towns dot the map along the highway, but stretches of wilderness threaten drivers with exhaustion and/or boredom. And the 'towns' are often no more than a collection of houses clustered around a store/gas station/hotel. When accidents occur, particularly in winter, it can be a long time before someone happens along to rescue a stranded or injured driver.

'I SURVIVED'

Despite the rigors of the road, more than 100,000 people make the trip every year. In Alaska, you'll often see cars sporting bumper stickers that proclaim 'I survived the Alcan Highway.' Most make the journey during the summer

months – June, July, and August, when the days are long and the weather poses fewer hazards. From Seattle it's about 2,300 miles (3,700km; including the route along Interstate 5 to Trans-Canada Highway 1 and then BC Highway 97 to Dawson Creek) and it will take at least four or five days. An excellent guide is *The Milepost*, a 700-page map book (updated yearly) that documents the Alcan, plus almost every mile of every major highway in the state. Also visit www.themilepost.com.

A road sign warns of slippery and icy conditions.

Local traffic.

Outdoor dining at the Pump House Restaurant.

FAIRBANKS

Beneath its workaday exterior, Fairbanks is a lively place with a friendly population. It offers the clearest view of the Northern Lights, and the museum at the University of Alaska Fairbanks is one of the best in the state.

On August 26 1901, E.T. Barnette had just been dropped on a high wooded bank along the Chena River, along with 130 tons of equipment. How did this riverboat captain, dog musher and aspiring entrepreneur become marooned in the middle of the Alaska wilderness? The answer has all the ingredients of a true Alaskan adventure tale.

THE BIRTH OF FAIRBANKS

Barnette journeyed to the Klondike in 1897, taking what was considered the rich man's route. He sailed from Seattle to St Michael (a coastal community on an island at the mouth of the Yukon River), where he was supposed to catch a sternwheeler to Dawson, British Columbia.

But when he arrived in St Michael, the boat had already departed. Undaunted, Barnette and several others bought a dilapidated sternwheeler, and set off for Dawson. Barnette piloted the craft to Circle and finally arrived at his destination via dogsled, after freeze-up. He prospered that winter selling much-needed supplies to men in the gold fields, but the Klondike was too tame for the likes of this man.

During the winter of 1901, Barnette returned south to Seattle, and arranged a deal that, he speculated, would make him a rich man. He and a partner purchased $20,000 worth of equipment to outfit a trading post, not in the Klondike

Kayaking on the Chena River.

but at the halfway point of the trail connecting Valdez, on the coast, with Eagle, on the Yukon River. Barnette considered this to be a strategically sound location to build what he hoped would become the 'Chicago of the North,' the industrial hub of the territory. It was at this point that the Valdez-to-Eagle Trail crossed the Tanana River, and he planned to accommodate both overland and river traffic.

Barnette shipped the equipment to St Michael and departed for Circle to purchase a sternwheeler. He arrived in St

Main attractions

Immaculate Conception
Church
St Matthew's Episcopal
Church
Old Federal Courthouse
Empress Theater
Pioneer Park
Sternwheeler Nenana
University of Alaska
Fairbanks
Geophysical Institute
Gold Dredge No. 8

Maps on pages 164, 244

Michael without incident, but there the sternwheeler struck a submerged rock, and the bottom was torn from the boat. At this point, Barnette was more than 1,000 miles (1,600km) from his destination with 260,000lbs (120,000kg) of equipment, a horse, a quantity of food, no ready cash, and a worthless sternwheeler. It was time for another partner. He convinced the customs agent in St Michael to co-sign notes and made him a full partner.

Barnette struck a deal with the captain of the sternwheeler *Lavelle Young* to take him to Tanacross (Tanana Crossing). The fine print on the contract stated that if the *Lavelle Young* went beyond the point where the Chena joined the Tanana River and could go no farther, Captain E.T. Barnette would then disembark with his entire load of supplies, no matter where they were.

As destiny would have it, the *Lavelle Young* could not float through the Tanana shallows, called Bates Rapids, so the captain steamed up the Chena River, convinced by the increasingly desperate Barnette that it would join up again with the Tanana River. It did not. Captain Barnette had no choice but to offload his massive pile of gear on a high bank with a good stand of trees. It seemed that his string of bad luck could get no worse.

THE NEW GOLD RUSH

Two down-and-out prospectors watched the sternwheeler's progress up the Chena from a hillside, now called Pedro Dome, about 20 miles (32km) north of where Fairbanks is now located. The miners had found some 'color' but no major strike, and were faced with the frustration of a 330-mile (530km) round-trip hike back to Circle City to replenish much-needed supplies. The prospectors, Felix Pedro, an Italian immigrant, and Tom Gilmore, eagerly set off for the stranded boat, hoping to purchase necessities.

Barnette was surprised to see the prospectors but pleased to sell them anything they needed. Still possessed by his wild scheme to establish a trading post at Tanacross, Barnette sent to Montana for Frank Cleary, his brother-in-law. Cleary would guard the cache of supplies

The Unknown First Family statue.

while Barnette and his wife returned to Seattle to obtain a boat capable of travelling the remaining 200 miles (320km) up the Tanana River to Tanacross. Braving the −40°F (−40°C) temperature, the Barnettes then departed for Valdez and points south in March 1903.

In their absence Cleary decided to outfit Felix Pedro again, on credit this time because Pedro had no collateral. Although this broke Barnette's rule, Cleary's decision proved wise and shaped the future of the Interior. Just three months later, in July 1902, Pedro quietly announced to Cleary that he had struck pay dirt.

Learning of the strike upon their return to the Chena camp later that summer, the Barnettes immediately abandoned all thoughts of moving to Tanacross. They had two shiploads of supplies in hand and were on the brink of the next gold rush. Clearly, there was money to be made.

Hundreds of gold-hungry prospectors swarmed out of Circle City, Dawson and Nome, and stampeded to the newest gold fields in the north. By the time they arrived, much of the promising land was already staked, most of it by 'pencil miners' like Barnette who secured the claims only for the purpose of selling them later.

These clever businessmen staked as many as 100 claims of 20 acres (8 hectares) each, thus controlling vast amounts of potentially rich ground. And still the stampede continued.

On the return trip from Seattle, Barnette had spoken with Judge Wickersham about naming his little settlement. The judge offered his support to Barnette if he would use the name 'Fairbanks,' for Senator Charles Fairbanks of Indiana, who later became Vice President under Teddy Roosevelt; Fairbanks it was.

The community of Fairbanks in 1903 consisted of Barnette's trading post, numerous tents, a few log houses, and wooden sidewalks where the mud was particularly deep. What a fine tribute to the senator from Indiana.

FAIRBANKS TODAY

Unless you have driven up the Alaska and Richardson or Parks highways,

Tourists panning for gold.

you'll arrive in **Fairbanks** ⑯ at the airport. You will have to handle your own luggage as there are no porter services. Many hotels offer guests free transportation and will send a vehicle if called, and taxis are usually plentiful.

While around 32,000 people call Fairbanks home, few people visit the town in winter, unless they absolutely have to; the city's short days and frigid temperatures are hardly a draw; on the winter solstice, Fairbanks gets just three hours and 42 minutes of sunlight. Temperatures plummet to –40°F (–40°C) or even lower for days or weeks at a time, with the average December temperature registering –6.5°F (–21.4°C) in the city. A rather unpleasant side effect of temperatures below –20°F (–29°C) is ice fog, which hangs in the still air. The fog results from a temperature inversion trapping ice crystals, smoke, and exhaust fumes in a blanket of cold air.

ORIENTATION

To begin your Fairbanks adventure, visit the riverside park, **Golden Heart Plaza**.

There you'll find the bronze statue, *The Unknown First Family*, and the attractive **Morris Thompson Cultural and Visitors Center** Ⓐ (101 Dunkel Street; tel: 907-459-3700; www.morristhompsoncenter.org; daily summer 8am–9pm, winter 8am–5pm). In addition to showing films and hosting art exhibits, the center is home to the Alaska Public Lands Information Center (tel: 907-459-3730), and the Fairbanks Convention and Visitors Bureau (tel: 907-456-5774; www.explorefairbanks.com), which offers a comprehensive guide to the Interior and a brochure for a self-guided tour of the town,

A STROLL THROUGH TOWN

The monument to E.T. Barnette, located near First Avenue and Lacey Street marks the spot where the town was born and is a good starting place for modern-day explorers. Here, too, is the obelisk that marks **Milepost 1,523** of the Alaska Highway. The milepost is hidden behind posing tourists most of the summer. Even with the completion of the Dalton Highway to Prudhoe

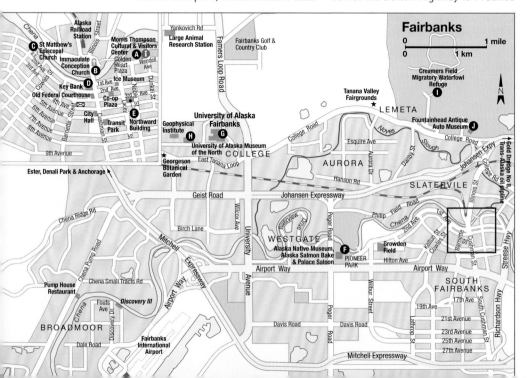

Bay, Fairbanks has, since World War II, been touted as the end of the highway. Residents like to say this is where the road ends and the wilderness begins.

Turn right across the Cushman Street Bridge pausing for a look at the Chena River. The **Immaculate Conception Church**  stands across the river from the Visitors Center. The church originally stood on the opposite side of the river at the corner of First and Dunkel. In 1911, Father Francis Monroe decided it should be closer to the hospital on the north side of the Chena. Many Catholics pitched in to move the building across the frozen river. Visitors are welcome to come inside and admire the stained-glass windows and the pressed-tin ceiling paneling.

Half a block north on the opposite side of the street is the *Fairbanks Daily News Miner* building at 200 N. Cushman Street. The *News Miner* (www.newsminer.com) publishes seven days a week, carrying on a long tradition. Judge Wickersham (the man who originally suggested to Barnette that the town should be called Fairbanks) published the first paper, the *Fairbanks Miner*, on May 9, 1903. All seven copies sold for $5 each, making the first edition one of the most expensive in the world. He used the money to help finance his 1903 expedition to climb Denali – the first group to ever make such an attempt. Wickersham's pioneering group reached an elevation of about 11,000ft (3,350 meters) before being turned back by near-vertical walls and tremendous avalanches.

Recross the Chena River to **St Matthew's Episcopal Church** at 1029 First Avenue. The altar of St Matthew's was carved from a single piece of wood, but no one is quite sure of the origin of the huge chunk. The stained-glass windows are of special interest; they portray images of Jesus, Mary, and Joseph with Alaskan Native features. Located in a log cabin, services were first held here in 1905.

Near the church, at the corner of First and Cushman, is the **Key Bank**, which was started as a First National Bank on that very site in June of the same year. 'Square Sam' Bonnifield and his brother John founded the bank, now the oldest national bank in Alaska. 'Square Sam' was given his nickname because he had been an honest gambler in Circle City, and miners could turn their backs while he was weighing a poke of gold.

DOWNTOWN

Head south down Cushman Street, the heart of downtown Fairbanks – although not exactly a fast-throbbing one. The **Old Federal Courthouse** stands near the intersection of Second Avenue and Cushman. When Judge Wickersham officially moved the Federal Court here in 1903, he built the courthouse on this piece of real estate, donated by Barnette, securing the future of the young settlement.

The original wooden structure burned down, and the present building was completed in 1934. It included the first elevator in the Interior. Federal offices

The Immaculate Conception Church.

⊘ SPOT THE DIFFERENCE IN GOLDEN DAYS

Felix Pedro, the prospector who hit gold back in 1902, sported a beard, and so does most of the male population during the third week of July when Fairbanks celebrates Golden Days. One event is a Felix Pedro Look-Alike Contest, and there is a re-enactment of Pedro's ride into town after his discovery.

His ride is part of the festival's biggest attraction, a parade through downtown Fairbanks complete with antique cars, clowns, and marching bands. Innocents need to be aware of the roving jail, because those not wearing a fundraising button are liable to be incarcerated for as long as it takes them to bribe the jail keeper.

Other party events include an E.T. Barnette Look-Alike Contest and a Hairy Legs, Chest, Beard and Mustache Contest. A Rubber Duckie Race offers prizes worth more than $25,000. Spectators buy numbered tickets, after which the Golden Days executive committee drops about 6,000 yellow ducks, each carrying a number, from the Wendell Street Bridge into the Chena River. The numbered ducks float downstream to the finish line at the Golden Heart Plaza.

Golden Days has been described as a politically incorrect blend of Mardi Gras, Halloween, and Founders' Day – with a decidedly Alaskan twist.

Tip

You can get a relaxed view of Fairbanks by hiring a canoe and spending the day paddling around the Chena River. Canoes can be rented for $37 to $52 a day from Canoe Alaska (1101 Pegger Road, Pioneer Park; tel: 907-457-2453).

soon required more space and were relocated, leaving the building open for remodeling into offices and shops.

The next stop is **Co-op Plaza** at 535 Second Avenue. Of 1927 vintage, this building was Captain Lathrop's gift to the people of Fairbanks. Before then, the buildings in Fairbanks were constructed of wood because, it was believed, no other material could withstand the test of a –60°F (–51°C) winter. This concrete affair was originally the **Empress Theater**, with 670 seats and the first pipe organ in the Interior. Locals tend to use 'the Co-op' as a meeting place.

During the mid-1970s, while the trans-Alaska oil pipeline was under construction, Second Avenue was the scene of incessant activity, with bars packed at all hours. Workers flew to town during rest periods from remote construction camps, only to spend most of their time (and money) along Second Avenue.

If you carry on down Cushman, you will come to the area known as **The Line**, the block of Fourth Avenue to your right, as far as Barnette Street. The boulevard was lined with small log cabins housing prostitutes, and to ensure that no one unwittingly wandered into this sinful area, the booming city of Fairbanks erected Victorian wooden gates at both ends. The Line has disappeared now, replaced by less colorful downtown businesses and parking lots.

THE ICE PALACE

Cross Cushman Street again and continue on Fourth Avenue past Lacey Street. On the next block, bounded by Lacey and Noble streets and Third and Fourth avenues, towers the 'Ice Palace.' Officially the **Northward Building** Ⓔ, it was the first steel-girded skyscraper built in the Interior, and became the inspiration for Edna Ferber's 1958 novel *Ice Palace*.

The 'palace' in the novel is a modern skyscraper built by a ruthless millionaire named Czar Kennedy. Fairbanks' locals recognized in Czar Kennedy the reflection of a prominent businessman, developer and politician, Captain Austin E. Lathrop.

A couple study a monument downtown.

ICE SCULPTING

Competitors in the World Ice Art Championships (www.icealaska.org), held in Fairbanks in March, carve their masterpieces from mammoth blocks of ice cut from ponds. Freezing together blocks, lifted into position by forklifts, can enable sculptures up to 24ft (7 meters) high. These can survive for three or four weeks in a park by the Chena River, depending on the weather. From May to September, you can view ice carvings at **Fairbanks Ice Museum** (500 2nd Avenue; tel: 907-451-8222; icemuseum. com; May–Sept daily 10am–8pm). Located in the Lacey Street Theater, built in 1936, the museum features a film chronicling the championships. You can also have your picture taken sitting in an ice chair, or slip down a 20ft (6-meter) ice slide for a brief thrill, and there's a Northern Lights program at 8pm.

CITY SHOPPING

Fairbanks offers a cornucopia of gifts for the traveler. Gold nugget jewelry, always a favorite, is priced by the pennyweight (dwt) with 20dwt equal to one troy ounce (1dwt = 1.555 grams). Remember that nuggets used in jewelry command a premium price, which is higher than that for raw gold.

Native handicrafts from the Interior are also treasured souvenirs. The Authentic Native Handicraft Symbol assures visitors that they are buying the genuine article. Be careful, as counterfeits abound. Favorite items include beaded slippers, beaded mittens and gloves, birch bark baskets, porcupine quill jewelry, and dolls made with fur.

PIONEER PARK

Pioneer Park F, a 44-acre (18-hectare) city park at the corner of Airport Way and Peger Road, to the south of the downtown area, is filled with a number of attractions offering a snapshot of life in the 'golden heart of Alaska' (tel: 907-459-1087; summer daily noon–8pm, other months daily noon–6pm;

free). You can get a shuttle bus to the park from the Visitors Bureau and from many of the main hotels in town.

The southeast corner of the park is devoted to Fairbanks history, in particular the gold rush. It includes an assortment of original structures rescued from the boomtown period. Every building is a piece of history, including Judge Wickersham's home, the first frame house in Fairbanks, which was built by the judge in 1904 as a surprise for his wife. It is a rather melancholy reminder of life in early Fairbanks: the bedridden Mrs Wickersham spent most of that summer sleeping in a tent as fresh air was thought to help cure tuberculosis.

Within the park you'll also find the **Alaska Native Museum**, with artifacts and demonstrations of crafts still carried out in remote parts of the Interior. Nearby, the **Sternwheeler Nenana** is listed in the National Register of Historic Places because so few of these vessels remain. It is a classic paddlewheeler with a colorful history on the waterways of the Interior. Imagine leaning back in the captain's chair, the stack

Tip

The Alaskan Interior produces some of the finest lynx, marten, wolverine, fox, and wolf fur in the world. Many people disapprove of buying furs; if you want them, Fairbanks is the place to purchase raw or tanned furs and fur coats, jackets, and hats – but be aware of customs regulations if you are taking such items out of the United States.

Morris Thompson Cultural and Visitors' Center.

belching sparks, and the crew scurrying about the deck as you maneuver the craft through the Yukon River.

Even the building that now houses the **Park Office** had a spicy past as a brothel, and the **Gold Rush Town** is packed with small shops containing an interesting array of crafts.

If you get hungry, follow your nose to the **Alaska Salmon Bake** – great value for a tasty Alaskan meal: king salmon, halibut, and ribs are grilled over an open alder fire to give them a very special flavor. After dinner, you could saunter over to the **Palace Saloon** and enjoy a drink while cancan girls entertain you.

UNIVERSITY PURSUITS

The **University of Alaska Fairbanks** (UAF) is located on a bluff overlooking Fairbanks and the Tanana Valley (take a Red or Blue Line bus from the town center). Established in 1917 as the Alaska Agricultural College and School of Mines, UAF is the main campus for a system that operates four-year satellites in Anchorage and Juneau. An emphasis on high latitude and Alaska research has earned UAF an excellent reputation.

The 2,250-acre (910-hectare) campus is a town unto itself, with its own post office, radio and TV stations, a fire department, and the traditional college facilities. A trip to the UAF campus is well worthwhile, and it's also a good opportunity to relax en route at the turnout on Yukon Drive and absorb the view of the Alaska Range. The large marker, with mountain silhouettes and elevations, helps you identify the splendid peaks fringing the southern horizon. It's the best Fairbanks view you'll get of Denali. Free guided walking tours of the university are offered Monday through Friday at 10am and 2.30pm (tel: 907-474-7500; www.uaf.edu/visituaf).

The **University of Alaska Museum of the North** on the UAF campus is a great idea for visitors to the Interior (1962 Yukon Drive; tel: 907-474-7505; www.uaf.edu/museum; summer daily 9am–7pm, other months Mon–Sat 9am–5pm). The museum is one of the best in the state, combining cultural artifacts, scientific equipment, and displays such as

Winter sunset over the University of Alaska.

⊘ MIDNIGHT BASEBALL

Fairbanks residents do not allow the summer solstice to slip by uncelebrated. On June 21, the semi-pro Alaska Goldpanners baseball team plays the Midnight Sun game at Growden Field with the first pitch crossing the plate at 10.30pm – and the entire game is played under natural light. Also known as the 'high noon at midnight classic' the annual event celebrated its 100-year anniversary during the 2005 summer solstice. There is also an arts and crafts fair, a midnight fun run (attracting 3,000-plus runners), and speedboat racing, when sleek racing boats propelled by twin 50-horsepower outboard motors zoom down the Chena, Tanana and Yukon rivers to Galena, returning at breakneck speed to Fairbanks and the finish line at Pike's Landing.

prehistoric objects extricated from the permanently frozen ground. A huge, 36,000-year-old bison carcass (nicknamed Blue Babe) found near Fairbanks, preserved in the permafrost, is displayed here, complete with skin.

The Native Cultures displays are an educational introduction to the Athabascan, Eskimo, Aleut, and Tlingit cultures. The collections date back to 1926, when the president of the school assigned Otto William Geist the task of amassing Eskimo artifacts. In the summer, there are daily shows on the aurora and native culture.

Tours are also provided at the **Geophysical Institute** (tel: 907-474-7558; www.gi.alaska.edu), a world center for Arctic and aurora research, during which a spectacular film of the aurora borealis is shown. Free tours are offered at the **Large Animal Research Station** (Yankovich Road; 1am, noon and 2pm; www.uaf.edu/lars), formerly known as the Musk Ox Farm. These woolly prehistoric creatures graze in research pastures together with moose, reindeer, and caribou.

A WILDLIFE TRAIL

Save a little shoe leather for a very special wildlife trail situated within the city limits of Fairbanks. **Creamers Field ❶** (tel: 907-452-6152; www.adfg.alaska.gov/index.cfm?adfg=creamersfield.main) at 1300 College Road was originally Charles Creamers' dairy farm, started in 1920. The 250 acres (100 hectares) remained in active production until the land was purchased by the state and was set aside as a waterfowl refuge in 1967. It now boasts 2,000 acres (809 hectares), and is one of Alaska's most easily accessible birding areas.

While hiking the nature trails you can see many species of animals, including diving ducks, shorebirds, cranes, foxes, or even a moose. The real show, however, takes place in late April to early May and again in August and September when the sandhill cranes, Canadian honkers, and ducks congregate in the field – it really is something to see. Take a Red Line bus to the trailhead, where the Department of Fish and Game office housed in the white farmhouse will provide you with a map and trail guide.

Bluebells in bloom.

Barbecue at Pioneer Park.

Motoring enthusiasts should definitely visit the nearby Fountainhead Antique Auto Museum (212 Wedgewood Dr, tel: 907-450-2100; www.fountainhead museum.com; summer Sun–Thu 10am–7pm, Fri–Sat 11am–6pm, other months Wed & Sun noon–6pm) showing more than 85 antique cars. There is also a section dedicated to vintage motoring fashion and historic clothing, with selections from the 600 outfits in the collection.

RIVERBOAT EXCURSIONS

Riverboats have never been far removed from the history of Fairbanks since E.T. Barnette's load of supplies was put ashore. In 1950 the late Jim and Mary Binkley continued the tradition with river tours aboard a boat made in the Binkley's backyard. Today, the company remains in family hands operating the 700-passenger *Discovery III* for excursions on the Chena and Tanana rivers. The Binkleys' narration brings history to life along the river banks.

A riverboat cruises down the Chena.

The sternwheeler's port of departure is at the end of Discovery Drive, just off Airport Way. Reservations are recommended (1975 Discovery Drive; tel: 907-479-6673/866-479-6673; www.river boatdiscovery.com).

Take note of the **Pump House Restaurant**, where you can enjoy grilled Alaskan halibut and a glass of wine after your river tour in a replica of a gold rush-era building.

SPECIAL EVENTS IN FAIRBANKS

The winter festival spirit has been revived in Fairbanks and is now called the **Winter Carnival**, celebrated during the second and third weeks of March. Fairbanks has traditionally hosted the **North American Open Sled Dog Championship** at this time. The 'North American,' as locals refer to it, was first run in 1946 and is not to be missed. The sprint race is run on three consecutive days (20 miles/32km the first two days and a tough 30 miles/48km the third day), with the start and finish line in downtown Fairbanks on Second Avenue. It attracts the finest sprint dog mushers, racing teams of up to 20 dogs.

Another sled dog race, not a sprint, is the **Yukon Quest**, a grueling 1,000-mile (1,600km) race between Whitehorse, Yukon Territory, Canada, and Fairbanks, following the old Gold Rush and mail delivery routes. Held in February, the race, first run in 1984, ends in Fairbanks in odd-numbered years and runs in the opposite direction in even-numbered years. The fastest ever recorded time, in 2010, was nine days and 26 minutes.

A full slate of events continues throughout the festival including ice carving. The **Festival of Native Arts** takes place in March at the university's main campus, along with Native-style potlatches.

THE OLYMPICS

For those in Fairbanks during July, the **World Eskimo-Indian Olympics** is recommended. The list of games includes some surprises as well as the expected: the blanket toss competition is fun to watch, as is the Native Baby Contest; the Knuckle Hop, Ear Pulling, and Ear Weight competitions are exactly what they say, and seem excruciatingly painful; and the muktuk-eating contest (muktuk is whale blubber), fish-cutting and seal-skinning competitions are opportunities to learn more about the Native cultures. It is also a rare opportunity for travelers to buy arts and crafts directly from Native artisans – beadwork, baskets, skin garments, masks, and carvings (see page 254).

The **Tanana Valley Fair**, held at the College Road fairgrounds during the second or third week of August, has grown to be the most popular event in the Interior, with attendances of more than 100,000 people. The prime attraction for travelers is the Harvest Hall filled with colossal vegetables. Here you will see what the long hours of summer daylight can produce in the Interior, including huge radishes and 70lb (32kg) cabbages.

Then there is nature's own special event, the Northern Lights (aurora borealis), which are seen frequently and vividly in and around Fairbanks from late August through early April (when skies are darkest). In winter this extraordinary show can last for hours; in mid-summer the sky is too light for it to be visible.

THE 'REPUBLIC OF ESTER'

To enjoy a trip back in time, head for the settlement of **Ester**, 7 miles (11km) from Fairbanks off the Parks Highway. To the outsider, Ester is just another faded mining community, but now with a population of over 2,400 it is a bedroom community of Fairbanks, albeit very rustic with a distinct artistic flavor. Also called the 'Republic of Ester,' this small town boasts a saloon, a couple of shops, a local newspaper, and a library. It was once home to the Malemute Saloon, where you could see vaudeville acts and hear readings of Robert Service, known as the 'bard of the Yukon.' Alas, the famous saloon has closed

⊙ Fact

A winter draw in Fairbanks is the aurora borealis; Japanese tourists, in particular, have been visiting the city to watch the spectacular Northern Lights ripple and wave in winter skies. Visible on average 243 days a year, the lights perform a matching display in the Southern Hemisphere, but at that time it is usually too light to see them.

A log pavilion at Creamers Field.

its doors, even though residents keep their fingers crossed that it will soon reopen. The time to visit is in the summer during the farmers' market on Thurdays from 4.30 to 7.30pm, when local farmers and artists sell their wares.

The gold dredges in the vicinity of Fairbanks, mute since 1966, stand like aging, silent dinosaurs, with necks outstretched, waiting. The dredges, like so many pieces of local history, are strewn about the hills waiting for some new purpose.

The easiest of the dredges to visit from town is **Gold Dredge No. 8** (tel: 907-479-6673; www.alaska.org/detail/ gold-dredge-8; summer daily 8am–5pm), rusting at Mile 9 Old Steese Highway, open during the summer. The five-deck ship, over 250ft (76 meters) long, displaced 1,065 tons as it plied the gold pay dirt of Goldstream and Engineer creeks. An admission fee includes a self-guided walking tour, with plenty of staff on hand to answer questions. A lunch of miner's stew in the historic dining hall is also included.

The dredge is only 600ft (180 metres) from the **trans-Alaska oil pipeline** (at Mile 8.4), which parallels the highway above the permafrost-rich ground.

THE DAVIDSON DITCH

Large-scale mining demands lots of water. J.M. Davidson proposed building an 80-mile (130km) water system to bring water from the Chatanika River to the diggings on Fox, Cleary, and Goldstream creeks. A 5,000-kilowatt power plant was erected, as well as six or seven dredges, and shops and camps to maintain the equipment and house the crews.

During construction of the **Davidson Ditch**, sections of the Steese Highway were built to facilitate access. The Ditch was completed in 1930 and was capable of carrying 56,000 gallons (254,500 liters) of water a minute. After the dredges were put to rest, this system continued to generate electricity until the flood of 1967 destroyed it. Remnants of the Ditch are visible in several places along the Steese Highway.

Visitors view the trans-Alaska pipeline.

'Age of the Mechanical Musher,'
World Ice Art Championships.

THE WORLD ESKIMO-INDIAN OLYMPICS

The annual games in Fairbanks may seem pretty wacky, but each event is a test of strength, courage, and dexterity needed for life in the far north.

To those unfamiliar with Alaskan native tradition and lifestyle, the athletic feats performed during the annual World Eskimo-Indian Olympics (www.weio.org) in Fairbanks each July may seem bizarre. What are those people doing hopping around on their toes and knuckles? And why are they playing tug-o-war with their ears? You won't see "conventional" events here, such as the pole vault or the 100-meter dash. Instead, be prepared for games of raw strength, endurance, agility, and concentration.

GAMES OF SURVIVAL

Survival has been the name of the game for Alaska's native people for thousands of years. It was essential to be disciplined both mentally and physically, to be ready for the unexpected. It was also important to work together for the common good.

The four-man carry, for example, represents the strength needed to haul firewood or moose or caribou carcasses back home. During this game four men hang from a fifth, who walks as far as he can before collapsing. The one- and two-foot high kicks require contestants to jump off the floor and kick a suspended object before landing on the kicking foot. Other events include the blanket toss, fish-cutting competition, and seal-skinning contest.

The games, first held in 1961, bring to life a time when Alaska's original peoples would gather in villages for friendly competitions, storytelling, dancing, and games. The host village provided food and lodging and visitors brought news from the surrounding areas.

A young competitor concentrates hard as she tries to maintain her balance on the greasy pole, one of the events most popular with the games' onlookers.

A competitor kicks the ball with her feet during the two-feet high kick contest. This contest originated from the Eskimo's celebration after whaling. A good competitor can reach as high as 2.5 meters (just over 8ft).

A man is launched into the air in the blanket toss competition, which originated from a successful walrus hunt. The blanket is made from walrus leather and held by 44 people.

Snow Sculpting: an Ephemeral Art

Anchorage is a long way from Fairbanks and the Eskimo-Indian Olympics, but it has its own crowd-pulling event, the annual Fur Rendezvous. Snow sculpting is among its most popular attractions, and holds its own against zany games of snowshoe softball and sled dog races. The finished creations draw hundreds to the display site north of Downtown.

Sculptors create their whimsical masterpieces from giant blocks of soft, clean, hard-packed snow. Each block stands 10ft (3 meters) tall and stretches 8ft (2.5 meters) across. Towering lights allow participants to work round the clock during the week

Snow sculptures in Anchorage are a winter tradition during the Fur Rendezvous festival.

preceding the festival. The rules are straightforward: no power tools, props, or extra snow; other than that, almost anything goes.

Unlike ice sculpting, which is more precise and requires greater skill, snow sculpting attracts a wide variety of participants, from scout troops and high-school students to corporate executives – anyone crazy enough to want to spend hours in the cold turning a block of snow into a gold rush-era saloon, a family of seals or a wing-spread dragon reading amongst a pile of books.

The ear pull, among the most painful of the games' events, is strictly a game of endurance. Elders say the ability to withstand great pain was necessary for survival. Contestants sit on the floor facing each other with a piece of twine looped over one of their ears. A tug of war begins. If the twine slips from a participant's ear, the other contestant wins the round. The winner is the one who wins two out of three rounds.

Two women fight for a stick applied with grease during the Indian stick pull contest. This contest simulates the action of the fisherman, who must grasp a fish so that it won't slip out of his hand.

Many of the contests, like the high kick seen here, challenge the participants' endurance of pain, and their balance and agility – skills needed for hunting and whaling.

The Northern Lights.

BEYOND FAIRBANKS

Mining trails, dogsled tracks, and rivers provided early transportation links connecting Fairbanks to the surrounding communities, with the rest of Alaska, and frequently with rewarding hot springs.

Trails, like the threads of a spider's web, spun into Fairbanks from every direction in the early 1900s. The more popular routes were eventually transformed from dogsled tracks to the roadways that now link the rest of Alaska to Fairbanks, the commercial hub of the Interior.

The first trail-cum-highway in all of Alaska, the **Richardson**, was originally a pack trail between the then-bustling mining settlements of Eagle and Valdez. Following the gold rush, the trail was extended to Fairbanks, linking the Interior to an ice-free port. Today, the Richardson joins with the Alaska Highway for the 98 miles (157km) between Fairbanks and Delta Junction.

NORTH POLE

If you take the Richardson Highway, your first stop may well be 14 miles (22km) southeast of Fairbanks at **North Pole** ⑰, the home, children are delighted to learn, of Santa Claus. Every year the tiny post office receives hundreds of thousands of letters addressed to Santa. Unfortunately, postal workers have to forward the mail to his winter residence 1,700 miles (2,700km) north at the geographic North Pole.

The town of North Pole was put on the map during the 1930s and 1940s

when a new wave of enterprising homesteaders found Fairbanks too crowded and didn't mind living in this low-lying basin where winter temperatures are severe enough for the nickname 'North Pole' to stick and become official.

Today, North Pole is home to more than 2,100 people and a surrounding population of 13,000. It has its own utilities, brand-new shopping malls and a large Williams petroleum refinery taking crude from the nearby trans-Alaska pipeline. It is best known as the town where it is Christmas all year, and

Main attractions
North Pole
Delta Junction
Eagle
Nenana
Central
Circle
Chena Hot Springs Resort
Aurora Ice Museum
Manley Hot Springs
Livengood

Map on page 164

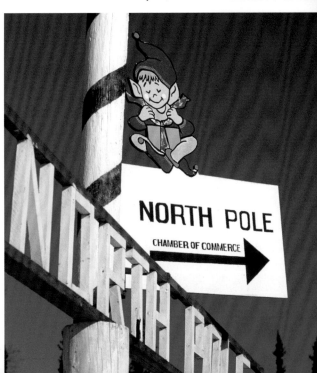

The North Pole, said to be the home of Santa Claus.

the holiday-themed streets (Snowman Lane and Saint Nicholas Drive), along with the candy canes adorning the town's street lights, prove it.

As surely as there is gold in the hills, there are buffalo and barley in **Delta Junction** . The **Tanana Valley** is one of the state's largest agricultural areas, with most of the farming centered in Big Delta and Delta Junction. Despite the typical Interior winter climate, the valley supports a variety of cereal grains, from barely to wheat. Many farmers also raise root vegetables and livestock including cattle, yak, and elk.

But what about the buffalo? Although they could be the spirit watchers of the shaggy bison who ranged the Interior millennia ago, this herd was actually imported from Montana and introduced to the area specifically as a game animal. The original 23-member herd now numbers a few hundred in the Tanana Valley, while other descendants established herds around the Copper and Chitina rivers. Recognizing that the bison, despite their tendency to graze on grain fields, brought an economic boon to the community, the state established the 90,000-acre (36,000-hectare) Delta Bison Range in 1979. Look for them at Mile 225.4 near the Black Rapids overlook.

LANDING UP AT EAGLE

After Delta Junction, the road forks; the southern extension being the Richardson Highway, while the Alaska Highway stretches east. Continue east some 110 miles (175km) to Tetlin Junction and take the rough gravel Taylor Highway for a further 160 miles (255km) and you will come to **Eagle** , where the road ends (the road closes in winter and snow isolates the community). This is a jumping-off place for Yukon River paddlers, as well as an official stop for river explorers floating from Dawson City. The first city on the American side of the Yukon, Eagle has a post office where river travelers check in with US customs.

Present day Eagle (population 86) had its beginnings in 1874, when the far-reaching and powerful Northern Commercial Company (NC) stretched its commercial fingers along the Yukon River and established a trading post near here. With the arrival of prospectors overflowing from the 1898 Klondike gold rush at Dawson City, just upriver over the border in Canada, this quiet riverbank was transformed into a brazen mining town of 1,700 people.

Judge James Wickersham built a federal courthouse here in 1900, a major army fort was established, and the Valdez-to-Eagle telegraph line spun out a historic message in 1905 when Roald Amundsen, passing through after his successful expedition into the Northwest Passage, made his announcement to the world from Eagle. By 1910 the gold muckers had vanished, trekking after even richer dreams near Fairbanks. They left behind 178 people. The population

Judge Wickersham's Courthouse.

has continued to dwindle since. but the buildings still stand and Eagle has undertaken a program to restore many of its fine older structures.

The Eagle Historical Society (tel: 907-547-2325; www.eaglehistoricalsociety.com) conducts a two-hour walking tour that includes **Judge Wickersham's Courthouse**, built by fines he imposed on gamblers and prostitutes in the rowdy mining town. Inside are the judge's desk and an early map of the country constructed of papier-mâché and moose blood. Also open for inspection is US Army **Fort Egbert**, abandoned in 1911, and the only remaining frontier fort of its type left in the state.

Summer visitors will find the basic necessities – laundry, lodging, groceries, gas station, airstrip, and mechanic shop. For those who want to go paddling through the Yukon–Charley Rivers National Preserve this is a good place to start. Contact the National Park Service Visitor Center, just off First Avenue across the airstrip from town (tel: 907-547-2233; www.nps.gov/yuch), for more information.

RAILWAY TOWN

Just over 60 miles (100km) south of Fairbanks, State Highway 3, the **George Parks Highway**, leads you to **Nenana** ㉠. Taken from the Athabascan word Nenashna, Nenana loosely translates as 'a good place to camp between two rivers,' and it's appropriately situated at the confluence of the Tanana and Nenana rivers. Always one of the main river-freighting centers in Alaska, the town changed when the Alaska Railroad was completed in 1923.

The railroad made headlines in 1985 when it was purchased from the US government by the state of Alaska. Shortly after, the station was listed on the National Register of Historic Sites, and now incorporates the **Alaska State Railroad Museum** (tel: 907-832-5556 year-round, 907-832-5500 in summer; summer daily 9am–6pm; free). The train still chugs along at about 50mph (80kmh) but it doesn't make scheduled trips.

Nenana is also the terminus port for tug and barge fleets that still service the villages along the Tanana and

The Lost Chicken Hill Mine was established in 1895.

Heaving up the tripod used in the annual Nenana Ice Classic, an event in which individuals attempt to guess the exact time the Tanana River ice will break up at Nenana.

⊙ Fact

Gamblers gained notoriety in the saloons of the boom- and-bust towns. One who went on to national fame was Tex Rickard, who was 24 years old when he trekked into Circle City in 1895. He later built Madison Square Garden in New York City.

Yukon rivers, loaded with supplies, fuel and tons of freight. For a closer inspection of an old tug, visit the refurbished *Taku Chief* behind the **Visitor Information Center** on the corner of A Street and Parks Highway.

Nenana is home to the **Nenana Ice Classic**, Alaska's coolest lottery. In an event that could only be held in the land of ice and cabin fever, cash prizes totaling $300,000 are awarded to those who guess the exact time – to the minute – of spring break-up on the Tanana. Break-up is that moment when suddenly there's more water than ice on the river, when massive blocks of ice surge and grind against one another in a spectacular release of winter energy. A tripod frozen into the river and attached by wire to a clock tips over when break-up occurs.

The Tanana River again becomes the focal point a month or so later with **River Daze**, celebrated during the first weekend in June. One event is the raft race down the Tanana from Fairbanks to Nenana, when participants create a variety of floating contraptions and enter them as rafts. Anything goes in this race, providing it floats and utilizes only 'natural' power.

OFF TO THE GOLD FIELDS

To drive the **Steese Highway** northeast of Fairbanks is to travel with the spirits of the old gold prospectors. The road angles to the northeast for 162 miles (260km) before ending at the Yukon River. Go past the Gold Dredge No. 8 and the viewing point for the trans-Alaska pipeline, and you will come first to the community of **Fox** at Mile 11, an early mining encampment which took its name from a nearby creek. The community is best known now for its excellent spring water. The symmetrical piles of gravel surrounding Fox are the dregs of the mighty earth-eating dredges.

Next stop is the **Monument to Felix Pedro** at Mile 17 (27km), a reminder of the Italian immigrant who was the first to strike it rich in these valleys in 1902 – a find that provoked a full-scale stampede. Gravel in the creek on the opposite side of the road has shown

Fireweed along the Dalton Highway.

some 'color,' so you could practice panning here.

The subsequent 3 miles (5km) of road gradually ascend to **Cleary Summit**, offering a magnificent panoramic view of the Tanana Valley, the White Mountains and the Alaska Range. Back in 1905, the notorious 'Blue Parka Bandit' found this encompassing lookout quite handy for his nefarious trade: Charles Hendrickson, engineer-turned-robber and terror of the trails, haunted these granite crags, pinching the pokes of unsuspecting gold miners.

PIONEER CAMPS

Anyone interested in Alaskan gold rush lore will not want to miss **Fairbanks Creek Road**. Leave the Steese Highway and Cleary Summit and travel south along the ridgeline for 8 miles (13km) to Alder Creek Camp. Beyond this, there's a 1-mile (1.5km) walk to **Meehan**, an abandoned machine-shop area where maintenance was done on mining equipment, and rusted equipment can still be found strewn along the trail.

Fairbanks Creek Camp is an additional 2 miles (3km) below Meehan. Tusks, teeth, and bones of Pleistocene mammals were uncovered here during stripping operations. One famous fossil is a well-preserved baby woolly mammoth found in 1949.

CENTRAL'S SUMMER INFLUX

The old Circle District is not yet devoid of gold or the miners who search for it. Some of them live in **Central ㉑**, a small mining community strung out along the Steese Highway, 'three miles long and one block wide.' An active winter population of over 100 swells to nearly 1,000 during the summer when miners and vacationers return. Since the addition of a permanent school in 1981, more and more 'summer people' have stayed on late into fall. Overnight accommodations, camping facilities, and general 'pit-stop' services are available in town.

A worthwhile stop is at the **Circle District Historical Society Museum**, located on the highway (tel: 907-520-1893, www.cdhs.us; summer daily

Well prepared for a winter hike.

⊘ A TOWN CALLED CHICKEN

The Interior town of Chicken, Alaska is located about 100 road miles southwest of Eagle, at Mile 66 of the Taylor Highway. The original inhabitants of the area were Han Kutchin Indians. Following the discovery of gold on (what is now) Upper Chicken Creek in 1886, a settlement was soon established as a hub for miners of the Fortymile Mining District. The residents wanted to name their new town 'Ptarmigan,' after the plump, ground-dwelling, game bird which were abundant in the area (now the state bird of Alaska), but couldn't agree on the correct spelling. To avoid any embarrassment they eventually settled on the more easily spelled 'Chicken.'

The author Robert Specht brought considerable notoriety to the area with the publication of *Tisha*, in 1984. Based on a true story, the book told of a 19-year-old schoolteacher, Anne Purdy, who traveled to Chicken in 1927, taught the children, married a local Indian man and remained in the community throughout much of her life. The dozen or so buildings of the original town site are listed on the National Register of Historic Places.

Today, the town's 17 residents enjoy lives of quiet isolation, home schooling their children and fur trapping during winters, and panning for gold or working in tourism in summer.

Picking wild blueberries in the tundra.

noon–5pm). The museum displays authentic pieces of mining equipment alongside gold nuggets, dogsleds, a period cabin containing genuine artifacts, and examples of some of the hardy alpine wildflowers that are found on Eagle Summit.

CIRCLE

All roads end some place. For the Steese, it's all over at **Circle** ㉒, a tiny community 50 miles (80km) south of the Arctic Circle, poised along a bend in the Yukon River. In gold rush days Circle had a population of 1,000; today that has dwindled to about 100.

Once the largest gold mining town on the Yukon, Circle was nearly abandoned after the gold strikes in the Klondike and Fairbanks areas and little now remains to be seen by visitors. Gone are Jack McQuesten's two-story log store, two dozen saloons, eight dance halls, theaters, and the music hall that earned Circle City the somewhat exaggerated title of the 'Paris of the North.' In their places reign a modern-day trading post with a motel, a café,

Enjoying a dip at Chena Hot Springs Resort.

a general store, a bar, and a gas station. Rudimentary tourist facilities are geared for summer visitors. Chartered flightseeing trips and boat tours are available, but it's wise to call ahead.

There's usually plenty of waterfront activity in this popular stopping-off place for canoeists and rafters traveling the Yukon River. One popular river trip begins in either Eagle or Circle and terminates at Fort Yukon or farther downstream under the Dalton Highway Bridge.

Circle, so named because early miners thought they were camped at the Arctic Circle (although they actually had about another 50 miles/80km to go), still offers some activity. Fish wheels smack the water as they turn in the current, flat-bottomed boats zoom up and down the river, and barges still make their way to points upriver. River travelers could easily miss all of this; the 'land' in front of Circle is actually an island concealing another channel of the mighty Yukon.

To get a real feel for the town, wander upriver to the Pioneer Cemetery

and look at some of the weathered gravestones of the early settlers. Circle is home to the Circle Hot Springs, once known for its lodge and its resident ghost that haunted the top floor. Unfortunately, the lodge and access to the springs have closed, though campgrounds are located nearby.

CHENA HOT SPRINGS RESORT

If you are interested in taking advantage of the Interior's thermal baths, one of the best places is the **Chena Hot Springs Resort ㉓** (tel: 907-451-8104; www.chenahotsprings.com).

To get there, take a right turn at Mile 3 on the Steese Highway. You will rollercoaster through some stunning country on Chena Hot Springs Road, passing through the middle of the 254,000-acre (103,000-hectare) **Chena River State Recreation Area**. At the end of the 56 mile (90km) road you will find the gates to the closest thermal resort to Fairbanks. Fully developed for the complete comfort of the guests, the resort is commercially equipped with all the necessities for extended, year-round visits, and has winter ski trails. The **Aurora Ice Museum** (year round daily 11am–7pm) is sculpted from 1,000 tons of ice and snow and has an average temperature of 28°F (–2°C). Most alluring are the steaming hot-water pools of **Monument Creek Valley**, and the indoor swimming and indoor and outdoor soaking facilities.

Those interested in a cool chance to witness the spectacular Northern Lights may do so during a winter visit to the resort, while soaking in the 110°F (43°C) water of Rock Lake. Or you can hop on one of the resort's large track vehicles and rumble to the top of a nearby ridge for unobstructed views. There's even a yurt for your comfort, complete with tea, cider, and hot chocolate. The cost for a day at the pools is only $10, payable at the front desk. The pools are open from 7am to midnight.

THE ELLIOTT HIGHWAY

The last of the four major highways in the Interior extending out of Fairbanks is the **Elliott Highway**, running northwest, and continuing on to the Dalton Highway. The Elliott branches off the Steese 11 miles (18km) north of Fairbanks and winds through 152 miles (245km) of gold mining country trimmed with broad valleys, bubbling creeks, blueberries and poppies, homesteads, and mining camps. You'll also catch glimpses of Denali on clear days and have views of the Minto Flats. The Athabascan village of **Minto** on the Tolovana River sits at the end of Minto Road at Mile 110.

MANLEY HOT SPRINGS

The Manley Hot Springs are the reward if you decide to venture to the end of the Elliott Highway. The lodge that once housed the springs is now closed, but a local couple gladly keeps up the four private concrete pools. It is located in a greenhouse, and you will soak surrounded by carefully tended grapes, flowers,

⊙ Tip

Chena River State Recreation Area shelters one of the state's most visible moose populations. Other wildlife includes bears, caribou, wolves, wolverines, lynx, and river otters. Hikes of varying length, from one hour to three days, are possible on the park's trails.

Snow plow at Chena Hot Springs Resort.

and pears. One hour costs $5, and it is encouraged that you call ahead (tel: 907-672-3231).

Further down the road, the small community of Manley Hot Springs has campgrounds and a historic roadhouse. Reportedly the first in the state, the Manley Roadhouse was built in 1906 and has a full bar, restaurant, and 13 rooms (tel: 907-672-3161; www.manleylodge.com).

THE DALTON HIGHWAY

Livengood 24, near the junction of the Elliott and Dalton highways, once held the 'end-of-the-road' position, but the isolated little community was transformed into a pipeline construction camp. Five months of intensive labor, and millions of tons of gravel created a 414-mile (666km) service road paralleling one of the most ambitious projects ever undertaken in the North American Arctic – the trans-Alaska pipeline.

This service road-cum-state highway, officially called the **Dalton Highway** but often known as the 'Haul Road,' opened up thousands of acres of wilderness territory that can be explored from the comfort of a vehicle. The road is maintained from Livengood to Prudhoe Bay, and although privately owned vehicles used to be allowed only as far as **Disaster Creek** near Dietrich Camp, about 280 miles (450km) north of Fairbanks and 200 miles (322km) south of the Arctic Ocean, the whole length of the road is now open to the public.

A journey north on the Dalton Highway, above the Arctic Circle, through the land of sheep, bears, wolves, and foxes is a challenge. Several tour companies offer excursions to the Arctic Circle and Prudhoe Bay. But if you choose to do it alone, beware. Conditions are hazardous; the roadway is rough and dusty in summer and slippery in winter.

Because this is primarily a service road, heavily loaded 18-wheelers rule the route. Automobile towing charges on the highway are expensive, and rental agencies do not allow their cars to be driven on it.

The Dalton Highway will take you beyond the Arctic Circle.

YUKON VILLAGES

Labor-saving devices and the other benefits of modern technology could transform life in the remote Interior, but each comes with its drawbacks showing that life here is a delicate balance.

What lies beyond Pedro Dome, Cleary Summit, and the White Mountains? What is it that the Chena, the Chatanika, and the Tanana rivers are all drawn toward? It is, of course, the Yukon River, flowing north of Fairbanks, and seemingly possessing a magnetic force of its own.

If Fairbanks is the heart of the Interior, the Yukon is a life-supporting artery. Not unlike the pioneers, today's visitors to Fairbanks often feel the urge to soar over the mountain peaks or float with the river current right to its mouth.

Centuries before European explorers spread out over the land, the Yukon River and its many tributaries were a common link in the survival of the nomadic Athabascan tribes living in the Interior. Ironically, the Yukon then provided access to intruders who came up-river in their sternwheelers from St Michael on the Bering Sea to reap the benefits of the fur country and the gold fields.

When explorers, missionaries, and fortune hunters penetrated this wilderness in the 19th century, the Athabascans were living as they had for generations, subsisting on salmon, moose or caribou, berries, and waterbirds. They were survivors in a harsh and unmerciful land, still living a semi-nomadic life, but with the arrival of outsiders, they congregated into small, year-round communities.

Scattered along the Yukon are the Athabascan river villages. The historical perspective of each community varies, but, remarkably, they are part of 21st-century Alaska, while paying silent tributes to the Athabascans of the past.

It would be naive to believe that the villages are untouched by the modern world. Conversely, it would be presumptuous to assume that they continue to provide a viable existence due only to space-age technology. Generally, villagers maintain a traditional subsistence lifestyle, hunting, fishing, trapping, gardening, and gathering berries. Daily life embraces the rhythm of the seasons, and survival demands adjusting to weather conditions and unpredictable wildlife cycles, just as it has always done, only today, there is the persistent hum of diesel generators in the background. Snowmachines, all-terrain vehicles, and motorboats compete with the traditional dogsled and canoe, and families now gather around flat-screen TVs watching the latest on satellite, or spend hours playing their X-Boxes. Today, many communities are looking past diesel to wind and hydro energy to power these modern luxuries.

Elementary schools are a part of every village, and many villages also offer high school education to their young people. Sponsored by a new state program, every student from 5th to 12th grade gets a laptop with internet hookup to use for the duration of the school year. Typical village teenagers, carrying the dreams of their ancestors, often find themselves at a crossroads, both personally and culturally.

The village elders, those keepers of the culture, go on dispensing wisdom, and village pride seems to have deepened in recent years. Almost forgotten dialects now roll easily from the lips of youngsters. Ancient drumbeats and dances are as popular as the latest rock music. The village is a microcosm of contrast, evoking a strong sense of the past as it surges toward the future.

An Athabascan indian girl displays furs for sale.

A lone phone booth sits beneath the northern lights in the Arctic Circle.

The Far North

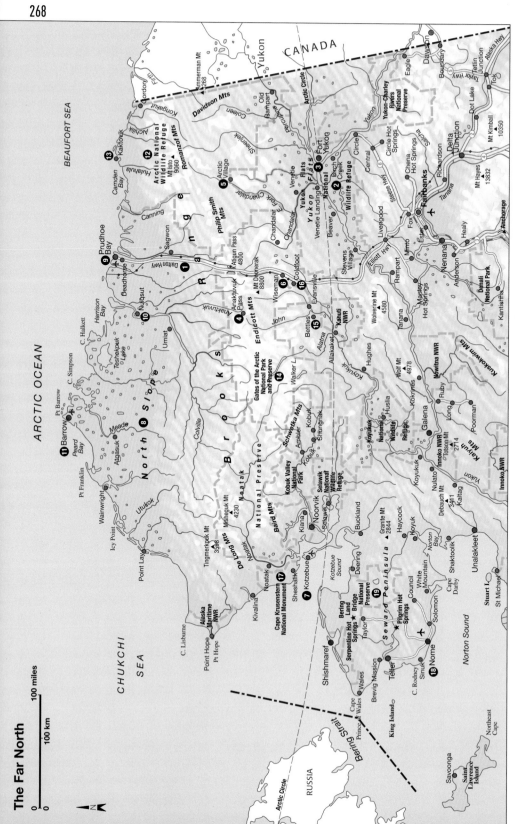

THE FAR NORTH

This vast land of caribou migrations, oil fields, and protected wilderness is the least visited in the state, but provides countless opportunities to the backcountry explorer.

The Arctic Sea.

When people think of Alaska, they're usually not picturing the moss-laden, towering Sitka spruce of Southeast, nor picturesque fishing communities like Cordova or Dillingham, and certainly not the modern high-rise apartment buildings, satellite dishes, or trendy restaurants of Anchorage; they're envisioning vast, desolate stretches of windswept, treeless tundra, pack ice dotted with prowling polar bears, or Native Alaskans venturing out on whale hunts in walrus-skin boats. They're thinking 'land of the midnight sun' or perhaps of endless, dark frigid winters – all of which are accurate descriptions of Alaska's Far North. However, this is by no means a complete list. This northernmost part of the state is, indeed, a place of extremes. It's a wilderness where self-sufficiency will save your life, while carelessness will surely claim it. It's a treasure trove of scarce and invaluable natural resources, located beneath an incredibly fragile Arctic ecosystem that could easily and forever be destroyed.

DIVERSE REGIONS

Alaska's Far North includes many diverse regions, each with distinct climates, peoples, wildlife, and other distinguishing characteristics, and the resultant lures and liabilities for travelers. The remote **Yukon Flats** area, for example, extends eastward from the Dalton Highway to the Canadian border. The Flats are situated in a marshy area near the Yukon River and its Porcupine and Chandalar river tributaries.

A raw gravel road leading to the Arctic Circle.

The glorious and remote mountains of the Brooks Range extend east-west across the wide expanse of northern Alaska. And nestled right in the 'heart' of the Range is the stunning **Gates of the Arctic National Park and Preserve**. It's important to note that this Preserve has no roads, no grocery stores, no amenities or services whatsoever – not even medical help.

Yet it is a wilderness historically inhabited by native Inupiat Eskimos and Athabascan Indians, and also by trappers and homesteaders, who together add up to a whopping one person per every 5,000 acres (2,000 hectares). The Preserve does offer 8 million acres (3.2 million hectares) of pristine wilderness for those who are adequately prepared, self-sufficient and in need of a prolonged ramble, river-run, or climb within a wild, unpeopled land.

ARCTIC NATIONAL WILDLIFE REFUGE

East of Gates of the Arctic, between the Dalton Highway and Canada, and north from the Brooks Range to the coastal tundra is much-discussed **Arctic National Wildlife Refuge** (ANWR). The Refuge encompasses traditional subsistence areas and homelands of both the coastal Inupiat Eskimos and the interior Athabascan Indians. Its Arctic and subarctic ecosystems support the greatest variety of plant and animal life in any Park or Refuge in the circumpolar region. Probably the most noted mammals in ANWR are the nearly 200,000 caribou that make up the Porcupine and Central Arctic herds. These herds

make yearly migrations from the boreal forests of Interior Alaska and Canada to summer calving grounds in ANWR's coastal plains – the same area thought by many to contain significant quantities of oil and gas. Of the 19 million total acres (7.7 million hectares) of the refuge, it is these 1.5 million acres of coastal plains that have spawned national and even international debate on whether to allow oil and gas development in the Refuge, or to preserve it as a wilderness area for future generations.

An arctic gateway of sorts to Barrow, made of Bowhead whale bones and whaling boat frames.

Farther west along the northern coast of Alaska's Far North is the **North Slope** and the industrial oil facility called **Prudhoe Bay**. But the North Slope is considerably more than just Prudhoe Bay. Continued westerly travel along the coastline of the Arctic Ocean leads to the tiny Inupiat community of **Nuiqsut** (population 400) and then the lethally cold **Barrow** (population 4,373), which has the twin distinction of being the largest Eskimo settlement in the world and the northernmost community in North America.

In the western coastal area of the Far North, located just above the Arctic Circle on Kotzebue Sound is the City of **Kotzebue**. A major transportation and services hub for northwestern Alaska, this predominantly Inupiat Eskimo community of approximately 3,300 residents also serves as the jumping-off point for treks into **Noatak National Preserve, Kobuk Valley National Park, Bering Land Bridge National Preserve**, and **Cape Krusenstern National Monument**. Finally, southwest of Kotzebue is the Seward Peninsula and, on the southwest corner of the Peninsula, the city of **Nome**, a resilient town that's endured countless boom-and-bust cycles.

An Arctic fox.

WILD AND BEWILDERING

Travelers considering a trip to Alaska's Far North – particularly to the most remote refuges, monuments and preserves – should give the idea the most careful consideration and thoughtful planning. While a regular scheduled airline service is available in the larger communities of Barrow, Kozebue, and Nome, far-flung destinations are generally accessible by floatplane or bush plane alone. Most flights depart from Fairbanks, though you can find flights from Anchorage as well. You can also drive to the Arctic via the Dalton Highway, a 414-mile stretch of dirt that runs from the town of Livengood.

In the Far North, all possible contingencies must be carefully planned out in advance. It is a wild, even bewildering locale, unlike any other, featuring polarized extremes of weather, temperatures, daylight, resources, geography, peoples, and even politics. It's the sort of place adventurers often dream of, but are only rarely gifted with the opportunity, skills, and tenacity to experience.

The far north is a long way from pretty much everywhere.

The piercing eyes of a husky.

THE ARCTIC

The lands north of the Arctic Circle are defined and shaped by the rugged and desolate Brooks Range and the rich and fertile flats stretching to the Arctic Ocean.

Stretching east–west from the Canadian border to the Bering Sea and north–south from the Arctic Ocean to the Arctic Circle, (66° 33' north latitude), Alaska's vast Arctic region comprises about a quarter of the state's mainland. It's a region characterized by extremes of light and temperature; rural communities of mostly Native Alaskan inhabitants; vast stretches of wilderness; several of the state's wildest parklands and refuges; America's largest oil field – and its largest caribou herds.

Only a small percentage of travelers come this far north; but those who do will find wilderness on a scale unmatched anywhere else in Alaska or the other 49 states. Here too they will find a thriving Inupiat Eskimo culture that balances its centuries-old subsistence lifestyle – including the annual hunt for whales – with modern technology and western culture.

The majority of visitors to this region get here by plane, but each year a few thousand also drive the **Dalton Highway** ❶, the only road into the Arctic that connects with Alaska's statewide highway system (see page 283).

THE YUKON FLATS

Extending from the Canadian border to foothills just east of the Dalton Highway, this is a flat, marshy, lake-dotted area dominated by the northernmost segment of the **Yukon River** and several large tributaries, including the Porcupine and Chandalar rivers. Few visitors come here, both because it is remote and expensive to reach, and because it is difficult to get around; it is also a major mosquito-breeding ground in summer.

The primary recreational activities are boating and fishing, within the **Yukon Flats National Wildlife Refuge** ❷ (tel: 907-456-0440; http://yukon flats.fws.gov). Encompassing 8.6 million

Main attractions
Dalton Highway
Yukon Flats National
  Wildlife Refuge
Fort Yukon
Anaktuvuk Pass
Wiseman
Kotzebue
North Slope
Prudhoe Bay
Nuiqsut
Barrow

Map on page 268

Ice floes on the Arctic Sea.

acres (3.5 million hectares) of lowland lakes, streams, and wetlands, the aptly named **Yukon Flats** is best known for its avian breeding habitat; the refuge is one of North America's premier waterfowl nesting grounds. Ducks and geese and other migratory birds come here from such varied wintering grounds as Costa Rica, Mexico, and Russia.

By summer's end, some 2 million ducks and geese – including one-fifth of the continent's canvasback ducks and large numbers of Canada and white-fronted geese – will prepare to leave the refuge's 40,000 lakes and ponds on southbound migrations. Large numbers of common, Pacific, and red-throated loons are among the 150 species of birds to breed here each year.

Nearly all those birds leave in fall, though 13 species live here year-round, from boreal chickadees to great gray owls, spruce grouse, and ravens.

As might be expected the flats' many rivers are important spawning grounds for fish, including three species of salmon – chinook (or king), chum, and coho – that travel more than a thousand river miles to reach these waters.

The Yukon Flats has some of the continent's greatest annual temperature extremes. In deepest winter, temperatures may drop to −50°F (−45°C) or even lower for weeks at a time. In such extreme cold, trees may crack and ice shatter, while sounds are carried for miles in the dense, dry air. In summer, by contrast, temperatures of up to 100°F (38°C) have been recorded here – the highest temperatures ever noted north of the Arctic Circle.

The region is home to Athabascan Indians, but few communities are located here. The largest, **Fort Yukon ❸**, is located near the confluence of the Yukon and Porcupine rivers. Home to nearly 600 people, mostly Athabascans, Fort Yukon is used as a jumping-off spot by visitors to the Yukon Flats and Arctic National wildlife refuges.

THE BROOKS RANGE

Extending east-west across the width of Alaska, the **Brooks Range** is Alaska's northernmost chain of mountains,

Peering out over the Brooks Range.

the farthest-north extension of the Rocky Mountains. More than 700 miles long and up to 200 miles across (1,000 by 320km), the Brooks Range is considered by many to be Alaska's premier alpine wilderness. Within the chain are several distinct groups of peaks, from the Baird and De Long Mountains in the west, to the Endicott and Schwatka mountains in the central Brooks and the Philip Smith, Romanzof, and Davidson mountains in the east. Here too are several of Alaska's premier conservation units, protecting much of the range's wild lands and wildlife.

Remote and expensive to reach – and therefore visited by few people – this range is relatively subdued by Alaskan standards; its tallest peak, **Mount Isto**, is just under 9,000ft (2,743 meters) high and few others reach higher than 6,000ft (1,820 meters). But that is one of its beauties. Wave after wave of mountain ridges can be ascended by adventurers with little or no mountaineering experience. And once upon a ridgeline or mountaintop, you can look across a mountain wilderness that seems to go on forever.

That's not to say these mountains are easy to climb; ascents of tundra and bare rock require stamina and good conditioning. And while many of the mountains are rounded domes or sedimentary rocks, several groups within the chain rise precipitously into the sky. The most notable of those are the **Arrigetch Peaks**, in the central Brooks Range. Taken from the Nunamiut Eskimo people, the name for this group of granite spires means 'fingers of the hand, extended.'

For a mountain chain, the Brooks Range gives a sense of wide-open spaces. In part this is because much of the range is north of the treeline, and ground-hugging tundra plants populate valley bottoms as well as high alpine meadows. But the openness is also accentuated by the broad glacially carved river valleys that cut through the mountains north and south.

Like other portions of the Arctic, the Brooks Range is a place of extremes. Winters are long, cold, and dark. The sun disappears for days to weeks at a time (the farther north you go, the longer the winter night lasts) and temperatures drop to –40°F (–40°C) or even colder for long stretches. Winter's first snows may arrive in August and the landscape doesn't thaw and begin to 'green up' until May or even sometimes June. Summer's short season is marked by weeks of light, low rainfall – much of the Brooks Range qualifies as a desert climate because of its low precipitation – and bursting life.

SUMMER WILDLIFE

A surprising diversity of wildlife can be found here in summer. Dozens of bird species nest in lowlands and alpine meadows; most avoid the long, harsh winter by migrating long distances each spring and fall but a few – for instance, chickadees, ravens,

A pair of caribou.

and ptarmigan – somehow survive year-round.

Mammals include the grizzly and black bear, moose, Dall sheep, wolves, foxes, wolverines, porcupines, and caribou. The caribou, as much as grizzlies and wolves, symbolize this northern mountain chain. Hundreds of thousands migrate through the Brooks Range each year on yearly migrations; after wintering on the range's southern fringes, they head north in late winter toward calving grounds on the North Slope, then return south at summer's end.

ANAKTUVUK PASS

Only a handful of human settlements are located here; most of those are along the mountain's fringes and number a few dozen people or less. Most of them are Native communities, of Athabascan or Eskimo origin. One village, **Anaktuvuk Pass ❹**, is deep within the Central Brooks range, at 2,200ft (670 meters) along the Arctic Divide. This is the only remaining settlement of Alaska's Nunamiut people, a tribe of inland Eskimos whose nomadic ancestors followed migratory herds of caribou across the western Arctic.

The Nunamiut maintained a semi-nomadic lifestyle deep into the 20th century, following caribou and other game across the landscape in small groups. Not until 1949 did they permanently settle at Anaktuvuk Pass.

About 340 people now live in Anaktuvuk; all but a few are Nunamiut. Nearly everyone depends on subsistence harvesting – hunting, fishing, trapping, berry picking – to some degree, with caribou at the center of it all. No longer do residents need caribou for tools and shelter, but the animals remain a chief source of food. Some still use caribou parts for clothing: boots, parkas, gloves, and hats.

ARCTIC VILLAGE

Much farther to the east is **Arctic Village ❺**, a community of about 152 people, mostly Athabascan Gwich'in. Like the Nunamiut, the Gwich'in were once a semi-nomadic people. They remain dependent on the Porcupine

Red bear berry foliage at the village of Anaktuvuk Pass.

caribou herd, which numbers more than 120,000 animals and ranges through northeastern Alaska and northwestern Canada.

Both Arctic Village and Anaktuvuk Pass are located within preservation units (the Arctic National Wildlife Refuge and Gates of the Arctic National Park, respectively) and are sometimes visited by Brooks Range adventurers; however, both communities have limited visitor facilities.

The small town of **Wiseman** ❻ represents a third culture: white gold miners. Prospectors were drawn to the area in the early 1900s, but that boom has long passed. Today the town's 14 or so residents are a mix of miners, trappers, and homesteaders who've found a niche along the Middle Fork of the Koyukuk, not far from the Dalton Highway.

PARKS AND PRESERVES

Much of the Brooks Range wilderness is protected within a series of seldom-visited parks, preserves, and refuges that have few or no traveler facilities:

from west to east, these include the **Noatak National Preserve** (tel: 907-442-3890; www.nps.gov/noat), **Kobuk Valley National Park** (tel: 907-442-3890; www.nps.gov/kova), **Gates of the Arctic National Park and Preserve** (tel: 907-692-5494; www.nps.gov/gaar), and the **Arctic National Wildlife Refuge** (tel: 907-456-0250; http://arctic.fws.gov).

NORTHWEST ALASKA

At the Arctic's far western end, from lowland flats south of the Brooks Range then north along the mountain chain's western fringes, is an area inhabited by several Inupiat Eskimo communities, the majority of whom still depend on traditional subsistence lifestyles. Several small Inupiat villages are located along the **Kobuk River** just south of the Brooks Range: **Kobuk**, **Shungnak**, **Ambler**, and **Kiana**, to name a few. Other communities are along the coast, from Selawik in the south up to Kivalina and Point Hope.

The landscape is varied, ranging from the tundra-topped hills and mountains of the Brooks Range to

The Ishivak Pass.

Salmon hanging out to dry at Kotzebue.

lowland forests and wetlands south of the mountains, and coastal marshes and beaches where marine mammals such as walruses and seals haul out. Polar bears roam the offshore sea ice, occasionally coming onto land and whales migrate past the region on seasonal travels.

Crystal clear streams born in the mountains feed the region's largest waterway, the Kobuk River. Approximately 300 miles (483km) long, the Kobuk's headwaters are in the Schwatka Mountains; the river then flows south a short way before turning west, where it eventually empties into Kotzebue Sound. The Kobuk is critically important to the Inupiat, both for transportation and as a source of food: fish, birds, and the caribou that cross the river each year.

IN AND AROUND KOTZEBUE

The cultural center of Northwest Alaska is **Kotzebue** ❼, a large, predominantly Eskimo community that is served by daily jet service out of Anchorage and Fairbanks. Kotzebue is the headquarters for NANA (www.nana.com), one of the regional Native corporations established in 1971 with the passage of the Alaska Native Claims Settlement Act. That act granted Alaskan Natives nearly $1 billion in cash and title to some 44 million acres (18 million hectares) of land. Thirteen Native corporations, formed to manage the sudden wealth, divided up the money and the ground. NANA's share was significant and it is now one of the more successful of the corporations. Several other business ventures of a more contemporary nature round out NANA's holdings in industries, including mining, oil, and tourism. The company is a significant economic force in northwestern Alaska.

Northeast of Kotzebue, NANA also helped develop the **Red Dog Mine**, a world-class zinc mine that provides hundreds of local jobs, transforming the economy of this sparsely populated area. Cominco, a Canadian-based mining concern, has helped to develop the roads and other

infrastructure necessary to support the venture. Zinc deposits are expected to last for at least 20 years, and recoverable quantities of silver, lead, and other minerals are also being mined.

But Kotzebue is still traditional. Fishermen tend nets in Kotzebue Sound and nearby streams. Native walrus, seal, whale, and polar bear hunters still brave the elements in pursuit of their quarries. Kotzebue is a rare combination of the old and the new, and one of the few places where traditional and contemporary lifestyles are blending in reasonable harmony.

In the heart of downtown Kotzebue is the Park Service's **Northwest Arctic Heritage Center** (100 Shore Avenue; tel: 907-442-3890; year-round Mon–Fri 8am–5pm). It features a bookstore and interesting displays of the region's human and natural history.

You can also find information on the Western Arctic National Parklands, which include Noatak National Preserve, Kobuk Valley National Park, Cape Krusenstern National Monument, and Bering Land Bridge National Preserve. Unlike most national parks, there are no fees, permits, or reservations necessary to enter the backcountry.

The helpful staff will, however, let you know if your planned route overlaps with a commercial reindeer drive, which are still allowed in many of these lands. They will also give you tips to finding a guide or to book a charter plane, which at $500 an hour easily makes up for any savings in park fees.

To experience Arctic life a little closer to town and for considerably less money, take a trip to **LaVonne's Fish Camp** (tel: winter 907-276-0976, summer 907-442-6013; www.fishcamp. org). At this compound of cabins just five miles (8km) from town, you can pick berries, set traditional Eskimo salmon nets, or observe a nearby reindeer herd. Birdwatching is plentiful, as are Native stories, crafts, and dancing. LaVonne's offers a rare look into the Eskimo existence on the Chukchi coast.

The traditional parka provides good protection against the cold.

The tundra ablaze in autumnal colors.

Tip

Tour companies offer flights to the Prudhoe Bay oil fields, often with a return by bus across 500 miles (800km) of gravel road to Fairbanks. A fixed fee provides a bed for the two-night trip, meals at a North Slope dining facility, and round-trip airfare. Four-hour tours of the oil fields round out the arrangement. It is also possible to take a one-day package, flying both ways.

THE NORTH SLOPE

Bush pilots on Alaska's north coast have little use for aerial charts, because there are few usable landmarks that can be depicted on a map to aid a pilot in this world of myriad tiny lakes and meandering rivers. Pilots usually plot their positions by counting the number of rivers crossed from a known starting point. Rivers flow from south to north on the **North Slope 8**, a vaguely defined but huge chunk of territory that includes everything north of the Brooks Range. Once a pilot locates a particular river by flying east or west, he turns inland toward terrain with more features, the treeless northern side of the mountains about 100 miles (160km) to the south.

There are no roads between communities and distances are great, so most people fly bush planes to get from one place to another; in winter many residents also depend on snowmobiles (and, to a lesser degree, sled dog teams). Fog is a year-round hazard: a 1,500ft (460-meter) thick cloud of mist blankets the north coast of Alaska for many days of the year. It often stretches inland for about 20 miles (32km), thus hiding the airports of North Slope villages, which are concentrated along the coast.

Stark, trackless beauty and the undisturbed miracles of nature surround you on the North Slope. Almost every stone or fossil is a clue to the varying layers of rock underlying the flat coastal plain, a clue that can lead – and has led – to the discovery of oil. Such clues are zealously guarded by the company that finds them, for finding and developing oil is the name of the game on the North Slope. Initial explorations by geologists are just the first move by the players.

In 2015, falling oil prices triggered a financial crisis which hit the Alaskan government hard. Since then, Alaska has been in a slow state of economic rebound. Its economy still floats on an ocean of black gold, most of it pumped from beneath the tundra on the North Slope. Oil generates about 90 percent of the state government's income and provides a reasonable living for a large transient population of oil-industry workers who commute to and from the Arctic coast.

PRUDHOE BAY

Prudhoe Bay 9 is a working person's world, visited by only a handful of tourists. Several hundred people live and work at the industrial facility – there are no schools, no public roads and few entertainment facilities. The workday is 12 hours long, seven days a week. The pace, though, is temporary. After two or three weeks on the job, workers fly to Anchorage, Fairbanks or even Dallas, Texas, for a week or sometimes two of vacation. It's not uncommon for a worker on the slope to make $75,000 per year for only 26 actual weeks on the job.

The larger oil companies house and feed their personnel, at no expense to employees. Living quarters may

Barrow is the northernmost tip of North America.

include a library, a gymnasium with an indoor track, weights room, game rooms, and satellite television, but they tend to be quiet places where the workers settle into a routine – and there is little time for more than working, sleeping, and eating.

Visitors to the Prudhoe Bay oil fields are usually impressed by the neatness of the facility and how little the buildings disturb the landscape. The silver slash of the trans-Alaska oil pipeline originates here, then winds south toward the Brooks Range. Seeing all this, you realize that here beats the heart that pumps black gold, the lifeblood of Alaska's contemporary economy.

NORTH SLOPE NATIVE LIFE

West of Prudhoe Bay and east of Barrow, **Nuiqsut** ⑩ is geographically placed between oil and tradition. Unlike most northern communities, this Inupiat Eskimo village is several miles inland from the coast, at the apex of the Colville River delta, about 60 miles (100km) from Prudhoe. Inupiat men still hunt whales off the coast (although regulations now strictly limit the number of whales they may take each year), as well as polar bears and seals.

Although most continue to lead a traditional lifestyle of hunting and gathering, a few jobs are available, mostly in government-run organizations. But for those who still venture onto the frozen sea in search of animal food and skins, their safety is less in the hands of chance these days. If they are late returning to their modern frame houses in the village, one quick telephone call launches a helicopter to search the coastline near the delta's mouth.

BARROW

Located to the west and just south of Point Barrow, the northernmost tip of North America, **Barrow** ⑪ is Alaska's largest Eskimo settlement. It is the headquarters of the Arctic Slope Regional Corporation, a Native corporation like the NANA corporation in Kotzebue. When the US Congress approved the Alaska Claims Settlement Act, Barrow and other key Native villages in Alaska instantly became corporate centers, modern enclaves of big business in a traditional land. Barrow today stands as the ultimate contrast between tradition and technology.

Skin whaling boats are still used for the spring hunt, while modern aluminum craft are used for the fall hunt, when sea ice is farther from shore, which means that whalers may have to travel greater distances to find whales. Whaling is now very strictly regulated, but captains teach their sons the secrets of harpooning and landing the bowhead whale, more as a means of keeping the culture alive than as a necessary tool of survival.

The opportunity to see an ancient culture and its traditions lure some visitors to Barrow; others come to see the midnight sun, which does not set here from mid-May to early August

A summer swim in the Beaufort Sea.

An Inuit hunter at sunset in Nuiqsut.

The blanket toss is a traditional native summer celebration.

Barrow, Alaska's largest Eskimo settlement.

Most people come here as part of a package tour. Travel agencies and tour companies offer overnight trips to Barrow from Anchorage and Fairbanks for a fee that covers a hotel room, a few local tours, and the use of a parka.

Visitors may be lucky enough to witness a traditional blanket toss (part of a festival celebrating a successful whaling season), or try a bite of seal meat or muktuk (whale blubber). But these local treats are available only sporadically, and visitors who like to live on the culinary edge may have to search for them.

INUPIAT CULTURE

It is unfortunate that most trips to Barrow are so brief. Inupiat culture is varied and ancient, but it is difficult and time-consuming for an outsider to gain a detailed knowledge of it. And, although English is spoken by most Inupiat (except for the very old), traditional behavior may be confusing and interfere with communication.

For example, Inupiat are not being impolite when they fail to respond immediately to a question or acknowledge a statement. It is simply not their custom to do so, but outsiders may find their long pauses uncomfortable. Saying 'thank you' is also not customary: traditionally, Inupiat people will simply return a favor – and expect no thanks from the recipient.

Perhaps the best advice for tourists to Barrow – or any part of the Arctic for that matter – is to assume a slower-paced style of speaking and behaving, a pace more attuned to traditional lifestyles, and to remember that the Inupiat people live not by the clock but by the change of seasons. Changing one's behavior takes a conscious effort, and may be hard at first, but a journey to the Arctic is an unparalleled opportunity to live, albeit briefly, in a different way and experience an unfamiliar culture.

(continually shining for 82 days), and for a chance to stand momentarily on the continent's northern edge – for many visitors the most vivid memory of their Barrow trip.

For winter visitors, the Northern Lights are a major attraction, but they are equally apparent in Fairbanks, which is a great deal more accessible than Barrow.

THE DALTON HIGHWAY

Once used solely by truckers serving the pipeline, this remote, unforgiving road is now being used by hunters, anglers, and those looking for adventure at the top of the world.

The only road north of the Arctic Circle to connect with Alaska's highway system, the Dalton Highway – named after James Dalton, an Alaska-born engineer – ties Interior Alaska to the oil fields at Prudhoe Bay. Some 414 miles (666km) long, the Dalton was built in 1974, during the state's oil-boom days, so that trucks could haul supplies to Prudhoe and pipeline construction camps in Alaska's northern reaches. Hence the Dalton's other name: the Haul Road.

Thousands of 18-wheeler rigs still drive the Dalton each year, but they now share it with hunters, anglers, and sightseers. Parts were opened to the public in 1981, but the entire route didn't officially open until 1995. That summer, 6,000 people signed the Bureau of Land Management's (BLM) guest register, a large jump from previous years. Numbers have risen only slightly since then.

That doesn't mean the Dalton has suddenly become an easy drive. It's narrow as highways go, often winding, and has several steep grades where it passes through mountains. Sections may be heavily potholed or washboarded and its coarse gravel is easily kicked up into headlights and windshields by trucks that travel 65 or 70mph (105 to 112kmh) along some straight sections.

Besides being tough on vehicles, the road has few visitor facilities. From its start at the Elliott Highway (84 road miles/135km northwest of Fairbanks) to its endpoint at Deadhorse (the small construction community that serves the Prudhoe Bay oil field workers), there are only three places to get fuel, lodging, and food – and two of those are within the first 60 miles/100km (Mile 56, at the Yukon River Crossing Visitor Contact Station and Mile 60.3, the Hot Spot Cafe); the third and last food-and-fuel stop before reaching the end of the road is at Coldfoot, Mile 175.

Drivers are therefore urged to take four-wheel-drive cars or trucks, loaded with extra provisions: reserve gas, spare tires, several engine belts, drinking water, enough clothing to survive an alpine snowstorm (which may occur at any time of year), and food and fuel for two weeks of camping. Because of the road hazards, car rental companies normally prohibit their vehicles from being taken up the Haul Road.

The great majority of Dalton Highway adventurers travel no farther than the Arctic Circle, at Mile 115.3, most just to be able to say they've been there. A Bureau of Land Management wayside has picnic tables, grills, outhouses, and interpretive displays. There's also a nearby primitive campground. Other designated campgrounds are few and far between; a popular one is the BLM's Marion Creek Campground at Mile 179.7.

Beyond Coldfoot, road traffic diminishes greatly, as the road ascends gradually into the heart of the Brooks Range Mountains. Though much of the highway's first 180 miles (290km) is bordered by monotonous lowland forest, here the landscape is grandly, ruggedly beautiful.

At Mile 244.7, the Haul Road tops out at 4,800ft (1,460-meter) Atigun Pass, along the Arctic Divide; it's the highest highway pass in Alaska and conditions may be wintry, even in mid-summer.

For an update on road conditions at any time of the year, telephone 511 (in Alaska) or 866-282-7577; http://511.Alaska.gov.

A truck makes its way along the Dalton Highway.

ARCTIC NATIONAL WILDLIFE REFUGE

In Alaska's far northeast corner, the refuge is home to grizzlies, packs of wolves, and a thundering herd of caribou, but you can go days or weeks without seeing another person.

Map on page 268

Drifting off to sleep his first night in the Aichilik River Valley, a backcountry explorer hears, or perhaps imagines, the distant howling of *Canis lupus*. Entering the visitor's dreams, wolves celebrate a successful hunt with wolf song. Several hours later the camper is awakened by the cries of *Homo sapiens*, singing the praises of a glorious Arctic morning. He quickly leaves his tent and joins the rest of his party for breakfast beneath a cloudless cerulean sky. Stirred by breezes that keep mosquitoes away,

the late-summer air is surprisingly warm. By mid-morning the group's thermometer registers 68°F (20°C) in the shade and in sunlight the air is 10 to 15°F (5.6 to 8.4°C) warmer.

The party of six – three Bostonians, two Alaskans, one Californian – have been flown into the remote and roadless **Arctic National Wildlife Refuge ⑫** (tel: 907-456-0250; http://arctic.fws.gov), in extreme northeastern Alaska. The refuge was established in 1960 as an 8.9-million-acre (3.6 million-hectare) 'wildlife range' whose primary intent was to preserve unique wildlife, wilderness, and recreational values. The range was expanded and upgraded to refuge status in 1980. Stretching from Alaska's Interior to the Arctic's North Slope and Beaufort Sea, it protects 19 million acres (7.7 million hectares), 42 percent of which is designated wilderness.

It is home to a remarkable assemblage of birds and mammals, including some of North America's most charismatic animals: grizzly and polar bears, wolves, musk oxen, Dall sheep, moose, golden eagles, and peregrine falcons. But its most famous inhabitants belong to the Porcupine caribou herd, which over the past decade has ranged from 90,000 to 180,000 members.

A porcupine caribou herd.

THE OIL ISSUE

The Porcupine is North America's only international herd of caribou, with a range that encompasses tens of thousands of square miles in both Canada and Alaska. But that isn't the herd's only – or chief – claim to fame. Since the early 1980s, it has been at the center of a national debate: whether to allow oil and gas development in the Arctic Refuge's 1.5-million-acre (600,000-hectare) coastal plain.

The oil industry and its supporters – including most Alaskans and the state's governor – push hard for oil and gas development, while those desiring a wilderness designation fight just as hard to save the wild landscape, which is a seasonal home for dozens of species that use it for all sorts of activities: denning, breeding, nesting, spawning, hunting, grazing, and calving. In 2019, the Trump administration said they would like to see the entire coastal plain opened for gas and oil exploration.

The caribou have become a symbol of what's at stake, largely because portions of the coastal plain serve as a traditional 'core calving area' where caribou cows give birth each spring. It's also where the caribou gather in huge, densely packed crowds from mid-June to mid-July to get some relief from mosquitoes and parasitic flies. The largest single group seen by biologists numbered more than 94,000 caribou.

While fierce debates have raged over the Arctic refuge's coastal plain, relatively little attention has been given to the refuge's other 17.5 million acres (7 million hectares), though they encompass some of the world's wildest Arctic lands, including the eastern third of the Brooks Range, Alaska's northernmost mountain chain.

THE NORTHERN FOOTHILLS

Stretching east–west across the state, the **Brooks Range** is a gently subdued mountain kingdom, with wave after wave of ridgelines and mountaintops – mostly under 5,000ft (1,500 meters) – that can be easily ascended in a day or less by hikers in good physical

Admiring the view over the Arctic National Wildlife Refuge.

condition (this is no place for couch potatoes). Dissecting the mountains are wide, U-shaped, north-south trending river valleys that create a sense of wide-open spaces. The **Aichilik River Valley** is one of those.

Rather than backpack or float a river, as most refuge visitors do, this group of explorers has established a 'base camp' on one of the Aichilik's many gravel bars; from here they will explore the surrounding landscape on day hikes. By setting their four tents on the river's sand and gravel, the campers avoid trampling the tundra: such low-impact practices are especially important in fragile Arctic ecosystems.

It's equally important, on any Alaska backcountry trip, to bring gear that can withstand winter-like storms, which may occur at almost any time of year, and to keep a clean camp and store food away from tents and in such a way that animals – whether grizzlies or ground squirrels – aren't likely to get into it. There are no trees here, so the group has brought plastic bear-proof

Preparing to fly out.

food canisters, and built a rock cairn around them.

ARCTIC FLORA AND FAUNA

This Aichilik River camp is nestled among the Brooks Range's northern foothills, within 3 miles (5km) of the coastal plain. The valley is one of many corridors used by the Porcupine caribou herd during seasonal migrations to and from the plain. The caribou have already moved through, but their signs are everywhere: hundreds of deep rutted trails crisscross the landscape, thick clumps of caribou hair hang from willow bushes, and whitened, sunbleached bones and antlers lay scattered on gravel bars, tundra wetlands, and limestone ridges.

Their first morning in the wilds, the hikers walk to a gray, nameless, cone-shaped mountain overlooking the coastal plain. Leaving the river, they cut across lowland tundra. From a distance, it appears smooth and monotonous, a green rolling carpet spread between gray and brown hills. Up close, that monotone green

is transformed into a complex mix of grasses, shrubs, mosses, lichens, and wildflowers. And it's anything but smooth. They pick their way through a maze of sedge tussocks, mushroom-shaped grass mounds that are the stuff of Arctic legend.

Narrow at the base and wide on top, the tussocks are unstable to walk upon; any step slightly off center makes them lean this way or that. It's possible to walk between the tussocks, but the boggy ground between them quickly soaks boots. There's no easy solution, but at least the day hikers don't have heavy packs to balance.

As the group gradually ascends, the tussocks give way to alpine tundra; this is pleasant, like walking on a dry, spongy cushion. After a stop for lunch – the usual mix of nuts, fruit, cheese, chocolate – on a wind-swept knoll, the three men and three women jump across a clearwater creek, and leave tundra for talus. Forty minutes of strenuous rock-scrambling brings them to the hilltop, where they look upon an immense landscape of lakes, tundra plains, braided rivers, and craggy peaks. It's a wild and ancient land, one that inspires reverence.

AN ABUNDANCE OF WILDLIFE

Returning to camp, the visitors spot two golden eagles soaring above the ridge they've just left. Later in the week they will see Dall sheep, red foxes, songbirds, ptarmigan, a couple of caribou – stragglers from the Porcupine herd – and a grizzly bear sow with two cubs. The anglers among them will also catch grayling and Arctic char in the Aichilik's cold waters.

Continued hot weather prompts some members of the group to switch from daytime to evening walkabouts for their last few days in the refuge; temperatures here may drop 10, 20, or more degrees at night. Their final evening, a pair ascends a 2,500ft (760-meter) limestone hill southwest of camp and are again rewarded with expansive views in all directions. To the north, beyond a series of

Tundra flora.

Brooks Range from the air, with the Kongakut River below.

humpbacked hills, is the undulating coastal plain stretching to the Arctic coast, where earth and sky meet in a white line: the ice-covered Beaufort Sea. To the east, across the Aichilik, are lowland plains, grading gently into tundra-covered knobs.

To the south and west are row after row of rugged ridges, culminating in the snow-capped tops of 8,000- and 9,000ft (2,400- and 2,700-meter) peaks, 30 miles (50km) away. The landscape invites further exploration; the hikers wonder what's over the next pass.

The couple descends as the sun drops behind the mountains. Above the darkening landscape a twilight glow paints the northern sky yellow, then orange, and crimson. Even at midnight, in mid-August, it's too bright for stars. For much of the summer, the sun never leaves the Arctic sky, though it may briefly hide behind high peaks. The pilot arrives on schedule and too quickly the backcountry visitors are headed south, back to sidewalks and restaurants and

hot showers. In seven days they have seen no other humans. The solitude and wildness have been a blessing.

FLOAT TRIPS

One of the most popular ways to explore the Arctic Refuge is by float trip. Although hundreds of rivers and creeks flow out of the mountains, both north and south, only a few are large and deep enough to permit easy travel by raft, canoe, or kayak. These include the Sheenjek, Coleen, Kongakut, Canning, and Hulahula. Most refuge visitors go on guided trips that last one to two weeks.

Some trips combine river floating with overland backpacking; nearly all allow opportunities for hiking through the mountains. Contact refuge headquarters in Fairbanks (101 12th Avenue, AK 99701; tel: 907-456-0250/800-362-4546; http://arctic.fws. gov) for a list of commercial outfitters and guides permitted to work here.

The **Hulahula** is the most challenging of the Arctic Refuge's floatable streams, with a few stretches of Class

III whitewater (on a scale of VI). At high water, some rapids might even be graded higher. It therefore isn't a good stream for unguided beginners, but it's popular with guided groups.

Born near the Arctic Divide, the Hulahula is one of the Arctic Refuge's largest and most heavily used north-flowing rivers. Fed by remnant glaciers as well as numerous clearwater tributaries, it passes two of the Brooks Range's three highest peaks (9,020ft/ 2,749-meter Mount Chamberlain and 8,855ft/2,699-meter Mount Michelson) while flowing 100 miles (160km) to the sea.

The river was given its name – originally spelled Hoolahoola – by whalers and was taken from a Hawaiian word meaning 'to dance.' Exactly to what dance the whalers referred is unknown but the name stuck.

River-runners who travel the Hulahula, or other north-bound streams, are likely to see Dall sheep, grizzlies, and sometimes wolves while passing through the mountains. Depending on the time of year, floaters may also cross paths with migrating members of the Porcupine caribou herd. Once out on the rolling and swampy coastal plain, rafters and other river travelers may see musk oxen, large prehistoric-like beasts with curved horns and long shaggy coats. These living relics of the ice age disappeared from Alaska's North Slope in the late 1800s, probably because of human overhunting. Reintroduced to the Arctic Refuge in 1969 and 1970, the species population now numbers in the hundreds.

Most river trips into the refuge are done between early June and mid-July, when the streams are running highest. Even then, rivers don't always have enough water for easy floating. It's sometimes necessary to lift and carry rafts through shallow, riffled sections of rivers. Not only does early summer offer the best river-travel conditions, it also features prime wildlife viewing opportunities, especially on the coastal plain. And mosquito numbers are usually still low, particularly in June.

GETTING TO THE REFUGE

Nearly all visitors enter the refuge by plane, using air-taxi services. The two most popular jumping-off spots are **Kaktovik ⓭**, an Inupiat Eskimo village along the Beaufort Sea on the refuge's northern border, and **Fort Yukon**, a small, predominantly Athabascan village 140 air miles (225km) from Fairbanks and about 450 miles (720km) from Anchorage. Both Kaktovik and Fort Yukon are served by commercial flights out of Fairbanks.

Once inside the refuge, visitors traveling on their own must be self-sufficient. There are no campgrounds or other facilities and backcountry travelers are expected to practice low-impact camping techniques. Here, as in other parts of the Arctic, it's also wise to come prepared for a wide range of weather conditions.

Ice-jumping along the Kongakut River.

GATES OF THE ARCTIC

If you hear the call of the wilderness, the Gates of the Arctic may be the place you are looking for, but plan your trip with care, because you really are on your own.

Map on page 268

In 1929, Robert Marshall, a founder of the Wilderness Society, proposed that most of Alaska north of the Yukon River be preserved as wilderness. His vision wasn't realized, but much of northern Alaska is in fact now so protected; and the place most dear to Marshall, the central Brooks Range, is preserved in **Gates of the Arctic National Park and Preserve** ⑭ (tel: 907-692-5494; www.nps.gov/gaar/index.htm). In the heart of northern Alaska, the park is 200 miles (320km) northwest of Fairbanks, and 200 miles (320km) southeast of Barrow, Alaska's largest Eskimo community.

No maintained roads or trails exist within the park – no phones, TVs, radios, gas stations, restaurants, stores, or hotels. No emergency services are available: no hospitals, first-aid stations, ambulances, police, or fire stations. There is one permanent ranger station at **Anaktuvuk Pass**, a Native village in the middle of the park.

The culture of the Nunamiut Inupiat is being documented in the **Simon Paneak Memorial Museum** (Anaktuvak Pass; tel: 907-661-3413; Mon–Fri 8.30am–5pm). Emphasis is put on the importance of the caribou in determining the Nunamiut people's nomadic lifestyle. Local artwork and crafts are on sale.

OUTDOOR ACTIVITIES

Such wilderness provides freedom from the trappings of civilization – one that relatively few people experience each year. In summer, there are opportunities for mountaineering, backpacking, hiking, and camping. The lakes, rivers, and streams allow for rafting, canoeing, kayaking, and fishing. Also popular are birding, flightseeing, and wildlife viewing.

Fall activities include blueberry and cranberry picking, and hunting for bear, Dall sheep, caribou, moose, ducks, geese, rabbits, and ptarmigan

Inquisitive polar bear.

(non-subsistence 'sport' hunting can be done only in the preserve). In winter, however, the park is quiet. The sun drops below the horizon in December and doesn't appear again until January. The record low temperature has been recorded as −70°F (−57°C). In March and April, as daylight hours again exceed darkness, a few hardy adventurers use the park for cross-country skiing, dogsledding and snowshoeing.

The Gates of the Arctic area is known as 'inhabited wilderness.' Visitors, floating past a Native fish camp, may see orange-red salmon strips drying on birch poles or a fish net bobbing with the flow of the river. They may even encounter a trapper's secluded log home with a snowmachine outside, traps, and a bearskin hanging from the cabin walls. But people are rarely seen. The area's population density is less than one person per 5,000 acres (2,000 hectares).

BETTLES

Gates of the Arctic National Park and Preserve is remote, pristine wilderness. The meaning of 'remote' becomes immediately evident when trying to get here. **Bettles** ⓑ is the primary gateway to Gates. You can take a scheduled flight from Fairbanks to this friendly little outpost, then hire an air taxi to fly into the park. Before going, check in at the park's ranger station and discuss your itinerary with staff. Bettles also provides visitors to Gates with potential outfitters, guides, and a lodge.

From here, any number of trips are possible into the park, but they all cost a lot. If you want to cut costs, it's sensible to travel in a group. A trip for six from Bettles can cost less than half what it costs for two. Compare services to prices and ask for references. Reputable guides will have names of people to contact who have taken their trips.

If you are short of money but have the time and the physical stamina you can backpack the many miles to the park, after driving along the Dalton Highway, built during the creation of the trans-Alaska pipeline. Check for road conditions on the Highway by calling 511 (within Alaska, or 866-282 7577; http://511.alaska.gov).

A gray wolf in the tundra.

Bettles Ranger Station can give you all sorts of advice.

⊙ **Fact**

In the 1930s the mining community of Wiseman had a population of 80 men, 22 women, and 25 children. Its raw life was vividly captured by Robert Marshall in his book Arctic Village: A 1930s Portrait of Wiseman, Alaska.

Fairbanks is also a recommended stop for maps, information and supplies. The **Alaska Public Lands Information Center** (101 Dunkel Street; tel: 907-459-3700; www.explorefairbanks.com; summer daily 8am–9pm, winter daily 8am–5pm) has a complete list of air services, commercial services, information books, and maps. Information is also available directly from the park visitor centers located in Bettles (tel: 907-692-5494) and Anaktuvuk Pass (tel: 907-661-3520; summer only).

Fairbanks is generally the last stop to shop for supplies, including stove fuel and food. Since all fuel must be flown in, many communities have erratic or non-existent supplies; camp stove fuel is not allowed on scheduled airlines. Villages are often not equipped with facilities for visitors, so travelers should have adequate food supplies and should have arranged return transportation in advance.

The Dalton Highway winds through wild and beautiful wilderness and nears Gates's eastern boundary at **Coldfoot** ⑯, approximately 250 miles (400km) north

A long-tailed jaeger perches on a boulder beside a caribou antler.

of Fairbanks. In early September, when the birch leaves are golden in the hills and the weather is sunny and dry, the drive alone is worth the trip – though early winter snowstorms may temporarily block the road in September or even August. A stop at the **Coldfoot Services Truckstop** is a must for any visitor. In the lodge-style dining hall restaurant, meals are eaten on oilcloth-covered tables with wooden benches, mining camp-style. Motel rooms are available.

The National Park Service and other federal agencies jointly operate a summer visitor center at Coldfoot. Another visitor center, the **Arctic Interagency Visitor Center**, is located just north of the Yukon River Bridge (tel: 678-5209; summer daily).

TRIPS AND TRAILS

The most easily accessed trail into the park is in **Wiseman**, 15 miles (24km) north of Coldfoot. Wiseman is a turn-of-the-20th-century mining community. Its weathered buildings are still home to a few miners. The road from Dalton Highway to Wiseman extends on to several

trails that enter the park. The **Nolan-Wiseman Creek Trail** goes through the historic mining area to the Glacier River. Another approved trail follows the Hammond River north from Wiseman.

One of the most popular areas in Gates is the North Fork of the Koyukuk River, where the peaks, **Frigid Craigs** and **Boreal Mountain**, form 'The Gates' for which the park is named. The Gates can be reached either by backpacking out of Anaktuvuk or by floating the North Fork from Summit Lake. Another favored excursion involves flightseeing out of the village of Bettles.

Float trips – and combination backpacking/float trips – can be arranged throughout the park. Or seek fish-filled **Walker Lake**, a blue jewel nestled in the deep forested hills in the southern part of the park. Winter cross-country ski trips, dogsled rides, and ice fishing are available here. A few private cabins and lodges are the only places where a visitor can sleep indoors in or near the park.

Sport hunting is allowed only in the park's preserve section, and non-Alaskans must have a guide if they want to hunt for certain big game animals. A guide familiar with local conditions is recommended even if not required. Some game can be taken only by permit. Contact the Alaska Department of Fish and Game for specifics (tel: 907-459-7206; www.adfg.alaska.gov).

THE MOSQUITO MENACE

As well as being home to grizzlies, wolves, and caribou, Gates is also host to hordes of mosquitoes. During certain times of the year – July in particular – wilderness travelers can best endure the ever-present swarm of bugs by keeping their entire body, including their hands, completely covered, and wearing a head net. Always carry a good mosquito repellent, preferably one with a high DEET concentration, and a finely screened tent.

Another wilderness creature that inhabits Gates is *Giardia lamblia*, a microscopic water organism that causes 'beaver fever,' an unpleasant intestinal disorder. The best prevention is to boil all drinking water or use chemical disinfectants such as iodine.

July and August are the wettest months. Thunderstorms are common. Rain has been known to start in mid-August and not stop until it turns to snow in September. Temperatures range from –70°F (–57°C) to 92°F (32°C). Snow may fall in any month. The average summer temperature ranges from freezing to 85°F (29°C), prime hypothermia (body-chilling) conditions. Wool or synthetic clothing such as fleece keeps you warm and dry, and high-quality hiking boots are needed in rocky and soggy conditions.

People have drowned sleeping on sandbars; others have found that a gentle stream can become a raging whitewater river after a downpour. Three to 10 days' leeway should be allowed for water level changes if any river or creek crossings are involved. Anyone who wants to visit the Gates of the Arctic needs to do considerable research beforehand: topographical maps are vital, and every problem must be anticipated and planned for.

Bear and human tracks in wet sand.

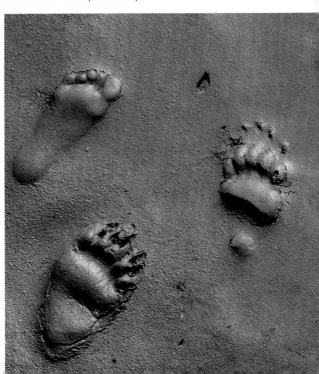

CAPE KRUSENSTERN

The remote lands of Cape Krusenstern, whose archeological treasures reach back 4,000 years, are only for the self-sufficient and intrepid traveler, but the rewards are great.

⊙ Main attractions

Cape Krusenstern
  National Monument
Kivalina
Noatak
Sheshalik
Kotlik Lagoon
Krusenstern Lagoon

Map on page 268

It's hard to imagine a less likely place for buried treasure. There's nothing particularly conspicuous about **Cape Krusenstern** – no towering mountains, magnificent waterfalls, verdant forests. Only a low, ridged spit with deep furrows, dotted with countless ponds, and bordered by a relentless sea on one side and a large lagoon on the other.

Clipping the waves of the Chukchi Sea, Cape Krusenstern stretches into polar waters in northwestern Alaska just north of Kotzebue. Hidden beneath beach ridges on the cape are archeological treasures dating back at least 4,000 years. This earth-bound chronicle of early man in Alaska brought about the establishment in 1980 of the 560,000-acre (226,600-hectare) **Cape Krusenstern National Monument ⑰** (tel: 907-442-3890/907-442-3760 in summer only; www.nps.gov/cakr/index.htm).

Charter planes and boats headquartered in **Kotzebue** take infrequent visitors to the monument, 10 miles (16km) northwest across Kotzebue Sound at its southern border. The monument lacks visitor services and receives only a few thousand visitors a year. Nevertheless, in 2015 it welcomed its most important visitor in centuries, when President Obama visited the town during a tour of Alaska.

REMOTE VILLAGES

The small village of **Kivalina** stretches out along the Chukchi shore north of the monument and to the east of Krusenstern, across the Mulgrave Hills, lies the village of **Noatak**. Kivalina and Noatak have airstrips but most visitors arrive via Kotzebue, which has service from Anchorage and Fairbanks.

Cape Krusenstern is a bring-your-own-shelter place, and that goes for stove, food, and water. Highlands

Native Inupiat grand-mother and granddaughter from Noatak.

beyond the beaches have freshwater streams, but it's still best to take some – and either boil or treat any local water you do use, to prevent the risk of giardia. Planes can land on some beaches of the monument, and float-planes put down on nearby lagoons. Many beach areas are privately owned; visitors should check with monument headquarters staff in Kotzebue for specific locations of private property, as they are not marked. Travelers are free to explore archeological zones located throughout 114 beach ridges adjacent to the Krusenstern Lagoon. No digging for artifacts or causing other disturbances is allowed.

Winds sweep almost constantly across the lowlands of Cape Krusenstern. In winter they bring instant freezing to an already cold land. In summer, fog blankets coastal areas, although temperatures are 40–65°F (4–18°C). Inland, the skies are often clear in June and July, but visitors should always carry rain gear and be alert for hypothermia.

FORMATION OF THE CAPE

The cape at Krusenstern didn't always exist. About 10,000 years ago, the coastline angled straight southeast from Point Hope, skirted a small mountain, and turned east. Kotzebue Sound was mostly a giant sandy lowland, not the open water-way it is today. During the Pleistocene Era, from approximately 2 million to 10,000–15,000 years ago, great ice sheets covered much of the northern hemisphere. These ice masses absorbed water, causing the sea level to recede. As the sea shrank away from the shore, it exposed a land bridge connecting North America and Asia. When the ice sheets melted, the sea level rose once again and covered the so-called Bering Land Bridge.

Sweeping down the newly aligned coastline, prevailing winds from the northwest propelled waves, which carried bits of gravel in their churning surf, down the beach. When the waves hit the turn where the coastline swung east, they dropped the gravel offshore. Every so often, usually in the spring, the winds shifted to the southwest. Great chunks of ice were driven onshore, but not before the ice scooped up gravel from shallow offshore beds and deposited it on the beach beyond the surf. Ridge after ridge built up on the outer shore of the cape.

Slowly the cape pushed seaward. Hardy beach plants colonized the ridges, their root systems helping to stabilize the gravels. Year after year the birth and death of beach plants built up a thin layer of soil, creating suitable habitat for other plants. Over the centuries, a carpet of green followed the shoreline, advancing seaward, until 114 ridges lined an approximately 3-mile (5km) -wide spit. Lt Otto von Kotzebue, sailing with the Imperial Russian Navy, gave geographical recognition to the cape by

Snow-bound home of an Alaska Native in Cape Krusenstern National Monument.

naming it Krusenstern after the first Russian admiral to circumnavigate the globe in 1803–4.

THE OLD WHALERS

Every once in a while the continuity of the archeological record was broken when scientists unearthed artifacts from a culture that did not fit in to the spectrum of early man in northwestern Alaska that was dominated by the Choris and Ipiutak cultures.

One such find was the record of Old Whalers on the beach ridge inland from the Choris remains. These prehistoric people, who lived for a brief time at the cape sometime between 1800 and 1500 BC, relied almost exclusively on the sea for sustenance. Their record indicates a greater use of whales than either preceding or subsequent cultures.

THE CAPE TODAY

Each spring, the rivers and streams of Kotzebue basin cleanse themselves when snowmelt fills the channels, which dump their load into Kotzebue

An Eskimo examines the remains of a whale as they dry out.

Sound. Whitefish join this migration, leaving their inland wintering grounds and moving into summer feeding areas in coastal estuaries. This annual flooding acts as a catalyst for one of the region's major subsistence hauls.

As the floodwaters fan out into Kotzebue Sound, several species of whitefish swarm into sloughs along the Krusenstern coast, fattening throughout the summer in the brackish waters. Local residents congregate at the sloughs each fall when groundswells from the Chukchi Sea push gravel and sand across the channels by which whitefish exit the saltwater areas on their return migration. Residents harvest the fish trapped in the sloughs, to add to their winter staples.

Travelers should take extra care not to disturb fishing nets, boats or other gear on which local residents rely.

Also crucial is the 6-mile (10km) flatland at the monument's southern tip, **Sheshalik**, 'Place of White Whales.' Several families maintain year-round homes at Sheshalik, which is a traditional gathering place for hunters of beluga: the small, white, toothed whale. Life in the community revolves around stockpiling the meat, fish, berries, and greens that see these families through nine months of harsh winter.

KOTLIK AND KRUSENSTERN LAGOONS

For centuries, hunters have gathered at **sealing points** on the narrow isthmus separating the Chukchi from these inner lagoons. Returning, their boats loaded with sea mammal carcasses, the hunters portage the isthmus and continue their southerly journey over calm lagoon waters rather than fighting the waves of the open sea.

In May, waterfowl return from their winter sojourn, and head for Krusenstern where snow melt has weakened the ice and open water spreads early throughout the lagoons. Several species of geese and ducks nest on the ponds, joined by their cousins on stilts, the sandhill cranes.

Later in the summer residents harvest salmonberries, cranberries, and blueberries. Women pick greens, preserving some in seal oil for later use. Fish are hung to dry on wooden racks. Chum salmon are taken for subsistence as well as for the commercial fishery in Kotzebue Sound.

HUNTING TERRITORY

After waterfowl leave in the fall, hunters turn to caribou, ptarmigan, and sometimes walrus or – rarely nowadays – bear. Both black and brown bears have been found on the cape; polar bears roam offshore ice in winter and spring and occasionally come ashore.

Agile Arctic foxes follow behind these northern barons, ready to inspect any tidbit they leave behind. Onshore, elusive furbearers – wolves, wolverines, red foxes, lynx, mink, weasels, snowshoe and tundra hare, and Arctic ground squirrels – patrol the tundra.

Hunters take moose in low-lying areas or Dall sheep in the Igichuk Hills.

A small group of musk ox, descendants of the shaggy mammals that once roamed all Arctic North America but were wiped out by hunters in Alaska in the mid-1800s, thunder across the tundra of the Mulgrave Hills.

Other species, generally not part of the subsistence catch, share Krusenstern's bounty. Birds such as the lesser golden plovers, sandpipers, whimbrels, Lapland longspurs, and Savannah sparrows add their beauty and song. Arctic and Aleutian terns float gracefully above the tundra, ready to defend their nests from the purposeful forays of glaucous gulls and jaegers. An Asian migrant, the handsome yellow wagtail, builds its nest in tiny cavities in the beach ridges. Overhead, rough-legged hawks soar from their nests in the highlands to hover over the tundra.

The ambiance at Krusenstern is understated, but for the curious and the thorough, the history of early man in the north and its modern translation in the subsistence world of local residents are only a step away.

More than 10 million ducks, swans, and geese nest in Alaska.

A seal hunter on the Cape.

📷 NATIVE ART AND ARTIFACTS

Items that once had specific purposes are now highly prized as tourist souvenirs, although to the Native people their traditional cultural values are still important.

In early times, all Alaska Native art served a definite purpose. The items created had either a practical or a cultural use. For instance, carvers created masks for ceremonies, totem poles to tell the histories of clans, and Chilkat blankets for special dancing, or to present as tokens of esteem.

These days, although much Native art continues to serve traditional purposes, many objects are sold into private hands. Dance fans and masks, for example, are still used in ceremonies today, but they are regularly sold as souvenirs. Often, these sales are a welcome source of income for the villages. Visitors to Alaska eagerly seek ivory scrimshaw, carvings of bone, wood, and stone, and baskets woven with colorful grasses or formed from birch bark.

REGIONAL DIFFERENCES

Natives from different parts of Alaska excel in various types of art. Doll making has been an Eskimo art form for at least 2,000 years. The Athabascans are known for colorful beadwork, usually flowers created on tanned moose hide, and incorporating porcupine quills and buttons. The Aleuts are masters at making tightly woven grass baskets, decorated with multicolored embroidery. Some baskets can take up to 15 hours an inch to complete. Southeast tribes are known for their blankets and totem poles.

Facial tattoos and face painting have traditionally been used to imitate and honor animals that bring good fortune.

A handcrafted doll made by Alaska Natives out of fur, ivory and whale bone.

Elaborate masks and headdresses such as this one have great symbolic importance, as they portray the relationship of a particular tribe with the spirits, and are worn during special ceremonies.

Totem Poles: Legends in Wood

Totem poles, some as high as 60ft (18 meters) tall, are one of the most popular examples of Northwest Native woodworking. Figures, or totems, on the poles are comparable to family crests and are used to tell a story, legend, or event. The totemic symbols are usually animals, such as bears, eagles, or killer whales. Their significance lies in myth – stories passed down through generations about how certain animals may have affected the destiny of ancestors.

Poles could usually be found clustered along the village's shore in front of clan houses or directly on the fronts of private houses, or in cemeteries. According to early accounts of Tlingit life, deceased clan members were cremated and their ashes placed in these poles.

Missionaries and other outsiders contributed to the destruction and neglect of many totem poles. Since the 1930s, many have been restored, some of which now stand in totem parks near villages like Klawock and Saxman, and at the Totem Heritage Center in Ketchikan. See www.ktn-ak.us for details.

An example of a traditional totem pole.

Chilkat blankets can take over a year to make, and were once highly sought after by Native nobility. Each told a legend and was used for a special occasion: to cover a body lying in state, or as a gift to an honored guest.

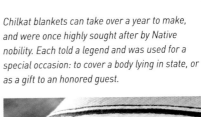
Traditional Athabaskan dancing boots with beads and rabbit fur.

This carving is from a mask in Hoonah. It is typical of the traditional designs used by the Tlingit people when carving their ceremonial masks, rattles and everyday utensils, each with its own story to tell.

NOME AND THE SEWARD PENINSULA

Once a Wild West gold mining boomtown, Nome is now best known as the end of the Iditarod Trail and the Seward Peninsula's commercial hub.

Main attractions
Midnight Sun Festival
Nome River Raft Race
Iditarod Trail Sled Dog Race
Bering Sea Ice Golf- Classic
Pilgrim Hot Springs
Bering Land Bridge National Preserve
Serpentine Hot Springs

Map on page 268

This remote community has long been known as the city that wouldn't die, although it has had more than enough reason to disappear many times since its founding in 1899. **Nome** ⑱ has been burned to the ground; pounded by relentless gales; attacked by flu, diphtheria, and countless other maladies; and almost starved out of existence, yet its population has always rebuilt and struggled on. Nowadays, this one-time boomtown is best known for its connection to the Iditarod Trail Sled Dog Race; and it's the commercial center of the Seward Peninsula, whose wind-whipped tundra landscape was first inhabited thousands of years ago by peoples migrating from Asia into northwest Alaska.

It was gold, discovered in 1898, that brought men, and later women, to this windswept, wave-battered beach on the Seward Peninsula, 75 miles (120km) or more from the nearest tree. Of all the Alaska gold rush towns, Nome was the largest and the rowdiest. Best estimates put the population in excess of 20,000 people by the summer of 1900, but nobody knows for sure.

By the time gold-bearing creeks around the area were discovered, claim jumping (stealing another miner's mineral rich land) and other less-than-ethical mining practices were well advanced in Alaska. Claim-jumping was so rampant that it took a dozen years or more before everything was straightened out. By then the boom was dying and Nome had little more than 5,000 residents. Over the years the permanent population has shrunk as low as 500. It has more or less stabilized at around 3,800 residents.

GOLD ON THE WATERFRONT
Nome hosted a whole series of gold rushes, each almost blending into

The Nugget Inn, Nome.

the next. The first gold came the traditional way – it was found in the streams flowing into Norton Sound. The thousands of prospectors who rushed to Nome set their tents on the beach and explored the nearby gullies, not realizing that all they had to do was sift the sand that was their floor for the precious yellow metal.

The famed black-sand beaches of Nome count as the 'second' gold rush. Since nobody could legally stake a claim on the beach, a man could work any ground he could stand on near the shoreline. The sands were turned over dozens of times and yielded millions of dollars in gold.

Then geologists pointed out that Nome had more than one beach. Over the centuries, as rivers carried silt away to the ocean, the beach line had gradually extended out to sea. The geologists predicted that under the tundra a few yards back from the water, miners would find an ancient beach and, with it, more deposits of gold. And so it was that later years saw yet a third gold rush as ground behind

the seawall was dug and re-dug to extract the precious metal.

Fortune seekers still sift the sands in front of Nome. In 1984 a Nome resident walking on the beach picked up a gold nugget weighing over an ounce from under a piece of driftwood. Such are the rewards of fresh air and exercise. The beach at Nome is still open to the public. Anyone with a gold pan or a sluice box can search for gold along the waterfront, and camping is permitted. If you're serious about finding more than a trace of gold, it's hard, backbreaking work, but then riches have never come easy for miners. Perhaps the only ones who found easy money were the gamblers and the tricksters who made their living relieving miners of their hard-earned gold.

WYATT EARP VISITS

Some shifty characters who learned their crafts in the boomtowns of America's Wild West converged on Nome as practiced, professional con artists – men like Wyatt Earp, the frontier

A gold dredger brought up from San Francisco in 1906.

marshal, who arrived in Nome as a paunchy, 51-year-old saloon keeper.

Yet Nome's gold rush years spawned a hero or two amid the unscrupulous. Shortly after Wyatt Earp arrived, a family named Doolittle moved to the town. One of the boys, Jimmy, delivered newspapers for the Nome Nugget, the oldest continually published newspaper in Alaska. Young Jimmy grew up to lead Doolittle's Raiders, the daring group of army pilots who launched their oversized, overloaded bombers from the decks of a Navy aircraft carrier in the darkest days of World War II.

ENERGETIC CELEBRATIONS

The ability to face all comers, whatever the odds, is what makes Nome the rollicking place it is today. Nomites bring a special energy to every project they embark on.

The **Midnight Sun Festival** is a good example. Held on the weekend closest to the solstice (June 21), the two-day festival includes a late-night softball tournament, a street dance, a chicken barbecue, food stalls (selling reindeer hot dogs and cotton candy), and a darts tournament. The **Nome River Raft Race** is part of the Midnight Sun Festival, and its only rule seems to be that there are no rules.

Less than two weeks later, Nome gets ready to party again with the 4th of July celebration. This event includes street games, a raffle, free ice cream (provided by the fire department) and the **Anvil Mountain Run**. Participants are required to run up the mountain on the road, but are allowed to take any path they want on the way down; the tundra is a shorter route, but it's not as smooth going.

As with most civic celebrations, each event has its own parade. There are hardly any spectators because most of the local residents are in the parade. And what would the 4th of July be without fireworks? In the early 1980s Nome's city council wanted to stop such devices being sold within the city limits because of the fire hazard. This particularly affected the mayor of the time, as he was one of the largest fireworks dealers in the area. He solved

Aerial view of Nome.

the problem by setting up his firework stand a few steps outside the city line and gleefully sold all manner of pyrotechnics to the people, who were more than willing to use them.

There are advantages to living in a remote frontier town. Nome is a close community, with almost anyone available to lend a hand. Consider Christmas. Christmas trees are traditional decorations in local homes just as elsewhere in the United States. The problem with this arises because the last ship of the season usually departs in October, just before Norton Sound freezes. Trees can be flown in, but that's expensive.

However, about 80 miles (130km) to the east is a convenient (at least by rural Alaska standards) forest, and in the weeks before Christmas residents band together and dispatch truckloads of volunteers along a bone-crunching road leading to the forest. The trucks are then filled with small spruce trees, enough to ensure that every household gets one. These aren't the magnificent Douglas firs that are favored in the Lower 48. Instead, they're straggly tundra spruces, but they fit the bill.

At the end of the holidays, residents take their old trees out to 'Nome National Forest' – a stretch of ice outside town – and 'plant' them.

In March, another highpoint is the combined **Spring Carnival** and **Iditarod Trail Sled Dog Race** (see page 306). Also in March is the **Bering Sea Ice Golf Classic**. Participants, dressed in wacky outfits, play on artificial grass on top of the ice, next to the 'Nome National Forest.'

A team in the Iditarod Trail Sled Dog Race.

WESTERN HUB

Today Nome is the transportation hub of western Alaska. It has a major airport with jet service to and from Anchorage, Fairbanks, and Kotzebue, and provides commuter plane service to every village in the region. Almost everyone touring northwestern Alaska must at least pass through Nome.

A small museum, the **Carrie McLain Museum** (in the public library at 233 Front Street; tel: 907-443-6630;

A Golfing Championship held in Nome, during the finish of the Iditarod race.

⊘ SEWARD PENINSULA ROAD TRIPS

Though travel to Nome must be by air or sea, the area boasts the second-largest city road system in the state. Three unmaintained gravel roads extend for a total of 300 miles (480km) across broad regions of the southwest portion of the Seward Peninsula.

These roads allow visitors opportunities – uncommon in remote bush communities – to drive or bike past small, outlying Native villages or through prime birding or wildlife-sighting areas. The Visitors Bureau (tel: 907-443-6555; www.visitnomealaska.com) provides a road guide and a list of businesses offering car rentals. Check with the Alaska Department of Fish and Game Division of Wildlife Preservation (tel: 907-465-4190) for local information on roadside fishing or wildlife-viewing opportunities.

There are no services available along any of these remote roadways, so be sure to bring along adequate fuel, food, a spare tire, and bug repellent. Current weather and driving conditions for any Alaska roadway are available from the Alaska Department of Transportation and Public Facilities by dialing 511 or 866-282-7577; or online at http://511.alaska.gov.

In Alaska as a whole, only one-third of the 300 or so communities are located on the road system. Travel to the others, as well as deliveries of goods and tourists, must generally be via boat, airplane, all-terrain vehicle, and/or snowmachine.

May–Sept daily 10am–5pm, winter Tue–Sat 1–5pm) concentrates mostly on gold rush memorabilia, and visitors can learn how to wield a gold pan. There are the abandoned gold dredges just outside town to explore, and several shops selling ivory carvings and other Native artwork.

Information on Nome's tourist businesses and rental companies can be obtained from the **Nome Convention and Visitors Bureau** (301 Front Street; tel: 907-443-6555; www.visitnomealaska.com; May–Aug Mon–Fri 8am–7pm, Sat–Sun 10am–6pm, winter Mon–Fri 9am–5pm).

ADVENTURES BEYOND NOME

The Seward Peninsula's road network can lead to all kinds of adventures: fishing, hiking, wildlife viewing, birding, and mountain biking, to name a few. Roads connect Nome with other peninsula communities, including **Teller** (population 237) and the ghost town of **Council**. There's another ghost town, **Solomon**, along the Nome Council Road, and the Last Train to Nowhere is

Granite outcrop near Serpentine Hot Springs.

a rusting hulk of a gold rush-era train, stranded on the tundra.

The Anvil Mountain Road goes (appropriately) to the top of **Anvil Mountain**, which presents panoramic views of Nome, the surrounding countryside, and the Bering Sea.

The Nome-Taylor Highway leads to **Pilgrim Hot Springs**; about 7 miles (11km) off the main road, this former Catholic mission and orphanage is open to the public, but visitors must obtain a permit available at the Nome Visitors Bureau located at 301 Front Street.

BERING LAND BRIDGE PRESERVE

Another hot spot, the **Serpentine Hot Springs**, is located within the **Bering Land Bridge National Preserve ⑲** (tel: 907-471-2352; www.nps.gov/bela; Mon–Fri 8am–5pm, also Sat 9am–3pm in summer), a 2.8-million-acre (1.1-million-hectare) parkland at the northern edge of the Seward Peninsula. Much closer to Siberia (55 miles/88km away as the raven flies) than Alaska's urban center, this preserve is among the most remote and least visited units in America's National Park System.

Its landscape is dominated by volcanic features such as lava flows and maars (former volcanic craters that are now lakes). Though barren in appearance throughout much of the year, the preserve is brightened each summer by vivid tundra flowers, and in late-June a carpet of cotton grass covers the tundra as far as the eye can see.

Surprisingly, more than 250 species of flowering plants have been found here, enduring the region's harsh climate. Thousands of birds come each year to breed and raise their young. Over 100 species are known to migrate to the preserve, including sandhill cranes, loons, geese, swans, and a wide variety of shorebirds and songbirds.

Other residents include grizzlies, wolves, caribou, musk oxen, and moose. Also of interest is the culture of neighboring Inuits – their villages, reindeer herds, and arts and crafts.

Thousands of years ago, during the Pleistocene Ice Age, this region was part of the Bering Land Bridge, which connected what is today North America with Asia. Up to 1,000 miles (1,600km) wide, the bridge allowed humans to migrate from Siberia into what we now call Alaska.

The Bering Land Bridge National Preserve celebrates that past while protecting the present landscape and its wild inhabitants. As with most parklands in remote Alaska, this has no visitor facilities and is most easily reached by plane.

SERPENTINE HOT SPRINGS

Known for their healing powers, Serpentine Hot Springs have been popular with Eskimo and Native people over the centuries. You can't actually climb into the springs for a soak, because the water's too hot. There

is nearby, however, a hot tub housed in a rustic bathhouse, with two pipes leading into it: one bringing hot water from the springs and the other cold water from a nearby creek. On days when the cold-water creek dries up, those hoping to enjoy a warm soak simply fill the tub early in the day, and let it cool.

You can also spend a few days hiking among huge granite outcroppings and sleeping in a bunkhouse-style cabin, which operates on a first-come, first-served basis.

It's not effortless to visit Serpentine Hot Springs, however. Summertime travelers must charter a plane from Nome or Kotzebue to fly out to the Preserve. In winter, travel may be by snowmachine and dogsled, as well.

For more information, contact the Bering Land Bridge National Preserve (www.nps.gov/bela), or to find an air charter service or tour operator in the area, contact the Nome Convention and Visitors Bureau (www.nomealaska.org) or the City of Kotzebue (www.cityofkotzebue.com).

A weasel at home in the park.

Cottonwood Creek cabin in the Bering Land Bridge National Preserve.

📷 THE IDITAROD TRAIL SLED DOG RACE

They don't call it 'the last great race on earth' for nothing. The Iditarod takes place over 1,150 grueling miles, taking 10 to 17 days to complete.

The race (http://iditarod.com) starts officially in downtown Anchorage on the first Saturday in March, although this is strictly ceremonial, as mushers drive their teams 20 miles (32km) to Eagle River.

The following day, mushers and dogs begin the race for real in Wasilla. In all, teams travel a circuitous route of more than 1,100 miles (1,770km) before reaching the finish line in Nome (the distance from Anchorage to Nome by air would be 650 miles).

A wide range of mushers compete, from professionals with large kennels to adventurers making a once-in-lifetime sled dog trip through Alaska. Alaska Native John Baker holds the race's speed record, finishing in fewer than nine days in 2011. Mushers compete with teams of up to 16 dogs against themselves, each other and the wilderness.

The first fully fledged race ran to Nome in 1973, recalling the 1925 'race for life,' when 20 mushers relayed life-saving serum to Nome to fight a diphtheria epidemic. Many said it could not be done, yet 22 mushers got to the finishing line.

The **Knik Museum and Sled Dog Mushers Hall of Fame**, 40 miles (64km) from Anchorage, is located in a former pool hall at Knik (Mile 13.9 Knik Road, south of Wasilla). The museum tells the story of the Iditarod Trail and Alaskan mushers.

Four-time Iditarod champion Dallas Seavey and his dog team cross the frozen Yukon River.

The race starts in downtown Anchorage in early March. For many the race signifies that winter is nearly over.

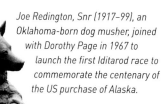

Joe Redington, Snr (1917–99), an Oklahoma-born dog musher, joined with Dorothy Page in 1967 to launch the first Iditarod race to commemorate the centenary of the US purchase of Alaska.

The Mushers who Defied the Odds

For the 60 to 70 racers who attempt the 'the last great race,' the trail is a grueling test of grit, stamina, and will. On the nine to fifteen day trek, mushers must contend with frostbite, violent moose encounters, blinding snow storms, and temperatures that drop to forty below freezing. Dog injury is not uncommon, and sadly neither is death. In 2009, six dogs perished on the trail, the highest number since 1985. The fatalities renewed the debate over animal cruelty that has cast a shadow over the race (see page).

Still, despite these tragedies, dozens of competitors are lured by the adventure and challenge of driving a sled dog team across Alaska each year. Since the race's start in 1973, six mushers have won the Iditarod title four times – Susan Butcher, Martin Buser, Jeff King, Lance Mackey, Doug Swingley, and Dallas Seavey – while Rick Swenson holds the all-time record with five championships.

In 2005 Rachael Scdoris of Bend, Oregon upped the ante against the famously fierce competitors, hostile terrain and biting elements when she entered the race as its first blind musher. With the help of a guide who was under strict instructions to only provide visual assistance, Scdoris competed in four Iditarods. In 2009 she achieved her best ever result, placing 45 out of the 52 finalists.

Veteran Iditarod musher Mitch Seavey from Sterling; for the ceremonial run the mushers have paying passengers.

A dog waits in a truck before the race begins. Over 1,200 dogs take part in the race, and there's usually at least one fatality.

Chicago-born musher Pat Moon travels the Kuskokwim River toward McGrath in the 2012 Iditarod.

Iditarod musher Trent Herbst, a teacher from Ketchum, at the start of the race. Mushers train for years to participate.

A bull moose in the wild.

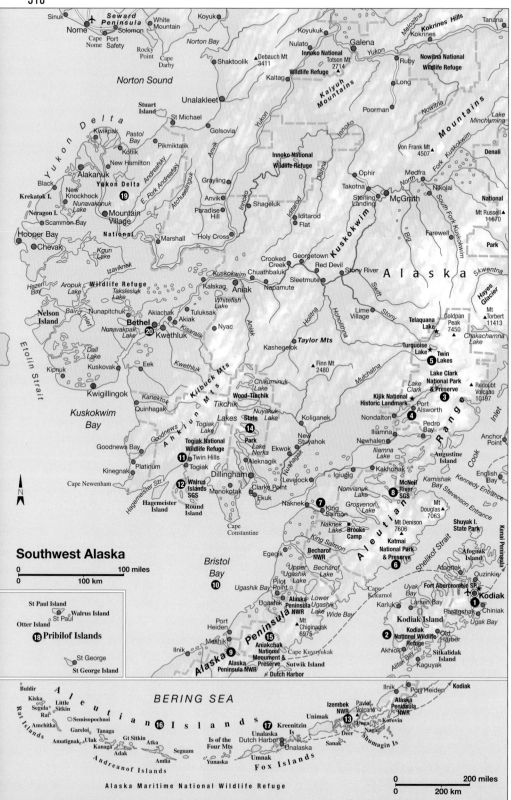

Southwest Alaska

0 ——————— 100 miles
0 ——————— 100 km

Pribilof Islands 18
St Paul Island
St Paul
Walrus Island
Otter Island
St George
St George Island

BERING SEA

Alaska Maritime National Wildlife Refuge

0 ——————— 200 miles
0 ——————— 200 km

THE SOUTHWEST

Stretching from the Alaska Peninsula to the Aleutian Chain, from the Kodiak Archipelago to the Pribilofs, Alaska's Southwest is one of the state's most remote regions.

Aleut fisherman with net, Dutch Harbor.

Far from Alaska's urban centers, Southwest Alaska is a broad and diverse region that includes the Kodiak Archipelago, Alaska Peninsula, Aleutian Islands, Bering Sea Islands, and Yukon-Kuskokwim Delta. It's a place of active volcanoes, windswept tundra, rugged coastal shores, and storm-wracked islands. It's also home to some of the world's largest bird rookeries and marine mammal populations, and the cultural center of the Aleut, Alutiiq, and Yup'ik Eskimo peoples, who have lived off the region's lands and waters for centuries.

Though often inhospitable to humans (and perhaps because of that), the Southwest region's landscape and climate support a diverse – and in some instances, rich – population of fish, birds, and mammals. Here too are the world's largest – and densest populations of – brown bears. And here are the continent's largest runs of sockeye; tens of millions of these salmon return each year to the region's river-and-lake systems, but the largest runs, by far, are centered in the Bristol Bay region.

A bull northern fur seal on St Paul Island, one of the Pribilof Islands.

NATIVE VILLAGES

More than 80 communities are scattered through the region, most of them small villages of indigenous peoples who are still largely dependent on traditional subsistence lifestyles in which they hunt, fish, trap, and gather plants, just as they have for untold generations. Most towns and villages have 200 residents or fewer, though a few commercial centers have between 1,000 and 6,000 people. Few roads link any of the communities and travel is primarily by air or boat year-round, plus snowmobile or dog team in winter.

In the northern Gulf of Alaska, and separated from the mainland by stormy Shelikof Strait, the **Kodiak Archipelago** consists of a couple of dozen islands, most a few miles across or less. But Kodiak itself is the largest island in the US after Hawaii. Sometimes called Alaska's 'emerald isle,' **Kodiak** is 100 miles long and more than 50 miles across at its widest point (160 by 80km). Other large islands in the chain include **Afognak** and **Shuyak**, at the northernmost tip.

THE ALASKA PENINSULA

Directly west of Kodiak, sandwiched between Shelikof Strait and Bristol Bay, the **Alaska Peninsula** stretches more than 500 miles (800km) from the southern boundary of Alaska's mainland to the beginning of the Aleutian Islands. A traditional home for Yup'ik Eskimo, Aleut, and Alutiiq peoples, the area also includes Lake Iliamna, Alaska's largest lake, encompassing 1,100 sq miles (2,850 sq km).

In the peninsula's northeast, Lake Clark National Park and Preserve covers 4 million acres (1.6 million hectares) of some of the most spectacular and least visited parkland in the state. At the intersection of coastal and Interior Alaska, the park has an astounding level of biological diversity and is also home to Mount Redoubt, an active volcano in the Aleutian Range. Since 1900, it has erupted five times; the most recent occurring in 2009 when plumes of ash and steam rose 15,000ft (4,500 meters) to disrupt air travel for three days.

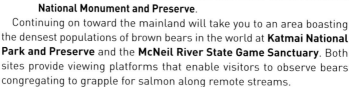

Sunrise on Kodiak Island.

The **Izembek National Wildlife Refuge**, an international crossroads for migrating shorebirds and waterfowl, is located at the southern tip of the peninsula. Following the curve of land to the northeast, you'll find ample support for Alaska's inclusion in the North Pacific's 'ring of fire' at the **Aniakchak Caldera** within the seldom-visited **Aniakchak National Monument and Preserve**.

Continuing on toward the mainland will take you to an area boasting the densest populations of brown bears in the world at **Katmai National Park and Preserve** and the **McNeil River State Game Sanctuary**. Both sites provide viewing platforms that enable visitors to observe bears congregating to grapple for salmon along remote streams.

The community of **King Salmon** is the access point for many of the activities of the peninsula, including not only wildlife viewing, but also world-class sportfishing, hiking, backpacking and river running. **Dillingham** serves as a hub for similar activities in the western Bristol Bay area. Trips can be arranged out of Dillingham to **Togiak National Wildlife Refuge** or to the nearby **Walrus Islands State Game Sanctuary**.

THE ALEUTIAN AND PRIBILOF ISLANDS

The **Aleutian Islands** extend southwest from the tip of the Alaska Peninsula in a 1,000-mile (1,600km) arc toward Asia. These windswept islands are the traditional homeland of the Aleut people. This area of Alaska is of particular interest to birders and sport fishers, as well as those interested in the islands' rich history of Aleut culture, Russian influence and remnants of Alaska's World War II involvement.

A brown bear fishing.

The **Yukon-Kuskokwim (Y-K) Delta** region of Southwest is mostly encompassed within the 19 million-acre (7.7 million-hectare) **Yukon Delta National Wildlife Refuge**. Both the Yukon and the Kuskokwim Rivers traverse the flat, treeless plains and tundra of the Delta and empty into the Bering Sea. Among the most populated regions of rural Alaska, the Yukon Delta is home to nearly 25,000 Yup'ik Eskimo people.

Three hundred miles west of the Y-K Delta area, and 200 miles (320km) north of the Aleutian Islands in the Bering Sea lie the treeless **Pribilof Islands**. St Paul and St George are the only inhabited islands of the group, and fishing and tourism are their emerging economic mainstays.

A bald eagle.

Horned puffin, Kodiak Island.

KODIAK

Two-thirds of mountainous Kodiak Island is a wildlife reserve, famous for its brown bears, while the city of Kodiak has a strong and visible legacy from its Russian past.

A shift of the wind can transform **Kodiak Island** from a desolate, windswept, rain-pounded rock isolated from the rest of the world by fog, to a shimmering emerald of grass, spruce trees, and snowcapped mountains glowing pink in the sunrise. But while the winds may shift, they remain predominantly from the north. Both the island itself and the city of Kodiak are places whose characters change with the weather, the seasons, and the observer.

At first glance, the city of **Kodiak ❶** seems to be near world's end; it is a town of 6,130 people perched precariously on a small ledge of land between ocean swells and jagged mountains (nearly 14,000 people inhabit the entire island). A look into Kodiak's economy reveals a major fishing port – one of the top three in the United States. Kodiak is home to a multi-milliondollar fishing fleet, which ranges from the Pacific Northwest to Norton Sound.

PAST CULTURES

Over 200 years of recorded history have swept across Kodiak, each one leaving traces of its passing. Artifacts of the indigenous Koniag culture surface near remnants of the Russian period or World War II bunkers, derelict whaling stations, collapsing herring-rendering plants, or fish-processing facilities. Just under the topsoil is a layer of

Kodiak's harbor.

volcanic ash, which covered the town in 1912 and still drifts about, leaving a coating of fine, white dust. White spruce tree skeletons guard the salt marshes, monuments to the land subsidence that occurred during the 1964 earthquake and tidal wave.

From the air Kodiak Island, beyond the city, seems an untouched wilderness, 3,588 sq miles (9,293 sq km) of rugged mountains deeply indented by bays. The northern half is covered with spruce trees, the southern half with grass. Foresters say the spruce forest

☉ Main attractions
Alutiiq Museum
Baranov Museum
Holy Resurrection Church
Fort Abercrombie State
  Historical Park
Pillar Mountain
St Paul Harbor
Buskin River State
  Recreation Area
Fossil Beach
Kodiak National Wildlife
  Refuge

**Maps on pages
310, 316**

You can't miss the Russian influence in Kodiak; seen here is the dome of the Holy Resurrection Russian Orthodox Church.

is invading and advancing down the island at the rate of a mile a century.

Landing in Kodiak can be an adventure (Alaska Airlines fly twice a day from Anchorage, except on Saturday). As the jet approaches the airport, it drops lower and lower over the water until its landing gear seems to skim the waves. Just beyond where the runway appears to emerge from the water, the plane sets down. At the other end of the runway sits **Barometer Mountain** (2,450ft/745 meters), so called because the peak is visible only in good weather.

The airport is about 5 miles (8km) from the city of Kodiak and there's a connecting bus. Spruce trees cast shadows across the highway, then the road twists in sharp turns around Pillar Mountain. In the winter bald eagles, sometimes 10 to a tree, perch in cottonwoods above the highway. The road then dips down into town.

THE RUSSIAN LEGACY

Hunting for ducks in Kodiak.

Drawn by his search for sea otter pelts, Grigor Ivanovich Shelikof arrived in Three Saints Bay on the southeast corner of Kodiak Island in 1784 with two ships, the *Three Saints* and the *St Simon*. He was not welcomed by the indigenous Alutiiq people, who proceeded to harass the Russian party (see page 48).

Having established his authority with brutal force, Shelikof founded the first Russian settlement in Alaska on **Three Saints Bay**, built a school to teach the Natives to read and write Russian, and introduced the Russian Orthodox religion.

In 1790 Alexander Andreyevich Baranov arrived at Three Saints Bay to take over leadership of the Russian settlement. He moved the colony to the northeast end of the island where timber was available, and which was closer to Cook Inlet and Prince William Sound. The site chosen by Baranov is now the city of Kodiak.

Russian members of the colony took Alutiiq wives and started family lines whose names still continue – Panamaroff, Pestrikoff, Kvasnikoff. Russian heritage in the city of Kodiak is also found on its street signs: Baranov,

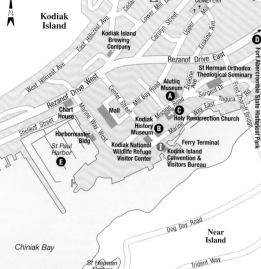

Rezanoff, Shelikof. The island's Native culture is also apparent, and can be seen at a performance by the Kodiak Alutiiq Dancers, which includes 50 dancers who wear traditional dress and perform ethnic songs and dances. The troupe performs throughout the state, with daily summer performances in Kodiak (tel: 907-486-4449; www.sunaq.org).

MUSEUMS IN KODIAK

Much of the rich culture of the Alutiiqs was absorbed by the Russian culture and can only be guessed at through artifacts and the diaries of the early Russian settlers. The best window on the culture is at the **Alutiiq Museum Ⓐ** (215 Mission Road; tel: 844-425-8844; www.alutiiqmuseum.org; Tue–Fri 10am–4pm, Sat noon–4pm). This Native-owned research museum collects and preserves artifacts from ongoing archeological digs.

The **Kodiak History Museum Ⓑ** (tel: 907-486-5920; www.kodiakhistorymuseum.org; summer Mon–Thu, Sat 10am–4pm Fri noon–7pm , winter Tue–Sat 10am–3pm) is across from the Visitors Bureau on Marine Way and next to the ferry dock. It too contains displays of Alutiiq artifacts and clothing as well as items from the Russian and early American periods. The museum also houses a 26ft (8-meter) -long Alutiiq *baidarka* (kayak) covered in sea lion skin, made in the late 1800s. The small museum is located in the **Erskine House**. Once a storehouse for furs, this was designated a National Historic Landmark in 1962, and is North America's oldest Russian building.

HOLY RESURRECTION CHURCH

When the US bought Alaska from Imperial Russia, the Russian citizens left, but the Russian Orthodox churches remained. The two blue onion domes of the **Holy Resurrection Church Ⓒ** on Mission Road are the town's most outstanding landmarks. Orthodoxy still plays a significant role in the Kodiak community, and is the predominant religion in the six villages in the island area.

In 1974, the **St Herman Orthodox Theological Seminary** was relocated to Kodiak: the white buildings stand near the church. Father Herman arrived in Kodiak in 1794 and settled on **Spruce Island**, where he established a school and became renowned as an ascetic and miracle worker. He was canonized in Kodiak in 1970, the first Orthodox canonization to take place on American soil. His remains are kept in the church and the Russian Orthodox faithful make pilgrimages every August to his shrine. Other treasures of the Holy Resurrection Orthodox Church include many brilliantly colored icons. Visitors are welcome to attend services.

The Russian Orthodox Church follows the Julian calendar, making Kodiak a town of two Christmases, December 25 and January 7, and two New Years, January 1 and January 14.

View from Pillar Mountain looking down on Kodiak.

Inside the Baranov Museum.

Kodiak Culture 1867-Present

FORT ABERCROMBIE

During World War II, Kodiak served as a major supply center for the Aleutian campaign. Military personnel and construction workers changed the city from a fishing village of 500 residents to a boomtown of 4,000 people with another 20,000 in nearby areas. The US Navy built a major base on the site, which is now used as a US Coast Guard facility. Today all that remains of the war years are moss-covered bunkers. **Fort Abercrombie State Historical Park** , some 4 miles (6km) from the city, is dedicated to the memory of those days and includes ruins of World War II coastal defence installations. A large bunker and the remains of gun emplacements overlook the sea from a cliff. Other bunkers can be found by walking through an alpine meadow and along the cliff edge. The visitor center at the entrance of the park on Abercrombie Drive provides trail maps as well as information about camping inside the park.

There are also bunkers on **Pillar Mountain** (1,270ft/385 meters) behind the city. Hikers working their way through the alders and spruce forests along the tops of shale cliffs often find others. Crowned with radar towers, Pillar Mountain also provides wonderful views of the surrounding mountains, beaches, and islands.

EARTHQUAKE AND TIDAL WAVE

Natural events have left indelible marks on Kodiak Island. Twice in the 20th century the landscape was altered, first by a volcanic ash fall in 1912 when Mount Novarupta on the Alaska Peninsula exploded, plunging Kodiak into three days of darkness, and again by the great earthquake and tsunami in 1964.

The Good Friday earthquake in 1964, which devastated much of South Central Alaska, also triggered a tidal wave that swept into the city of Kodiak and destroyed the downtown buildings, canneries, and docks. Many residents fled up Pillar Mountain and watched helplessly while the sea ran out, leaving the harbor dry, and then rolled back in across the land. Those who didn't reach high ground were swept away.

Herman's Harbor, Kodiak.

After the tidal wave, most of downtown Kodiak was redesigned and rebuilt. Residents who lived through the tidal wave and stayed to rebuild the town have formed a special bond. Though the tidal wave was a tragedy, it left behind a feeling of unity that still envelops the community.

A THRIVING FISHING INDUSTRY

Kodiak's economic dependence on the sea has been constant and its harbor is home to 800 year-round fishing vessels. Ask Kodiak residents what season it is and, if it is summer, they're likely to answer, 'salmon season.' Fall is king crab season; winter is marked by the Tanner crab, marketed as snow crab; spring is herring season; halibut and black cod are harvested in spring and summer, and whitefish species most of the year.

Fish harvesting dominates the employment opportunities in Kodiak and Kodiak's fishermen work year-round, switching from fishery to fishery as the seasons change. Between seasons the waterfront throbs with activity. Crane trucks and flatbeds move 500lb (230kg) steel crab pots from storage to the boat and back to storage. In spring, herring seines and gillnets are stretched out on the docks where crewmen with shuttles can attach float and lead lines.

Visitors are welcome to wander down the ramp behind the Harbormaster Building and walk along the floats in **St Paul Harbor** Ⓔ. Across the channel, on **Near Island**, is **St Herman Harbor**. In St Paul Harbor there are two loading docks where skippers load gear onboard their boats. The harbor is also home to exhibits of the **Maritime Museum** (www.kodiakmaritimemuseum.org; tel: 907-486-0384), which itself does not have a physical location. Dedicated to the recognition and preservation of Alaska's maritime heritage, the museum presents fishermen's tales and photographs. A restored old salmon ship, *Thelma C*, serves as a permanent outdoor exhibition near the harbor.

Like its fishing industry, Kodiak's population is diverse, and you'll overhear a mixture of languages and accents as you wander around the harbor.

TOURING KODIAK ISLAND

Except for several Native villages, the populated portion of Kodiak Island is confined to the road system, and there are fewer than 100 miles (160km) of it. Some stretches are only fit for four-wheel-drive vehicles. The six coastal villages on the island are accessible only by plane or boat; to visit one of them, you need to make arrangements in advance.

Crossing fish-laden rivers, curving around deep bays, and climbing through headlands thick with Sitka spruce, the road out to Fossil Beach is a great afternoon trek. Heading south from the city of Kodiak, the Chiniak Highway passes the **Buskin River State Recreation Area** (dnr.alaska.gov/

Heed the rules when near bear habitats.

Lush vegetation and Fireweed in Abercrombie State Historical Park.

parks/aspunits/kodiak/buskinriversrs.htm),
where the headquarters and visitor
center for the Kodiak National Wildlife
Refuge is located. The Buskin River
is a popular sport-fishing stream for
salmon and steelhead.

Eventually, you will reach a
T-intersection. A left turn will take you
to the community of **Chiniak** (population less than 50) and to Cape Chiank,
with windswept World War II military
installations. To reach Fossil Beach,
turn right onto Pasagshak Road,
which travels through cattle country where ranchers run about 2,000
head of beef cattle. Ahead the ocean
comes into view again by **Pasagshak
State Recreation Site**, a popular river
for fishing silver salmon with a small
campground on its banks.

The road continues past the sand
dunes of a surf-beaten beach and ends
at **Fossil Beach**, where fossil shells lie
loosely in the clay and rocks. During
the fall, gray whales pass Pasagshak
and Fossil Beach on their migration
to California from the Bering Sea. In
spring, the whales pass the island

again as they migrate to their northern
summer feeding grounds.

KODIAK WILDLIFE REFUGE

By traveling along the roads you will
see some of the loveliest scenery on
the island. But if you want real wilderness, and bears, you must visit
the **Kodiak National Wildlife Refuge**
❷ (tel: 907-487-2600; kodiak.fws.
gov), which can be reached only by
air or sea. This mountainous wilderness, covering two-thirds of the island,
belongs to bears and foxes, rabbits and
birds, muskrats, and otters.

Most people come here to see the
brown bears. For those who aren't
experienced in traveling through bear
country, the best and safest way to see
them is to take one of the bear-viewing
tours based in Kodiak, but be warned
– they are not cheap. Information on
local guides can be obtained from the
refuge headquarters. Wilderness hikers should always remember to walk
noisily through Kodiak's backcountry to
reduce the chances of any confronta-
tions with bears.

*Bird Nest Rock, off
Kodiak Island.*

🔍 WILDLIFE REFUGES

Alaska's network of preserves, some of which are among the oldest in the country, has played a critical role in preserving sensitive habitat in this rapidly developing state.

Put aside by President Teddy Roosevelt in 1909, areas that are now a part of the Yukon Delta and Alaska Maritime National Wildlife Refuges were among the 53 original sites designated to become the bold new National Wildlife Refuge System. Protecting wildlife, it began to play a critical role in preserving sensitive habitat in the rapidly developing state. In 1980, Congress added millions of acres to protected land by creating nine new refuges and expanding several others. Alaska now has 16 National Wildlife Refuges, ranging in size from 300,000 to 19.5 million acres (120,000 to 7.9 million hectares), with nearly 77 million acres protected in total.

The refuges encompass some of the world's most spectacular wildlands and present all sorts of opportunities for backcountry adventure. A few can be reached by road, but most are remote, easily accessible by plane and in some instances, boat. And though several are popular with hikers, others hardly ever see people, or are used primarily by subsistence hunters and fishermen. Suggest drilling for possible oil beneath one of them, though, and political storms will rage.

While the Arctic National Wildlife Refuge garners the most international attention, the Southwest has the greatest diversity and concentration of Alaska's refuges, including the smallest national refuge in Alaska, 315,000-acre (127,000-hectare) **Izembek** NWR, on the lower Alaska Peninsula, an international crossroads for migrating waterfowl and shorebirds. Its heart is Izembeck Lagoon, where thousands of waterfowl converge each fall. Brown bears fish salmon-rich streams, caribou migrate across the tundra. In addition, The Aghileen Pinnacles here, a group of volcanic spires, present a little-known mountaineering challenge.

The **Alaska Peninsula** and **Becharof** refuges in Southwest encompass towering volcanic peaks, rugged coastal fjords, rolling tundra, and glacially carved lakes. There are 14 major volcanoes, including nine that have erupted in historic times. Best known for hunting and fishing opportunities, these refuges are also prime candidates for backpackers, climbers, and coastal kayakers seeking extreme challenges.

The **Alaska Maritime** refuge consists of 3.4 million acres (1.4 million hectares) and includes areas of the Pribilof Islands, the Aleutian Chain, and the remote coast of the Chukchi Sea. About 80 percent of the state's 40 million nesting seabirds gather here. Marine life also includes whales, sea lions, walrus, porpoises, and sea otters. The refuge is outstanding for birdwatching and for the kayak trip of a lifetime.

The **Togiak** refuge, also located in Southwest Alaska, has more than 30 species of mammals and clearwater streams with some of the continent's finest salmon and trout fishing. Coastal areas are rich with brown bears and marine mammals. The uplands have 2.3 million acres 930,000 hectares) of designated wilderness to explore on foot or by boat.

The Yukon Delta National Wildlife Refuge covers over 21 million acres of mostly treeless waterlogged expanse. Home to the largest aggregations of waterbirds in the world, it is a popular place for boating, birding, fishing, and hunting.

For more information contact the US Fish and Wildlife Service office (1011 East Tudor Road, Anchorage, AK 99503; tel: 907-786-3309; https://fws.gov).

Alaska has five species of loon.

📷 A SERENGETI OF THE NORTH

Wildlife watching draws many visitors to the state. They are rarely disappointed, for the seas, parks, and wilderness areas contain a remarkable variety of wildlife.

Alaska is sometimes called the 'Serengeti of the North.' That's a bit of an exaggeration, but not much. The seas are the habitat of humpback, beluga, minke, and gray whales, porpoises and dolphins, walrus, sea lions, sea otters, and polar bears; while the land is inhabited by 105 species of mammals, including hoary marmots, Dall sheep, little brown bats, flying squirrels, and ferocious wolverines. The state is also seasonal or permanent home for more than 400 kinds of fish and nearly 300 bird species.

The Pribilof Islands in the Bering Sea are the summer home to a million fur seals and to millions of seabirds, while thousands of bull walrus haul out each year on Round Island, in Bristol Bay. The McNeil River, on the Alaska Peninsula, has the world's largest gathering of brown bears: more than 100 individuals have been observed at McNeil Falls during a single summer, feeding on the salmon runs.

Farther north, some 400,000 caribou roam the state's northwest region, perpetually on the move, while 120,000 or more form the Porcupine caribou herd, which ranges through northeastern Alaska and western Canada. And each fall between thousands of bald eagles gather in Southeast Alaska's Chilkat Valley near Haines to feed on a late run of salmon.

Alaska's wild bison occur alone or in groups ranging up to several hundred animals or more.

A walrus bull displays its tusks along the rocky coast of Round Island, part of the Walrus Islands State Game Sanctuary in Bristol Bay. They're bulky creatures: an adult male may weigh up to 4,000lbs (1,800kg).

The largest members of the deer family, moose are the most important game animals in the state. They are herbivores and feed on a variety of plants, including aquatic weeds.

Gray wolves are the ultimate symbols of the wild. They range through much of Alaska but they tend to inhabit remote wilderness and avoid humans as much as possible.

Bear Country

There's a good reason why Alaska is called 'bear country.' It's the only one of the 50 states to be inhabited by all three of North America's bears: the black bear, the polar bear, and the brown bear – also called the grizzly.

Polar bears roam the ice of the Beaufort, Chukchi and Bering seas. Both black and brown bears are found throughout most of the state, though the smaller black bears tend to be forest creatures. Browns and grizzlies prefer open areas: mountain meadows, Arctic tundra, and coastal beaches.

Brown bears and grizzlies are members of the same species: the former are coastal creatures while the latter live in the interior. Grizzlies have longer claws and a bigger hump and are generally smaller than their coastal cousins. This is thought to be because brown bears have access to energy-rich foods, especially salmon. Though classified as carnivores, brown, grizzly, and black bears eat both vegetation and meat; the polar bear is a true carnivore and its favorite prey is the ringed seal.

A total of eight whale species can be seen in the waters off Alaska.

A grizzy bear, one of Alaska's most famed inhabitants.

The red fox is most often found south of the Arctic tundra. It is also present in tundra regions, which it shares with the Arctic fox. In these areas, red foxes have been observed digging Arctic foxes from their dens and killing them.

LAKE CLARK NATIONAL PARK

Lake Clark may be the quintessential Alaska parkland, with volcanoes, rugged coastline, several major river systems, and a wide diversity of plants and animals.

◉ Main attractions

Turquoise Lake
Mount Redoubt
Port Alsworth
Twin Lakes
Telaquana Trail
Kijik
Telaquana Lake

Map on page 310

It's 11pm on a late July evening. The sun has disappeared behind a gentle hill, but the northwest horizon remains brightened by an afterglow of rich pastels. A band of yellow gradually yields to orange, then rose and finally purple. Winds that swept in with an early evening rain shower have died, leaving the air utterly still yet surprisingly bug-free despite the mid-summer warmth.

With the wind and rain's departure, a shroud of silence has fallen over **Turquoise Lake**. The quiet is broken only by the soft crunching of boots on beach gravel, the occasional splash of grayling, and the intermittent screeches of two young terns calling for their parents, out busily fishing for the evening meal.

It is a magical, paradisical evening along the lake – serene, yet bursting with life. Sandpipers and plovers prowl the shoreline, skittering and dipping in their frenetic search for food. Just a few yards offshore, a family of old squaws swims past. And across the lake, an eagle circles over a small group of caribou, crossing tundra brightened by multi-colored fields of wildflowers: blue monkshood and Jacob's ladder, yellow tundra rose, pink fireweed, and prickly rose.

Yet less than 10 miles (16km) to the east is an ominous and desolate world where the tundra's greens and yellows and pinks give way to the blacks and grays and whites of rock, snow, and ice. Rising darkly into the sky, 8,020ft (2,444-meter) **Telaquana Mountain** is a natural fortress of solitude, its upper reaches guarded by jagged spires and pale-blue glaciers that overhang sheer rock cliffs. It's forbidding and impenetrable. In fading light, it is a magnificent spectacle.

THE ESSENCE OF WILD ALASKA

The 4 million-acre (1.6 million-hectare) **Lake Clark National Park**

A hiker wades across a stream.

and Preserve ❸ may indeed be the quintessential Alaskan parkland. Within its boundaries are two active volcanoes, including one – 10,197ft (3,108-meter) **Mount Redoubt** – that erupted in 1990 and again in early 2009; rugged coastline whose rocky cliffs serve as rookeries for multitudes of puffins, cormorants, kittiwakes, and other seabirds; two major mountain systems, the Aleutian and Alaska ranges, which join to produce the Chigmit and Neacola mountains (snowcapped and glacially carved, most of the park's high peaks remain unclimbed and unexplored); and several major river and lake systems – including three designated wild rivers – that offer world-class sportfishing opportunities for all five species of Pacific salmon and rainbow trout.

Lake Clark is home to a remarkably diverse mix of plant communities. Along the coast is one of the northernmost stands of Sitka spruce rainforest, while inland are lowland boreal forests typical of Interior Alaska and several varieties of tundra, including Arctic tundra usually found in northern Alaska. Those varied ecosystems support more than 100 species of birds and nearly 40 species of mammals, including black and brown bears, wolves, Dall sheep, caribou, and moose. Also within the park boundaries is the Kijik National Historic Landmark, where more than a dozen archeological sites mark the abandoned village belonging to the Dena'ina Athabascan people.

AN UNDISCOVERED PARK

Here, then, is a national park with fantastic scenery, easy access by air, and diverse recreational opportunities. One would expect it to be among Alaska's most popular destinations. But it's not. In fact, Lake Clark is among the state's least-known and least-appreciated national parks. In a sense, it remains one of Alaska's undiscovered parks.

There are a few reasons why. For one thing, it doesn't have one or two major attractions. Denali National

Flyfishing on Turquoise Lake near a Cessna floatplane.

> **Tip**

Lake Clark National Park can't be reached by road. Most visitors charter a flight from Anchorage, about 90 minutes from Lake Clark. Charter flights can also be taken from the Kenai Peninsula. Commercial airlines fly between Anchorage and Iliamna, a base for many charter airlines.

A plane about to land on the lake.

Park, for example, has Denali and wildlife viewing. Katmai has its bears. Glacier Bay has its spectacular glacier-sculpted landscape and marine wildlife tours. An even bigger factor, perhaps, is that Lake Clark is not accessible by road (or cruise line). Sure it's easy to reach by plane, and relatively inexpensive. But 'bush plane' travel is still very foreign to most travelers. And most visitors don't like the idea of being dropped 'in the middle of nowhere.'

There's one other factor that likely acts as a crowd deterrent: the lack of visitor facilities. The National Park Service has intentionally kept development to a minimum. The park's visitor center (tel: 907-781-2117; www.nps.gov/lacl) and a field headquarters are located in **Port Alsworth** ❹ (tel: 907-781-2218) on Lake Clark's southeast shore. There are no other public facilities within the park, although rangers may be seasonally based in the backcountry. Several privately owned wilderness lodges, most of them catering to hunters and anglers, are located in and around the park; several are at Port Alsworth, the entry point for many visitors. In addition, dozens of guide services operate within the park. The majority specialize in sportfishing, but other guided activities include backpacking, hiking, lake-touring, mountaineering, photography, and river running.

Several air taxi operators offer flightseeing trips into the park and transport big-game hunters. Information on commercial visitor services authorized to conduct business within Lake Clark National Park and Preserve can be obtained from the park's Anchorage office. However, with no connection to Alaska's highway system, no singular attraction to catch the public's fancy, and minimal visitor facilities, Lake Clark is likely to remain a low-profile park, at least for the near future.

WILDERNESS LODGES

Before Congress established Lake Clark National Park and Preserve

⊘ FISHING ON LAKE CLARK

Sportfishing is extraordinary in the lakes and streams of Lake Clark National Park, thanks largely to the abundance of rainbow trout, Dolly Varden, Arctic grayling, whitefish, lake trout, northern pike, and, particularly in the Cook Inlet drainage, silver and king salmon.

The Chilikadrotna and Mulchatna rivers offer some of the park's best prospects. Many anglers arrange to be dropped off in the upper reaches of one of these rivers, and, after inflating a raft, drift and cast their way downstream for a few days. There's also good fishing in Kontrashibuna, Telaquana, and Turquoise lakes and in the streams that flow in and out of them. Lake Clark itself has given up trout larger than 50 pounds (23kg).

It takes years for the region's trout, grayling, and char to reach trophy size, so most anglers practice catch-and-release fishing, playing a fish as briefly as possible and avoiding removing it from the water as they remove the hook and let it swim away.

For many, that means fly-fishing. Spinning gear works well, too, particularly if anglers use single, barbless hooks, rather than treble hooks on spinners and spoons. Fish taken on bait tend to swallow hooks, damaging delicate gill tissue and internal organs, which leads to bleeding and, ultimately, death.

in 1980, the region's resources were utilized by two main groups: local residents (most of whom lead a subsistence lifestyle in Dena'ina Indian villages near the park's southern edge); and sport hunters and anglers seeking trophy wildlife and fish.

Much of the fishing pressure comes from wilderness lodges. Prime fly-in fishing grounds include the Chilika-drotna and Mulchatna rivers – also popular with river floaters – as well as the Stony, Crescent, Silver Salmon and Nondalton rivers, and Telaquana, Crescent and Tazmina lakes.

And then there's the actual lake: Lake Clark, 42 miles (68km) long, up to 860ft (262 meters) deep and covering 110 sq miles (285 sq km), Alaska's sixth-largest lake is a critical sockeye salmon spawning ground. Many of the park's lake and river systems contribute significantly to Bristol Bay's world-famous commercial sockeye salmon fishery. In fact, one of its primary functions is to protect watersheds that feed the salmon fishery. Rainbows and salmon get most of the angling attention, but lake trout, pike, Dolly Varden, Arctic char, and Arctic grayling are also popular target species.

While sportfishing is permissible anywhere within the parkland, trophy hunting is restricted to Lake Clark's 1.4-million-acre (570-hectare) preserve, where tundra-covered foothills and lowland forests support healthy populations of caribou, moose, and brown bear. Prior to 1980, however, the Chigmit Mountains' Dall sheep populations were also fair game. Many of these hunters immortalized their conquest by tallying their kills on the walls of their cabins. Today, in some of the older park service cabins you can find such scribblings as, 'Dr Norbert Conrad, Michigan. 1 sheep, 1 caribou, 1 black bear, 1 nice grizzly and lots of walking.'

EXPLORING TWIN LAKES

Nearly three decades later, **Twin Lakes** ❺ remains a popular backcountry destination, but it now attracts a different sort of crowd. Some visitors use it as a starting point for float trips down the Chilikadrotna, while others are more interested in backpacking. A few simply come to set up camp along the beach and relax.

Twin Lakes is a prime visitor destination for several reasons but access is probably the most significant one; it's only a half-hour flight from Port Alsworth. Founded in the 1940s by bush pilot Leon 'Babe' Alsworth and wife Mary, Port Alsworth has become the region's 'hub of activity' despite its small size (population 159). For many visitors, this community on Lake Clark's southeast shore serves as the gateway to Lake Clark National Park and it's where the National Park Service has established its local headquarters.

The Alsworth family maintains its strong presence in the community; a structure first built by Babe and Mary Alsworth in the 1940s has been

A hiker at Lower Twin, Twin Lakes.

Lake Clark National Park.

Richard Proennicke's cabin is now a designated National Historic Site.

Hikers on one of the many trails.

remodeled and converted into 'The Farm Lodge' run by their son Glen and his wife Patty. The Alsworths also own Lake Clark Air, which runs daily commuter flights between Port Alsworth and Anchorage in the summer months. Call for information on flights (tel: 800-662-7661) or accommodations (tel: 888-440-2281), or visit www.lakeclarkair.com.

Then there was Richard Proennicke, who settled at Upper Twin Lake in the 1960s and became something of an Alaskan legend when he wrote the book *One Man's Wilderness: An Alaskan Odyssey*. Now deceased, Dick Proennicke lived alone in the wilderness for three decades, and people would travel to Twin Lakes just to meet him. Though hospitable to those who passed his way, Proennicke sometimes second-guessed the wisdom of writing a book that so affected his solitary lifestyle. People are still drawn to the homestead where he lived.

DIVERSE WILDLIFE

The scenery around Twin Lakes is spectacular, the wildlife diverse – everything from Dall sheep, moose, and grizzlies to beavers, eagles, shorebirds, waterfowl, ground squirrels, and voles. And the hiking is superb. Fed in part by glaciers born in the Neacola Mountains, the Twin Lakes are a vivid, penetrating aquamarine hue. Much of their shoreline is bordered by boreal forest that offers easy walking – at least by Alaskan standards

Above the open white-spruce forest is dry alpine tundra, which in turn gives way to lightly vegetated or bare volcanic hills whose canyons provide endless avenues for exploration and whose ridges offer awe-inspiring vistas of the Twin Lakes valley.

Kayaks, canoes or inflatables are wonderful means of exploring Lower and Upper Twin Lakes, 5 and 7 miles (8 and 11km) long, respectively. But beware: the valley often acts as a wind funnel and what had been a mirror-smooth lake surface may, in a matter of minutes, become a white-capped chop with waves 2ft to 3ft (60 to 90cm) high.

THE TELAQUANA TRAIL

Another way to see the park is along the 50-mile (80km) Telaquana Trail. This historic Athabascan trading route originates in the village site of Kijik, once home to over 90 people and a Russian Orthodox church, but abandoned by the early 20th century. From Kijik, the Telaquana Trail winds through boreal forest, mountain passes, alpine tundra, and crosses multiple glacial rivers. The trail passes the Twin Lakes, the aptly named Turquoise Lake, and ends at the Old Village site on **Telaquana Lake**. In addition to being within the park's Historic District, the trail has been designated a Cultural Landscape.

Another area of historical interest is Tanalian Point, a former trapping and trading center on Lake Clark's

southeastern shore. Much of it falls on private property, so contact rangers at the Visitor Center for more information.

TAKING PRECAUTIONS

The weather often changes rapidly throughout Lake Clark because the park is located in a region where marine air masses from the Bering Sea and Gulf of Alaska frequently collide with drier, continental systems from Alaska's Interior. The result is extremely variable weather. The prime visitor season is June through August, when temperatures normally range from 50 to 65°F (10 to 18°C). Yet even in summer temperatures may drop into the 30s, especially at higher elevations. They may also, on occasion, climb above 80°F (27°C).

Windy, wet weather is the rule, rather than the exception, especially in the park's eastern sections. The region's wettest months are August and September; winter is comparatively dry, but temperatures may plummet to –40° or colder.

Visitors exploring Lake Clark's backcountry on their own should plan to be totally self-sufficient. Quality clothing is a must, because hypothermia is a risk even in summer. Other 'shoulds' include insect repellent, tents that can endure high winds and long spells of rain, and extra food. It's not uncommon for stormy weather to delay pick-up flights.

BEAR-AWARE

The Lake Clark region, like most of Alaska, is bear country, and visitors should take appropriate measures to avoid close encounters with the park's ursine residents; that includes clean camping and noise-making when traveling in areas with low visibility. Bear-awareness brochures are available from the Park Service. Giardia may be a problem in some areas; when in doubt, it's best to treat drinking water. Before heading into the backcountry, it's also a good idea to leave a trip itinerary with someone reliable.

⊙ Tip

For those eager to take Lake Clark National Park's Telaquana Trail, remember that it is old and unmaintained, so keen overland navigation skills as well as backpacking experience are a must. A guide to the trail is available from Alaska Geographic.

Telaquana Mountain overlooking Turquoise Lake.

⊘ WATCHING VOLCANOES

Once a political punch line illustrating Alaska's legislators' unique ability to pull federal dollars for arcane projects, the Alaska Volcano Observatory established in 1988 successfully predicted Mount Redoubt's eruption in 2009. Beginning on March 15, the eruption lasted until April 4 and coated the Southcentral region as far north as Delta Junction with a fine layer of ash. The observatory recorded 26 eruptions, the largest sending an ash plume 65,000ft (19,800 meters) high and triggering massive mudslides of melted snow and ice around the volcano's slopes. While Mount Redoubt remains quiet for the moment, the observatory is now keeping an eye on Cleveland Volcano in the Aleutian Islands. It has erupted 22 times over 230 years, including twice in 2010, and once in 2012.

KATMAI NATIONAL PARK

Take a trip to Katmai on the Alaska Peninsula to fish and paddle, and see the strange lunar landscape created by a volcanic eruption.

◎ **Main attractions**

King Salmon
Brooks River and Camp
Valley of Ten Thousand
  Smokes
Novarupta Volcano
Grosvenor Lake

📍 Map on page 310

Nature in **Katmai National Park and Preserve ⑥** is awesome. Here in this isolated location the scenery is breathtaking, the weather is unstable, the winds can be life threatening, and the past is reckoned in terms of before and after the volcanic eruption of 1912. The park receives more than 60,000 visits a year by sightseers and flightseers, fishermen, hikers, climbers, and canoeists.

Located 290 air miles (465km) from Anchorage on the Alaska Peninsula, the park is a haven for lovers of the unspoiled wilderness. No highway system touches this area; access is primarily by small plane, or by boat out of **King Salmon ⑦**, the park's gateway community. Most visitors take a one-hour commuter flight from Anchorage to King Salmon, then fly by floatplane into Katmai's backcountry. It's also possible to arrange boat rides to some destinations, most notably **Brooks Camp**, the primary attraction on **Naknek Lake**, where a large run of sockeye salmon each summer attracts dozens of brown bears, the coastal cousins of grizzlies.

You can pick up information at the Park Service's office in King Salmon or at the Brooks Camp Visitor Center (daily, June–mid-Sept), where you're required to check in when visiting Brooks (be sure to ask about the ranger-led programs); or check the park's website before visiting (tel: 907-246-3305; www. nps.gov/katm). Some people fly in for only a few hours, have a look at the bears, and then leave. Please note that only authorised companies are allowed to operate within the park. Check the complete list at www.nps.gov/locations/alaska/services-katmai.htm.

VIEWING THE BEARS

Book well in advance if you hope to stay in **Brooks Lodge** (tel: 800-544-0551; www.katmailand.com). Besides

River canyons were cut in the Valley of Ten Thousand Smokes after the 1912 eruption.

the lodge, there's also a campground that takes reservations on a first-come, first-served basis (tel: 877-444-6777/518-885-3639; www.recreation.gov). Visitors to Brooks Camp are required to begin their stay by checking-in at the visitor center for Bear Etiquette training.There are several easy walks in the immediate vicinity, and bears can be viewed in summer from safe viewing platforms as they feed on spawning salmon in the Brooks River, particularly at Brooks Falls. The best time to see bears along the Brooks River is in July and again in September.

You can also book a place on a tour bus that provides transportation to the scene of volcanic devastation in the **Valley of Ten Thousand Smokes**. The bus takes visitors to Griggs Visitor Center, at the end of the road, from where you can see the valley and take a gentle, ranger-led hike, or set off on a more ambitious one on your own.

More than 90 years after the eruption, the valley remains awe-inspiring, though most of its 'smokes' stopped steaming decades ago. Ash, pumice, and rocks produced over 40 sq miles (100 sq km) of lunar landscape, sculpted by wind and water. The once-verdant valley floor, covered with shifting pumice, resists vegetation and quickly erases the imprint of hikers' boots.

Before the great eruption of 1912, a portion of the historic Katmai Trail passed through this valley. The trail was traveled by Russian fur traders and missionaries, then by a flood of gold seekers taking a shortcut to Nome. Prospectors and mail carriers used it to avoid a stormy sea passage around the Alaska Peninsula but by 1912 the gold rush had subsided and the trail was seldom traveled.

Today the ancient route is no longer visible and is a path of blowing ash, rugged terrain, dense undergrowth, quicksand and narrow canyons. During severe weather, travelers are warned against the old route; the interchange of air between the Gulf of Alaska and the Bering Sea streams through this pass and can cause winds of over 100mph (160kmh) – strong enough to blow hikers off their feet.

⊙ Fact

In 2003, Katmai National Park gained unwelcome attention when Timothy Treadwell, famous for his up-close documentation of its bears, was mauled to death. Two years later the incident was immortalized by Werner Herzog's movie *Grizzly Man*. Most Alaskans believe that Treadwell behaved recklessly and brought the danger on himself.

Wildlife watching in Katmai.

TREMORS AND ERUPTIONS

When the great eruption occurred, news was slow to reach the world outside Alaska because the area was so isolated, but its impact was felt hundreds of miles away. The closest account was given by a Native, American Pete, who was on the Katmai Trail only 18 miles (30km) north-east of Mount Katmai when the violent explosions began. Earth tremors that preceded the eruption were so severe that the residents of Katmai and Savon-oski, small Native villages on the Alaska Peninsula, gathered their possessions and fled to Naknek, on Bristol Bay.

Later research gave credit for the devastation not to Mount Katmai, but to **Novarupta Volcano**, a volcano formed by the eruption itself. The explosion was heard up to 750 miles (1,200km) away in Juneau, and associated earth tremors caused immense avalanches on Denali, hundreds of miles to the north. Most heavily impacted were the Native villages of Katmai and Savonoski, later abandoned because of heavy ash fall, and the town of Kodiak on Kodiak Island, across Shelikof Strait.

Enjoying the view near the Brooks River Falls, Katmai National Park.

THE SMOKING VALLEY

In the following years several expeditions were sent to the eruption site by the National Geographic Society to satisfy worldwide interest and carry out scientific research. Scientists were initially prevented from reaching the source of the eruption by seas of mud, ash slides as deep as 1,500ft (450 meters), and evidence of one of the most powerful water surges ever.

In 1916 the crater of Mount Katmai was reached and a smoking valley discovered at Katmai Pass. The valley was named by botanist Robert Griggs, who found it 'one of the most amazing visions ever beheld by mortal eye. The whole valley as far as the eye could reach was full of hundreds, no, thousands – literally tens of thousands – of smokes curling up from its fissured floor.' The landscape's fiery desolation prompted Griggs and his colleagues to call one stream the **River Lethe**, which in Greek mythology flows through the centre of Hades.

In 1918 the Valley of Ten Thousand Smokes was made a national monument

in order to preserve an area important to the study of volcanism. In 1980 the monument was upgraded in status and greatly expanded: the new Katmai National Park and Preserve protected 4 million acres (1.6 million hectares) of coastal lands, forests, rivers, lakes, volcanic mountains, and alpine valleys.

When the Katmai monument was first created it was believed that the Valley of Ten Thousand Smokes would become a geyser-filled attraction to rival Yellowstone National Park in Wyoming, because scientists thought that the geyser field at Yellowstone was dying. But the reverse has come about. The Yellowstone geysers are still active, but the fumaroles at the Valley of Ten Thousand Smokes have subsided.

A RUGGED WILDERNESS

Katmai National Park and Preserve makes available to visitors not only an area of amazing volcanic involvement but a representative and undisturbed portion of the Alaska Peninsula. Great varieties of terrain in Katmai include the rugged coastal habitat of Shelikof Strait on one side of the Alaskan range and the rivers and lakes of the Naknek River watershed on the other. Mixed spruce and birch forests, dense willow and alder thickets, and moist tundra are found at lower elevations, with alpine tundra on the higher slopes.

A series of small lakes and rivers provide opportunities for canoeing, kayaking, and fishing. You can paddle to a group of tiny islands on Naknek Lake's north arm, but it's about a 60-mile (100km) round trip.

VARIED WILDLIFE

Rainbow trout, lake trout, char, pike, and grayling are popular sport fish here, and nearly one million salmon return each year to the Naknek River. Wilderness lodges at **Kulik** and **Grosvenor lakes** cater to serious fishing enthusiasts who want backcountry comfort and guided

fishing, while other park visitors arrange their own fishing and float trips.

The brown bears are the main attraction, but there is a great deal of other wildlife. Moose, caribou, land otter, wolverine, marten, weasel, mink, lynx, fox, wolf, muskrat, beaver, and hare all inhabit the park.

Offshore, in coastal waters, seals, sea lions, sea otters, and beluga and gray whales can be seen. Birdwatching is also a popular pastime – the park has more than 40 songbird species.

THE CLIMATE

The weather in Katmai is variable as this is a coastal region where different weather systems meet; heavy rain is characteristic in the summer months. The northwestern slope of the Aleutian Range has the most comfortable weather: at Brooks Camp the average daytime temperature is 60°F (15°C).

Here, skies are only expected to be clear or partially cloudy 20 percent of the time. Warm clothing, rain gear and boots are highly recommended at any time of the year.

An island in the park.

Mount Douglas.

Grizzly bears fishing.

MCNEIL RIVER STATE GAME SANCTUARY

Getting close to bears allows you to recognize their individual personalities – some are aggressive by nature but others are mild-mannered or even timid while some are playful.

The bears have always come first at **McNeil River State Game Sanctuary** ❽. Created in 1967 by the Alaska Legislature, the sanctuary is intended, above all else, to protect the world's largest known concentration of brown bears, the coastal cousins of grizzlies. The focal point of the gathering is **McNeil Falls**, where bears come each summer to feed on chum salmon, returning to the river to spawn. Typically, the salmon begin arriving in late June or early July and remain in large numbers until mid- to late August. As many as 144 individual bears (adults and cubs) have been identified along the river in a single season, and up to 72 bears have been seen feasting at the falls at one time.

By nature, adult brown bears tend to be fairly solitary creatures, with the exception of females that are raising families, or bears that temporarily pair up during mating season. For them to gather in such large numbers – and in such close quarters – is exceptional. For 40 years, Alaska's Division of Wildlife Conservation has enacted and enforced a series of restrictions to ensure that this unique gathering of bears is not disrupted by problems and conflicts with humans.

State regulations make it clear that viewing the brown bears is the primary human activity in the sanctuary, which

is located at the upper end of the Alaska Peninsula, just north of Katmai National Park and Preserve. Hunting and trapping are prohibited, and all other use by individuals is allowed only as long as it does not significantly alter the bears' behavior. To limit human impacts, a permit system has been established to regulate the number of people who can watch and photograph the bears.

A DEADLY ENCOUNTER

Through the late 1960s, McNeil River was virtually unknown as a

⊙ Main attractions
McNeil Falls
Mikfik Creek

Map on page 310

A brown bear shows his teeth.

Catch of the day.

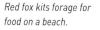

Red fox kits forage for food on a beach.

bear-viewing site. Jim Faro, a state biologist who managed the sanctuary in its early years, recalls that only a half-dozen or so people visited in 1969. Because of that, there were few rules to govern visitor behavior. By 1970, however, the media had begun to bring McNeil to the public's attention. Vistation jumped. And because there were no rules to regulate public use, human activities got out of hand.

'We had people running up and down both sides of the river,' Faro recalls. 'There were even people fishing for salmon right at the falls, where the bears feed. If all the horror stories you heard about bears were true, we should have had lots of dead people.'

Instead, the bears went into hiding. 'It was like the bears were saying, 'We don't have to put up with this.' They took one look at all the people and left,' Faro says. Only a handful of bears remained.

That same summer, a bear was killed by one of the sanctuary visitors. A photography guide decided to take some close-up pictures of a female with cubs, as they fed on the coastal mudflats. Crawling on his hands and knees, the photographer made his approach. The adult bear saw the movement and charged. It's likely she thought another bear was approaching and threatening her young. The bear came more than 300ft (90 metres) across the flats. Expecting a false charge, the photographer remained on his hands and knees, rather than standing and identifying himself as human. Finally, when the bear was only 60 to 70ft (18 to 21 meters) away, the man made his move: he shot the sow with a .44 pistol. On being hit, the bear turned and fled, shot fatally in the lungs.

Tighter controls were needed, both to prevent future injurious encounters between bears and humans and to bring the bears back to McNeil in large numbers. In 1973, the Alaska Board of game approved proposals to regulate visitor activities in the sanctuary during the prime-time bear-viewing period.

THE PERMIT SYSTEM

Since 1973, the primary visitor control has been a permit system that limits viewing and photography opportunities. Only 185 permits, allowing guided visits to the sanctuary's bear-viewing areas, are issued each season; permit holders must be accompanied by one or two state biologists in attendance here. The permit period runs from June through August 25.

That permit system has been extraordinarily successful. Since the state enacted its visitor restrictions, the number of bears visiting the falls has increased nearly tenfold. Just as important, no bears have been killed within the sanctuary and no humans have been injured by bears – this despite thousands of human-bear encounters, often at close range.

APPLYING FOR PERMITS

The permits are issued through a lottery held each year in late March. Applications must be postmarked or sent in online by March 1 and accompanied by a nonrefundable application fee of $30 per person (group applications are limited to three people).

Non-resident permit winners pay $525 per person to visit the sanctuary for the four-day permit period, while Alaskans pay $225. An additional 57 Camp-Standby permits are issued each summer (for half the fee) for visitors to view bears from the camp only (they get to experience the guided experience only if a visitor with a Guided Access permit cannot attend one of their guided sessions).

Normally, bears 'trespassing' within the campground is not a problem. But occasionally a local resident – usually an adolescent bear – has to be taught the campground is off limits. The education proceeds in stages. Stage One is usually limited to loud, aggressive yelling. If that doesn't work, sanctuary staff step it up a notch. That next step involves the use of a 'shell cracker,' which gives off a loud bang much like a firecracker. If there's still a problem, rubber pellets or even birdshot are

Remote accommodation at McNeil River State Game Sanctuary.

⊘ BE PREPARED

Nearly all visitors reach the sanctuary by air, using air charters based in Homer. McNeil visitors must be self-sufficient and prepared for a wilderness experience; no commercial facilities are available. Visitors must bring their own tents, camping gear, and food. Even in midsummer, equipment and clothing must be suitable for cold, wet weather. Visitors are also cautioned that bad weather can delay flights for several days. Visitors should also be in good physical shape; the 4-mile (6.4km) round-trip hike to McNeil Falls is not especially hazardous, but it does require strenuous slogging across mud flats and crossing Mikfik Creek. A typical day at the falls lasts six to eight hours, on a narrow gravel pad that's about 15ft (4.6 meters) long.

⊙ Tip

To obtain an application packet for McNeil River State Game Sanctuary, contact the Alaska Department of Fish and Game, Division of Wildlife Conservation, (333 Raspberry Road, Anchorage, AK 99518-1599; tel: 907-267-2257; www.adfg.alaska.gov/index.cfm?adfg=mcneilriver.main).

used. But only rarely – and never in recent years – have the sanctuary staff had to go as far as Stage Three.

MIKFIK CREEK

Until the mid-1980s, few people visited McNeil sanctuary before July 1. That's when the chum salmon – and the bears – began to arrive at McNeil River. But in 1982, a new pattern began to emerge, because of changes at **Mikfik Creek**, a small, shallow, clearwater stream that flows through the sanctuary and enters a saltwater lagoon less than a mile from McNeil River. It hosts a run of sockeye salmon from early to mid-June, but historically the run has been so small that bears largely ignored the fish.

Then, mysteriously, Mikfik's salmon return began to swell dramatically. Tens of thousands of sockeye (or red) salmon entered the creek each year. Not surprisingly, larger numbers of bears were attracted to Mikfik's increased fishing opportunities. And following closely behind the bears were bear watchers and photographers.

MCNEIL FALLS

While Mikfik has made the sanctuary's bear-viewing more diverse, **McNeil Falls** remains the primary focus in July and August. Located a mile above the river's mouth, McNeil Falls is actually a step-like series of small waterfalls, pools, and rapids that stretch along the stream for several hundred yards. Individual bears take up their fishing positions based on their place in the ursine pecking order.

The prime spots are located along the western bank, opposite the two viewing pads used by humans. Here the most dominant bears – adult males, some weighing 1,000lbs (450kg) or more – jockey for position.

The bears use a variety of fishing techniques. Some stand motionless in mid-stream. When a chum salmon swims by, the bear pins it to the river bottom with its paws, then bites into it. Others use snorkeling techniques, and a few even dive for fish. Cubs watch their mothers from the shore, closely observing mom's technique; now and then an especially bold cub will make its own attempt. But normally they'll wait until their mother brings a fish to shore. Adolescent bears – the equivalent of teenagers – that have been weaned from their mothers patrol the shorelines, hoping to find a scrap or two. Gulls and bald eagles, too, crowd the river, fighting over carcasses.

The best fishers may catch dozens of salmon in just one day. One particularly adept male once caught more than 70 fish in less than eight hours. When hungry, bears will consume the entire fish, including head and bones. But as they become satiated, bears will go for the highest calorie parts: the brain, eggs, and skin.

The chum run ends in mid- to late August, but bears begin to disperse even before then, as they go in search of another nutritious food: berries.

Brown bears gather at McNeil River Falls for salmon fishing.

🔍 MIXING BEARS AND PEOPLE

Getting close to bears allows you to recognize their individuality – some of them are aggressive by nature but others are mild-mannered or even timid.

'It's widely assumed that bears and people don't mix,' says Larry Aumiller, the former long-time manager of the McNeil River State Game Sanctuary. 'But here we've shown that they can mix, if you do the right things. To me, that's the most important message of McNeil: humans can peacefully coexist with bears.'

Such peaceful coexistence is possible because of a simple fact: McNeil bears are habituated to humans, but view them as neutral objects – almost a part of the landscape. People do not pose a threat nor are they a source of food. To prevent any such association, feeding of bears is prohibited at McNeil (as it is throughout Alaska). Furthermore, a designated wood-frame building is provided for food storage, cooking, and eating. And a no-bears-allowed policy is strictly enforced within its well-defined campground area.

CAMPGROUND RULES

Aumiller's education of McNeil's bears went beyond campground discipline. Through the years he made it easier for the bears to 'read' people. The close supervision of sanctuary visitors is, in part, intended to make humans more predictable to the bears. For example, visitors are permitted to watch and photograph bears from a single, defined viewing area; only 10 per day are allowed there; and viewing is done from late morning through early evening. Such routines and restrictions have made it easier for McNeil's bears to tolerate people.

THE TRUTH ABOUT BEARS

Bears aren't the only ones to receive an education at McNeil. The sanctuary is a valuable learning ground for humans as well. Many visitors come to McNeil filled with irrational fears born of ignorance or sensationalized accounts of bear attacks. They carry the simplistic and inaccurate image of bears as menacing, dangerous creatures – unpredictable killers lurking in the shadows and waiting to attack. McNeil helps to change such misconceptions. Visitors discover first-hand that bears aren't man-eating monsters as so often portrayed in literature and news accounts.

'The first day people come here,' says Aumiller, 'many are fearful, usually because of things they've heard or read. But after they've seen a few bears up close and the bears go about their business, people get incredibly blasé about them. After that, they have to be cautioned about getting too careless. The transformation is almost universal.'

Watching them for hours each day, for up to four days in a row, visitors gain glimpses into the animals' lives. People start to recognize the bears as individuals, with different mannerisms and personalities. Some are aggressive, even bullies, others mild-mannered or timid around their own kind. Some are excellent fishers, others fare poorly.

Aumiller believes that McNeil's visitors feel safe around the bears largely because the sanctuary provides a controlled situation. The biologists act as guides. And they're armed, though they've never had to shoot a bear. The removal of irrational fears makes it easier to accept the bears on their own terms. And there's no better place to watch bears being bears.

A favorite lunch.

REMOTE COMMUNITIES AND WILDLANDS

Alaska

Anchorage

Part of the north Pacific's volcanic 'Ring of Fire,' the Alaska Peninsula has many Native American settlements as well as some notable wildlife reserves, excellent fishing and bird watching opportunities.

Map on page 310

Extending more than 500 miles (800km) from top to tip, the **Alaska Peninsula ❾** is a rugged, storm-blasted, mostly treeless landscape inhabited by the world's densest population of brown bears: more than one bear per square mile. The greatest of these concentrations occur in **Katmai National Park and Preserve** and **McNeil River State Game Sanctuary** (see page 335), at the upper end of the peninsula. Dozens of brown bears gather along peninsula streams each year to feed

on the spawning salmon, and both the National Park Service and Alaska Department of Fish and Game have established bear-viewing programs that give people unmatched oppor-tunities to observe the fishing bears.

BRISTOL BAY

The largest salmon runs are those of the sockeye that return to **Bristol Bay ❿** streams each summer; tens of millions of the salmon spawn here, providing nutrients for all manner of predators and scavengers, including bears, eagles, gulls, foxes, rainbow trout, and char. And humans, too. The Bristol Bay region is home to North America's largest commercial salmon fleet; and the streams that feed the bay are known around the world as a fish-erman's paradise.

Though many anglers come to catch the region's salmon, rainbow trout are an even bigger draw. Doz-ens of fishing lodges are scattered through the Bristol Bay and Alaska Peninsula region. Other companies have fish camps or do guided day trips out of the region's communities.

Besides bears, salmon, and rain-bows, Bristol Bay and the Alaska Peninsula are seasonal or year-round homes to numerous other species of mammals and birds; among the most spectacular concentrations are migrating herds of caribou, numerous

Bristol Bay has large colonies of walrus.

colonies of seabirds and large marine mammal haul-outs. Some of the world's greatest concentrations of walrus occur in Bristol Bay; one is at the **Togiak National Wildlife Refuge** ⓫; the other is at **Round Island**, within the **Walrus Islands State Game Sanctuary** ⓬ (tel: 907-267-2189; www.adfg. alaska.gov/index.cfm?adfg=walrusislands. main). On the lower Alaska Peninsula, the **Izembek National Wildlife Refuge** ⓭ (tel: 907-532-2445; www.adfg. alaska.gov/index.cfm?adfg=izembek.main) serves as an 'international crossroads' for migrating waterfowl and shorebirds.

The refuge's heart is **Izembeck Lagoon**, where hundreds of thousands of migratory waterfowl converge each fall, including the entire world population of black brant.

Besides being home to large concentrations of wildlife, the Alaska Peninsula is also a seismically active place that is part of the North Pacific's 'Ring of Fire.' Dozens of volcanoes dot the landscape, several of them still considered active. **Pavlof Volcano**, on the lower peninsula, has erupted more than 40 times since 1790; in 1986 it sent volcanic ash more than 10 miles (16km) into the atmosphere and continued to belch smoke and ash and lava off and on for more than two years.

One of the more spectacular volcanic landscapes is **Aniakchak Caldera**, a 6-mile (10km) wide crater formed thousands of years ago by the collapse of a huge volcano. Within the caldera are all sorts of volcanic features: lava fields, warm springs, and cinder cones. The caldera is the dominant feature of **Aniakchak National Monument and Preserve** ⓯ (tel: 907-246-3305; www. nps.gov/ania), one of the least visited units of the National Park System.

The Alaska Peninsula and Bristol Bay region is home to the Aleut and Yup'ik Eskimo peoples. Here, as in much of rural Alaska, most residents continue to depend on subsistence harvests of fish, mammals, birds, and plants. Dozens of small villages are scattered along the coast; the area's two hubs are **Dillingham**, in Bristol Bay, and **King Salmon**, on the upper Alaska Peninsula. Both communities are served by daily commuter flights from Anchorage and are jumping-off spots for trips into the area's parks and refuges. For information and visitor services, contact the King Salmon Visitors Center (tel: 907-246-3339; www.fws.gov/refuge/Becharof).

THE ALEUTIAN ISLANDS

Reaching southwest beyond the Alaska Peninsula, the **Aleutian Islands** ⓰ arc more than 1,000 miles (1,600km) in their bend toward Asia. More than 200 islands make up the chain, which separates the Pacific Ocean from the Bering Sea.

Nearly all of the islands are included within the **Alaska Maritime National Wildlife Refuge** (tel: 907-235-6546; www.fws.gov/refuge/alaska_maritime), which protects the coastal lands and waters used by the many seabirds, shorebirds, waterfowl, migratory

Fishing on one of the Aleutian Islands.

Bear spotting.

⊙ Fact

Students (grades 6 and above) in the Alaska Peninsula community of South Naknek (population 76) must cross the Naknek River each day to attend school. When the river is frozen, they can travel by car, ATV, or snowmachine; otherwise the daily school run is via bush plane.

birds, and marine mammals that inhabit the chain.

While the volcanic, tundra-covered islands that make up the chain have a rugged, barren appearance, the waters surrounding the Aleutians are among the richest in the world, supporting a billion-dollar fishing industry. The area is also home to some of the world's largest bird colonies and marine mammal populations, from sea otters to seals and sea lions and whales. Yet even here, there is evidence of ecological stress: two once-plentiful species, sea lions and harbor seals, have experienced great declines in recent decades; the populations of some birds, too, have been greatly reduced. Scientists have been studying the declines, which may be tied to overfishing, climate change, or other factors.

The weather in the Aleutians is generally cool and wet, and often stormy. Annual precipitation ranges from 20 to 80 inches (50 to 200cm) a year. Summer temperatures rarely get much above 50°F (10°C) and in winter don't often drop below 20°F (–6.7°C). Winds

seem to blow constantly and fog too is common. Visitors to the region must be prepared for weather delays, both coming and going.

DUTCH HARBOR

Aleuts have inhabited the island chain for centuries, depending on the marine ecosystem for their survival.

Small numbers of Aleuts (and even smaller numbers of non-Natives) still reside here, in several small communities. The Aleutians' largest city and commercial hub is **Dutch Harbor**, at the northern end of the chain on **Unalaska Island ⑰**. It is one of the top fishing ports in the US, both in terms of poundage and value.

With a combined population of about 4,500 people, Dutch Harbor and neighboring **Unalaska** also serve as the Aleutians' tourism center, complete with the world-class Grand Aleutian Hotel. Visitor activities here range from sportfishing for salmon and halibut to birdwatching, hiking, kayaking, and exploring World War II remnants. Japanese troops bombed

Dutch Harbor.

Dutch Harbor during the war and also landed on Attu and Kiska Islands; the US military later retook those islands, in the only battles fought on American soil during World War II.

Those who travel to Dutch Harbor can learn more about local history at the **Museum of the Aleutians** (314 Salmon Way; tel: 907-581-5150; www.aleutians.org; Tue–Sat 11am–4pm), which has exhibits about the Aleut culture, Russian occupation, World War II, and the fishing industry. Contact the Dutch Harbor/Unalaska Convention and Visitors Bureau (tel: 907-581-1251; www.ci.unalaska.ak.us) for more information about travel to and within the area.

THE PRIBILOF ISLANDS

Three hundred miles (480km) off the western coast of Alaska and 200 miles (320km) north of the Aleutians lie the **Pribilof Islands** ⓲, the nesting grounds for over 2 million seabirds of 240 different species, and the breeding grounds and summer home of nearly a million Pacific fur seals. Five volcanic, treeless islets make up the Pribilof group, but only two of those are inhabited by humans: **St Paul** and **St George**; with a population of nearly 600 people, nearly all Natives, the village of St Paul is the world's largest community of Aleuts. There are small hotels on both islands, but only St Paul has a restaurant. It also is visited in summer by packaged tours, the easiest way to visit the Pribilofs. Contact the Tanadgusix Village Corporation of St Paul Island for more tourism information, tel: 877-424-5637; www.alaskabirding.com.

Today, the fishing and tourism industries are being developed as St Paul's main economic supports. Past revenues were generated by the fur seal harvest and government aid. With the ending of the commericial harvest in 1985, the community was forced to find other means of support.

The recently completed harbor is a boon to local fishermen, who had no safe haven for their boats, and is expected to attract new industry. Tourism also helps; the Pribilofs are known as a birders' paradise.

⊘ Fact

Most visitors fly in from Anchorage to the Pribilofs. Contact PenAir (tel: 800-448-4226; www.penair.com) for more details. Founded in 1955 as Peninsula Airways, PenAir is now Alaska's biggest commuter airline, with a fleet of 40 aircraft and a service to 36 communities in the Southwest.

A Russian Orthodox shrine in a remote part of Saint Paul Island reflects the long standing effects of Russian colonization in the Bering Sea islands.

⊘ THE BEST FISHING

There are several lodges and fishing guide operations in Katmai National Park (tel: 907-246-3305; www.nps.gov/katm) and **Wood-Tikchik State Park** ⓮ (tel: 907-842-2641; http://dnr.alaska.gov/parks/asp units/woodtik/woodtiksp.htm); at 1.6 million acres (647,000 hectares), Wood-Tikchik is the largest of America's state parks, with two immense river-and-lake chains that are popular with boaters as well as anglers.

Guided sportfishing is also popular in three national wildlife refuges: the **Togiak Refuge** is on Bristol Bay's northern edge (tel: 907-842-1063; http://togiak.fws.gov), while the **Becharof and Alaska Peninsula refuges** (tel: 907-246-3339; www.fws.gov/refuge/alaska_peninsula) encompass much of the Alaska Peninsula.

Especially attractive to serious birders are the 'accidental' Asian migrants that sometimes get blown to the islands by strong western winds. These birds are rarely, if ever, seen anywhere else in North America.

Visitors to the Pribilofs should be prepared for cool and moist conditions. In June, the average daily high is 42°F (5.8°C) and nighttime lows fall into the 30s even in summer. And only rarely do the islands experience back-to-back sunny days.

YUKON-KUSKOKWIM DELTA

Encompassing 76,000 sq miles (200,000 sq km) in remote Southwest Alaska, the **Yukon-Kuskokwim Delta** is home to Alaska's Yup'ik Eskimos and one of the world's great waterfowl-nesting areas.

Much of the delta is within the **Yukon Delta National Wildlife Refuge ⑲**. (tel: 907-543-3151; www.fws.gov/refuge/yukon_delta). At nearly 22 million acres (8.9 million hectares), this refuge is the nation's second largest (just slightly smaller than the Arctic

National Wildlife Refuge). It's also the oldest refuge in Alaska; in 1909, President Theodore Roosevelt established the Yukon Delta Reservation.

That reservation and some later refuges were then consolidated and expanded in 1980 to form the present Yukon Delta NWR. Within the refuge, waters from two of Alaska's four largest rivers meander through immense, tundra wetlands. The Yukon flows 1,400 miles (2,250km) before emptying into the Bering Sea, while to the south, the Kuskokwim River winds 540 miles (870km) through Southwest Alaska.

This is as flat as Alaska gets: nearly 70 percent of the refuge is delta lands and waters less than 100ft (30 meters) in elevation. Innumerable streams and sloughs weave through this lowland, which is also dotted with tens of thousands of lakes, ponds, and marshes. In all, about a third of the refuge is covered in water. Higher and drier areas are covered by forests and range up to an elevation of 4,000ft (1,200 meters), in the gently rounded **Kuskokwim** and **Kilbuck Mountains**.

Sunset over the Alaska Peninsula.

The refuge's wetlands are seasonal home to millions of birds: seabirds, shorebirds, waterfowl, songbirds, and raptors. In both diversity and numbers, the refuge is considered America's most important shorebird nesting area and is also critically important for ducks and geese. Birds come here from the Atlantic coast as well as Asia.

SPAWNING GROUND

The Delta's waterways also serve as important spawning and rearing habitat for 44 species of fish, including Alaska's five species of Pacific salmon, Dolly Varden char, northern pike, grayling, and rainbow trout. Mammals range from grizzlies and black bears to caribou, moose, wolves, and musk oxen. Coastal waters are important to several types of seals, walrus, and whales.

Few people visit the refuge and those who do come here largely for the sportfishing or birdwatching. For information on recreational opportunities, contact the refuge headquarters in Bethel (tel: 907-543-3151).

BETHEL

The Delta's Yupik residents live in scattered villages along the coast and its main rivers. Most of the 50 or so communities are small, with few or no accommodations for travelers.

The commercial and social hub of the region is **Bethel ⑳**, a city of about 6,080 people on the Kuskokwim River. Here you'll find a theater, banks, restaurants, radio and TV stations, a college, a hospital, and lodging options. The Moravian Church established a mission here in 1884. Information on Bethel and outlying areas can be obtained from the Bethel Chamber of Commerce (tel: 907-543-2911; www.chamberofbethel.org).

From the flatlands of the Y-K Delta to the volcanic peaks and bear-rich salmon streams of the Alaska Peninsula and the wind-battered islands of the Aleutian chain and Pribilof Archipelago, the Southwest region presents adventurous visitors the opportunity to see parts of wild Alaska and aspects of the state's traditional culture that few travelers ever encounter.

Fact

The Dolly Varden char is named after a colorfully attired character in Charles Dickens's *Barnaby Rudge*. The fish was once mistakenly thought to endanger salmon by eating their eggs, and bounties were paid for the 6 million fish killed and discarded in the 1920s and 1930s.

A black oystercatcher.

Mount Shishaldin, Unimak Island.

ALASKA

TRAVEL TIPS

TRANSPORTATION

The 1.5 million yearly visitors to Alaska arrive in one of three ways: by air, sea, or road. The best choice for the individual traveler depends on the goals for the journey, the time available, and the costs involved. Arriving by train is not an option. No train system, neither US nor Canadian, connects with Alaska's railway service.

By Air

Generally speaking, the fastest and least expensive way to travel to Alaska is to fly. Several major airlines provide regularly scheduled flights into Anchorage's Ted Stevens International Airport (and some to Fairbanks International), especially during the summer season. Alaska Airlines offers, by far, the most comprehensive coverage, with non-stop flights to Anchorage from Vancouver (British Columbia), Seattle, Portland, San Diego, Los Angeles, Denver, San Francisco, Salt Lake City, and Chicago. Anchorage serves as the primary hub for travel to and within the state. Those wishing to travel to smaller, outlying towns and villages may do so from Anchorage by using Alaska Airlines, the smaller, regional airlines, or chartered air taxi companies.

The communities of Ketchikan, Juneau, Fairbanks, and Anchorage may be reached directly from Seattle via Alaska Airlines (see page 350 for a list of airline contacts) and act as a hub for nearby destinations.

There are no airport taxes in Alaska, but each passenger is assessed a small fee that is attached to the price of the ticket. The fee usually amounts to only a few cents and at most, a few dollars.

Private pilots planning to fly to Alaska should have the latest federal government flight information publication, the Alaska Chart Supplement, available from the Federal Aviation Administration, 222 West 7th Avenue, No. 14, Anchorage, AK, 99513; tel: 907-271-5645; www.faa.gov.

By Sea

Nearly half of all visitors to Alaska travel via **cruise ship**. There are several good reasons for this, beyond the effective marketing programs of the cruise industry. Most Alaska cruises begin – or end up – in Seattle or in Vancouver, British Columbia, Canada. They offer one-way or round-trip voyages through the protected (and therefore generally calm) waterways of the Inside Passage. Passengers may go ashore to experience the local culture and shop in various Southeast communities without having to pack and unpack, or sleep in a different bed every night.

Passengers generally have the option of adding shore excursions – even extended land tours – to the basic package. The entire cost of the trip, while admittedly expensive, is known at the outset.

Cruising Options

Big-ship cruise lines, such as Holland America, Princess, Celebrity, Norwegian, Regent Seven Seas, Disney, and Royal Caribbean transport thousands of passengers while offering not only luxurious travel to Alaska, but also an array of on-board entertainment for those who enjoy endless options of formal dinners (and formal dress), casinos, floor shows, spas, line dancing, art auctions, bingo, and kids' programs, to name a few.

Small-ship cruise lines, like Lindblad, Abercrombie & Kent, Un-Cruise Adventures, Alaska Sea Adventures, and Discovery Voyages, carry 12 to 250 passengers, and specialize in excellent food, casual dress, close-up (sea-level) wildlife and glacier viewing, and educational lectures by on-board naturalists. These smaller ships have the added advantage of being able to offer stops in less-traveled areas such as Wrangell or Petersburg.

Whether you decide to go large or small, all cruise passengers must pay a $34.50 'head tax.' While some of the money goes to monitoring the ship's environmental impact, most is used by local agencies for infrastructure upkeep.

Those who are more adventurous (and have plenty of time) might want to consider one of the more unusual Alaska cruises to the far north, around the Pribilof Islands (these are known to be superb for bird-watching) and into the Bering Sea. The smaller, specialist expedition cruise companies operate these.

Ferries

Independent travelers may choose another excellent option: traveling to Alaska aboard one of the **Alaska Marine Highway System** ferries. The state operates 11 ferries providing year-round service between Bellingham, Washington (or Prince Rupert, British Columbia, Canada), and many of Alaska's coastal communities. Although rarely is it a straight shot. The trip through British Columbia is beautiful and the

---

⊘ Airport Information

Fairbanks International Airport: tel: 907-474-2500; dot.alaska.gov/faiiap/index.shtml

Juneau International Airport: tel: 907-789-7821; www.juneau.org/airport

Ketchikan International Airport: tel: 907-225-6800; www.borough.ketchikan.ak.us/130/Airport

Anchorage Airport: tel: 907-266-2526; www.anchorageairport.com

best illustration of Alaska's isolation, but it will add an extra two to three days to your trip. It is recommended that you make reservations at least six months in advance, especially if traveling during the peak season.

Useful Contacts

Alaska Marine Highway System: tel: 800-642-0066 or 907-465-3941; www.ferryalaska.com.
Cruise Lines International Association: tel: 604-681-9515 (Vancouver), www.clia-nwc.com.

By Road

Cruise ships moored at the Railroad dock in Skagway.

Traveling the Alaska Highway is a great adventure. However, because of the great distance, you should only consider it if you are well prepared and have plenty of time.

By Bus

Bus service and motorcoach tours are available to Alaska by way of the Alaska Highway. From Seattle, Washington, Greyhound connects with Greyhound Canada (www.greyhound.ca), offering service to Whitehorse in the Yukon Territory, Canada. From Whitehorse, Alaska Direct Bus Line (http://fairbanks-alaska.com) and Alaska/Yukon Trails (www.alaskashuttle.com) connect with several Alaska communities, including Fairbanks, and Anchorage. Interior Alaska Bus Line (www.interioralaskabusline.com) offers year-round services, connecting Anchorage, Fairbanks, Tok, and Northway. Several companies offer motorcoach tours between the contiguous United States and Alaska.

By Car or RV

Improvements to the Alaska Highway have made driving enjoyable and safe, but distance may be a drawback. It is 1,488 miles (2,395km) from Dawson Creek, British Columbia to Fairbanks, and much of the trip will be through extremely remote, though spectacular, country.

For essential information about driving Alaska's highways, refer to the latest edition of *The Milepost*, published and updated yearly, which gives detailed descriptions of points of interest, food, gas, and lodging options, as well as road conditions. Log onto www.themilepost.com for additional information.

The Alaska State Department of Transportation also provides up-to-date information on weather, traffic, road conditions, and construction. Visit http://511.alaska.gov, or call 511 in Alaska or 866-282-7577.

GETTING AROUND

Because of Alaska's size, getting around is no small task. Destinations are dozens, if not hundreds of miles apart and often separated by waterways, steep mountain ranges, and endless tracts of uninhabited terrain. For this reason, many travelers choose to see the state via cruise tours that take trips into the Interior. (See page 94.)

For those who decide to go it alone, the state's few highways (six in total), numerous airports, and train system make traveling easy, if time-consuming. While cities in the Southeast are small and dense enough to navigate largely on foot, Anchorage and Fairbanks are sprawling and have limited public transportation. If you plan on spending any length of time in either, renting a car is advisable.

To and from the Airport

Most airports in Alaska are located within a few minutes' drive of the downtown area, and ground transportation is easily available via taxis, car rentals or the local bus service in the major cities of Anchorage, Fairbanks, and Juneau. In Anchorage, cruise-ship passengers can take the Alaska Railroad spur to downtown hotels. By contrast, the Ketchikan airport is located on a separate island, and a short ferry trip is necessary to reach the ground transportation – which you have to prearrange – to take you Downtown.

The ferry runs every half-hour and costs $6 per adult.

By Air

The secret to conquering Alaska's vastness is air travel. Commuter airlines and charter aircraft services are everywhere. More often than not, even the most remote cabins have some sort of airstrip nearby, or a stretch of hard-packed sand on a river bar to serve as a landing strip.

Thankfully this means that flying in Alaska is reasonably affordable, costing nearly the same as land-based travel, but taking considerably less time. Still, the more remote the location, the steeper the ticket price. While not always necessary, flights out of Anchorage are generally the cheapest. Alaska Airlines, Ravn Alaska, and Bering Air are the major carriers, and service out-of-the-way native villages. The easiest way to search routes, price-shop and make a reservation, is online.

Chartering a plane is also possible, particularly to remote wilderness locations. Most local carriers, including Ravn Alaska and Bering Air, offer charter services. The tourist information center of your destination will also have a number of good recommendations. Costs typically begin at $600 an hour (flight time) to charter a pilot and plane that can carry four passengers, depending on the amount of baggage. If you're traveling with a large group, it's even possible to charter a vintage DC-3, a twin-engine plane capable of hauling large loads for long distances. Going standby (willing to wait for an available seat) is considerably cheaper, reducing the price, often, by over half.

See the tint panel on 'Airline Contacts' for a list of many of the carriers offering scheduled and chartered intrastate air service.

By Rail

The 470-mile (756km) Alaska Railroad connects Anchorage with Fairbanks to the north and Whittier and Seward to the south. Along the way passengers enjoy stops in Portage, Girdwood, Talkeetna, and Denali, among others. A flagstop train, the Hurricane Turn runs Thursday through Monday (in summer; first Thursday of the month only in winter with fewer stops), while all other trains run daily in the summer. In the winter, two weekly services (Tue and Sat)are available to Fairbanks aboard the Aurora Winter Train.

Summertime, one-way tickets from Anchorage to Fairbanks or Seward cost $249 or $175 respectively. All trains have domed vista cars that are open to everyone, but are first-come-first-served. Except for the Hurricane Turn, light meals, along with beer and wine, are available on all trains, while the Denali Star and the Coastal Classic have full-service dining cars. The Alaska Railroad also offers packaged tours that range from day trips to dogsled camps near Girdwood to the 'Deluxe Alaska Sampler,' a sevennight journey from the Kenai Fjords to the Denali backcountry. For more information and ticket reservations,

contact: Alaska Railroad (tel: 907-265-2494/800-544-0552; www.alaskarailroad.com).

Princess Cruises and Holland America/Grayline Alaska own several luxurious domed cars that travel as part of Alaska Railroads trains. Grayline Alaska offers rail tours to non-cruise-ship passengers that include hotel stays and wilderness activities. Destinations include Denali National Park, Talkeetna, Kenai and Copper River. To make reservations, contact Grayline Alaska (tel: 888-425-1737; www.graylinealaska.com).

By Ferry

For many coastal communities, ferry travel is a basic form of transportation, but for the traveler, it is a relaxed, affordable way to travel.

On-Board Facilities

The ferries range in size from the 181ft, 125-passenger M/V *Lituya* to the 418ft, 499-passenger M/V *Columbia*. The larger ferries offer comfortable staterooms, some with private baths. There are large, clean, public restrooms and showers. After 10pm, you may roll out a sleeping bag in one of the spacious lounges, kick back in a recliner, or pitch a tent (at any time) near the solarium on the upper deck. The ferries offer inexpensive cafeterias or snack bars, gift shops, video game

rooms, occasional movies, a play area for toddlers, a full bar serving $3 pints of Alaskan beer, and plenty of scenery at no extra charge. During the summer, USDA Forest Service offers interpretive programs on the observation deck.

Destinations and Timetables

In addition to the popular Southeast, the Alaska Marine Highway ferries (www.dot.state.ak.us/amhs; tel: 800-642-0066) cross the Gulf of Alaska to the communities of Whittier, Valdez, and Cordova in the Prince William Sound. From Homer, you can jump to Kodiak and venture out along the Alaskan Peninsula to the Aleutian Islands. Passage through the gulf can be rocky compared to the smooth sailing in the Southeast.

Building your own itinerary is easy. The ferry docks between one to six hours at every location and passengers are encouraged to step ashore. Where the dock is located far from town, as in Sitka, a shuttle is usually provided for little additional cost. Extending your stay doesn't greatly affect the overall cost, but it may be a couple days until the next ferry. Gulf crossings occur twice a month in the summer and are significantly reduced in the winter, as is service to all Southcentral and Southwestern communities.

Day trips are also available, between certain destinations in the Southeast and in Prince William Sound. From May until September, there is a weekly service to Gustavus in Glacier Bay.

Reservations and Fares

Fares can be as little as $25, but walk-on passengers from Bellingham to Skagway, for example, can expect to pay around $504 (one way). Coin-operated lockers are available to keep valuables, as is storage for bicycles or kayaks for an additional charge of at least $120, depending on the vessel. A stateroom (for two) with a bath will add at least $450 more, while a small automobile will increase the ticket approximately $1,100 (considerably more for larger vehicles, including RVs).

While summertime travelers ought to book in advance, particularly to snag a stateroom, spontaneity does not need to fall by the wayside. Tickets may be purchased up to one hour before departure time at the ticket office or ferry terminal.

By Bus

Despite Alaska's wide-open spaces, traveling by bus (or 'shuttle') is a surprisingly easy, comfortable, and affordable way to go. Trips from Anchorage to Fairbanks, Denali, Talkeetna, Seward, and Whittier occur daily in the summer and cost anywhere from $100 (to Fairbanks) to $65 (to Seward). Service to more distant locations such as Valdez and the Yukon Territory are also available.

Alaska's three largest cities offer municipal bus service. Fares cost between $1.50 and $2.00 one way and must be paid with exact change. Service is infrequent, with waits between buses anywhere from 30 minutes to one hour. Depending on your schedule and needs, the city bus can be a cheap way to move around Alaska's spread-out cities.

Useful Contacts
Interior Alaska Direct Bus Line: tel: 800-770-6652; www.interioralaskabus line.com.
Alaska Park Connection: tel: 800-266-8625; www.alaskacoach.com.
Alaska/Yukon Trails: tel: 907-888-5659; www.alaskashuttle.com.
Anchorage People Mover: tel: 907-343-6543; www.muni.org/departments/transit/peoplemover
Metropolitan Area Commuter System (MACS): tel: 907-459-1002; www.co.fairbanks.ak.us/transportation.
Capital Transit System (CTS): tel: 907-789-6901

Private Transportation

Taxis
Taxis are nice for getting around town, but can be extremely expensive for long distances.

Anchorage
Alaska Checker Cab, tel: 907-644-4444; http://akcheckercab.com
Alaska Yellow Cab, tel: 907-222-2222; www.alaskayellowdispatch.com

Fairbanks
Alaska and King Cab, tel: 907-452-2222; http://kingalaskacab.com

Juneau
Capital Cab and Evergreen Taxi, tel: 907-586-2121/2772; www.evergreen taxi.com

Car Rentals

Renting a car is a great option for those eager to explore Alaska's interior on their own. It is advisable to make a reservation far in advance, especially during the summer. You should also check the policy to make sure there aren't any travel restrictions. For example, many companies will not allow you to drive into Canada or take the car on a gravel road like the Steese or Dalton Highways. In the summer, rates run about $150 per day and $740 per week for a mid-size sedan. Hefty taxes and surcharges are added, raising the price between $50 and $150. Four-wheel-drive, sports utility vehicles, and passenger vans are also available and occasionally come with additional coverage for rougher terrain.

Anchorage
Midnight Sun Car & Van Rental, tel: 888-877-3585; www.ineedacarrental.com
The companies listed below have desks inside the terminals of the Anchorage, Fairbanks, and Juneau airports:
Alamo www.alamo.com
Avis www.avis.com
Budget www.budget.com

Recreational Vehicles
For maximum independence throughout the Interior, consider renting an RV camper. Not only are you freed from train and bus schedules, but bedding down for the night means simply finding a beautiful (and accessible) spot. With beds, dining, kitchen, and bathroom facilities, rates run generally $259 to $279 per night for a standard or large vehicle. As with car rentals, rates do not include the taxes and surcharges that can hike the price 30 percent, and companies often stipulate that their vehicles are not driven on dirt or gravel roads. The price of gas is another consideration as it is perhaps surprisingly expensive in Alaska. Linens and dishware rental is often available for an additional charge of $20.

Anchorage
ABC Motorhome & RV, tel: 907-279-2000 or 800-421-7456; www.abcmo torhome.com

Fairbanks
Go North, tel: 907-479-7272; www.go north-alaska.com

Motoring Advice

The speed limit on most Alaska highways is 55mph (88kmh), although speeds of up to 65mph (104kmh) are allowed on some sections (rural freeways). Speed limits are lower within cities, in residential areas and especially near schools. Alaska law requires drivers to pull over at the first, safe opportunity whenever five or more vehicles are following behind them.

A right turn is permitted against a red light unless otherwise posted, but only after you stop long enough to confirm there is no traffic with which you will interfere. All drivers in both directions are required to stop for a school bus with its warning lights operating. Drivers may not proceed around or past a school bus until the lights have been turned off.

Drivers in Alaska may see hitchhikers, but not nearly as many as in the past. Hitchhiking is most common during the summer season, when both residents and visitors are in search of a ride when traveling to jobs or adventures along major routes. Pick up hitchhikers at your own risk.

Prudence dictates that you slow your speed during the winter months. Highways in Alaska are not the best in the world, and in combination with ice and snow, can be treacherous. For the latest information on road conditions, dial 511, or go to http://511.alaska.gov.

Car Breakdown
When driving the highways in Alaska, it's always a good idea to be prepared. While excellent, dependable towing and repair services are available in cities and even smaller towns in the state, you may break down in the middle of nowhere. It's very important that your vehicle be in reliable condition if you're planning a drive to remote areas. Check to be sure you have a working spare tire, a jack, flares, a basic tool kit, jumper cables, and a first aid kit, as well as food and drink. An extra can of oil as well as transmission and brake fluids could be a godsend. If you do break down along the road, you'll likely find that other drivers in Alaska will probably stop and see if they can help. Do not rely on your cell phone as cell service throughout much of Alaska is erratic at best.

A – Z

A

Accomodations

Accommodations vary greatly, from the glossy mega hotels owned by the cruise ship companies to the homey digs of a B&B, to the isolation of a forest service cabin to the adventure of a wilderness lodge. Because of this, Alaska can satisfy our greatest sense of adventure and our deepest need for luxury. Anchorage offers the widest range of hotels, but the further you travel from the city, the slimmer (and funkier) your lodging options become. Don't be surprised if the mediocre small-town motel costs nearly as much as a better-appointed Anchorage option. Prices are high everywhere, especially in more remote areas and in summer. A 'bed tax' is attached to all bills, but varies between 5 percent and 12 percent of the total depending on the city or borough. These motels are very popular. Winter sees great deals, and most accommodations are now smoke-free (or at least offer smoke-free rooms) and provide free internet access. Kitchen amenities, also frequently found, help save money on dining, which in Alaska is often expensive. Freezer storage is usually standard in fishing communities.

Admission Charges

The larger museums and attractions in Alaska's main cities usually charge $2 to $6. The Alaska Native Heritage Center charges by far the highest at $24.95 for general admission. During winter, visitors to the museum are asked to make a donation to cover their entry cost. Seniors (individuals 65 and older) generally get a small discount at most places, as do students and children. Young children under the age of three – or

six in the case of the Alaska Native Heritage Center – frequently get in for free. In smaller, out of the way attractions, a donation is suggested. Here, a few dollars is usually sufficient. Check websites for any fee changes or special deals. Admission is often reduced in the winter season.

Age Restrictions

To drive a car in the US, you have to be at least 16 or 17, though rental cars usually require you be at least 21. The legal age for drinking and purchasing alcohol is 21, while cigarettes can be bought at age 18.

Alcohol

To purchase alcohol, identification is required to verify the buyer's age. Alcohol is sold or served in liquor stores, lounges and restaurants licensed by the state. Unlike most of the US, grocery stores cannot sell alcohol, but they may have a separate liquor store attached or nearby. Don't be surprised if you can't get a drink on Election Day: the state prohibits the serving of any alcohol while the polling areas are open.

Alaska state law requires a mandatory three-day jail sentence for drivers found to be driving under the influence of alcohol – even for first-time offenders. Some small rural communities have banned alcohol – and they take it seriously. You could be arrested and finedfor violating the local ordinances. Before traveling to a remote destination, make sure you know the local liquor laws.

B

Budgeting for Your Trip

Traveling within Alaska is expensive. The further you roam from

urban locations, the more expensive food, lodging and services may become. This is due, in part, to the transportation costs involved in shipping goods to far-flung regions in a vast state. Here are some examples of what you might pay in US dollars when this book went to press.

Camping: Expect to pay $20 to $28 per night (tent site) at a state or federally managed campground. Contact Alaska Campgroung Owner's Association (www.alaskacampgrounds.net) for details.

Hotels: During the summer season, basic hotel rooms are generally over $100 per night, and can be as high as $300 (or more) per night during periods of highest demand. Advance reservations in summer are strongly recommended.

Meals: A fast-food meal for one will typically cost less than $10. A meal in a casual restaurant will likely run between $15 and $20. Evening meals in a nice restaurant may cost $20 to $30 per person, and often that's just for the entrée. Add a dessert and a glass of wine, and the price is likely to be close to $50 per person, before the tip (see page 356).

Transportation: Most Alaska cities, of even modest size, offer **taxi** services. A trip from Anchorage airport to the downtown area in a taxi will cost around $25 (before the expected tip). Larger cities offer municipal **bus** lines. In Anchorage, a ride on the People Mover costs $2 (one way) for adults, $1 for youth and is free for children aged four and under.

Rental cars are available in larger cities, and you can expect to pay from $100 to $200 or even more per day, depending upon the size vehicle you want. Be sure to reserve early. In peak season it can be very difficult to find a rental car at any price. Regular travel on the Alaska **Railroad** between Anchorage and Denali National Park and Preserve costs about $319 per person, one way.

Attractions. Here's a sample of prices for Anchorage-area attractions: **Anchorage Museum** at the Rasmuson Center: $18 adults, $12 seniors, $9 children 3 to 12, and ages 2 and under free, but $2 donation suggested; **Alaska Native Heritage Center**: $24.95 adults, $21.15 for seniors and military, $16.95 for children ages 7 to 16, free for ages 6 and under; **Alaska Zoo**: $15 adults, $10 seniors, $7 ages 3 to 17; **H2Oasis Indoor Water Park**: $24.99 adults, $19.99 ages 3 to 12.

Children

Bringing your children along on an Alaska vacation is a wonderful idea, because most of the things that interest you will delight them as well.

Accommodations: Many hotels in Alaska allow young children to stay for free in their parents' room, but some backcountry lodges and smaller B&Bs don't allow children under ten.

Eating: Many of Alaska's restaurants offer children's menus and even crayons and paper to help them wait for their food.

Places of Special Interest: Just getting to Alaska can be exciting, whether it's driving the highway watching for moose, or flying up and looking out the window at all those snow-covered mountains. Day cruises out of any Southeast or Southcentral coastal community would likely involve watching for marine mammals and glacier viewing.

There are also many exciting options within the larger cities. Here are some fun things to do with kids in the Anchorage area: The Discovery Center (625 C Street; tel: 907-929-9200; www.anchoragemuseum.org) features a planetarium, hourly science demonstrations, an Alaska marine touch tank, a life-sized dinosaur, and more. The Alaska Zoo (4731 O'Malley Road; tel: 907-346-2133; www.alaska zoo.org) gives kids (and their parents) a chance to get a close-up look at some of Alaska's wildlife; the

H2Oasis Indoor Waterpark's (11030 Chelea Street; tel: 907-522-4420; www.h2oasiswaterpark.com) wave pool, lazy river, pirate-ship lagoon, and Master Blaster 505ft water-coaster ride could make for an exciting day.

You could take a day trip south to Seward (by road or train) for a cruise into Kenai Fjords National Park, and while you're there visit the Alaska Sealife Center (301 Railway Avenue; tel: 907-224-6300; www.alaskasealife.org) to check out the sea lions, puffins and seals. Or you could travel north to visit Denali National Park and Preserve. Spend the night in a nearby hotel (advance reservations essential) and the next day enjoy a bus tour into the park as you watch for bears, moose, sheep, wolves, and more.

Possible Concerns: Your children will enjoy their time in Alaska more if you remember to bring sunscreen; the summer sun will still cause sunburn, even though the temperatures may seem mild. Another essential item is insect repellent. While Alaska has yet to have any problems with the West Nile or Zika viruses, mosquitoes are plentiful and may take much of the fun out of an otherwise splendid hike or picnic. If your plans take you onto the water, even in summer, dress your children (and yourself) warmly in layers. A T-shirt, then a light fleece jacket, topped with a wind/waterproof jacket, lightweight gloves and knit cap will allow for any changes in weather.

Climate

Alaska's vastness defies attempts to categorize its climate. For convenience, however, the state can be divided into five regions about which some climatic generalizations can be made.

Southeast: This is Alaska's Panhandle, a narrow ribbon of mountainous, mostly forested mainland and islands extending along the western edge of British Columbia. Wet and mild are the best terms to describe its climate. Certain communities in the region can receive more than 200 inches (5 meters) of precipitation annually. On rare, sunny days in summer, high temperatures might reach the mid-70s°F (21°C+) range. High 40s (4°C) to mid-60s (15°C) are the summer

norms, under cloudy skies. Winter temperatures rarely fall much below freezing. Skagway and Haines are usually drier and cooler in winter.

Southcentral: Anchorage and most of the gulf coast comprise this part of Alaska. Some coastal communities are nearly as wet as southeastern cities, but the amount of rainfall lessens considerably just a short distance inland. Anchorage occasionally has summer highs in the 80s (26°C) but the 60s (15°C) and low 70s (21°C) are more common.

Interior: The broad expanse of inland Alaska, loosely centered on Fairbanks, gets an average of 10 inches (25 cm) of precipitation annually. Summer temperatures have reached 100°F (37°C) on occasions; 70s and 80s (21°C and 26°C) temperatures are common, with typical winter lows to –40°F (–40°C).

Northwest and Arctic Coast: This region encompasses Alaska's northern fringe and the west coast as far south as Kotzebue. High winds are common, and average temperatures are too cool to permit trees to grow. Near Nome, summer temperatures can climb into the 80s (27°C), but the mid 60s (16°C) are more common. Winter temperatures, though extreme, are never as low as some Interior temperatures. This is also an extremely dry area, receiving only minimal amounts of moisture every year. Barrow, for example, receives just 4.7 inches (11.5cm) of precipitation annually.

Southwest and the Aleutians: The Aleutian Islands are justly known for some of the most miserable weather on earth. High winds (williwaws) can rise without warning and smash through the islands at speeds of 100mph (165kmh). Heavy fog is

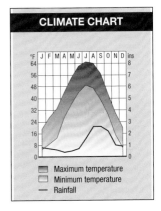

CLIMATE CHART

Maximum temperature
Minimum temperature
Rainfall

common, as are rain and cool temperatures. The southwestern mainland is the meeting point for Aleutian weather and Interior weather, and often experiences unsettled conditions, frequently accompanied by high winds.

Average Daily High Temperatures

CITY: JANUARY/JULY
Fahrenheit
Anchorage: 21.4°/65.2°
Barrow: −7.4°/45°
Cold Bay: 33.1°/55.1°
Fairbanks: −1.6°/72°
Juneau: 29.4°/63.9°
Kodiak: 35°/60.5°
Nome: 14.7°/57.7°
Centigrade
Anchorage: −6°/18.4°
Barrow: −22°/7.2°
Cold Bay: 0.6°/12.8°
Fairbanks: −18.6°/22.2°
Juneau: −1.5°/17.7°
Kodiak: 1.6°/15.8°
Nome: −9.6°/14.3°

What to Wear

When packing for Alaska, remember you are traveling north. While Alaskans may describe the climate as warm in the summer, those from warmer climates find even the summer chilly. No matter what part of the state you are visiting, bring along a warm coat and a synthetic pile or fleece jacket. A wool or synthetic sweater, hat, and gloves or mittens, are also necessities.

Layering clothing is the best way to stay warm. While you may be able to run around in shirtsleeves on a warm summer day, the evenings often require a sweater or light jacket. Tour companies sometimes furnish specialty items such as parkas for overnight trips to Barrow, Kotzebue, Prudhoe Bay and other colder areas.

No matter where you visit in Alaska, you are likely to run into periods of rain, so good-quality rainwear is needed. If your travel plans include flying to a remote area in a small plane, it is advisable to wear durable warm clothing; survival gear is required for cross-country flights in small planes.

Air services and charter flight operators normally carry sufficient survival gear as required by law; it's up to passengers to dress appropriately.

Because of its location on the Gulf of Alaska, weather conditions change rapidly, so be prepared for everything.

Customs Regulations

Visitors entering Alaska from anywhere other than a US port of embarkation will proceed through US customs. Personal effects, such as camping gear and fishing rods, are exempt from duties. Visitors who are over the age of 21 may also bring in small amounts (for personal use) of liquor, cigarettes and cigars (not from Cuba). You may also bring personal gifts, as long as the total value is not more than $100. These exemptions may only be claimed if you plan to spend at least 72 hours in the US, and if you have not claimed them within the preceding six months. A flat-rate duty may apply to other or pricier goods brought into the US. While the rates vary, it is usually around 3 percent.

Don't wrap any gifts you bring into the country; they will need to be available for inspection. Don't try to bring raw food or plant material into the US without a special license. Don't bring more than $10,000 in cash (US or foreign) unless you want the hassle of filling out additional documentation.

When leaving Alaska, you will need to have a permit for any souvenir purchased that is made from protected mammals, such as certain Native handicrafts. You can get a permit from the US Fish & Wildlife Service in Anchorage (tel: 907-271-6198), a process that may take a few days. If your souvenir contains *marine* mammal parts, the permit must come from the Washington, DC office, and may take considerably longer. The simple solution is to have the store (where you purchase the item) ship it to your home, and handle all the needed documentation. Information is also available at www.alaska.gov.

For the latest information on what documentation you will need to cross any US/Canadian border, contact:

Canada Border Service Agency: tel: 800-461-9999; www.cbsa.gc.ca
US Customs and Border Protection: tel: 877-CBP-5511

E

Embassies and Consulates

Great Britain: University of Alaska, Anchorage College of Arts and Sciences, Room 362, 2311 Providence Drive, Anchorage, AK; tel: 907-786-4848.

Emergencies

In the event of any emergency requiring police, fire or ambulance service, go to the nearest telephone and dial 911. It is a toll free call; no coins will be needed for a public telephone.

For less serious accidents, call the local police department or the state troopers non-emergency lines. Dial 907-555-1212 for directory assistance in locating the

Camping in Alaska is best reserved for the experienced camper.

⊘ Electricity

The standard for electricity throughout the US is 110 to 120 volts (60 cycle) AC. The plugs have two flat, parallel pins. Foreign visitors who don't have dual-voltage appliances will need a 110-volt transformer and an adaptor plug.

appropriate non-emergency police or trooper telephone number.

Etiquette

As when visiting any small town, particularly a Native American community, be mindful that you are in someone's home, not a museum or exhibit. Ask before taking photos, and don't assume that it is okay to enter into people's houses. Be sure to introduce yourself, and ask permission to walk around the village.

Buying something at a store with ties to these communities is a great way to strike up conversation. (See page 65.)

Food and Drink

Except for indigenous villages and remote bush communities, it is safe to assume that every population center has microbrew beer, espresso, and some kind of halibut sandwich on the menu. Alaskans love their fried fish almost as much as their locally brewed beer. Coffee, however, is supreme, and it could be argued that the drive-through espresso stand was perfected here.

The larger cities and destinations have a wide range of dining options, from sandwich shops to high-end restaurants. Expect to find diners serving large portions of 'American food' (ie hamburgers, steaks, bacon and eggs) in most small communities.

Mexican food is becoming increasingly popular and is often the better and more affordable option. Prices are extremely high in this state, so don't expect to have dinner for under $20, even at the most modest, out-of-the-way joint.

Health and Medical Care

Two major hospitals serve the general public in Anchorage, and there is one in Fairbanks and another in Juneau. Additionally, there is a hospital in Anchorage run by a number of Native Americanowned corporations. Treatment there is free for anyone who is one-quarter or more Native American. There is also a hospital on Elmendorf Air Force Base, in Anchorage, which serves military personnel and their families.

If you need to visit a doctor, larger cities in Alaska have walk-in clinics open daily with no appointment necessary. Clinics typically are staffed by some combination of physicians, nurses, and, occasionally, dentists. The service will be expensive, and you will need to pay first, and then apply for any reimbursement from your personal insurance company. Alaska hospitals will render 24-hour emergency aid to anyone in critical need, but short of that standard, payment will be required before care will be given. A trip to the emergency room due to an accident or serious illness can easily cost $1,000 or more. Adequate travel insurance is essential.

The Covid-19 pandemic caused school closures and the cancellation of various festivals in 2020. For ongoing restrictions, vistors to Alaska should check the most up-to-date state guidance at https://covid19.alaska.gov/travelers.

Alaska Native Medical Center
4315 Diplomacy Drive, Anchorage
Tel: 907-563-2662
www.anmc.org

Alaska Regional Hospital
2801 DeBarr Road, Anchorage
Tel: 907-276-1131
www.alaskaregional.com

Bartlett Regional Hospital
3260 Hospital Drive, Juneau
Tel: 907-796-8900
www.bartletthospital.org

Fairbanks Memorial Hospital
1650 Cowles Street, Fairbanks
Tel: 907-452-8181
www.foundationhealth.org

Providence Alaska Medical Center
3200 Providence Drive, Anchorage
Tel: 907-562-2211
http://alaska.providence.org

Internet

Internet access is available at most public libraries, hotels, cafés, and airports. Even smaller cities generally offer some online access.

LGBTQ Travelers

In Alaska's 'live and let live' spirit, homosexuality is widely accepted. However, it is important to exercise caution in some remote areas. Anchorage and Fairbanks have a fairly thriving LGBTQ scene. In downtown Anchorage, Identity, Inc. runs the Gay and Lesbian Community Center at 336 East Fifth Avenue, Anchorage, AK 99520-0070, tel: 907-929-4528, www.identityalaska.org. A gay, lesbian, bisexual, and transgender organization, their mission is to build the Alaska GLBTA community through programs, education, and collaboration. The Southeast Alaska Gay and Lesbian Alliance is also a great resource. Visit their website, www.seagla.org, for gay-friendly restaurants, lodging, and tours around the state.

Lost Property

Here are some numbers you may need if you lose personal belongings:
Alaska Marine Highway System: tel: 800-642-0066
Alaska Railroad: tel: 907-265-2494
Fairbanks International Airport: tel: 907-474-2500
Juneau International Airport: tel: 907 789 7821
Ted Steven's International Airport (Anchorage): tel: 907-266-2526

Maps

An excellent source for topographic maps of Alaska is US Geological Survey, 4210 University Drive, Room 208, Anchorage, AK 99508; tel: 907-786-7000; http://usgs.gov/centers/asc/maps.

Media

Newspapers

The three major daily newspapers are the *Juneau Empire* (www.juneau empire.com), the *Alaska Dispatch News* (www.adn.com) and the *Fairbanks Daily News-Miner* (www.newsminer. com). Numerous smaller communities also put out newspapers, many of which tackle controversial local issues. For native issues, the *Tundra Drums* (Bethel; www.thetundradrums. com) is a good source.

Many bookstores and variety stores have one or more of the major Alaska dailies for sale, and in larger cities *The New York Times*, *The Wall Street Journal*, and *USA Today* are normally available.

Television

Only Anchorage has enough stations to affiliate actively with the four major television networks. Stations in other major cities generally run a mix of network and local programming. Public television is available in most of the state.

Radio Stations

The major radio networks have affiliates in all the larger cities, and most towns or villages will have a locally owned radio station. National Public Radio reaches communities throughout most of the state and is an excellent source of entertainment and information. For listings around Alaska, visit http://radio-locator.com/cgi-bin/finder?sr=Y&s=T&state=AK.

The vast majority of radio and television programs are broadcast in English, though many of the public stations also offer a limited number of programs in Spanish, Russian, or the Native dialect that is spoken in a particular village or region.

Money

Travelers' checks in US dollars are advised to ease problems in dealing with the currency. National banks in Alaska's major cities – Anchorage, Fairbanks, and Juneau – can convert foreign currency at the prevailing exchange rate. Automatic teller machines (ATMs) can be found in just about every town on the road system.

Outside these metropolitan areas the opportunities to convert foreign money are dramatically reduced.

Tipping

Airport porters usually receive $1 for each bag. (Don't expect porters outside of Anchorage.) Similar tips are appropriate for bellhops in the larger hotels.

Waiters and waitresses normally receive about 15 percent of the bill. Tipping can be as high as 20 percent for excellent restaurant service. Tips are inappropriate in most fast-food restaurants, although most cafés will have an (optional) tip jar on the counter. A dollar a drink is common for any well-poured cocktail. Bartenders should get 10 to 15 percent of the bill depending on the quality of service.

For tours, charters, or at small, backcountry lodges, expect to tip an additional 10 to 20 percent, depending on quality of service and length of stay.

O

Opening Hours

Government offices (except for Post Offices) are normally open from 8am to 4.30pm Monday through Friday, with banks and credit unions generally open from 10am to 6pm and, in some cases, during limited hours on Saturday. Except for necessary public services, most government offices and businesses are closed on public holidays (though the Post Office at the Anchorage airport is open every day from 6am to 11.59pm). Retailers, especially in peak summer months, are often open seven days a week, well into the evening. Some grocery stores are 24-hour. Many businesses and state run parks and agencies have different operating hours in the summer and winter. Generally 'summer' runs from May to October, while 'winter' simply can mean the rest of the year.

⊘ Time Zones

Alaska Standard Time equals Pacific Standard Time minus 1 hour (Eastern Standard Time minus 4 hours; GMT minus 10 hours). The Aleutian Chain and St Lawrence Island are in the Hawaii-Aleutian Time Zone, which is 1 hour earlier.

P

Postal Services

You can mail a letter at your hotel, at local post office, or in any of the official US Post Office's blue collection boxes located around town.

Public Holidays

Banks, offices, post offices, and state and federal agencies will probably be closed on the following state and national holidays:
January 1: New Year's Day
Third Monday in January: Martin Luther King, Jr. Day
Third Monday in February: Presidents' Day
Last Monday in March: Seward's Day
Last Monday in May: Memorial Day
July 4: Independence Day
First Monday in September: Labor Day
Second Monday in October: Columbus Day
October 18: Alaska Day
November 11: Veterans' Day
Fourth Thursday in November: Thanksgiving Day
December 25: Christmas Day

R

Religious Services

Although Alaska is perhaps the least religious state in the union, there are plenty of places of worship. The Wasilla/Palmer area has become a growing center of Evangelical Christianity, and has the highest church-per-person ratio in Alaska. Protestant, Catholic, and Russian Orthodox are the dominant religions.

S

Shopping

What to Buy

Many rare crafts and products are available to buy throughout the state. Popular items include jade jewelry, canned food products, and Alaskan native crafts. Gold nugget jewelry is also a local specialty and makes a wonderful Alaskan souvenir or gift. Somewhat expensive,

Alaskan goods are generally of high quality.

Although opportunities to pick up bargains from the actual artisans have declined markedly, it is occasionally possible to strike a good deal in the villages. Alaska is still sufficiently folksy for many of the most interesting shopping places to be 'Mom and Pop' operations. Your best bet for finding such establishments is to wander slowly through whatever town you're in and take time to check out the stock in even the most rundown-looking stores. Alaska is also home to many talented artists whose works can be purchased at local galleries and shops. Museums and major hotels all have gift shops hawking Alaskan products.

There are two ways to ensure you're buying authentic goods. If an item was manufactured in Alaska, the tag features a polar bear and the words, 'Made in Alaska.' Authentic Native-made products show a silver hand with the designation 'Native Handicraft.' Recently, Russian goods reading 'Alaskan made' have seeped into the state, becoming a popular scam. Make sure that the label has the proper insignia.

Native Crafts

Native crafts are abundant and include items carved from walrus ivory, soapstone, and jade. Also look for seal-oil candles, carved wooden totem poles, and clothing.

Alaskan women make some of the most intricately woven baskets in the world. Materials used for the baskets include beachgrass, birch bark, and whale baleen. These items have become very popular over the years and command a high price, some selling for several hundred dollars. Beaded slippers from sealskin and wolf hair are also handmade. Unusual porcupine quill earrings are affordable and attractive.

Jade and Ivory

Jade is found locally in Alaska, and is made into carvings, as well as jewelry. Jade stones come in various shades of green, brown, black, yellow, white, and red.

Scrimshawed walrus ivory – scenes are etched on the ivory – is another authentic handicraft. Visitors who wish to take ivory to a country other than the United States

With climate change the glaciers are receding.

must obtain an export permit from the US Fish and Wildlife Service. Be sure to ask about restrictions when your purchase is made.

Fur

Furriers remain a popular business, particularly in larger cities like Anchorage and Fairbanks. Most fur comes from trappers who live in the bush and are regulated by the state's Fish and Wildlife Department. Still, fur remains a controversial trade, particularly with regard to animal cruelty, but in this state of extreme cold and back-to-the-land self-reliance, it is much more accepted. If you plan on purchasing fur, ask its origin and any customs regulations that may apply when taking it out of the US.

Smoking

Like most of the US, Alaska is in a state of flux with regards to smoking. While it has long been popular here, restrictions have been voted in some cities and boroughs to limit or prohibit smoking in restaurants and bars.

Tax

There is no state sales tax in Alaska. However, different boroughs and municipalities across the state may impose a sales tax on all or some goods and services, including hotel stays. If uncertain as to whether or not there is a local sales tax, ask any cashier or hotel clerk. It is generally around 8 to 10 percent of the cost of the bill. All cruise passengers must pay a $34.50 'head tax'.

Telephones

Dial 411 for local numbers. Information on telephone listings anywhere in the state can be obtained by dialing 907-555-1212. Information for other states and Canada can be obtained by dialing 1, followed by the appropriate three-digit area code and then 555-1212. The three-digit area code for all telephone exchanges within Alaska is 907.

Cell phones can be used in most major communities and several smaller ones, such as Barrow, Fairbanks, Tok, Valdez, Anchorage, Cordova, Juneau, Kenai, Homer, and Whittier where there are stronger signals. Check with your phone provider before arriving in Alaska.

Toilets

Gas stations, bars and restaurants have public restrooms available. So will some retail stores, but if not, the clerk will direct you to the nearest one. The farther you get from population centers, the more popular outhouses become due to freezing water pipes. Most tourist areas have indoor plumbing, but it is likely you will encounter at least one Alaskan outhouse on your trip.

Tour Operators

Alaska has countless tour operators throughout the state that offer everything from birdwatching and hiking to fishing and mountain climbing.

Tourist Information

For information about visiting Alaska's parks, contact Public Land Information Centers at www.alaskacenters.gov. Every town and tourist destination has a visitors bureau, usually located Downtown.

The Alaska Travel Industry Association
610 East 5th Avenue, Suite 201, Anchorage AK 99503
Tel: 907-929-2842
www.travelalaska.com

Anchorage Convention and Visitors Bureau
524 West Fourth Avenue, Anchorage, AK 99501
Tel: 907-257-2363
www.anchorage.net

Fairbanks Convention and Visitors Bureau
101 Dunkel Street, Suite 111, Fairbanks, AK 99701
Tel: 907-456-5774 or 800-327-5774
www.explorefairbanks.com

Haines Convention and Visitors Bureau
PO Box 530, 122 Second Avenue, Haines, AK 99827
Tel: 907-766-2234
www.visithaines.com

Juneau Convention and Visitors Bureau
800 Glacier Avenue, Suite 201, Juneau, AK 99801
Tel: 907-586-2201/888-586-2201
www.traveljuneau.com

Kenai Convention and Visitors Bureau
35571 Kenai Spur Highway, Soldotna, AK 99669
Tel: 800-535-3624
www.kenaipeninsula.org

Ketchikan Visitors Bureau
131 Front Street, Ketchikan, AK 99901
Tel: 907-225-6166/800-770-3300
www.visit-ketchikan.com

Kodiak Island Convention and Visitors Bureau
100 East Marine Way, Suite 200, Kodiak, AK 99615
Tel: 907-486-4782/800-789-4782
https://kodiak.org

Mat-Su Convention and Visitors Bureau
610 South Bailey Street, Suite 201, Palmer, AK 99645
Tel: 907-746-5000
www.alaskavisit.com

Nome Convention and Visitors Bureau
301 Front Street, PO Box 240, Nome, AK 99762
Tel: 907-443-6555
www.visitnomealaska.com/

Petersburg Visitor Information Center
PO Box 649, Petersburg, AK 99833
Tel: 907-772-4636/866-484-4700
www.petersburg.org

Sitka Convention and Visitors Bureau
104 Lake Street, Sitka, AK 99835
Tel: 907-747-8604
www.visitsitka.org

Skagway Convention and Visitors Bureau
PO Box 1029, Skagway, AK 99840
Tel: 907-983-2854
www.skagway.com

Valdez Convention and Visitors Bureau
309 Fairbanks Drive, Valdez, AK 99686
Tel: 907-835-2984
www.valdezalaska.org

Wrangell Convention and Visitors Bureau
293 Campbell Drive (Nolan Center) PO Box 1350, Wrangell, AK 99929
Tel: 800-367-9745
www.wrangellalaska.org

Additional Websites

State of Alaska: www.alaska.gov
Visitor Information sites:
Bethel: www.cityofbethel.org
Cordova: www.cordovachamber.com
Gustavus: www.gustavusak.com
Homer: www.homeralaska.org
Kotzebue: www.cityofkotzebue.com
Seldovia: www.seldovia.com
Seward: www.seward.com
Soldotna: www.soldotnachamber.com
Unalaska/Dutch Harbor: www.ci.unalaska.ak.us
Whittier: www.whittieralaskachamber.org
Yakutat: www.yakutat.net

Travelers with Disabilities

Nearly all hotels, restaurants and tours in Alaska's larger cities welcome visitors with disabilities. It is important to specify your particular needs when making reservations. The US Coast Guard regulates tour-boat activities and therefore these vessels do not fall under the requirements of the Americans with Disabilities Act. While some smaller day-cruise boats are not structured to allow for wheelchair use, you will likely find that most tour operators make every effort to accommodate special-needs passengers.

A good contact is Challenge Alaska (3350 Commercial Drive, Suite 208, Anchorage, AK 99501; tel: 907-344-7399; www.challengealaska.org), a non-profit organization that specializes in providing sports and recreational opportunities for those with disabilities. The group operates an adaptive ski school at the Keil Center at the Alyeska Ski resort in Girdwood, just south of Anchorage. For more information, call 907-783-2925.

V

Visas and Passports

Visitors coming to the United States must have a valid passport, visa, or other accepted documentation. However, in an effort to attract more tourists, the US initiated the Visa Waiver Program for those coming on vacation for a maximum of 90 days. With 38 countries participating, the program allows for select travelers to enter the US with only a machine-readable passport. Travelers under this program can also make short trips to Canada without an additional visa. Increased security now requires all VWP participants to apply with the Electronic System for Travel Authorization. Online authorization can occur at any point before entry into the US; however, applying early is advisable. To check eligibility for the Visa Waiver program, and for complete and up-to-date information for all travelers, visit the US State Department (http://travel.state.gov/content/travel/en/us-visas/tourism-visit/visa-waiver-program.html).

For the latest travel restrictions related to the Covid-19 pandemic, please check online at https://travel.state.gov.

FICTION

Alaska, by James Michener. Beginning with the mastodons, Michener tells the history of Alaska in this big, sprawling work of historical fiction.

Call of the Wild; White Fang, by Jack London. Two classic tales, the first told through the eyes of Buck, a dog who makes the journey from pampered life to leader of a wolf pack, pulling sleds across Alaska before his return to the wild. White Fang tells the tale of a wild dog becoming tamed. Both stories give a good idea of both the hardship and the camaraderie inherent in the Alaskan experience.

The Cloud Atlas, by Liam Callanan. The last frontier becomes a place of magic realism during World War II as the army is dispatched to save a remote Aleutian Island from Japanese attack.

Drop City, by T.C. Boyle. A funny and entertaining novel chronicling a group of hippies as they attempt to build a commune along the Yukon River deep in the Alaska bush.

Tisha: Story of a Young Teacher in the Alaska Wilderness, by Robert Specht. A popular, heart-warming story about Anne Hobbs, a young teacher living in the remote gold-rush settlement of Chicken in 1927, who was determined to treat people as equals, despite great prejudice.

Yiddish Policeman's Union, by Michael Chabon. A fanciful account about what would have happened if the government's plan to establish a Jewish colony in Sitka during World War II had come to pass.

TRAVEL AND EXPLORATION

American Buffalo, by Steven Rinella. The author finds his obsession with bison leads him to the Wrangell Mountains, where one transplanted herd roams free in this hugely entertaining book.

Coming into the Country, John McPhee. Still one of the best accounts of all that is Alaska, interweaving vivid characters and descriptive narrative to cover both urban life and the total wilderness.

Final Frontiersman: Heimo Korth and his Family, Alone in Alaska's Arctic Wilderness, by James Campbell. Campbell recounts the story of his cousin Heimo, who left his native Wisconsin and settled far north of the Arctic Circle, over 100 miles

(160km) from his nearest neighbor. Hunting during spring visits to St Lawrence Island, Heimo's story is a glimpse into a dying way of life.

Green Alaska, by Nancy Lord. Alaskan writer and commercial fisherwoman, Nancy Lord, recounts the pivotal Harriman Expedition of 1899. Part history, part travel, part memoir, this is an entertaining and insightful read.

In the Shadow of Denali, by Jonathan Waterman. A modern mountaineering classic. Waterman examines the powerful draw of the wilderness and in particular, the passion of conquering Alaska's highest peaks.

Into the Wild, by John Krakauer. Made into a film in 2007 directed by Sean Penn, this is the story of Christopher McCandless, an idealistic young

⊘ Send us your thoughts

We do our best to ensure the information in our books is as accurate and up-to-date as possible. The books are updated on a regular basis using destination experts, who painstakingly add, amend and correct as required. However, some details (such as opening times or travel pass costs) are particularly liable to change, and we are ultimately reliant on our readers to put us in the picture.

We welcome your feedback, especially your experience of using the book "on the road", and if you came across a great new attraction we missed.

We will acknowledge all contributions and offer an Insight Guide to the best messages received. Please write to us at:

Insight Guides
PO Box 7910
London SE1 1WE
Or email us at:
hello@insightguides.com

man who tried to survive in the wilderness, cutting off his middle class family and renaming himself Alex Supertramp. He was found dead by moose hunters, probably killed by eating toxic seeds.

Looking for Alaska, by Peter Jenkins. Experiencing personal stagnation, author Peter Jenkins decides to try his hand at Alaska living.

Tracks across Alaska: A Dog Sled Journey, by Alastair Scott. This is a great read for anyone who romanticizes the great white north, or who dreams of abandoning the day job for a new life with a pack of huskies. In crisp, clear prose, the author describes how he took up dogsledding and followed the Iditarod trail.

Winterdance: The Fine Madness of Alaskan Dog Racing, by Gary Paulsen. No need to have an interest in dogsledding to enjoy this book; an entertaining and touching account of Paulsen's training for and then running the Iditarod sled dog race.

HISTORY AND POLITICS

Alaska: Saga of a Bold Land, by Walter Borneman. A detailed history of the Last Frontier. A good overview of the state.

The Thousand-Mile War: World War II in Alaska and the Aleutians, by Brian Garfield. A thrilling, deeply researched account of the "forgotten war" in Alaska.

REFERENCE

The Milepost (also at www.themilepost.com), edited by Kris Valencia. Known as the bible to Alaska with good reason, this is an incredibly detailed travel guide, listing gas stations, stream crossings, trash facilities, you name it. Excellent if you are planning on doing your own tour.

CREDITS

PHOTO CREDITS

Al Smith/NPS 291T
Alamy 13MR, 35, 57R, 124, 125, 148, 255TR, 259B, 265, 282T, 284, 299ML, 303B
Alaska Division of Community and Business Development 141T
Alaska Division of Tourism 21T, 21B, 22B, 22T, 69, 279T, 311T, 316T, 348, 354
Anchorage Convention & Visitors Bureau 177B
Anchorage Museum 11T, 173T, 173B
Andrei Taranchenko/Flickr 149
Angie Cerny/FCVB 242, 247, 249B, 252
AWL Images 266/267
Bigstock.com 111
Bill Eichenlaub/NPS 144, 146
Bill Sherwonit/Alaska Division of Community and Business 299BL
Bureau of Land Management 281T
Cathryn Posey/Anchorage Convention & Visitors Bureau 171T, 174, 176T
Cecil Sanders/Flickr 211, 216B, 218T, 219
Chris Russininiello/NPS 304, 305B, 305T
Cielo de la Paz/Flickr 139
Corbis 158/159T, 159ML, 159BR, 295, 296, 297B
Craig McCaa/Bureau of Land Management 87, 260
Danny Lehman/Princess Cruises 7TL, 94/95
Denise Ferree/Chena Hot Springs Resort 262B
Donna Dewhurst/US Fish & Wildlife Service 9BL
Dreamstime 34, 73, 78L, 79, 117, 141B, 142B, 156B, 176B, 184T, 189B, 206T, 223B, 224B, 239T, 256, 269T, 269B, 273, 283, 297T, 298BR, 313, 349
FCVB 243
FLPA 160
Fotolia 8T, 32, 59, 61, 80, 84, 116B, 156T, 245, 315, 316B, 321, 322BR, 334,

340
Frank Flavin/Visit Anchorage 169
Frank Kovalchek/Flickr 179, 187B, 199, 201, 217, 218B, 307ML, 307BL, 307TR
Gates of the Arctic NP 292, 293
Getty Images 14/15, 20, 23, 24, 36/37, 58, 60, 74, 104, 114, 126, 129, 131B, 135, 143, 151B, 157, 161, 171B, 191B, 209, 210, 222, 225, 282B, 299BR, 300, 302, 314, 322/323T, 327B, 333B, 344, 345, 346
Glacier Bay NP 6MR
Gray Line of Alaska 92
Holland America Line 7ML, 88, 89, 93
iStockphoto 6ML, 6BL, 6MR, 7MR, 7BL, 7BR, 9TL, 10B, 10T, 11B, 12B, 16/17, 25, 27, 28, 29, 33, 38B, 38T, 39, 47, 49, 56, 57L, 70, 71, 72, 76, 77, 78R, 81, 82, 83, 85, 86, 90, 91, 96, 97, 98/99, 105T, 105B, 109T, 109B, 110T, 110B, 112, 115, 118, 119T, 119B, 120, 122, 123, 127B, 130, 131T, 132, 150, 153, 154, 165T, 166T, 167, 177T, 184B, 186, 187T, 188, 190, 192, 193, 194, 195, 196B, 196T, 197, 198, 202, 203, 204T, 204B, 206B, 207T, 214, 215B, 215T, 216T, 220/221, 223T, 224T, 227, 229, 231B, 233B, 235T, 236, 237B, 239B, 248, 251, 259T, 262T, 270T, 270B, 271, 272, 275, 280, 290, 298BL, 299TR, 303T, 308/309, 311B, 312T, 312B, 319B, 319T, 322BL, 323ML, 323BL, 323TR, 330, 332, 333T, 335, 336T, 336B, 339, 342, 343, 352, 357, 359
Jade Frank/FCVB 246, 249T, 261
James McClean/Chena Hot Springs Resort 263
Janet Buckingham 317T, 318
Josh Steinitz/Flickr 286, 287, 288, 289
Karen Laubenstein/US Fish & Wildlife Service 208
Kent Miller/NPS 8B, 228, 230, 231T, 232, 233T, 234, 235B, 237T, 326, 328T, 328B, 329
Kevyn Jalone/NPS 327T

Klondike Gold Rush National Historical Park 155
Kodiak Island CVB 317B
Kristopher Volkman/Flickr 136
Library of Congress 41B, 42, 43, 44, 46, 48, 50, 51, 52, 53, 158BL, 159BL
Northern Alaska Tour Company 264
Peter Hamel/NPS 331
Photoshot 66, 75, 100/101, 151T, 254BR, 254BL, 254/255T, 255MR, 255BL, 255BR, 257, 307BR
Potlatch Park 116T
Ralph Hones/NPS 279B
Rex Features 306/307T, 306BR
Riverboat discovery 250
Robert Harding 128, 137, 147, 278
Ronald Laubenstein/US Fish and Wildlife Service 9TR, 213
Roy Caples Collection 258
Shutterstock 1, 4, 12ML, 12MR, 13TL, 13TR, 13BL, 62/63, 68, 102/103, 253, 281B, 320, 323BR
Skagway Convention & Visitors Bureau 152
Steve Chase/US Fish and Wildlife Service 285
Steve Hillebrand/US Fish & Wildlife Serevice 207B, 291B, 341T
SuperStock 18/19, 26, 30, 31, 64, 65, 67, 121, 134, 162/163, 168, 180, 181, 182, 185, 226, 238, 240, 241, 276, 277, 294, 298/299T, 301, 306BL, 324, 325, 337, 338
T. VandenBerg/NPS 7TR, 145B
Teri McMillan/NPS 274
Tim Rains/NPS 145T
TopFoto 158BR
Trail Mix, Inc 140, 142T
US Fish & Wildlife Service 40, 341B
US Geological Survey 41T, 45, 54, 55
USDA Forest Service NatureWatch 127T
USDA Forest Service 178, 189T, 191T
Visit Anchorage 166G
Wayde Carroll/Visit Anchorage 165B
Wendy Cutler 113

COVER CREDITS

Front cover: Bald eagle, Kenai *Shutterstock*
Back cover: Autumnal Denali *Shutterstock*

Front flap: (from top) Grizzly bear *Shutterstock*; Kayaking in Glacier Bay *Shutterstock*; Forest Loop Trail in Glacier Bay *Shutterstock*; Mount

Denali ridge *Shutterstock*
Back flap: Saxman Native Village *Shutterstock*
E book flap: Bear family *Shutterstock*

INSIGHT GUIDE CREDITS

Distribution
UK, Ireland and Europe
Apa Publications (UK) Ltd;
sales@insightguides.com
United States and Canada
Ingram Publisher Services;
ips@ingramcontent.com
Australia and New Zealand
Booktopia;
retailer@booktopia.com.au
Worldwide
Apa Publications (UK) Ltd;
sales@insightguides.com
Special Sales, Content Licensing and CoPublishing
Insight Guides can be purchased in bulk quantities at discounted prices. We can create special editions, personalised jackets and corporate imprints tailored to your needs.
sales@insightguides.com
www.insightguides.biz

Printed in China

All Rights Reserved
© 2021 Apa Digital AG
License edition © Apa Publications Ltd UK

First Edition 1988
Twelfth Edition 2021

Every effort has been made to provide accurate information in this publication, but changes are inevitable. The publisher cannot be responsible for any resulting loss, inconvenience or injury. We would appreciate it if readers would call our attention to any errors or outdated information. We also welcome your suggestions; please contact us at:
hello@insightguides.com
www.insightguides.com

Editors: Siobhan Warwicker & Annie Warren
Authors: Todd Obolsky, Elizabeth Linhart Money, Maciej Zglinicki
Cartography: original cartography Colin Earl, updated by Carte
Picture Editor: Tom Smyth
Layout: Aga Bylica
Head of DTP and Pre-Press: Rebeka Davies
Head of Publishing: Sarah Clark

CONTRIBUTORS

The latest edition of this long-time Insight bestseller was thoroughly updated by **Todd Obolsky**, a travel writer who has also written on Florida, New York City, Canada, Belize and Peru.

It builds on the previous work of the following contributors: **Brian Bell, Bill Bjork, Jeff Brady, Kris Capps, Alyse Dar, Lisa Dion, Debby Drong-Bjork, Elizabeth Linhart Money, Mike Miller,** and **Bill Sherwonit. Douglas Ward,** author of the renowned *Berlitz Complete Guide to Cruising and Cruise Ships,* wrote the chapter on Alaskan cruising.

The book was copyedited by **Siobhan Warwicker & Annie Warren.**

ABOUT INSIGHT GUIDES

Insight Guides have more than 45 years' experience of publishing high-quality, visual travel guides. We produce 400 full-colour titles, in both print and digital form, covering more than 200 destinations across the globe, in a variety of formats to meet your different needs.

Insight Guides are written by local authors, whose expertise is evident in the extensive historical and cultural background features. Each destination is carefully researched by regional experts to ensure our guides provide the very latest information. All the reviews in **Insight Guides** are independent; we strive to maintain an impartial view. Our reviews are carefully selected to guide you to the best places to eat, go out and shop, so you can be confident that when we say a place is special, we really mean it.

Legend

City maps

	Freeway/Highway/Motorway
	Divided Highway
	Main Roads
	Minor Roads
	Pedestrian Roads
	Steps
	Footpath
	Railway
	Funicular Railway
	Cable Car
	Tunnel
	City Wall
	Important Building
	Built Up Area
	Other Land
	Transport Hub
	Park
	Pedestrian Area
	Bus Station
	Tourist Information
	Main Post Office
	Cathedral/Church
	Mosque
	Synagogue
	Statue/Monument
	Beach
	Airport

Regional maps

	Freeway/Highway/Motorway (with junction)
	Freeway/Highway/Motorway (under construction)
	Divided Highway
	Main Road
	Secondary Road
	Minor Road
	Track
	Footpath
	International Boundary
	State/Province Boundary
	National Park/Reserve
	Marine Park
	Ferry Route
	Marshland/Swamp
	Glacier
	Salt Lake
	Airport/Airfield
	Ancient Site
	Border Control
	Cable Car
	Castle/Castle Ruins
	Cave
	Chateau/Stately Home
	Church/Church Ruins
	Crater
	Lighthouse
	Mountain Peak
	Place of Interest
	Viewpoint

INDEX

MAIN REFERENCES ARE IN BOLD TYPE

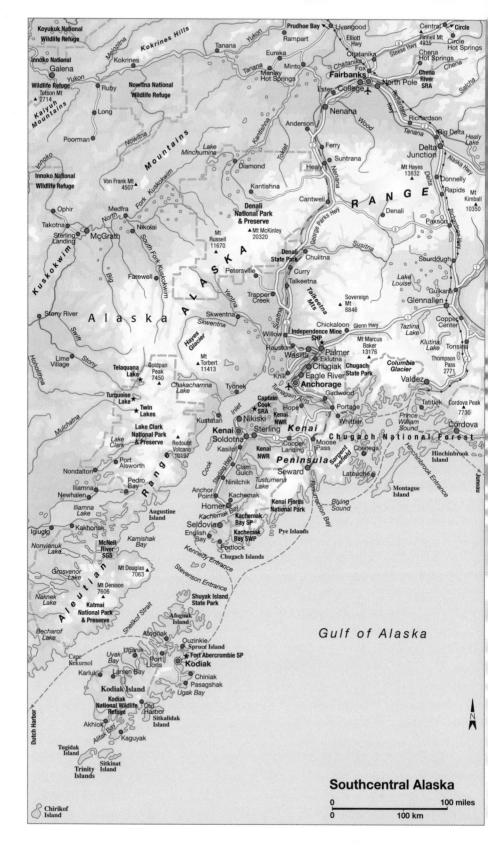

Southcentral Alaska

0   100 miles

0   100 km